Acclaim for Lawrence Lessig and

REPUBLIC, LOST

"Lessig's vision is at once profoundly pessimistic—and deeply optimistic...Lessig's analysis of the distorting effects of money is...dead on."
                                                            —*New York Times*

"A well-reasoned argument on the structural problems now paralyzing American government."
                                                            —*Kirkus Reviews*

"REPUBLIC, LOST is a powerful reminder that this problem goes deeper than poor legislative tactics or bad character. As progressives contemplate how best to pick up the pieces after recent setbacks, a robust agenda to change how business gets done in the capital needs to be part of the picture. This time, we'd better mean it."
                                                            —*American Prospect*

"Comprehensive and persuasive...enjoyable to read."
                                                            —*Atlantic*

"One of the many charms of REPUBLIC, LOST is its sympathy for the people involved...With lawyerly precision, Lessig parses the problem."
                                                            —Bloomberg.com

"The real crisis facing American politics is what elected officials have to do to raise the money...That, roughly, is the theme of Lawrence Lessig's stirring book, REPUBLIC, LOST...Without a doubt, the Lessig plan (which has been carefully designed to pass constitutional muster) would be a vast improvement over the current system."
                                                            —WashingtonMonthly.com

REPUBLIC, LOST

*The Corruption of Equality and
the Steps to End It*

Revised Edition

———— ★ ————

Lawrence Lessig

NEW YORK   BOSTON

Twelve

Hachette Book Group

1290 Avenue of the Americas

New York, NY 10104

www.HachetteBookGroup.com

Printed in the United States of America

RRD-C

First Revised Edition: October 2015

Original edition published in hardcover in October 2011

10 9 8 7 6 5 4 3 2 1

Twelve is an imprint of Grand Central Publishing.

The Twelve name and logo are trademarks of Hachette Book Group, Inc.

The Hachette Speakers Bureau provides a wide range of authors for speaking events. To find out more, go to www.hachettespeakersbureau.com or call (866) 376-6591.

The publisher is not responsible for websites (or their content) that are not owned by the publisher.

Additional copyright and image credits are on page 362.

Library of Congress Control Number: 2015949738

ISBN: 978-1-4555-3701-3

for aaron

Contents

Preface

At the end of December 2006, a friend came to visit me, to ask me to justify myself, and my work.

I was a visiting scholar at the American Academy in Berlin, finishing my fifth book about copyright and Internet policy, and preparing for my first TED talk. My friend was attending the Chaos Computer Congress, held in the week between Christmas and New Year's each year. His name was Aaron Swartz.

At the time, Swartz had just turned twenty. I had known him since he was in his early teens. We had first met at conferences about the Internet. I was the speaker; he was the most attentive member in the audience, usually in the first row, often with his chaperone (his mom or dad, for he was no more than twelve or thirteen). When a group of us first began developing Creative Commons—an alternative to traditional copyright, which would enable artists and authors to mark their creativity with the freedom they intended it to carry—Swartz was everyone's recommendation to be the technical lead. At fourteen, he had already helped to develop the RSS protocol, and was among the world's leading metadata experts. Quickly, and with almost no guidance from me, he developed the infrastructure that would define the Creative Commons project for its first fifteen years.

Beginning with that project, Aaron and I became friends. He was brilliant, if impatient. Rare among technical sorts, he had enormous humility and a keen sense of the public good. His single overriding purpose throughout the time I knew him was how to make the world a better place. What that "world" was started small. At first it was the universe of people trying to share content easily on the Web. Then people trying to share it freely. Then people trying to make science and culture available freely. And then, about the time he came to see me in Berlin, it was not really about making the Internet a better, freer place anymore. His focus, at less than twenty years old, was society more generally.

And that was his question for me. I had achieved a sort of petty prominence, within my own field at least: Internet policy generally, copyright policy in particular. My life was split between teaching, speaking, litigating, writing, and a growing family—intense and rewarding, but in the scale of things, a life focused on the small. I knew it was small, but I believed I was right, and the choice to become an academic is always the choice of a life of confident certainty within a tiny domain.

Aaron was not impressed with that tiny domain. He had come to challenge it: "How are you ever going to make any progress," he asked me, with just the suggestion of a smile, "so long as the government remains so fundamentally corrupt?"

I was a bit taken aback by the question. I had been describing my work to him, and my hopefulness for progress. He was impatient with hopefulness, and unimpressed with the work. And as I let his question hang for a bit, he just stared at me, directly into my eyes, waiting quietly for an answer.

"It's not my field," I told him.

"As an academic?" he asked.

"Yes, as an academic."

"What about as a citizen. Is it your field as a citizen?"

I didn't realize it at the time, but our friendship had grown in a very distinctive way. I was not his father—indeed, he had an incredibly loving and brilliant father—but in one sense, we were in a father-and-son-like relationship. He was testing me, testing my commitment to the idealism I spoke of, maybe trying a bit to set me up for failure by acting in a way that didn't live up to that idealism. And so his questions forced me to choose: If I had a good reason—a principled reason, a reason he could respect—for continuing on

in my way, then fine. But if I didn't—if I couldn't deny the truth in
what he said, and if I didn't have a good reason to ignore the impli-
cations of what he was asking—then our friendship would face a
test: I would either accept the premise of his question, and change
my work, or reject the premise of our relationship—respect—and
continue in the space of the small.

I didn't have the confidence to disappoint Aaron. He was right.
Every book I had written had included the arguments about why
he was right. I knew there was little progress to be had, not just
in copyright policy, but in every other field of important public
policy, until this corruption was ended. And so that night, sitting in
a chilly room in a beautiful estate on the Wannsee, I resolved with
Aaron to give up my work on copyright and Internet policy, and to
return to Stanford that fall focused exclusively on the question of
"corruption."

Almost seven years later, at the age of twenty-six, Aaron was
dead. He had helped me launch a project to attack this corruption ("Change Congress," which would eventually become "Root-
strikers"). With some friends he had met at a Y-Combinator event,
he had cofounded Reddit. He had launched his own progressive
reform organization, Demand Progress, convinced that Obama was
the great hope for progressives. He had helped architect the most
important Internet-driven political victory to date, the effort to
stop the "SOPA/PIPA" legislation. He had been a fellow at the center I directed at Harvard, the Edmond J. Safra Center for Ethics. He
had spent a stint working on Capitol Hill, understanding the beast
from the inside out.

But in January 2011, he had gotten himself arrested. He was
caught downloading a database of academic articles, contrary
to the rules of the site, with the intent, the prosecutors alleged,
of distributing them to others. The arrest began two years of hell,
as Aaron, through his lawyers, tried to talk fiercely over-eager
prosecutors down from the certainty that they had captured one
of America's most wanted. Upon announcing the indictment
against Swartz, U.S. Attorney Carmen Ortiz threatened thirty-five

years in prison. Eighteen months after that indictment, most of his resources exhausted, he himself exhausted, Aaron took his own life.

Ten months after he was arrested, Aaron wrote me to congratulate me about the first edition of this book. It was the best thing I had written, he said. "May its insights," he wrote, "come to seem obvious."

I never had the chance to say the same to him. Yet if there is one hope I have for my own young children, all of whom knew and miss Aaron dearly, it is that the commitment of his soul comes to seem obvious, too.

He was never someone to dream big. He worked, patiently, in a big direction.

May we all.

Introduction

We have entered an age of fantasy politics—when candidates from both parties parade promises for a better future before a public that recognizes, somewhere deep down, that it's all really just a show. A ritual. A way to get the blood flowing. No one believes the promises anymore. A solution to the student debt crisis. A way to end the public debt crisis. Health care reform (for real). Climate change legislation (finally). Tax reform. Tariff reform. Bridges that aren't crumbling. An education system to be proud of, again. But elections are scheduled, and one side has got to win. And usually that's the side that embraces the fantasy more firmly than the other. So both sides work hard to "believe." Both sides shut their eyes and dream.

This is not to say with Nader that there isn't a "dime's worth of difference" between the two parties. There plainly is, in important areas at least, if not in enough areas. And it's not to say that there isn't a reason to fight for one side or the other, at least with the presidency. The Supreme Court is reason enough.

But it is to say that a basic idea of a representative democracy—one that argues over fundamental choices of policy, through the battle between differently committed representatives—is not the reality of our democracy anymore. We've settled into what Francis Fukuyama calls a "vetocracy," where change of almost any kind, whether from the Right or the Left, is practically always stopped.[1]

It is not hard to see why, even if it is easy to be confused about why. Some say it is polarization—and it is, in part, but the polarization that we can fix is just a symptom of a much deeper problem. Some say it is gerrymandering—and again, in part it is, but fixing gerrymandering before we address this deeper problem won't fix anything. Some say it is the inevitable consequence of a plutocracy, as if the inability to act *at all* is bias in favor of one side. Sometimes it is, but in this case, it is not. The problem of America is not capture. The problem of America is collapse—a collapse in the ability to govern, because of the corrupting influence of money in campaigns. Because of this influence—not only this, but this first—we have lost the ability to rule. The steering wheel has detached from the axle. Regardless of which direction "the people" turn, the bus trundles on, oblivious. And as it does, confidence in the institution of Congress collapses. In no institution identified by Gallup did Americans show less confidence in June 2015:

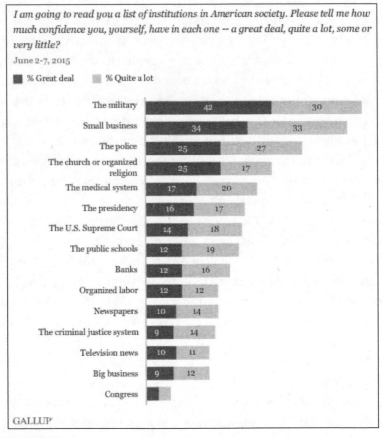

FIGURE 1[2]

June 2015 was not an anomaly:

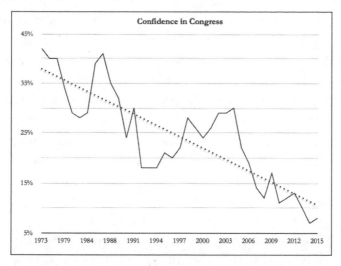

FIGURE 2. *Percent expressing at least "quite a lot" of confidence in Congress*

And who would say that America was being unfair to its core representative body? We are a nation that gives billions in subsidies to one of the world's most profitable industries (oil); we give the middle class and the rich a tax deduction for mortgage interest, but not for interest on credit cards; our government spends billions buying drugs for the elderly and for some covered by Obamacare, but by law, it's not permitted to negotiate with drug companies for lower prices; we subsidize the production of unhealthy "food" (high fructose corn syrup), but not fruits or vegetables; our tax system gives one of its lowest rates to its richest taxpayers (hedge fund managers); we spend billions to buy weapons for a kind of war that our nation will never see again; we run a farm subsidy program in which the biggest and richest 10 percent get almost 70 percent of the subsidies; we subsidize flood insurance for the owners of beach houses—and these are just the small things. As well as these, we are a nation yet to pass federal legislation addressing climate change, yet to rationalize an insanely complicated tax system, yet to confront sensibly the high cost of health care, yet to reform the banking industry in a way that would avoid the kind of collapse of 2008, yet to even acknowledge the long-term costs of endless debt, and yet to find a way to speak sensibly about a defense budget that seems only ever to grow. We are a bipolar nation: on the one hand, with the most creative and innovative people anywhere, and with the world's most generous middle class; on the other hand, with a government in collapse, filled with "leaders" who can do nothing more than position for the next election. As great as "we, the people" are, our government is, in the same degree, awful. It is the best of times, and the worst of times. It is a nation that can inspire more than any in the world, when the focus is on us, but a nation that cannot inspire less, when the focus is on the USG.

As I have studied this problem, my understanding of this collapse has evolved. As I described it in the first edition of this book, *Republic, Lost*, the core problem is a kind of *corruption*: a dependence, contrary to the one intended by our Framers, that has infected the way our government works, and that now, at its extreme, has rendered it incapable of governing. Not the corruption of criminals, but the corruption of a system. Not the wrong of "quid pro quo bribery," but a problem with the incentives for responsiveness that we have allowed to evolve within our Republic.

I continue to believe in that account. But as I've thought more deeply about its nature—and more important, as I've experienced the hopelessness of so many when they think about this problem solely as a problem of corruption—I've come to see the importance of linking that understanding to a more fundamental way to see its nature, and to give voice to its remedy.

This is the idea of equality. Not wealth equality, or speech equality, or the idea that somehow, the government must make us all "equal speakers." Instead, an equality of citizenship. Our Republic has been corrupted, because it betrays a basic commitment of a representative democracy to this equality. By ending that corruption, we could realize this equality.

Yet here we confront a familiar problem. In the first edition of this book, I felled many trees introducing a conception of "corruption" that was familiar to historians, our Framers, and geeks, but that had fallen out of use among lawyers and politicians.

And so, too, is it with the particular conception of "equality" that I mean to defend here. That equality would also have been obvious to the Framers, yet it, too, is almost lost to us today. It is not an equality of stuff. It is an equality of status. It is, as Danielle Allen describes in her powerful book, *Our Declaration* (2014), a political equality, or as I'll call it, an equality of citizens. Our Republic has been corrupted, because we've allowed it to evolve a *structure of influence* that denies the equality of citizens. That inequality is a corruption of the idea of a "representative democracy," or of what the Framers would have called "a Republic."

This idea, more clearly than talk about "corruption" alone, speaks its own remedy. It gives moral force to the movement that demands it. And it shows more clearly than corruption talk one way forward.

I am obviously not the first to use the idea of equality as a way to understand the problem with our democracy. The field is filled with brilliant work from incredibly talented theorists and practitioners, emphasizing the radical inequality that we've allowed to seep within our democracy.[3]

But that debate has too often been framed as a choice: Either we say that our democracy is corrupted, or we say that our democracy is unequal. That framing in turn has been forced on us by the Supreme Court: In the terms the Court uses, if the problem is "corruption," there is something Congress can do about it. But if it is mere inequality, the First Amendment blocks Congress from remedying it. Those pressing "corruption" thus want to give Congress a way to fix it. Those insisting it is "inequality" have given up on this Supreme Court, and wait for the day when equality can rule.

If there is a contribution in this book, it is a way to see just how both sides in this debate could be right. The Court is right to insist that we limit Congress's rules to remedies for "corruption." And the Court is right to deny Congress the power to "equalize" speech as a way to achieve equality. The traditions that ground both resolutions are important and valuable, and we should not move too quickly to abandon them.

But the Court has missed how—on its own terms—the current

system *is* a corruption, and how equality justifies a remedy to that corruption, even if it doesn't justify "equalizing speech." Put differently, there is no reason, consistent with its values, that the Supreme Court could not permit the remedies this democracy needs. Indeed, it is *because of those values* that we can see the remedies that this democracy requires.

This book is not, however, a letter to the Supreme Court. I take the terms of the debate as they have set them not because I want to engage with them, but because those terms point an obvious way forward. I believe there is a way forward; I believe there are reforms that are both feasible and effective; and I want more than anything to see the movement step in this direction, if only because I want it to win.

If, indeed, you believe that there is a way forward. Because in response to my claim that we've entered the age of fantasy politics, there will be many who say that I've entered a world of fantasy reform. The overwhelming sense of anyone close to this story is that there's nothing that can be done. Or when that seems too hopeless, the skeptic invokes the universal *deus ex machina*—a massive grassroots political movement[4] that will somehow rise up and fix everything.

I get just how impossible reform seems just now, and hence, how fantastic a plan for fixing it seems. But the witchcraft of "a massive grassroots movement" isn't a plan, and not fixing it is not an option.

So to the skeptic, the critic, or the unconvinced reformer, I offer John Snow (*Game of Thrones*):

> "You're right. It's a bad plan." [pause]
> "What's your plan?"

One that doesn't rely on magic ("a grassroots movement..."), that doesn't simply wait for a disaster ("ongoing scandal"), and that doesn't assume the people are idiots.

The people are not idiots. We can't wait for a disaster—it's already here. And the only magic that there is is the magic we make, through the movement that understanding makes possible.

PART I

★

THE FLAW

CHAPTER 1

Tweedism

In the early fall of 2014, protests erupted across Hong Kong, led first by students, and then joined by hundreds of thousands of ordinary citizens.

These protests were in response to the Chinese government's plans for that state's "democracy." Seven years before, Hong Kong had been promised that its chief executive would be popularly elected by 2017. In August 2014, the Standing Committee of China's Twelfth National People's Congress released its plans for that popular election three years hence. According to the committee:

> The ultimate aim is the selection of the Chief Executive by universal suffrage upon nomination by a broadly representative nominating committee in accordance with democratic procedures.[1]

This "nominating committee" was to be small, at least relative to the population of Hong Kong. Twelve hundred citizens—about .02 percent of Hong Kong's population (and remember that number, .02 percent, for at least a couple pages here)—would have the power to nominate the candidates that the voters would then select among.

Yet those 1,200 were not to be randomly selected. They were instead to be chosen through a complicated procedure that would produce a committee, critics charged, representing a "pro-Beijing, business elite" more than the average Hong Kong citizen.[2]

This was not, the protesters insisted, "democracy." It was instead, as Martin Lee, Chairman of the Hong Kong Democratic Party, put it, "democracy with Chinese characteristics."[3]

The flaw in the Hong Kong system is not hard for us to see. China had proposed a two-step process for selecting its governor. Yet in the first step, the system introduced an obvious bias. That bias wasn't an accident. Indeed, it was explicitly defended by Hong Kong's current governor, Leung Chun-ying. As he said in response to the protests:

> If it's entirely a numbers game and numeric representation, then obviously you would be talking to half of the people in Hong Kong who earn less than $1,800 a month.[4]

Obviously, you can't have a democracy that represents all people equally. Obviously some must be more equal than others.

Ninety years before Hong Kong protested the inequality that was about to be pressed upon them, Lawrence Nixon was protesting a similar inequality that had just been forced upon him.

Nixon was a physician living in El Paso, Texas. He had moved to El Paso in 1910, and in every election between 1910 and 1924, Nixon had walked to his polling place, paid his poll tax, and voted.

But in 1924, when he arrived at the polls, he was told by the precinct judges, "Dr. Nixon, you know we can't let you vote." "I know you can't," Nixon replied, "but I've got to try."

Nixon was black. In 1923, Texas had enacted a law that forbade blacks from voting in the Democratic Primary.[5] Nixon was recruited by the NAACP to challenge that restriction—twice. Yet in some form, the "White Primary" would survive in Texas for another thirty years. Blacks were free to vote in the ultimate election (assuming, of course, that they could register). But in the first step of choosing who would govern Texas, and the only step that really mattered ("as of 1940, no Texas Republican had been elected to a major state or federal office in over seventy years"[6]), only whites had a role.

All men may have been created equal in Texas, but some were more equal than others.

* * *

The link between Hong Kong's future and Texas's past is not an accident. It is an obvious system design. Boss Tweed, the infamous leader of New York's Tammany Hall, famously quipped, "I don't care who does the electing, as long as I get to do the nominating." That's precisely the idea behind both of these schemes—a multi-stage process, with a biased filter in the first stage, intended to benefit those who control the "nominating" power. None but rogues reject "rule by the people" anymore. But *tweedism* is the trick by which fraud democracies guarantee that "the people" need not actually govern a state "rule[d] by the people."

Not because the tweeds are few—were the "nominating committee" in Hong Kong truly representative, the scheme would not be tweedist in the sense I mean here.

Not because to be a tweed requires a certain qualification—party primaries are typically open to members of a party only. That, too, is not tweedism.

But instead because the tweeds do not represent the people that the democracy is to govern. Tweedism defeats democracy, by twisting democracy's representative function, through a procedure—a system—that assures that representatives are not representative.

Sometimes this tweedism is quite crude. In Iran, the Guardian Council (twelve theologians and jurists) selects the candidates that 80 million Iranian citizens get to vote among.[7]

Sometimes it is quite subtle. Hong Kong's is more obscure than Iran's and certainly more subtle than the Jim Crow of Texas.

And sometimes, it is so subtle as to be all but invisible, at least to the natives.

This last form is the tweedism that is the focus of this book: the tweedism in modern America.

Because, like Hong Kong, America has a nominating process, too. I don't mean the primaries, the formal procedure by which a candidate gets to be a candidate. I mean a much more fundamental nominating process—one that determines who can even consider becoming a candidate, or at least a "credible candidate," and one that determines who has any chance of prevailing within any contested election.

This more fundamental process doesn't involve any formal vote. Instead, this more fundamental process is tied to money.

The Green Primary

We take it for granted in America that political campaigns will be privately funded. Not all campaigns—some states, like Maine, Connecticut, and Arizona, publicly fund elections. And in theory at least, candidates for the presidency still have an option for public funding. But for every other federal contest, the first real contest that a candidate must engage in is the contest to raise the money necessary to become a viable candidate.

That contest is a kind of primary. Not a voting primary, but a money primary. Not the "White Primary," but a "Green Primary."[8]

Unless a candidate self-funds, this primary is as mandatory as any. It determines whether the candidate will be visible in the weeks leading up to a vote. Just as important, it determines whether a candidate will be deemed "credible" by the press, and hence, credible by the public. We live in a time when what makes a candidate "credible" is that she comes to the election with money. Money is the measure of a campaign, long before anyone is thinking about votes.

In 2012, for example, the most qualified candidate running for president in the Republican Primary was a three-term congressman, a former governor, and the founder of a successful community bank (think Newt Gingrich and Tim Pawlenty and Herman Cain wrapped in one).

But you can't remember who that candidate was because that most qualified candidate was not "a viable candidate." Buddy Roemer had made money the issue in his campaign, by refusing contributions greater than $100. That decision disqualified Roemer from serious consideration in the primary. *Literally, because of the money.* Roemer was not "viable," his campaign was told, and hence could not be in the debates, unless he could raise $500,000 within six weeks. And once he was deemed not viable, he was deemed not credible. Credibility turned on the money.

The same is true for Democrats, too. In 2014, a brilliant young woman challenged New York Governor Andrew Cuomo in the Democratic Primary. Zephyr Teachout had made corruption the issue in her campaign. After Cuomo, the anticorruption governor, had been charged with corruptly manipulating an anticorruption commission to protect his friends while attacking his enemies, Teachout's candidacy began to take off.[9]

But Cuomo refused even to debate Teachout, not because she wasn't qualified, not because she was a woman, and not because she wasn't popular (she would eventually win 33 percent of the primary vote, winning 25 of 62 counties).[10] Cuomo refused to debate her because she was not a credible candidate.

And what made her not credible? The money. *Only* the money. Cuomo had raised more than $40 million. Teachout eventually raised just about $600,000.[11]

We take this for granted in America today: a democracy in which the first test of credibility is not votes, or broad public support, but money. And not money that comes from all of us. Money that comes from the very few. Every single campaign, from the president to members of the House of Representatives, gets tested first on this first question: Can you raise enough money from this tiny tiny few?

Just how tiny is this few I'll describe in a bit. But before we get to the numbers, let's be clear about the psychology.

Why is it a problem that our politicians are so dependent on so few? What is the consequence of this dependency? How does it threaten a democracy?

The dynamic here is not hard to understand, at least with a bit of empathetic imagination.

No one knows how much time members of Congress and candidates spend raising money. Estimates range anywhere between 30 and 70 percent.[12] But regardless of the exact number, it's perfectly clear that fund-raising has become their job. They are instructed to do this by the leadership of their party. They are practically forced to do this by their own staff. (In 2015, Congressman Brad Ashford (D-Nebr., 2015–) lost his staff because of his refusal to fund-raise "enough." As Ashford commented, "I spend half of my day just dealing with the ISIS....The fundraising, obviously everybody needs money to run campaigns but it's got to be a secondary consideration."[13]) This is the one thing they need to get very good at. Not debating members on the floor of Congress. Not giving speeches to voters in their district. Not working out solutions to America's problems. What they need to be good at is raising money.

So think about how such a life would affect you—*you*, not Spock of *Star Trek*, but you. Imagine spending hours every day dialing for dollars—calling people you've likely never met, asking those people for their support. Your success depends upon telling these people what they need to hear, to inspire them to give you the support that you need. If you've become good at your job, it's because you've become good at saying what you need to say to make the people you're begging for money give you that money. If you've become good, it's because you've become *responsive* to *them*.

So *who they are* matters. If congressmen were calling people randomly, the way Gallup or Rasmussen calls people to conduct a poll, this discipline might well be a good thing. For a couple hours each day, members of Congress would practice saying the things that a representative public would like to hear. Such calls might well make our Congress more representative.

But of course, members are not calling people randomly. They're calling instead a very targeted and specific few: the large donor. And not millions of large donors, because obviously, large donors are very few.

So we have evolved a system for funding campaigns in which members and candidates spend an extraordinary amount of time learning what a tiny tiny unrepresentative few cares about—so that they can respond to that tiny few in a way that might induce the few to do something very specific: send them money.

If these targets do send money, then again, because congressmen are human, a bond has been created. The congressman has been obliged. Congressmen are dependent on funders; the funders have obliged, by giving. And through this process of dependence, we develop a Congress not "dependent on the people alone," as James Madison promised.[14] Through this process, we develop a Congress dependent also on these funders, too.

But it's even worse than this.

"Leaders" are supposed to be leaders. But what sort of leadership gets bred from constant prostration before the most powerful in society? How can you lead when you spend so much time begging?

The point isn't rhetorical. It is as practical as mud. What does this sort of life do to an ordinary person? What should we expect it would do? Congressmen say that they are not affected by this constant begging for money. But if that were true, they would be sociopaths. Normal human beings can't resist the pull of ordinary reciprocity. That is precisely what *normal* modifying *human* means. As any human would, as congressmen do their No. 1 job (aka fund-raising), they become dependent and subservient and responsive to their funders.

So who are these funders?

Let's start with the numbers.[15] In 2014, 5.4 million Americans gave at least something to any congressional campaign or political party or PAC. That's about 1.75 percent of America.

But of that 5.4 million, the top 100 gave almost as much as the bottom 4.75 million.[16] The top 100 individuals and organizations gave 60 percent of the super PAC money given.[17]

.2 percent (610,000) of the contributors gave as much as 66 percent of the contributors.

.04 percent (122,000) gave the equivalent of the maximum allowed in one election—$2,600.

About a fifth as many—26,000, or .008 percent—gave at least $10,000 to any set of candidates.

But between those final two numbers stands a number that quite accidentally has a very significant reference.

Consider the number of Americans who gave the equivalent of the maximum amount you are permitted to give to any candidate in both the primary and the general elections—$5,200.

$5,200 is a lot of money. That's the equivalent of what the average American spends each year on her retirement.[18] It's also a handy target for candidates as they try to raise money for their campaigns. If we're trying to imagine who the *relevant funders* of campaigns are—those who give enough to matter to a candidate as that candidate is thinking about the positions that candidate should take— $5,200 is not a bad target. I've had many incumbents tell me it is wildly too low. I've had some tell me it "gets someone on the radar."

So if we assume that $5,200 is not too low, if we assume it is a good measure of how much you must give to matter to the candidates as they spend their time dialing for dollars, then we can identify the number of Americans who matter, in this way, in our democracy.

In 2014, that number was 57,854. That is, 57,854 gave the equivalent of $5,200 to candidates running for Congress.

57,854 is .02 percent of America.

.02 percent.

You remember that number, right? .02 percent is the percentage of Hong Kong citizens that China said could sit on Hong Kong's "nominating committee." That was the number that triggered outrage across Hong Kong in the fall of 2014. A biased .02 percent wasn't "democracy," Martin Lee said. It was "democracy with Chinese characteristics."[19]

But *at the very most*, it's .02 percent who dominates the Green Primary in America. At the very most, it is this Chinese percentage of the public who gets to say who is credible, and who is not. In both cases, it is a tiny and *unrepresentative* slice of the so-called democratic populace that gets to decide who is allowed to run in the elections. In both cases, the system denies the basic equality of a representative democracy, by allowing an unrepresentative few to set the choice for the rest.[20]

This is *tweedism*. Even though we, the people, have the *ultimate* influence over elected officials—since there is, ultimately, an election in which we all have the right to participate—the way we fund campaigns *means* that we don't have equal influence within this "representative democracy." In our democracy, too, some are more equal than others.

In a single line, then, this is the core problem with America's democracy today: We have concentrated the funding of campaigns in the tiniest fraction of us, and thus made candidates for public office dependent upon this tiny fraction of us. *They* do the nominating while we do the *electing*. In this tweedist process, the design of our Framers is *corrupted*, and we, the citizens, are rendered *unequal*—just like blacks in Jim Crow Texas, or the average citizen in Hong Kong's threatened future.

Corrupt and unequal.

CHAPTER 2

Corrupt Because *Unequal*

*C*orrupt.

Tweedism corrupts representative democracy. Not in a criminal sense, but in a design sense. Tweedism defeats the design of a representative democracy, by introducing an influence that weakens the dependency a representative democracy is meant to create. That systemic defeat is "corruption."

In the first edition of this book, I introduced a particular way to understand the idea of "corruption," as a way to understand the corruption of Congress.

As I argued there, when we ordinarily use the term, "corrupt" is something we say of a person. And when we say it of a person, we mean something quite nasty. A corrupt person is an evil person, for corruption is a crime. There's no ambiguity or uncertainty in the term. Like the death penalty or pregnancy, "corrupt" in this sense is binary.

But as well as corrupt individuals, there are corrupt institutions. And not corrupt in the sense that the crime has just metastasized from one to many. But corrupt in the sense that the institution has lost its way. For at least some institutions, there is a clear sense of the institution's purpose. That purpose has been corrupted when an economy of influence has steered that institution away from its purpose. That steering is the corruption.

Yet here there need be no crime. An institution could be corrupt even if every individual within that institution was not corrupt. The only wrong necessarily attaching to any individual within a corrupt institution is the wrong of not repairing the corruption. It is the failure, as trustee, of maintaining that institution's trust.

Our Congress is corrupt in this institutional sense. There may or may not be criminals among the members of Congress. If there are, they are very few. In the main, Congress is filled, in the words of former Senator Bill Bradley (D-N.J.; 1979–1997), with "fine public servants...stuck in a bad system."[1]

But relative to the baseline intended by our Framers, Congress is plainly lost. Tweedism shows why.

The Framers meant Congress—or more precisely at the time, the House of Representatives, since at the founding the Senate was chosen by state legislatures—to be dependent in a very specific way. As James Madison described it, the House was to be "dependent on the people alone."[2]

Think about what that means. *Dependent.* We say that a child is dependent upon her parents, in the sense that she needs her parents to sustain herself. We say that a court is dependent on the law, in the sense that it is to draw its judgment from the substance of the law, and not from the politics of its judges. We say that a young man is dependent upon himself, in the sense that he draws his sustenance from his own industry and savings, and not from his parents or the state. We say the president is dependent upon the people, in the sense that she is selected in an election by the people. (At the framing convention, delegate James Wilson worried that if the president was selected by the Senate, his "dependence on them" would mean that "the President will not be the man of the people as he ought to be," but would instead be a "minion of the Senate."[3])

In all these cases, dependence speaks to a relation governing a person or an institution over time. It describes the health or character of that person or institution. It provides a test for the loss of that character, or for its failing health.

Dependencies, of course, can be multiple. And they can conflict. A drug addict could be dependent on his employer for his income or career. But he is also dependent on the drug to which he is addicted. These dependencies are different. These dependencies conflict.

Tweedism describes a system within which there are multiple dependencies built into a democracy. In its simplest form, it

describes an additional dependence within a democratic process—
a dependence beyond a dependence "on the people alone." Tweedism is a dependence on the tweeds *as well as* a dependence on
the people. Were the tweeds simply a snapshot of the people—
imagine the tweeds were a truly random and representative body
of 5,000—that additional dependence would not be a corrupting
dependence. Congress would be dependent on the tweeds and
"the people," but the tweeds would just be—in a statistical sense at
least—the people.

But in America, the tweeds are not the people. They in no sense
represent the people. The best political science demonstrates their
views are not the views of the people. Yet to get elected in America, a so-called "representative" must answer to these nonrepresen-
tative tweeds first.

We've thus allowed to evolve an additional dependence that
conflicts with a dependence on the people. We've thus allowed the
original design *to be corrupted*. As Zachary Brugman puts it:

> An additional relationship of dependence by a representative
> to attain office, beyond the dependence on the People, epito-
> mizes corruption—and results in aristocracy.[4]

That conclusion is important both rhetorically and legally. It is
important legally for a reason that I will return to in Chapter 12.
For now, stay focused on the rhetoric: We have allowed a structure
to develop that defeats a primary objective of the Framers' design.
That structure—the way we fund campaigns—is thus a corruption
of that design.

Because Unequal

Tweedism has also rendered us unequal.

"Unequal."

That word sits uncomfortably within American politics today.
In one sense, it is perfectly uncontroversial: No one defends race

discrimination, or sex discrimination, or at least no one defends them openly anymore. And almost no one defends sexual orientation discrimination—and amazingly so, given how quickly attitudes on that equality have changed. In this sense, we are all egalitarians, Republicans and Democrats alike. In this sense, at least, we all believe in "equality."

But when the sense of "equality" shifts from race or sex to class, the hums of "Kumbaya" fall silent. We all may believe in racial equality, but wealth equality? For a large majority of Americans, especially on the Right, *no way*.[5] The same is true for speech equality. Even for many on the Left, *no way*. We are all egalitarians in some spheres at least, but we are not egalitarians in all spheres. Americans embrace—indeed, celebrate—the inequalities among us, and for the vast majority of us, we believe that government has no place in trying to eliminate these inequalities.

Yet there is at least one more sense of equality—beyond race and sex and sexual orientation—that we all, Republicans, Democrats, and Independents alike, should be able to embrace, openly and warmly. A sense of equality that doesn't thereby commit us to equality of wealth or equality of speech. And a sense of equality that our Framers were clearest about, even if we've lost touch with their founding ideal.

This is the sense of equality *as citizens*: the idea that we should all have an equal place in a representative democracy. That as a "Republic" (by which the Framers meant a representative democracy), we weigh the voice of each citizen equally.

This is the sense of equality in John Adams's description of a legislature: "an exact portrait, in miniature of the people at large, as it should feel, reason and act like them."[6]

This is the sense of equality that James Madison had when he promised a branch "dependent on the people alone," in which "the people" were "not the rich more than the poor."[7]

This is the sense of equality that makes the very idea of a "representative democracy" make sense. Because representative of what? Of citizens, of course, and of course, of citizens equally.

Obviously, across our history, America has not lived up to this ideal equality. Blacks were slaves. Women were practically the property of men.

But the failures across our history are mistakes that we, as a people, discovered, not mistakes that were intended. We—all of us—see their mistake with race, and sex. They didn't. And the struggle of ideals that is the story of America is the fight to achieve equality when inequality is finally recognized. Some always saw the inequality as inequality. Eventually, everyone came to recognize what only some originally saw.

Yet the equality of citizens is an equality that our Framers saw then, but that we have forgotten now.

They saw then that a system that gave "the rich," again, as Madison put it, more power than "the poor" violated the core commitments of a representative democracy, what they called "a Republic." "The people" upon which Congress was to be "dependent alone" were not to be "the rich more than the poor."[8] "The people" upon whom our Congress is dependent today, however, are "the rich more than the poor."

But didn't the Framers restrict the vote to property owners only? How could that be a commitment to equality regardless of wealth?

They did—though at the time, as John Steele noted, "almost every man is a freeholder, and has the right of election."[9] And in any case, in the view of most at the time, the vote was reserved to property owners as a means to *avoid* aristocracy. As Gouverneur Morris stated, "Give the votes to the people who have no property, and they will sell them to the rich who will be able to buy them.... If you don't establish a qualification of property, you will have an Aristocracy."[10] This was Blackstone's view as well ("if these persons had votes [that] would give a great, an artful, or a wealthy man a larger share in elections than is consistent with general liberty").[11] Whether their prediction was right or not as a factual matter, their motive was not aristocracy.

The tweedism of American politics today thus violates their

sense of equality. It violates the equality of citizens. "The rich" plainly have a power that "the poor" (or the middle class, for that matter) don't, because of a system for funding campaigns that renders representatives dependent on "the rich" in a way that they aren't dependent on the poor. Just as the White Primary violated the equality of citizens by creating an impermissible dependence on whites at a critical first stage of an election, the Green Primary violates the equality of citizens by creating an impermissible dependence on the rich at a critical first stage of an election. That wrong is the inequality.

Yet to say "the people" means "not the rich more than the poor" is decidedly not to say that there should be no rich or no poor. It does not, in other words, mandate equal wealth. Likewise, to say that we are entitled to be equal citizens is not to say that we must equalize speech, or that everyone must have equal persuasive influence. Those kinds of equality might or might not make sense (and in the extremes, I would oppose both).

But whether you support these particular equalities or not, they are ideas that are distinct from the idea of equality as citizens. We can be equal citizens, even if Bill Gates has more money than you. And we can be equal citizens, even if Bill O'Reilly is more persuasive to more people than I. It is a *political* equality to which a Republic is committed. Political equality does not entail social, or economic, or persuasive equality.

Why we are so confused about the idea of equality today is a powerfully interesting question. We have been colored by the modern battles for race and sex equality—battles that have had at their core the claim of "equality as sameness." Women have the same ability as men. Blacks are as qualified as whites. This equation then feeds, as my colleague Danielle Allen puts it in her book, *Our Declaration* (2014), a choice that politicians, and political philosophers, have presented us with. As Allen describes:

> Too many of us think that to say two things are "equal" is to say that they are "the same." Consequently, we think the assertion

that "all men are created equal," is patently absurd....But "equal" and "same" are not synonyms. To be "the same" is to be "identical." But to be "equal" is to have an equivalent degree of some specific quality or attribute. We can be equal in height although we are not the same as people.[12]

Thus, when the Declaration of Independence began:

WHEN IN THE COURSE OF HUMAN EVENTS, IT BECOMES NECESSARY for one people to dissolve the political bands which have connected them with another, and to assume among the powers of the earth, *the separate and equal station* to which the Laws of Nature and of Nature's God entitle them...

no one believed that the United States was "equal" to Britain, in the sense of wealth, or power, or the ability to influence— despite the declaration that we would assume an "equal station." The United States was a developing nation; Britain was arguably the most powerful nation in the world. Whatever "equal station" means, it *could not possibly* mean "equal" in the sense of the equality of stuff. "Equal station" means the equal status of each nation, recognizing the vast differences that exist between these "equal" nations. Again, Allen:

[Equal] does not mean equal in all respects. It does not mean equal in wealth. It does not mean equal in military might. It does not mean equal in power. It means equal as a power.[13]

And political equality, or as I describe it, equality of citizens, thus means, as Allen puts it, "equal political empowerment."[14]

No doubt, *from our perspective*, the Framers practiced that equality poorly. Women were not equal citizens. African-Americans were slaves. Those were the great mistakes of our tradition, and (some of) our parents and grandparents and great-grandparents worked incredibly hard to correct those mistakes. After generations of struggle, we've made progress on those corrections, and there is still a great deal to be done.

But from the Framers' perspective, we, too, have practiced the ideal of equality poorly. Because from their perspective, the one idea of equality that was central to their design is the one ideal that we have all but given up on.

We can redeem their promise of equal citizenship, without contradicting their ideal of free speech. We can defend the ideal of equal citizenship, without questioning the dream of Horatio Alger. We can promise a people denied equal citizenship that the remedy to their injustice flows from a tradition we have all inherited: a tradition of a constant struggle for a more perfect union.

Tweedism is a corruption of the ideals of a Republic. It is a corruption *because* it denies citizens political equality.

But isn't unequal influence and access at the core of democracy? And hasn't the Supreme Court explicitly held that "equalizing the relative ability of individuals and groups to influence the outcome of elections" is not something that Congress is allowed to do?[15]

We will return to the details of the Supreme Court's cases in Chapter 12. But for now, let me surprise you by saying: I agree with the Court. Congress has no general, free-floating power to "equalize" the "influence of speech." *Speech equality* is "constitutionally suspect,"[16] as Dean Robert Post puts it. It is certainly not a founding principle. The First Amendment is pretty clear evidence of its rejection.

But to say that Congress has no power to equalize speech cannot mean that Congress has no power to eliminate tweedism. For tweedism isn't speech. Tweedism is a structure that has the formal effect of rendering certain citizens less represented. And as the Supreme Court has held in a related case that we'll consider in detail in Chapter 6, a structure that "defeat[s] the right of the people to choose representatives for Congress" is one that Congress can regulate. Indeed, it is one that Congress must regulate, if the "great purposes" of the Constitution are to be respected.[17]

Tweedism is such a structure. Tweedism reserves to some—the tweeds—first dibs on selecting the candidates that the rest of us get to vote among. Is that reservation constitutionally permitted?

Certainly sometimes it is—think about a party primary. There's nothing wrong in principle with a system that identifies the party candidates that get to compete in the general election. All citizens are equally free to join a political party. They might not like the choices, but they're not banned, formally or effectively, from joining.

But it is equally certain that sometimes such a reservation is permitted.

Think about the most extreme case: Imagine Congress said that in the next election, candidates for Congress shall be selected by "a nominating committee" of the 100 richest Americans.

There is no possible way that such a scheme could be constitutional, even though, as the Supreme Court said in *Citizens United*, "the people have the ultimate influence over elected officials,"[18] and even if, in abolishing it, Congress would be "equalizing" the speech of those 100 richest Americans with the rest of us.

The problem with this explicit tweedism is not unequal speech. The problem is a structure that defeats the potential for equal participation. That structure "defeat[s] the right of the people to choose representatives for Congress," because it makes members of Congress "dependent" on a group that cannot be said to represent "the people." This is a "democracy with Chinese characteristics," as Martin Lee put it.[19] It is a system that defeats the rights of the people. It is a system that *corrupts* the basic commitment to a branch "dependent on the people alone."

Now of course, there is a huge difference between a system that explicitly says "the 100 richest get to pick" and a private system for funding political campaigns. But as I'll show in Chapter 12, that difference should not matter for the Constitution. It is a corruption of the Framers' design whether the tweeds are selected or not. It is a corruption because it creates a dependence on something other than "the people alone."

To target tweedism is thus to target this systemic corruption. The consequence of that corruption is inequality, including speech inequality. But the power of Congress is not the power to remedy (at least) speech inequality. It is the power to remedy the corruption. From time immemorial, Congress has had the power to remedy corruption. It should have that power however that corruption evolves. Systems that corrupt the ideal of equal citizenship must be systems that Congress can change.

"But is the way we fund campaigns the only source of inequality?"

Obviously not. The way we fund campaigns is but one of many ways, some direct, some not, that our democracy defeats the ideal of representativeness. And most of these other inequalities Congress is perfectly free to fix without any concern raised by the First Amendment.

We vote on Tuesday, which means we make it more difficult for a significant portion of our population—ones without a flexible work schedule, or without easy child care—to vote. There's no First Amendment problem with Congress mandating weekend voting.

Thirty-four states demand IDs to vote, meaning the poor and old are disproportionally burdened, because they are least likely to have appropriate IDs.[20] The First Amendment wouldn't restrict rules that remedied that burden.

Districts in the House of Representatives are gerrymandered across the country, producing a Congress in which less than 100 seats are contested, meaning a Congress in which the minority in three fourths of the nation never have a shot at electing a representative. ("In a normal democracy," *The Economist* writes, "voters choose their representatives. In America, it is rapidly becoming the other way around."[21])

That gerrymandering plus single-member districts make the problem only worse. In 2012, though 40 percent of New England voters cast ballots for Republican Mitt Romney, Republicans won exactly zero seats from that region in that election.[22] (Don't feel too bad for the GOP: In the same year, nationally, the party won 52 percent of the vote, but because of the winner-take-all, single-member districts, got 57 percent of the seats.[23]) But it wouldn't violate the First Amendment for Congress to require multimember districts (again[24]), or to set rules that limit gerrymandering.

You might think this is just the nature of a democracy—there will always be losers, and it's not a political crime if the Flat Earth Party never wins an election.

But the issue isn't about losers. It is about choosing political structures that produce unnecessary unrepresentativeness. There are obvious ways to structure our representative democracy that would give more representation to a wider range of citizens. Removing partisan gerrymandering would be a first step. (In states where Republicans drew the lines, they won 72 percent of the seats with just 53 percent of the votes; in states where Democrats drew the lines, they won 71 percent of the seats with just 56 percent of the vote.[25] Eliminating winner-take-all districts (as was the practice at the founding[26]) would be a powerful next step. And adding a procedure by which people could rank their choices ("ranked choice voting") would give more people a better chance of real representation. Automatic registration. Strengthening, as Bruce Cain argues, the institutions that support pluralism.[27] If we set as our ideal the fundamental principle of any Republic—that citizens be represented equally—then there are a host of ways that we could make dramatic improvements on the system we have now—improvements, at least, from the perspective of the equality of citizens, without changing the Constitution,[28] and without triggering any First Amendment concern.

But of these inequalities, the money is the most significant. There is no other exclusion as dramatic in our democracy today, and none that is as consequential. Every other problem either flows from this inequality, or is exacerbated by this inequality. This is the one we must fix first.

CHAPTER 3

Consequences: Vetocracy

B ut so what?" the skeptic asks. "What's the real harm? There are rich Republicans and rich Democrats both. What reason is there to believe that the view of 'the people' gets lost in this mix?"

Equality *is* a fine ideal. It is a reason of principle to push for change.

But if principles don't get you going, something else here should.

Tweedism is a problem not just for the unequal among us. Tweedism is a problem for all of us. Tweedism doesn't just distort what our government does. Tweedism renders America ungovernable. Tweedism has produced not an aristocracy, not a plutocracy, nor a kleptocracy. Tweedism is the clearest way to understand why America is a "vetocracy."

A "vetocracy"—veto-ocracy—is a system in which governance has become impossible because so many have the effective power to block, or veto, any proposed change.

In his most recent book, *Political Order and Political Decay*, American political theorist Francis Fukuyama describes why America has always been ripe for vetocracy—a constitutional Republic obsessed with separating and checking power by design establishes veto mechanisms which give many in society the ability to stop reform.[1] That structure blocked critical change across the history of America, civil rights legislation most dramatically. That system was designed to block change, so long as a substantial minority didn't support it.

But when bundled with the extreme partisanship of America today, that constitutional design becomes a governance disaster. Partisanship is the motive; constitutionally separated power, the means; a government unable to address any important issue sensibly, Fukuyama argues, the consequence.[2] A vetocracy.

To this story, however, we must add the role of money. Because the mechanism by which this polarization matters (and as I'll describe later, by which it is also amplified) is money. The design of our Constitution renders us vulnerable, no doubt. The separation made manifest by polarization makes succumbing to that vulnerability more likely. But the thing that engenders it all is the money: the life of members in a Skinner box, fund-raising perpetually, and hence, perpetually susceptible to the influence of money. This is the dynamic that has made a constitutional design questionable in theory, flawed in fact.

It also begins to define the very nature of the power of a member. As Senator Tom Harkin (D-Ia., 1985–2015) put it, "A senator has his or her power not because of what we can do—but because of what we can stop."[3] That, in turn, incentivizes an obvious response among lobbyists. As Darrell West describes:

> Because of Senate rules granting unbridled authority to individual senators to block nominations through secret holds, object to "unanimous consent" motions, and engage in filibusters... a popular tactic among those with extensive political connections is to develop a close relationship with a senator who sits on a key committee... [to] persuade that person to block undesired nominations or bills.[4]

Vetocracy is thus a general condition. It is an equal opportunity inhibitor. It blocks the ability to pass climate change legislation. It blocks the ability to get fundamental tax reform. It blocks real health care reform. It blocks the willingness to deal with the debt. Regardless of the issue, so long as there exists on one side of a fight a sufficiently concentrated economic interest, vetocracy will give that concentrated interest the levers it needs to block change.

Not always. Not with every issue. And not regardless of the person in power. Nothing in politics is certain.

But just as the smoker who never gets lung cancer isn't proof that smoking doesn't cause cancer, so, too, are the sporadic victories for reform in Congress not evidence that the system is working. It is not working when we can stand back from the political battlefield and recognize that for a wide range of the most important questions facing America today, sensible reform, whether from the Right or the Left, is not possible.

Thus, the problem of vetocracy is a problem of structure. In its essence, it points to a certain instability. By concentrating the power of funding in the hands of a few, tweedism gives that few extraordinary power. They exercise that power, rationally from their perspective, but irrationally from ours.

Because beyond a few issues, this tiny few is not united by a common interest. They all benefit, of course, from lower taxes, but what motivates the most engaged is not actually taxes. Instead, it is a diversity of interests and wants that drive these funders to fund as they do. But that diversity has no consistent internal logic. It is a hodgepodge, not a plan. It is the erratic flailing of an out-of-control computer, not a Jack Welch–style strategic plan.

Think about this point, because it is too often overlooked yet critical for seeing just how unstable things have become.

If it were a landed aristocracy that controlled our government, there would be a relatively consistent set of wants that would guide government policy—at least where that policy affected the aristocracy. Or if it were GM that controlled our government, then the government would bend to benefit GM, yet be relatively free beyond the concerns of GM. Or the same with a criminal cartel. Or the king of France. The point is that if we were controlled by a very small few with a distinctive and coherent common view, that might be bad for the people, but it wouldn't be disastrous, or at least not necessarily so. If we thought of political society as a huddled mass, then any of these tiny few would be pulling that mass in not the best direction, for that mass, at least. But at least they'd be pulling in a consistent direction, at least for them.

Yet we don't even have that. We don't even have the benefit

of consistency. Because the tweedism that we've evolved permits equal power to tweeds with radically different purposes. And thus the rest of us get pulled in radically different directions. As Richard Painter puts it, "Despite all of the rhetoric about the top 1 percent or top .05 percent using the campaign finance system to control the Country, no cohesive group of people is in control."[5] There are funders demanding climate change legislation, and funders demanding none. There are funders eager for health insurance mandates and funders keen to avoid the competition of a public option. There are idealists pushing for free trade, and cronies pushing for sugar tariffs. There are funders pushing for simpler taxes and builders pushing for subsidies for mortgage companies.

The American democracy is not the victim of a hostile takeover by an organized clan eager to serve itself. Think instead of vultures feeding on the carcass of a gazelle. There is no consistency. There is no vision. There is no plan. There is just an increasingly frenetic effort by funders to get what they can while they can—since after all, everyone else is, too.

"But why isn't that just the description of a perfectly competitive market? Shouldn't we all want a system where many powerful interests are competing against each other? Won't the best policy then just rise to the top, just like competition among the sellers of pork bellies produces the cheapest pork bellies for all?"

This is a common view. It reflects a common mistake. As I've carried this fight across the country, I've heard it repeated again and again. The intuition begins solidly enough—competition in the market benefits us all. But the next step is simply a fallacy. As Milton Friedman famously wrote, we certainly want competition *within the rules* of a free market.[6] But we don't want the competitors in that market to compete to define those rules.

The reason is pretty obvious, and is the core argument made by those on the Right who rally against "crony capitalism."[7] If we create a market in regulation, we give the dinosaurs the power to block evolution. As libertarian economist Luigi Zingales puts it:

The incumbent large firms are politically powerful but not necessarily the most efficient. Thus they have a strong incentive to manipulate the power of the state to preserve their market power through political means. The winner take all economy, in other words, breeds crony capitalism.[8]

Imagine what would have happened if AT&T had been free to block the Internet. Or Comcast blocked YouTube. Or Verizon blocked Skype. In each case, the most powerful company today is last generation's great success. The great danger of capitalism is that the successful use government to protect themselves— from the next generation's success. Their aim is to knife the baby, because babies don't have lobbyists.

"But doesn't democracy itself pull in every direction? Isn't the battle of politics precisely a battle over the rules?"

It is, of course. There's no single or common "public good" that guides the votes of 146 million registered voters, let alone 535 representatives.

But here is the critical point: The danger in tweedism is not influence. It is the *concentration* of influence. The problem comes from concentrating this power in so few. No doubt government can make terrible decisions. But if you need to rally millions to support your terrible idea, the chances of you succeeding are pretty small.

Yet today, to block real health care reform, or climate change legislation, or tax reform, or regulatory relief, or cuts to defense spending, or the elimination of sugar baron tariffs, you don't need to win millions to your side. You need only a few thousand. A vetocracy is a system that has perfected the ability to make bad decisions, at least where that bad decision benefits the few with power, and harms the rest of us.

And this, in the end, points us to the best practical understanding of our present dilemma. But to set it up properly, we need to add some historical context.

In the late nineteenth and early twentieth centuries, the Supreme Court developed a set of constitutional rules that had a very profound consequence for regulation: Whole sectors of our economy were technically beyond the regulatory reach not just of the federal government, but of any government.

Limits on the federal government derived, the Supreme Court said, from the nature of our federal Constitution. The Framers gave us a government of "enumerated powers." In the early twentieth century, the Court interpreted those enumerated powers to be quite narrow. Those limits meant that powerful economic entities that were affecting the United States economy as whole could not be regulated by the federal government. According to the Court, the power to regulate those entities, in theory at least, lay with the state.

But only, it turned out, in theory. Because a different part of the Constitution—the Due Process Clause—turned out to restrict, the Supreme Court held, the power of *any* government to regulate economic activity. That Clause was interpreted to mean that states couldn't regulate these powerful economic entities either. So the result was that the Supreme Court interpreted the Constitution to effectively require laissez-faire, at least for hugely important swaths of the American economy. We were not permitted—either the states or the federal government—to regulate powerful economic actors. The Framers, it turned out, were economic libertarians—at least according to the Court, and bizarrely so, since at least the Framers of the Constitution were framing long before anyone understood the true foundations of modern "libertarianism."

This extreme position survived during the boom of the bubble that was the 1920s. But the crash of 1929 shook the constitutional certainties that had sustained this vision.[9] It may well be that less regulation is better than more regulation. But after a collapse that seemed so directly tied to wild irrationalities within the market, the view that whole chunks of our economy should be beyond the reach of the people—through regulators—was no longer even plausible. No doubt, government could screw it up. But so, too, could the market screw up—as it just had. And in any modern society, or so the view evolved, there needed to be at least the ability of a government to step in. Whatever the force of the theory had promised that things "eventually" would take care of themselves, in the face of 25 percent unemployment at the height of the Depression, no one was willing to believe anymore that things would take care of themselves.

Okay, that's the history. Here's the lesson: We are quickly approaching a similarly forced laissez-faire today, though with less principle, and with vastly worse consequences. Yet the forcing today is not constitutional. It is political. Powerful sectors of our economy are free of regulation not because the Supreme Court has ruled that the Constitution requires it to be so. Powerful sectors of our economy are instead free of regulation *because there could no longer be any sufficient political will to intervene* against them. The way we fund campaigns has rendered certain crucial sectors of the American economy sensible-regulation-free zones. And as we think about what sectors those are, there should grow within us a certain terror. In a world in which members of Congress spend 30 to 70 percent of their time raising money from a tiny fraction of America, small numbers matter. Whole industries become untouchable, because to regulate them would be political suicide for the party in power, or the party trying to get power.

Exhibit 1: the financial sector.

After the 2008 financial crisis, the one *relatively uncontroversial* reform that practically everyone agreed upon was the need to assure that private banks didn't get to gamble with the government as their backup. The most grotesque part of the 2008 collapse was that Wall Street had engaged in a massive one-way bet. Using the exploding market of derivatives and the like, Wall Street earned massive profits. But when the bet of those derivatives went south, we paid the bill, through government bailouts. It was the dumbest form of socialism known to man: We privatized the benefits, but socialized the loss.

The reason for this silliness was that the banks got to gamble, in effect, with government-backed funds. They believed we weren't going to let them fail, so they believed that if their bets went south, we'd pick up the tab. We knew and the market knew, because the bigger banks paid less for capital, because the markets expected that they would be bailed out.[10] And when those bets did go south, we did what the market predicted: We saved the banks, with the largest bailout in human history of one the most profitable sectors in America's economy.

The 2010 Dodd-Frank bill was meant to change all this. In effect, the law required that if banks were going to gamble with derivatives, they needed to do so with funds not guaranteed by the American taxpayer. Of course, the law didn't effect that result in any simple way. (The 1932 Glass-Steagall Act was 37 pages long; the Dodd-Frank Act is 848 pages long.[11]) But still, the intent was clear, and the purpose perfectly sensible. If there's any sector of our economy that doesn't need a guarantee from the taxpayers, it is the banks gambling with derivatives.

But in December 2014, Congress changed all that. In a rider to a bill designed to keep the government open, Democrats and Republicans agreed to relax the regulation on derivatives. Banks are once again permitted to gamble with taxpayer-backed funds. And the reason for this change isn't very hard to see.

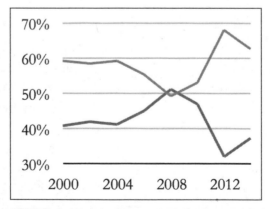

FIGURE 3. *Percentage of Finance, Insurance, and Real Estate contributions going to each party.*

After Dodd-Frank, the Democrats were punished.[12] The largest sector funding congressional campaigns turned against the party, dropping its contributions to a historic low. In 2014, "finance, insurance, and real estate" gave close to $500 million, with almost two thirds going to Republicans.[13] That change no doubt weighed on at least some of the 88 Democrats who joined Republicans to "deregulate derivatives."[14] Democrats could not afford to be Wall Street reformers, at least for long.

Robert Kaiser makes a similar point about Congress, long before this punishment began:

> In earlier eras real radicals could be found in Congress, men who were ready, even eager, to enact harsh measures to impinge on the privileges of the rich, though they almost never enjoyed majority support. By 2009 such firebrands were all but extinct.[15]
>
> What explains this "extinct[ion]"? Kaiser: "The moderation shown now even by liberal Democrats surely was influenced by the political money game."[16]

The general point is this: A tiny number of motivated citizens have an incredible power over our government today. As Mancur Olson pointed out a half-century ago, in *The Logic of Collective Action* (1965), in some sense that's always been true. But today the effect is much much worse. Today, because of the interaction between the collection action problem and the funding of campaigns, a tiny fraction has even more influence. Neither political party can afford to make Wall Street, or pharmaceuticals, or the energy sector, their enemy. Both parties are thus held hostage by these special interests, because both parties need their campaign contributions.[17]

Our problems today are not particular. They are systemic. We are not color blind—unable to see reds, or blues. We are simply blind. When most think about the corrupting effect of money in politics, they think about specific policies that this system blocks.

We'll never get climate change legislation, the enlightened climate activist reasons, until we change the way elections are funded. And the same with tax policy, or the debt, or health care reform, or defense spending: With each, the current system of dependence practically guarantees that no sensible reform within each of these areas is possible.

But the critical point is to connect the dots. This isn't a problem for a particular issue. It is a problem for government generally. We're not at a time when a small set of important problems can't be dealt with—as, for example, was the case with civil rights for the hundred years after the end of Reconstruction. We're at a time when practically every important issue, whether a concern of the Right or the Left, can't be dealt with—because of the corrupting influence of concentrated funding. This isn't a moment of a particular failure. This is a moment of general failure.

The cop on the beat is a drug addict. We can't rely on a drug addict to police his pusher. We need to find a way to break his addiction, if we're to have any chance to restore a government that works. We will only break that addiction by changing the way campaigns are funded.

It's just this simple: Change the way campaigns are funded, and we have a chance to save this Republic. Continue with the status quo, and we don't.

CHAPTER 4

The Fix

The fundamental problem with America's democracy is a problem of equality. Not the equality of wealth, or speech, or race, or
sex. Instead, the equality of citizens.

Shot through our system are a host of devices—winner-take-
all, single-member districts (as opposed to multimember districts,
where more than one representative gets selected), gerrymandering, Tuesday voting, etc.—that compromise that equality. Those
compromises defeat a founding ideal.

The way we fund campaigns corrupts that equality. The rules
governing elections corrupt that equality, too. In both contexts, we
have allowed systems to evolve that deny a fundamental equality.
In both contexts, we need reform to establish or restore that equality of citizens.

The reform for unequal elections is familiar enough. Ending partisan gerrymandering. Ending discriminatory voting restrictions.
Restoring a framing ideal of multimember districts.[1] Expanding the
technique of ranked-choice-voting (so voters can rank many different choices on the same ballot): All of these would restore the
power of a disenfranchised many, by restructuring the economy of
influence for ordinary politics. These changes have been described
extensively elsewhere, and most powerfully of late by Michael
Golden, in his book, *Unlock Congress* (2015).[2]

The remedy for the corrupting way that we fund campaigns is
more obscure.

In the view of most, there's nothing we can do to change the
influence of money in politics—short of banning it, which of
course some (but only a few) support. It's baked into the system,

most seem to believe. And given a Supreme Court seemingly bent on striking down almost every campaign finance rule, there seems little to be done to remedy this fundamental flaw.

But there is a remedy—or at least a remedy for 90 percent of today's problem. There is a change that is at once feasible (since it requires just a statute) and constitutional (as the Supreme Court has explained again and again). The work we need now is not the crafting of new amendments to the Constitution. That work is necessary, but it is not the first task. The work we need now is understanding, and a willingness to state the obvious.

The core flaw of the current system is the concentration of its funders. That concentration betrays the fundamental commitment of a *representative* democracy—of a government "dependent on the people alone," where "the people" mean "not the rich more than the poor."

But if that's the problem, the solution is not hard to describe. If the problem is *concentration*, the solution is *dilution*. If the problem is that too few exercise control over the funding of campaigns, the solution is for many more to exercise control over the funding of campaigns.

Yet the term we typically use to describe this solution—"public funding"—creates its own problem in American political culture today. Because that word is ambiguous between a solution and yet another version of the problem.

What we need is a kind of "public funding of campaigns." But that term—"public funding"—is too often associated with a different kind of centralization. If "public funding" means "government funding," then we're just replacing one system of centralized control with another.[3] Instead of working to please the few, candidates would work to please the government. And while the nature of that pleasing is very different—the 100 want to know your views on issues X, Y, and Z, while the government simply wants to know whether you've got enough signatures on your petitions—there's still something very twentieth century in the idea of erecting a massive federal bureaucracy to address the problem of a massive concentration of private power.[4]

I don't support *government public funding* of elections. Instead, the public funding that I support is *citizen public funding* of elections. It is public funding that gives more people the power to influence elections. It is a system of funding that democratizes campaign funding in just the way votes are meant to democratize candidate elections.

This is the kind of public funding of elections that the Framers knew. Yes, the Framers. Because here's the critical fact about our history that we as a political culture have all but forgotten: *In the beginning, there was public funding of campaigns. At the birth of the American Republic, the public funded the core costs of campaigns for public office with public funds.*

It is perhaps the least understood fact about our founders and the founding generation: They spent federal tax dollars to fund the political campaigns of federal officials. But in the main, they did this in the right way. The money they spent was fundamentally decentralizing. It spread political understanding without concentrating power in the few.

The biggest chunk of the federal budget at the founding—by far—was for the post office.[5] The post office gave political parties and pamphleteers the opportunity to send their publications to the public almost for free.[6] (Washington wanted free postage for all newspapers; Madison wanted a small charge—to encourage efficient delivery. Madison won.[7]) At a time when the Framers couldn't agree about whether the federal Constitution gave Congress the power to build highways (for horses and carriages), the single largest expenditure by the federal government was to support the construction of the first information superhighway (which the post office was back then, at least compared with the post office of today). Through the channels of the post office, ideas and argument would flow. Tax dollars funded that flow of (practically) free speech. Tax dollars thereby effectively knit together the political culture of the nation. As Theda Skocpol has quipped, "Early United States may have been not so much a country with a post office as a post office that gave popular reality to a fledgling nation."[8] Benjamin Rush, signer of the Declaration of Independence and delegate at the constitutional convention, described the mechanism:

> For the purpose of diffusing knowledge, as well as extending the living principle of government to every part of the United States—every state—city—county—village—and township in the union, should be tied together by means of the post-office....It should be a constant injunction to the postmasters, to convey newspapers free of all charge for postage. They are not only the vehicles of knowledge and intelligence, but the sentinels of the liberties of our country.[9]

Federal subsidies didn't stop there. Funding the post office is fairly neutral: (Practically) anyone could take advantage of the subsidy; money was not denied on the basis of the substance of what one speaker said.

But in addition to this "viewpoint neutral" subsidy, Congress also funded politics in a very partisan way.[10] It was one of the spoils of the system that the party in power gave government printing contracts to partisan newspapers, as a way to subsidize the partisan power of those newspapers to organize the public to support the party in power. Those subsidies were obviously not neutral. But they show quite clearly just how invested the Framers were in the idea that the government has a critical role in subsidizing the flow of political information to the public.

The public funding that we should support today has nothing to do with the post office. Nor should it be partisan in the way that the funding of the partisan press was. But it should be—as both of those techniques were—*decentralizing*. It should enable more to participate in the influencing of our representatives, not fewer.

In American politics today, there are at least two conceptually different public funding proposals that meet this standard—proposals that subsidize political speech, by decentralizing the funding power.

The first is an idea now pressed most vigorously by Republicans—*vouchers* to fund elections. The second is an idea pressed most strongly by Democrats—*matching funds* for small contributions.

Vouchers

Imagine if every registered voter received a stored-value card—like a Target card, or a Starbucks card—worth $50. And imagine that voter could allocate whatever part of that $50 she wanted to any candidate running for Congress—either Senate or House, but excluding the president.[11] Any allocation could be revoked within twenty-four hours of being made (this is important to avoid voucher fraud, as I'll explain a bit later in this section). But beginning nine months before an election, candidates could work to persuade voters to allocate their vouchers to them, as a way to fund their campaigns.

To qualify to receive these voucher funds, a candidate would have to demonstrate some minimal amount of public support—maybe "four score and seven" thousand $5 contributions (to play up the Lincoln link). And she would have to pledge to accept only two kinds of contributions to fund her campaign: vouchers and donations of up to $100 per citizen.

Fifty dollars doesn't sound like a lot. But it adds up quite quickly. Fifty dollars per voter is about $7 billion ($3.5 billion per year)—roughly 3.5 times as much as was raised by candidates for Congress in 2014. So this is real money, but it is real money from many people. It is decentralizing public funding, giving more the power to participate in the funding of elections, just as voting gives more the power to participate in the election of public officials.

What's more—and from a conservative perspective, what's even better—is that if the voucher is kept relatively small, no one is subsidizing anyone else's political speech. Sure, the voucher is funded by government funds. But you need to embrace your inner Tea Party here for a moment: Government funds are just *our* money. The voucher is just a *rebate* of the money that *we* have given the government (through taxes of whatever form); and all of us pay taxes to the federal government in some form. Not necessarily income taxes—most don't pay income tax. But the income tax is just one of six major (and many minor) kinds of taxes that the federal government has. Somewhere, and somehow, the government gets us for at least $50.

So the $50 is a simple rebate of the first $50 we send to DC—in a form that gives us the ability to secure *representative* government generally.

There have been voucher proposals for many years. Bruce Ackerman and Ian Ayres proposed them in 2004. Ed Foley and Rick Hasen proposed a different version a decade before. I proposed another version in 2011.[12]

But the most compelling arguments for vouchers today come from the Right. The former ethics czar for President George W. Bush, Richard Painter, for example, has advanced an incredibly ambitious voucher proposal. Painter motivates his proposal with a(n original) Tea Party slogan: No taxation without representation. His meaning should be pretty clear to the readers of this book so far. In the world of tweedism, all Americans might be represented equally, but some are more equal than others. Those who fund campaigns have a kind of representation that those who do not fund campaigns don't.

Painter takes that point, and builds upon it: The unequally represented should not be taxed until they are equally represented. And they would be equally represented only when representatives are equally dependent upon all of us. So Painter proposes a $200 per voter voucher, to cover all federal elections (president included), which, if enacted, would make everyone represented, and hence, subject to tax.

Similar arguments motivate the other powerful voucher proposal being pushed from the Right, this one from Jim Rubens of New Hampshire. Rubens was a New Hampshire state senator. In

2014, he ran in the Republican Primary to be that state's nominee for United States Senate. When he ran, he was the only Republican candidate running for Senate *in the nation* who made how campaigns are funded a central issue of his campaign. Rubens lost to Scott Brown (and full disclosure: the super PAC I helped start, Mayday.US, supported Rubens in his race). But as I watch Rubens's leadership on this issue (and also on another important issue that I'll describe in Chapter 9), I'm not sure whether he's more influential inside the Senate than out.

Rubens's proposal begins where I do—a tax rebate of $50 to every voter. He bundles that rebate with two other ideas—one which is relatively uncontroversial, and one which will appeal mainly to the Right.

The relatively uncontroversial proposal is disclosure: All contributions outside the $50 voucher must be disclosed immediately.

The controversial proposal is the repeal of any contribution limits: For candidates opting out of the voucher system, there would be no limits on contributions at all. Large funders who wish to support a candidate could therefore support that candidate directly. But any such direct funding would be reported to the public immediately.

There are parts of both Painter's and Rubens's proposals that I disagree with. But so what? Both would radically change the corrupting influence of money on our government. For rather than the funding coming from the few, both would make it possible for candidates to fund their campaigns from the many. And hence the influence of any few on the workings of our government would be radically decreased.

Yet a voucher system would do much more than this. In a word, it would *bind* representatives more completely to their supporters, just like the current dialing-for-dollars system binds representatives to their current funders.

As our elections are crafted now, representatives return to the voter every two years to secure their vote on Election Day. For the vast majority of representatives, there's only one election that really matters—the party primary. For some, there are two—the primary and the general election. But between those one or two voting days, representatives focus their attention elsewhere—on the funders of their campaigns.

The voucher system wouldn't change this mix, except again, and importantly, the funders would be the voters. So in the continuous engagement to recruit funders, candidates would be engaging an increasing number of voters. Each chance to speak is a chance to collect voucher dollars. And each neighborhood is a potential argument about why the incumbent or the challenger is the best representative for that neighborhood. As Ackerman and Ayres put it:

> [Vouchers] will give candidates a tremendous new incentive to reach out to the "silent majority" currently disconnected from the entire democratic process.[13]

Fund-raising would be continuous, but decentralized. And the role of the candidate would be radically changed. No one is going to be calling anyone to ask for $50 contributions. But campaigns will get increasingly good at reaching out to voucher holders to get them to support their candidate.

"But won't voters just sell their vouchers? Won't this system just fuel more bribery?"

This is an important concern, but is precisely the reason that any assignment must be (anonymously) revoked within twenty-four hours. By making the assignments revocable, you would destroy the market for vouchers.

Here's why: It would be a crime under the system to sell your voucher. But let's say someone tries, criminal law notwithstanding. He promises a campaign to transfer his $50 voucher to that campaign, if the campaign pays him $10.

The ability to revoke any transfer makes it highly unlikely that any rational soul would pay even $10 for the $50 voucher. Because if you're the sort of person who would sell your voucher—criminal law notwithstanding—you're also the sort of person who would sell your voucher twice. That is, you'd sell it to one campaign, then revoke the transfer, and sell it to another. Campaigns would recognize this, and hence recognize they're not getting much value for the dollar. And so just like vote buying in the twentieth century has essentially collapsed from its nineteenth-century high (in some communities, 25 percent of votes were sold[14]) because votes are anonymous and contracts to sell voters are therefore not verifiable, voucher buying in the twenty-first century would collapse, too. As Ackerman and Ayres put it, "Once a voter could promise to vote one way, and actually vote another, it was no longer easy for him to sell his vote."[15]

"Yes, but even if they can't sell the vouchers, they could bundle them. The AARP or NRA could gather millions of vouchers, and just replicate the problem of big money that we have today."

Vouchers certainly can be bundled. But that's not a bug. That's a feature. There is all the difference in the world between an organization that bundles 1 million $50 vouchers, and a system where billionaires write checks for $50 million. The first is democracy; the second is tweedism. The problem with our democracy today is not that there is money in politics; it is the concentration of the funders in politics. But once that concentration is removed, then aggregating small-dollar donations is the most effective way for groups to organize politically.

Thus, vouchers are one way to decentralize the funding of campaigns.[16] They would also encourage a wide range of other activity, all devoted to bringing more people into the political system. The effect would not just be to fund campaigns, but also to change the way campaigns mattered. Vouchers would give candidates an ongoing reason to be engaged with citizens—not a terrible thing in a democracy.

Matching Funds

The other major idea for decentralizing the funding of campaigns relies on matching funds, provided by the government, to encourage candidates to rely on small-dollar contributions alone. There are various versions of this matching funds idea—the most prominent being New York's system, which matches small contributions on a 6 to 1 ratio. But the most prominent federal proposal is the Government by the People Act by Congressman John Sarbanes

(D-Md., 2007–). Sarbanes's proposal would give candidates opting into the system up to a 9 to 1 match on contributions—depending on how much they limit their other contributions.

Sarbanes's proposal isn't exclusively a matching fund proposal. He also includes a pilot program for vouchers, as well as a fund to support small-dollar-funded candidates in the final days of a campaign.[17]

But the critical difference at the heart of the two proposals is whether the citizen has to put up his own money first. $20 is worth $200 under the Sarbanes program, and that will certainly give more people the incentive to (1) look for $20 contributions, and (2) give $20 contributions. But there can be little doubt that fewer will give 20 greenback dollars than would give 20 voucher dollars. The voucher would encourage more to participate; the matching funds give people the ability to participate with greater variance.

Both proposals thus do the same thing, even if they do it in different ways. Both would radically change the mix of funders in any campaign, by radically increasing the number of funders to any campaign. And by increasing the number of funders, both proposals would shift the attention of the candidates from large funders to the funders generally.

Would More Funders Make the Problems Worse?

There is some research to suggest that small-dollar contributions are more polarized than larger contributions. Moving to a small-dollar model only, skeptics such as Ezra Klein and Adam Bonica fear, would make the problem of polarization worse.[18]

But we can't extrapolate from the dynamic of small contributions *in a large-funder system* to the effect of small contributions *in a small-funder system*. In the current system, for most members of Congress, small contributions are gravy. And to the extent members make an appeal for them, the appeal draws directly on extreme and polarizing speech.

Yet in a system that was exclusively a small-dollar system, candidates could not afford to fund their campaigns from the extremes only. Instead, with, for example, a voucher system, they would need to reach a much wider range of citizens. That breadth would preclude extremism. Like a mandatory voting system, a small-dollar-funding regime would put constant pressure on representatives to hew to the mainstream.

This is the conclusion of perhaps the leading scholar studying the effects of small-dollar systems for funding elections. Michael Malbin of the Campaign Finance Institute has been at the center of research studying the effects of small-dollar systems, as compared to the dominant model of private funding. As he concludes from a wide range of empirical studies of actual small-dollar systems, from New York City's system for local elections, to Connecticut's and Maine's systems for state elections, small-dollar donors would widen the range of participation, and dilute the effect of the extremes within our system.[19]

These fears, however, should not be ignored. They tilt, in my view, toward the more inclusive small-dollar voucher systems pushed by Painter, or Rubens, or me. Those systems would at least guarantee more were in the mix of campaign funding, working against the existing pattern of donors coming from the extremes. If everyone were a funder, the funding system would be as polarized as the voters themselves are.[20]

But What Would All This Cost?

Public funding costs money. There's no hiding this fact, or imagining some special tax—on lobbyists, or television stations—would cover it. We as a democracy must be willing to invest in our democracy if that democracy is to function.

Of course, we've been keen to invest in democracies overseas. We've spent close to $1 trillion building democracy in the Middle East (not to mention the sacrifice in lives). So it's not unheard of for our nation to believe that investing in the infrastructure of freedom is a sensible way to spend tax dollars.

But the critical point to recognize about the cost of public funding in America is how small it would be relative to the other costs of government.

A $50 voucher program would cost $3.5 billion a year. No doubt, that's a lot of money. But compared to what?

The Cato Institute, for example, a libertarian think tank that is one of Washington's most respected (justifiably) and longstanding, tries each year to calculate the cost of "corporate welfare" in the federal budget. As they define it, "corporate welfare" includes "direct and indirect subsidies to small businesses, large corporations, and industry organizations."[21] In 2012, they estimated that the federal budget included $100 billion in corporate welfare.

Not everyone will object to the spending that Cato identifies. But if a newly independent Congress—meaning, one no longer dependent on corporate campaign cash—could reduce corporate welfare by just 10 percent, we could pay for public funding more than 2½ times over. No doubt, an independent Congress, like an independent judiciary, costs real money. But a dependent Congress, like a dependent judiciary, certainly costs more.

What These Changes Would Do for "Lobbying"

These proposals would also have an effect on a second economy of influence that is also at the center of the corruption of DC: lobbying.

This point is often overlooked. The conventional story says, "Campaign finance isn't the most important issue. Lobbying is the most important issue. Firms spend many times the money lobbying as they do funding."

But this ignores the critical support that lobbying gets from the way we fund campaigns.[22] If we chose differently—if we changed the way we fund campaigns—lobbying would be differently supported. And much less wealthy.

Lobbying is a critical part of any government. Lobbyists provide a crucial service, providing information and support to legislators as legislators do their job.

But as the system has evolved in America today, lobbyists provide a second service to our representatives in Congress. Directly or indirectly, the lobbyists help fund campaigns. Directly, by giving money themselves. Indirectly, by steering the funds of their clients to the candidates the lobbyists select.

This sounds like a burden for the lobbyists. In fact, it is an incredible benefit. Because as the members become dependent on the lobbyists, they become responsive to the requests of the lobbyists. And to the extent they become responsive, the lobbyists have a valuable product to sell to their clients. Mutual dependence thus works to produce mutual profit. The cronies are eager to find a reliable way to influence members of Congress; the lobbyists become an ever more reliable way.

But if the economy of campaign funding changed dramatically, this bit of the lobbyist's influence would disappear. Persuasive lobbyists would do better than unpersuasive lobbyists, just as good lawyers do better than bad lawyers. Beyond persuasion, the lobbyists would have no other lever to pull.

This change would in turn induce another important change. If the ability of a lobbyist to "persuade" is reduced, the value of being a lobbyist would fall as well. As the value of being a lobbyist falls, the ability to offer high salaries to former members of Congress or their staff from Capitol Hill would fall as well. And that means that the revolving door would slow, as members have less reason to leave Capitol Hill to move to K Street, and more reason either to return home, or to take up some other honest profession.

This change of the economy of lobbying is a critical, but underappreciated, shift that gives both more reason to want the fix, and more reason to doubt the fix will ever happen. Because if we got close, the lobbyists would notice. Yet if they noticed and fought a change in the way campaigns are funded—we would be fighting the most effective policy-making influence in America today.

We can overcome them. That's the argument of Part III. But before we get to that part, we need to clear up one final skepticism about the necessity in decentralizing campaign funding first. That skepticism expresses itself in a single sentence: "What about *Citizens United?*"

CHAPTER 5

Distractions

On January 21, 2010, the Supreme Court gave birth to a movement. The event was a decision in what many thought would be a tiny case, involving an obscure provision of an all but forgotten bit of "campaign finance reform" legislation—the McCain-Feingold Bipartisan Campaign Reform Act of 2002. Because in deciding the case, the Supreme Court set out a principle that both shocked practically everyone who heard about it, and gave birth to the most important reform movement since the progressives.

The case was *Citizens United v. Federal Election Commission* (2010), and the question was whether Congress had the power to forbid corporations and unions from spending funds from their treasury to support or oppose political candidates—at least independently of those candidates' campaigns.

In a closely divided vote, the Supreme Court held that Congress did not have that power. As the Court held, the only justification for restricting political speech was to avoid "corruption" or the "appearance of corruption." But because the Court conceived of "corruption" as "quid pro quo" corruption, by definition, an independent expenditure could not be a "quid pro quo"—since, by definition (and the Court was really treating it as if it was a matter of definition), "independent" *means* the quid is unrelated to the quo. Corporations and unions were thus free because of the Constitution to spend unlimited amounts to influence elections—"independently." The decision was shocking, not so much because of the particulars in the case, but because of how it came to be understood. Two slogans summarized the public's understanding of the Court's "mistake": First, the Court had treated "money as speech" (and obviously, as the critics insisted, money isn't speech; money is money); and second, the Court had treated "corporations as persons" (when obviously, as the critics insisted again, corporations are not persons any more than a Steve in *Minecraft* is a person).

These mistakes, its critics predicted, would bring about a radical change in campaign spending. Corporations would now flood the airways with political ads, radically altering the political landscape. The case was likened to *Dred Scott*, a case that may well have caused the Civil War.[1] It was, in the words of Senator John McCain (R-Ariz., 1987–), "one of the worst decisions I have ever seen."[2]

I was among the Chicken Littles predicting the worst from *Citizens United*. And certainly, we Chicken Littles were right to believe that *Citizens United* would bring about a radical change, and a change for the worse.

But we were wrong about just how. The case did not open up the floodgates of corporate money—at least not directly. It may well have not opened the floodgates of corporate money at all. We just don't know. In 2014, if every "dark" dollar contributed was contributed by a corporation, then just 4.6 percent of the money spent in 2014 came from corporations.[3] That's not a flood. That's a leak.

Yet *Citizens United* did lead to a much more consequential court decision that did change things in a much more significant way. This decision was not made by the Supreme Court. This decision was made by a lower court sitting in Washington, DC, and ultimately, unreviewed by the Supreme Court.

Two months after *Citizens United*, a court of appeals extended its reasoning in a dramatic (and I think ultimately mistaken) way.

As I've described, *Citizens United* held that the First Amendment gave corporations and unions *the right to spend* unlimited amounts independently of a political campaign. That left open the question of the *right to contribute* to support that spending. It's one thing to say that I have a constitutional right to spend my money to support my ideas. (Indeed, so has the Court directly held in *Buckley v. Valeo* [1976].) But it is quite a different thing to say that I have *right to contribute* unlimited amounts to an entity that will then spend it to support my ideas.

In *SpeechNow v. FEC*, however, the Court of Appeals for the DC Circuit did not see any difference. As the Court held, if unlimited independent *expenditures* were protected by the First Amendment, then so, too, were unlimited *contributions* to independent political action committees protected by the First Amendment. Anyone (except foreigners, for reasons never really explained) was just as free to give as to spend, so long as both were independent of a political campaign.

And thus was the super PAC born.[4] Corporations and unions didn't need to spend their money directly. They could give their money to a super PAC, which would spend it for them. And even better, because of a loophole in the way the law requires disclosures, corporations and unions could effectively use a super PAC to launder their contribution. All contributions to super PACs must be disclosed. But if the entity giving money to a super PAC is itself a nonprofit, then all that must be disclosed is the name of that nonprofit. That nonprofit may or may not disclose its contributors.

This trick is pretty cool (for the lovers of dark money, at least), so we should understand how it works.

If a corporation gives $10 million to an entity that tax geeks call a "c4"—call it, "Resolved for an American Tomorrow—Soon [RATS]"—that c4 can turn around and contribute some of that $10 million to a super PAC. That super PAC will have to disclose the contribution from RATS. But RATS need not disclose anything. This trick thus becomes a pretty effective way for the corporation to influence the election without the public necessarily knowing anything about the corporation. Imagine a sign on the highway of political influence: "Need to launder some influence? Take Exit C4."

This is the world of "dark money" in American politics. And no doubt, it is an absurd loophole. When the Supreme Court decided *Citizens United*, it didn't know about this loophole. Justice Kennedy assumed it wasn't there. As he assured the public:

With the advent of the Internet, prompt disclosure of expenditures can provide shareholders and citizens with the information needed to hold corporations and elected officials accountable for their positions and supporters.... This transparency enables the electorate to make informed decisions and give proper weight to different speakers and messages.[5]

Yet we should not exaggerate the significance of this loophole, or the significance of "dark money." In the 2014 election cycle, 5 percent of the money contributed to candidates or organizations was "dark." 1.5 percent was semi-dark. So that means, we know with certainty where 93.5 percent of the money came from in 2014.[6]

Dark money is a problem. But a much more important problem than the dark money is the super PAC itself. And no doubt, even with small-dollar public funding, we won't have real reform so long as super PACs continue to grow. Any ultimate solution for this corruption must ultimately reverse the rule that gave us the super PAC.

But the critical point to recognize just now is that *that* reversal is not a reversal of any Supreme Court decision. Again, *SpeechNow* was not reviewed by the Supreme Court. The Supreme Court has not had the chance to rule on whether *Citizens United* means that super PACs are constitutionally required.

And this is important because it speaks directly to what strategy makes the most sense right now. Should our efforts be directed at the Supreme Court? Or at an amendment to reverse the decisions of the Supreme Court? Should the fight be to demand that "money is not speech" or that "corporations are not persons"? Or should we be focusing our work more fundamentally?

Don't get me wrong: What I described as "the fix" in Chapter 4 won't fix anything if American politics continues its slide toward super-PAC-funded elections.[7] Small-dollar public funding could well be swamped by large-donor PACs, regardless of how many representatives participate.

But it's equally clear that even if we somehow reversed *Citizens*

United, and thereby reversed *Speech Now*, and thus eliminated all corporate and union money from independent expenditures, *we would still not have begun to address the core corruption in America's democracy*: For still, the tiniest fraction of the 1 percent would be dominating the first stage of our elections. Remember the .02 percent? There was no corporate money in that amount. Reversing *Citizens United* is not a cure for tweedism. And thus a campaign focused on *Citizens United* alone is not a campaign that will solve the essential corruption—and inequality—of our democracy.

Nor is it—and here is the hardest point for progressives to accept—a campaign that is likely to win.

Fundamental reform in America is always cross-partisan—and could only ever be cross-partisan. Is it always and only a movement that draws us together, and that inspires by reminding us of the most vital ideals that stand within our tradition.

The ideals that attack tweedism are ideals of equality: the equality of citizenship promised to us at the Founding, and now denied to us by tweedism. We are not equal citizens when the tiniest fraction of the 1 percent dominates the first and critical stage of our elections. We have given up on Madison's conception of "the people" when we permit "the rich more than the poor" to control our democratic life. The fight against tweedism is a fight for equality. Not equality of results, and not equality of income. But equality of citizenship: the right for all of us to have an equal say in how our government works.

The ideals that attack *Citizens United* are ideals of inequality. They seek to deny participation to a certain group or entity, by asserting the inferior status of that group or entity. Corporations (and unions) are not persons, this attack insists. They don't deserve the rights of persons. They are constitutionally lesser beings, and the movement that seeks to rally America to overturn *Citizens United* seeks to rally America against those lesser beings.

I agree that corporations and unions are, constitutionally, lesser beings. But I don't believe that movements focused on differences rally Americans as powerfully or as successfully as movements that focus on equality. The movement to deny corporations "the right to speak" is opposed by many on the Right. It is opposed by many on the Left as well. The ACLU defends *Citizens United* vigorously. The case was argued by one of America's most important free speech advocates, Floyd Abrams. Thus to win the fight against *Citizens United* requires converting not just a pro-business Right, but also a pro-free speech Left. And if an amendment to the Constitution is required, those conversions will have to be huge. No amendment can become part of our Constitution unless thirty-eight states ratify it.

These facts lead me to believe that our fight should be for equality first, by ending the corruption that has destroyed the equality within our Framers' design. That, in other words, we should focus our energy on getting a Congress that would pass fundamental reform in the way campaigns are funded first. And that while we are waging that fight, we also work to secure that equality constitutionally.

This doesn't mean giving up on the constitutional reforms being pushed by so many incredibly inspiring people-driven groups, such as MoveToAmend, or People for the American Way.[8] But it does mean shifting the focus of those movements to a more plausible path to victory. I will describe that shift in Part III below. But for now, the critical point is just this: We need to start with our strongest claim—that ours was to be a Republic committed to an equality of citizens. We have improved on that commitment in critical ways in the 200+ years since our Constitution was enacted. But we have forgotten its core—that our Congress at least was to be "dependent on the people alone," where "the people" means "not the rich more than the poor."

We can rediscover this core. We can make it central to our tradition again. But this must be our focus: the equality of citizens.

CHAPTER 6

What About "Free Speech"?

The standard response to an argument for equality is to invoke the First Amendment. Equality cannot be the norm, the argument goes, because the First Amendment protects "free speech." Or more precisely, the government can't try to make equality the norm because the First Amendment protects free speech.

This response in turn leads some to demand that we change the First Amendment: that we carve back on its protections so as to better protect the equality of citizens.

Nothing I've argued for here is about restricting the scope of "free speech." Indeed, as I see the problem, "speech" is not the issue. The inequality that I believe corrupts our democracy is not an inequality of speech. Indeed, the inequality that I believe corrupts our democracy would not even necessarily be corrected by achieving an equality of speech. Rather, the inequality that I'm describing is an *inequality of citizens*, produced not because some can speak more loudly than others, but because our representatives are more dependent on some than others. The inequality that I've described is systemic: It is a *system* that gives some of us a first shot at selecting the candidates that the rest of us get to select among. That system is an inequality because the difference it draws has no justification within any plausible theory of our government.

In a single line: The inequality in our democracy comes not from what the money buys; the inequality in our democracy *comes from how the money is raised*. The First Amendment certainly does prohibit taxing the *Wall Street Journal* to subsidize the *Huffington Post*. But leveling the playing field of speech is different from giving each citizen an equal role. One equality (the equality of speech) is not permitted by our constitutional tradition; one equality (the equality of citizens) is required.

This distinction should be fundamental to free speech analysis, but it is too often overlooked. We can orient the difference in a simple diagram.

FIGURE 4

When we think about influence within a political system, we can think either about the influence of speech *on citizens*, or about the influence of speech on our government, or *on representatives*.[1]

Political ads influence citizens. They make a citizen more likely to vote one way or the other. Given inequality in the resources behind political ads, some are more likely to affect citizens than others. That is the consequence of unequal speech.

The way candidates raise money for campaigns, however, doesn't influence citizens. It influences representatives. If a candidate must spend 50 percent of her time talking to billionaires in order to raise the money she needs to run, that affects the candidate. It doesn't, directly at least, affect the citizens. Likewise, if a candidate could get public funding to run her campaign, that would be a different economy of influence upon that candidate. It would not be a different influence on citizens.

Over the history of our Republic, governments have tried to regulate both kinds of influence.

The state of Michigan, for example, decided that corporations had too much influence over the voters in Michigan. It therefore decided to limit that influence, by forbidding corporations "from using corporate treasury funds for independent expenditures in support of, or in opposition to, any candidate in elections for state office."[2]

That was an effort to regulate the way speech affects citizens. And though the Supreme Court originally upheld that regulation, it eventually (and I believe, correctly) struck it down. It is not the government's place to decide which voices in the political marketplace need suppressing. Whether or not the speech is distorting, that problem is a problem that we, as citizens alone, must solve. It's too dangerous to make the government the guardian of truth—especially political truth. Or so a commitment to the First Amendment has properly been read to mean.

But very different from Michigan's regulation is the regulation the federal government still has on, for example, bribery, or on contributions to the campaigns of political candidates. These regulations are not trying to affect the way speech *affects us*. These regulations are trying to affect the way speech (and money) *affects representatives*. Their aim is to restrict certain influences on representatives, to avoid them becoming improperly dependent on those influences.

Thus the Supreme Court has upheld the power of the government to decide that large contributors create a risk of improper quid pro quo corruption. To avoid that improper dependence, the Supreme Court has permitted Congress to limit such large contributions. The reason the Court has done this is the concern that such influences would wrongly influence representatives.

This division in regulatory power—or more precisely, this difference in the First Amendment's restriction on regulatory power—makes perfect sense. A government must have the ability to protect *itself* from improper influence. But even granting that,

it doesn't follow that a government should have the power to protect *the public* against so-called improper influence. It makes good
sense, in other words, maybe perfect sense, to leave the public to
protect itself, while taking critical steps to protect the government.

When the government protects itself against improper influence, obviously, it is regulating speech. When someone wanting
to bribe a Member of Congress is told that he can't, he'd be perfectly correct to say, "But money is speech. How can you restrict
my speech?" The answer is obvious: Yes, your money is speech, in
the narrow sense that the government needs a very strong reason
if it's going to restrict your ability to use your money for expressive purposes. But avoiding the improper dependence produced by
bribery is just such a reason.

Yet there are few dangers greater than a government in the business of protecting us from speech that it deems too dangerous for
us. I may well agree with Michigan that the effect of corporation
political ads on the people of Michigan is distorting, or confusing,
or just silly. But I don't think it should be within Michigan's power
to do anything about it. The citizens of Michigan need to suck it
up, and learn how distinguish between fact and fluff. Centuries of
speech tyranny are enough to teach us how dangerous it is to trust
the government to do that for us.

Against the background of this distinction—between laws
focused on the influence of speech *on citizens* versus laws focused
on the influence of speech *on representatives*—my focus in this
book should be clear. My concern is always and only about how
the economy of influence that we have evolved for raising money
to fund campaigns affects our representatives. What does living in
the Skinner box of fund-raising do to them?

I may well despair—I do despair—about how political speech
affects citizens, but I have no regulatory agenda to do anything
about that influence. Thirty-second television ads *are the worst*.
Television campaigns in general are the worst. There is nothing
redeeming in how political campaigns work today. And until we
find a way to improve them, there's little hope for this democracy.

But the project of improving the way political speech affects citizens is not my project. My sole concern is about how influence affects representatives.

Too few are sensitive to this distinction. The Court speaks as if the question of whether Michigan bans corporate speech is the same sort of question as whether $400 is too strict a limit on contributions to candidates.[3] But once we tease these two questions apart, it becomes easier to understand the law regulating political speech. It is my view that the Court is right to be deeply skeptical of regulations meant to protect us from the so-called distorting effect of political speech. It is also my view that the Court has been overly restrictive on efforts to protect what Robert Post calls the representative integrity of the political process.[4]

It will take a lot to move the current debate (and Court) beyond this confusion between laws trying to regulate the effect of speech on citizens and those trying to regulate the effect of speech on representatives.

But it might help that progress to recognize that this is not the first time we've had to make such a move. That in our history, we were once confused in a very similar way. Hard as it is to recognize, we have had this debate before.

The White Primary lived in the Old South for a very long time. Discrimination against black voters by whatever means lived longer, of course. But it was a surprisingly hard struggle for the Supreme Court to finally find a way to end this obvious system of inequality. Or at least, obvious to us.

But why wasn't it obvious to them, too? What took them so long?

The answer has a familiar ring to anyone who has followed the fight against so-called "campaign finance reform" legislation. It is the First Amendment. Not directly, or precisely. But it was values protected by the First Amendment that made it difficult for the Court to end the White Primary.

That value was the "right of association." We all have the right to hang with whomever we want. We especially have the right to form whatever political associations with whomever we want. So the desire of white Democrats to hang together to form their own political association is at the very core of the freedom that the "right of association" is meant to protect. As the Texas Supreme Court wrote:

> Since the right to organize and maintain a political party is one guaranteed by the Bill of Rights of this state, it necessarily follows that every privilege essential or reasonably appropriate to the exercise of that right is likewise guaranteed, including, of course, the privilege of determining the policies of the party and its membership. Without the privilege of determining the policy of a political association and its membership, the right to organize such an association would be a mere mockery. We think these rights, that is, the right to determine the membership of a political party and to determine its policies, of necessity are to be exercised by the State Convention of such party, and cannot, under any circumstances, be conferred upon a state or governmental agency.[5]

At first, Texas couldn't rely on that freedom directly in justifying its exclusion of blacks. The rule restricting blacks from participating came from the Texas legislature, not the Democratic Party. It was therefore the state's decision, not the party's,[6] and thus could the Court hold, easily, that it violated the equality required by the Fourteenth Amendment.

When the Texas legislature tried to fix the problem, by delegating the right to choose party members to the party's "State Executive Committee," the Court balked again. The policies of a political party, the Court declared, are not determined by a "State Executive Committee." They are instead determined by "a party convention." Because the convention of the Democratic Party of Texas hadn't excluded African-Americans from its ranks, that exclusion was again, in effect, an exclusion by the Texas legislature. It had picked the committee that banned blacks; that ban was therefore, again, the state's responsibility.[7]

But the third time was the charm. For in response to its second

rebuke by the Supreme Court, a convention of the Texas Democratic Party did explicitly resolve to exclude blacks. And this
time, when the Court reviewed that restriction, it upheld it—
unanimously. It wasn't Texas doing the discriminating here, the
Supreme Court held. It was instead the (white Democratic) people
of Texas. And the constitutional right of them to associate however
they want was not going to be questioned in the Supreme Court.

Even though it plainly destroyed the right of blacks to participate equally in their democracy. The ideal of equality was not
enough to overcome the right to associate freely.

We can't begin to imagine just how depressing this decision
must have been for anyone in America who cared about equality—
and especially for blacks denied equality. For the decision seemed
to mean that there was nothing in the law that could end this practice of inequality. And not just any inequality, but inequality at the
core of a Republic: the right to participate equally in a representative democracy.

But then came *United States v. Classic*.[8] *Classic* did not arise in
Texas. It had nothing to do with the White Primary. The case grew
out of a controversy in Louisiana. Federal law protects against voter
fraud. But because of the limited power of our Constitution, federal
law can only protect against voter fraud in an "election." The question the Supreme Court had to answer in *Classic* was whether a
"primary election" was an "election" under the Constitution.

This question seems obvious to us today. It isn't obvious, and
certainly wasn't at the time of *Classic*. The thing about a Federal
"election" is that it chooses some federal officer. The winner gets
to be the representative (or senator or president). But a primary
doesn't choose an officer. A primary chooses a candidate. So how
could a process that didn't select an officer be an "election" for purposes of the Constitution?

There were no primaries at the time the Constitution was
adopted. But by the time of *Classic*, Louisiana had made it practically impossible for anyone to win who hadn't run in a primary.
The primary had thus become an effectively mandatory stage in

the process of an election. And the question the Supreme Court had to answer in *Classic* was whether laws protecting against ballot fraud in an election also applied to the effectively mandatory step in an election—a primary.

In answering that question, the Supreme Court, through Justice Stone, gave one of the most compelling arguments for why the Constitution reaches differently across time. As Stone wrote:

> We may assume that the framers of the Constitution in adopting that section, did not have specifically in mind the selection and elimination of candidates for Congress by the direct primary any more than they contemplated the application of the commerce clause to interstate telephone, telegraph and wireless communication which are concededly within it. But in determining whether a provision of the Constitution applies to a new subject matter, it is of little significance that it is one with which the framers were not familiar. For in setting up an enduring framework of government they undertook to carry out for the indefinite future and in all the vicissitudes of the changing affairs of men, those fundamental purposes which the instrument itself discloses. Hence we read its words, not as we read legislative codes which are subject to continuous revision with the changing course of events, but as the revelation of the great purposes which were intended to be achieved by the Constitution as a continuing instrument of government.[9]

Against the background of those "great purposes," the question for the Court was whether "changes [in] the mode of choice[—] from a single step, a general election, to two, of which the first is the choice at a primary of those candidates from whom, as a second step, the representative in Congress is to be chosen"[10]—change the application of the constitutional principles. Put differently, can a state evade the requirements of the constitution by splitting "a single step [process into]...two" steps?

Put like that, it was pretty clear how the Court was going to answer the question: Obviously, no. You can't evade the requirements of the Constitution for "an election" by simply creating in effect another election. As the Court wrote:

> Long before the adoption of the Constitution the form and mode of that expression had changed from time to time. There is no historical warrant for supposing that the framers were under the illusion that the method of effecting the choice of the electors would never change or that if it did, the change was for that reason to be permitted to defeat the right of the people to choose representatives for Congress which the Constitution had guaranteed.[11]

And so, the punch line:

> Where the state law has made the primary an integral part of the procedure of choice, or where in fact the primary effectively controls the choice, the right of the elector to have his ballot counted at the primary, is likewise included in the right protected by Article I, s 2.[12]

Classic changed everything, and after *Classic*, it was perfectly clear that the days of the White Primary were numbered. *Classic* meant that the rights one had in a general election extended to a primary as well. *Even though* the First Amendment protected the right of individuals to associate, the equality demanded by the Constitution required that such associations not deny citizens the equal right to participate. Even if the choice of membership in the party was private—and even if it was protected by the freedom to associate—the equal right to participate in an election overrode that right of association.

And so did the Supreme Court (finally!) hold in *Smith v. Allright* (1944), when it struck down the White Primary. Because the primary was an "election," every voter had an equal right to participate. The State of Texas may well not have chosen to exclude blacks from the primary; but Texas was not permitted through its inaction to allow blacks to be excluded from the primary. Even though it may have to restrict a First Amendment–like right to associate, elections had to be equal. Because the equal right to participate in a representative democracy was fundamental.

So let's return to the question that titles this chapter: What about "free speech"?

The campaign for political equality need have no quibble with speech libertarians. We can agree that the state has no right to equalize speech for speech equality's sake.

But that cannot mean that the state cannot protect the equality of citizens, regardless of whether that end also happens to equalize the persuasive power of speech.[13] Compare: The state is permitted to ban bribery. Banning bribery advances speech equality. But it cannot be that simply because bribery laws advance speech equality, bribery laws violate the First Amendment. They don't. Bribery laws are a permitted speech regulation because they protect against quid pro quo corruption—even if they also "equalize speech."

So imagine Congress passed a voucher proposal, giving every voter a $50 voucher to use to fund congressional campaigns. Imagine further that candidates could choose to accept those vouchers if they agreed not to take any large contributions in addition to those vouchers. And imagine finally the regulation did not restrict the ability of citizens to spend whatever money they want on their own, independent of contributions to a campaign.

That proposal would not be (1) "restricting" speech (2) for the purpose of equalizing speech. That's because the voucher wouldn't be a restriction and because the purpose of the voucher proposal would be to equalize citizenship, not speech. The speech libertarians should therefore have no problem at all with this minimal first step. Yet this minimal first step could still radically change the way campaigns are funded.

But let's take it one step further. Imagine the same proposal, but now mandatory. Imagine the law said the only contributions you could take for your campaign were vouchers and small contributions. Voters would still be free to spend their money independently. But as a candidate, you would be limited to small contributions of either cash or vouchers.

This proposal should still be unproblematic. Once again, what justifies the restriction here is not speech equality, but political equality. The aim of the state is to force its politicians to rely on the public generally to fund their campaigns, rather than depend upon the very few. The aim, in other words, is to *democratize dependence*, so as to avoid a corrupting dependence. No doubt, this regulation equalizes the ability to speak through contributions. But that equality is justified on the grounds of equal citizenship, not on the grounds of equalizing speech.

But still, doesn't this mandatory program at least burden free speech? Sure, I can spend whatever I want independently of a political campaign. But I can't express the intensity of my commitment to a particular candidate by giving that candidate more than others. Isn't that a burden on speech, too?

It is, of course—in just the sense that banning the White Primary was a burden on the right of association. No one thought that the reason the White Primary was banned was so that the right of association could be eliminated. The White Primary was banned to assure the political equality of all citizens regardless of race. That fundamental political equality was no doubt more important than the indirect burden it created for the right to associate. But that importance is completely appropriate, since the commitment of a Republic—a representative democracy—is to equal citizenship first.

The same argument can be made about the voucher program. Yes, a mandatory voucher program would limit the ability of some to express their super strong support for one candidate over another. But the reason for that limit is not to equalize speech. It is to democratize the dependence within a campaign funding market. The restriction on speech is real, but justified by a more fundamental commitment to political equality.

And it is here that *Classic* becomes so compelling. Because remember, in that case, the Court recognized that the method by which elections were run was going to change over time. ("There is no historical warrant for supposing that the framers were under the illusion that the method of effecting the choice of the electors would never change....") The only requirement was that the constitutional norms governing those elections could not change. So if a state went from a one-step election to a two-step election, the norms that governed step two must also govern step one.

The same point applies here. In America, we have changed the way elections are run—again. Not through the addition of another voting primary, but through the addition of a money primary. The money primary is also an essential step on the way to an election—as practically essential as the Democratic Primary was in Texas. And because it is essential, constitutional norms must apply to it, too. The government can't be allowed to defeat the obligations of equal elections by adding an effectively mandatory step to the process that only rich people or white people or Christian people or Masons for that matter could participate in. If the government adds an effectively mandatory step, it must assure that values of the Constitution apply to it.

In their fantastic book *The Wealth Primary* (1994), Jamin Raskin and John Bonifaz argue that those norms basically render privately funded campaigns unconstitutional. But whether one goes that far or not, we should at least be able to agree that those norms should permit a Congress to enact measures to respond to that inequality, by democratizing dependence. Bottom-up public funding, whether vouchers or matching funds, would do that. At the very least, *Classic* should sanction those.

We need not go even that far here. The public funding that I'm arguing for in this book is voluntary, not mandatory. It would be a critical first step to democratizing the dependence that has developed within this system. And while I'm happy to concede that the First Amendment questions with mandatory public funding are difficult, everyone should concede that the First Amendment questions with voluntary public funding are simple. We, the people, *at the very least* have the power to give our leaders the choice to fund their campaigns without depending upon a tiny fraction of us. At the very least, our Constitution must permit Congress to give politicians the freedom to choose the equality of citizens as the way to fund their campaign.

So what about the "First Amendment"? What about it, indeed. The First Amendment is a critical protection at the core of our constitutional Republic. But it does not demand an end to our constitutional Republic. We can have both political equality and free speech. It's time we take steps to get both.

PART II

DEEPER

The aim of Part I was to map the arc of an argument for why we must reform this Republic, now. The core problem with our democracy is a corruption of a fundamental idea of a democracy—equal political rights for all citizens. We have let the insiders evolve a system that denies that equality, simply to make it easier for them to manage the work of reelection.

We need to change this system, and in the first part, I have sketched the elements of that change, and how they fit within the current debates of the most prominent reformers.

But before I turn to the specifics of how this change could happen, I need to do some more work. We need to step back from the current crisis to fill in the details about how we got here, and what the system actually does. It is critical that we see just how this system hurts liberals, libertarians, and conservatives. And it is incredibly important to do some hard legal work to sketch just how the Supreme Court could uphold the essential reforms that change needs, even without a constitutional amendment.

Hence Part II. Readers of the first edition of *Republic, Lost* will recognize much in this part. I have updated the data, and changed the argument where it was wrong. But because the chapters about the Left and the Right are meant to be illustrative, not comprehensive, I've not added to the examples that might be multiplied with each. My aim in this edition was to keep this core intact as much as possible, before a very different final part describing the updated strategy for reform.

CHAPTER 7

Why So Damn Much Money

Midway through his extraordinary book *So Damn Much Money* (2009), Robert Kaiser, the now retired associate editor and senior correspondent at the *Washington Post*, reports a conversation with Joe Rothstein, campaign manager for former Alaska Senator Mike Gravel (D-Alaska, 1969–81). As Kaiser reports Rothstein to say:

> Money has been a part of American politics forever, on occasion—in the Gilded Age or the Harding administration, for example—much more blatantly than recently. But...: "the scale of it has just gotten way out of hand." The money may have come in brown paper bags in earlier eras, but the politicians needed, and took, much less of it than they take through more formal channels today.[1]

If we're going to understand the corruption that is our government, we need first to understand this change. What explains the explosion in campaign cash? What are its consequences? No doubt, things cost more today than they did in 1970. But the rise in campaign spending wildly outpaces the rate of inflation.[2] Between 1974 and 2008, "the average amount it took to run for reelection to the House went from $56,000 to more than $1.3 million."[3] In 2014, the average was $1.4 million.[4] In 1974, the total spent by all candidates for Congress (both House and Senate) was $77 million. By 1982, that number was $343 million—a 450 percent increase in eight years.[5] By 2010, it was $1.8 billion—a 525 percent increase again plus the same in outside spending.[6] In 2014, the direct spending dipped to $1.6 billion, but outside spending added another $2.2 billion.

Why? And how did this rise affect how Congress does its work?

To answer these questions, we need to review a bit of recent history. There have been real changes in the competitiveness of American democracy that help account for the increase in the demand for campaign cash. This increase in demand in turn inspired a change in how campaign cash gets supplied. And that change in supply, I will argue, has radically altered how our democracy functions. To build on an analogy first advanced by Samuel Issacharoff, if you're well fed, good manners are one thing. If you're starving, they become very different—fast.

Demand for Campaign Cash

If the political history of the twentieth century can be divided into three periods—a period before FDR, the period of FDR to Reagan, and the period of Reagan to Bush II—our picture of Congress, as taught to us in universities and as studied most extensively by scholars and political scientists, is the Congress of the middle period, FDR to Reagan. The Congress that gave us the New Deal. The Congress that enacted the Civil Rights Act. The Congress that would have impeached President Nixon.

This was a Democratic Congress. In the sixty-plus years between 1933 and 1995, Democrats controlled the House of Representatives in all but four years. It controlled the Senate in all but ten. If anything happened during this period, it was because the Democrats supported it. When things didn't happen, it was because they didn't support it strongly enough.

For most of this period, no sane Republican could imagine taking permanent control of both houses of Congress. Like mile runners before Roger Bannister cracked the four-minute mile, most Republicans, and most Democrats, simply believed that Republican control was politically impossible. The parties had a certain character. The nation had a certain character, too. Those two characters were going to produce a political world in which Democrats controlled and Republicans cooperated. That was the "nature" of politics in America.

Then nature changed. The seeds to that change were sown by a Democratic president, elected with the second-largest contested Electoral College vote in American history: Lyndon Baines Johnson.

Johnson is one of the twentieth century's two most important politicians. Pulling himself up from almost nothing, by means none would be proud to be forced to confess, Johnson became a key leader of the Democrats in Congress. He knew better than most how to play the game of compromise that moves bills through Congress. That moved him to the very top of the United States Senate—more quickly than anyone else in the history of the Senate.[7]

When an assassin's bullet thrust him into the presidency, however, Johnson changed his game. In his first speech to Congress, he placed civil rights at the core of his new administration, and hence at the core of the values of the Democratic Party.

The decision to do this was profoundly controversial. In a six-hour meeting before the speech, Johnson was advised strongly against making civil rights so central to his administration. As described by Randall Woods, Johnson was told, "Passage [of the Civil Rights Act] . . . looked pretty hopeless; the issue was as divisive as any . . . ; it would be suicide to wage and lose such a battle." The safe bet was the bet against the fight. Johnson replied, "Well, what the hell is the presidency for?"[8] These were not the words of a triangulator. These were the words of a man who had grown tired of the game, and wanted to try something new.

When he decided to make civil rights central to his party's platform, Johnson knew that he was forever changing the political dominance of the Democratic Party. His decision to pass the most important civil rights legislation in history was a guarantee that the Republicans would again become competitive. Yet his loyalty was more to truth, or justice, or his legacy—you pick—than to party politics. To that end, whichever end it was, he was willing to sacrifice a Democratic majority of tomorrow in order to use his Democratic majority of today.[9]

I don't mean to suggest that racism made Reagan possible. To the contrary: It was a wide range of focused and powerful ideas, first born in the idealism of politicians such as Goldwater and public intellectuals such as William F. Buckley, that made the new Republican Party compelling. I remember well the power of those ideas. I was a rabid Reaganite, and the youngest elected member of a delegation at the 1980 Republican Convention.

But there's no doubt that this decision by Johnson strengthened the Republican Party by alienating a large number of not-yet-enlightened Southern Democrats. That alienation encouraged a Republican return. And when Ronald Reagan rode a powerful set of ideals to power—none of them explicitly tied to race—he gave to all Republicans an idea that only dreamers in 1950 would have had: that their party could retake control of Congress. That Republicans might again become the majority party.

It was 1994 before this dream was finally realized. With the energy and passion of Newt Gingrich, with the ideals of a "Contract with America," and with a frustration about a young, triangulating Democratic president, the Republicans swept Congress. For the first time since 1954, the Republicans had control of both houses of Congress.

The Gingrich election changed everything: By putting the control of Congress in play, it gave both Republicans and Democrats something to fight to the death about. Whereas a comfortable, even if not ideal (for the Republicans, at least) détente had reigned for the prior forty-something years, now each side could taste majority status—or perhaps more important, minority status. Congress was up for grabs. And between 1995 and 2014, control of Congress changed hands as many times as it had in the forty-five years before.

It was within this period that the modern Fund-raising Congress was born. The Republicans came to power raising an unheard of amount of money to defeat the Democrats. Republicans in 1994 received $618.42 million (up from $534.64 million in 1992) in contrast to Democrats' $488.68 million (down from $498.45 million in 1992).[10] In the four years between 1994 and 1998, Republican candidates and party committees raised over $1 billion.[11] Never before had a party come anywhere close.

This fund-raising in turn changed what leadership in both parties would mean: If leaders had once been chosen on the basis of ideas, or seniority, or political ties, now, in both parties, leaders were chosen at least in part based on their ability to raise campaign cash. Leading fund-raisers became the new leaders. Fund-raising became the new game.

Campaigns now were not just about who won in any particular district; they were also about which party would control Congress. This control has its own value—especially if, as John Lott argues, the government is handing out more favors or, in the words of economists, "more rents."[12] Such rents drive demand for control. As corporate law scholars would describe it, they make the "control premium" all the more valuable.[13]

At the same time that demand for winning was increasing, the core costs of campaigns were increasing as well. Part of the reason for this change was the rising cost of media. But a bigger part was an advance in campaign technology. The machine of politics was more complicated and more expensive. "Campaigns dependent on pollsters, consultants, and television commercials," Kaiser notes, "were many times more expensive than campaigns in the prehistoric eras before these inventions took hold. . . . So congressmen and senators who used the new technologies . . . quite suddenly needed much more money than ever before to run for re-election."[14]

These two changes together—if not immediately, then certainly over a very short time—put the monkey on the back of every member of Congress. An activity that for most of the history of Congress was a simple road stop—fund-raising—now became the central activity of most congressmen. Each member had to raise more,

not just for his own seat but also for his own party. Yet because
the most obvious solution to this increase in demand for campaign
cash—collecting more from each contributor—was not legally possible, the only way to raise more money was to scurry to find more
people to give.[15] Congress had tried to limit political expenditures
in 1974.[16] The Supreme Court had struck down that limit, while
upholding the limit on contributions. As Professor James Sample
describes it, quoting Professors Pam Karlan and Sam Issacharoff,
"The effect is much like giving a starving man unlimited trips to
the buffet table but only a thimble-sized spoon with which to eat:
chances are great that the constricted means to satisfy his appetite
will create a singular obsession with consumption."[17]

"No rational regulatory system," Issacharoff writes, "would
seek to limit the manner by which money is supplied to political
campaigns, then leave...spending uncapped."[18] Yet ours did. And
the result, as Josh Rosenkranz puts it, was a system that turned
"decent, honest politicians [into] junkies."[19]

Junkies.

Supply of Campaign Cash: Substance

As the demand for campaign cash rose, the political economy for
its supply changed. The Fund-raising Congress became different
from Congresses before. Its values and its ideals, at least as they
related to raising campaign funds, were different.

One part of this difference was substantive: The political message of both parties changed in a direction that enhanced the ability of each to raise campaign funds.

First, the economic message of Democrats became much more
pro-business.[20] Beginning almost immediately after the 1994
Republican sweep, leaders in the Democratic Party launched a
massive campaign to convince corporate America that the Democrats could show them as much love as the Republicans traditionally had. President Clinton led the campaign, especially on Wall

Street, as his administration worked feverishly to convince Wall Street funders that Democrats were as committed to deregulation as Republicans were. At least with respect to the economy, America didn't have two major parties anymore. Instead, as Dan Clawson, Alan Neustadtl, and Mark Weller wrote: "The country... has just one: the money party."[21] The Democrats' "populist tradition," Hacker and Pierson describe, "more and more appeared like a costume—something to be donned from time to time when campaigning—rather than a basis for governing."[22]

This change is familiar and extensively debated. So, too, is the question of its causation. Many "new Democrats" defend the probusiness shift on grounds of principle. Many more find this explanation a bit too convenient. But whether the initial shift was for the money or not, as the shift in fact did produce more money, the change was reinforced. Given the increasing dependency on cash, the cause was conveniently ignored.

Second, and less frequently remarked, the noneconomic messages of both Democrats and Republicans became more extreme. Conservatives on the Right became (even to Reagan Republicans) unrecognizably right-wing. And many on the Left grabbed signature liberal issues to frame their whole movement. It may be true that the Right moved more than the Left did,[23] but both sides still moved.

The reasons for this shift are many, and complicated. But without hazarding a strong claim about causation, it is important to recognize that *for both the Right and the Left, a shift to the extremes made fund-raising easier.*

Direct marketers told campaigns that a strong and clear message to the party base is more likely to elicit a large financial response than a balanced, moderate message to the middle. Extremism, in other words, pays—literally. As one study summarized the research, "An incumbent's ideological extremism improves his or her chances of raising a greater proportion of funds from individual donors in general and small individual contributors in particular.

Extremism is not the only way to raise money, [...but] to some legislators, extremism is an advantage."[24]

But, you wonder, doesn't extremism hurt a candidate's chances with swing voters?

Of course it does. But that doesn't matter if swing voters don't matter—which they don't in so-called "safe seats." Safe seats are gerrymandered to produce no realistic possibility for one party to oust the other. Throughout this period, between 75 and 85 percent of the districts in the House remained safe seats. In those districts at least, the fund-raisers had a comfortable cushion within which to message to the extremes. The demand for fund-raising plus the supply of safe seats meant American politics could afford to become more polarized, as a means (or at least a by-product) of making fund-raising easier.[25]

To claim that American politics became more polarized, however, is not to say that *America* became more polarized. Politically active Americans don't represent America. As Morris Fiorina and Samuel Abrams write, "The political class is a relatively small proportion of the American citizenry, but it is...the face that the media portray as an accurate image of the American public. It is not."[26]

Instead, the distribution of political attitudes for most Americans follows a classic bell curve. As Hacker and Pierson summarize the research, "the ideological polarization of the electorate as a whole—the degree of disagreement on left-right issues overall—is modest and has changed little over time,"[27] even though "the two parties are further apart ideologically than at any point since Reconstruction."[28] Their point from 2010 has only gotten worse in the time since.[29] Today, as the *National Journal* reported in its study of the 111th Congress, "For the first time in modern history, in both the House and Senate, the most conservative Democrat is slightly more liberal than the most liberal Republican."[30] Here's how the trend is represented in the *Vital Statistics on Congress*:

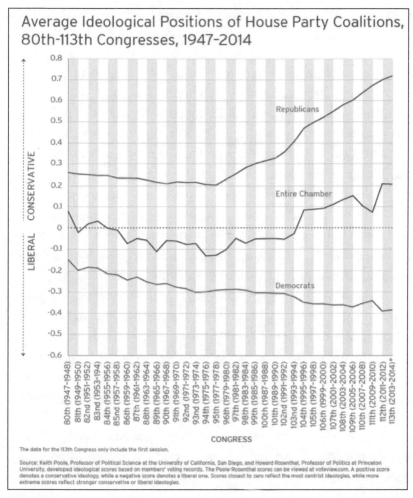

Average Ideological Positions of House Party Coalitions, 80th–113th Congresses, 1947–2014

FIGURE 5

Yet even though these activists are "not like most people," power in the American government gets "transferred to [the] political activists."[31] Not just because "only zealots vote,"[32] but increasingly because the zealots especially fund the campaigns that get people to vote. Fund-raising happens most among the politically active and extreme, and that puts pressure on the extremists to become even more extreme. As Fiorina and Abrams put it, "The natural place to look for campaign money is in the ranks of the single-issue groups, and a natural strategy to motivate their members is to exaggerate the threats their enemies pose."[33] On the Right, this is especially pronounced: As Lee Drutman has argued, "The more Republicans depend on the 1 percent of the 1 percent donors, the more conservative they tend to be."[34]

In this odd and certainly unintended way, then, the demand for cash could also be changing the substance of American politics. Could be, because all I've described is correlation, not causation. But at a minimum the correlation should concern us: On some issues, the parties become more united—those issues that appeal to corporate America. On other issues, the parties become more divided— the more campaign funds an issue inspires, the more extremely it gets framed. In both cases, the change correlates with a strategy designed to maximize campaign cash, while weakening the connection between what Congress does (or at least campaigns on) and the desires of ordinary Americans. So long as there is a demand for endless campaign cash, one simple way to supply it is to sing the message that inspires the money—even if that message is far from the views of most. This is why, as Darrell West writes, "part of the polarization" problem is driven "not just by self-interested behavior but by the current system of campaign finance."[35] And why, as Mann and Ornstein write, "pursuing a new framework for campaign finance remains a key component for reducing dysfunction in the American polity."[36]

Supply of Campaign Cash: New Norms

The increasing pressure to raise money correlates not only with changing party policies, but also with radically different congressional norms.

Consider, for example, the case of former Senator Max Baucus (D-Mont.; 1978–2014), chairman of the Senate Committee on Finance, arguably the most powerful senator during the debate over the details of Obama's heath care program. Between 2003 and his retirement in 2014, Senator Baucus raised more than $7 million from the financial, insurance, and health care industries—precisely the industries whose regulation he oversaw.[37] According to *Public Citizen*, between 1999 and 2005, "Baucus took in more interest group money than any other senator with the exception of Republican Bill Frist."[38] Baucus is not embarrassed by this fact. Indeed, he should be proud of it. It is a measure of his status, and the power he yields. It is a way to demonstrate that power: They give to him because of it.

Compare Baucus to another powerful committee chairman, Mississippi Senator John Stennis (D-Miss.; 1947–1989). As Robert Kaiser describes, in 1982, Stennis was chairman of the Armed Services Committee. That committee oversaw the spending of hundreds of billions of defense dollars. But when Stennis was asked by a colleague to hold a fund-raiser at which defense contractors would be present, Stennis balked. Said Stennis: "Would that be proper? I hold life and death over those companies. I don't think it would be proper for me to take money from them."[39]

The difference between Stennis and Baucus is not idiosyncratic. It is culture. Stennis was no choirboy. But his hesitation reflected an understanding that I doubt a majority of Congress today would even recognize. There were limits—even just thirty years ago—that seem as antiquated today as the wigs our Framers wore while drafting the Constitution. As Congressman Jim Bacchus (D-Fla.; 1991–1995) said of the practice of raising money from the very people you regulate, it "compromises the integrity of the institution."[40] After that practice became the norm, Senator Chuck Hagel (R-Neb.; 1997–2009) commented: "There's no shame anymore. We've blown past the ethical standards, we now play on the edge of the legal standards."[41] As former super-lobbyist Jeff Connaughton describes the change:

> It used to be verboten to bring up an issue at a fundraiser... Of course, they'd call the next day. But over the years, primarily because Congress is so pressured for time and the need to raise huge sums of cash, it's literally become the Senator or Member going around the table, one-by-one, "What's your issue?" How can anyone feel good about how that must look to the American people?[42]

Again, it is hard to say with integrity that one thing caused the other. We just don't have the data to prove it. The most that we can say is that the new norms make fund-raising easier, just at the moment when the demand for raising funds rises dramatically. That should concern us, too.

Supply of Campaign Cash: New Suppliers

The story of the last thirty-five years, however, is not just about political parties whistling a new (and more financially attractive) tune. Nor is it about politicians getting more comfortable with leveraging power into campaign cash. The most important bit is the rise of a new army of campaign cash suppliers happy and eager to oblige policymakers with the wonder of their rainmaking techniques.

Some of these suppliers are relatively benign. Campaigns have finance committees, with increasingly professional fund-raisers at the top. These fund-raisers deploy the best techniques to raise money. Those techniques may tilt the message of the campaign slightly. But at least these fund-raisers are the agents of the candidate. They have just one boss, and their interest is in advancing the interests of that boss.

Some of these suppliers, however, are not so benign. For some are not agents of the candidate or the campaign. Instead, a critical and newly significant part of this army of campaign cash suppliers works not for the candidate, but for special-interest clients. Their salary is paid not by a campaign, but by a firm that sells their services directly to interests eager to persuade policymakers to bend policy in one way or another.

These less benign suppliers are two: the modern American lobbyist, and the modern political action committee—the super PAC. I will address the questions of the super PAC in Chapter 12. Consider now the economy of the lobbyists.

Lobbyist$

Lobbying is nothing new to the American republic. Some say the moniker dates back to President Grant, but the practice certainly predates him. Grant would sit with friends for hours in the lobby at the Willard Hotel "enjoying cigars and brandy."[43] Influence peddlers, or "those lobbyists,"[44] as Grant called them, would approach him while he sat there. Grant's sneer, however, suggests correctly that the relationship of these "peddlers" to democracy has always been uncertain, and for many, troubling. Georgia's constitution explicitly banned the lobbying of state legislators in 1877.[45] The Supreme Court tried to stanch at least one brand of lobbying three years before, in *Trist v. Child* (1874), when it invalidated contingency contracts for lobbyists. As the Court wrote:

> If any of the great corporations of the country were to hire adventurers who make market of themselves in this way, to procure the passage of a general law with a view to the promotion of their private interests, the moral sense of every right-minded man would instinctively denounce the employer and employed as steeped in corruption, and the employment as infamous. If the instances were numerous, open and tolerated, they would be regarded as measuring the decay of the public morals and the degeneracy of the times.[46]

"Degeneracy" notwithstanding, even without contingency contracts, the industry has thrived, especially as the reach of government has grown.

For most of the history of lobbying, the techniques of lobbyists, and their relationship to Congress, were, in a word, grotesque. Well into the twentieth century, lobbyists wooed members with wine, women, and wages. Congressmen were lavishly entertained. They frequented "cat houses" paid for by lobbyists.[47] They kept safes in their offices to hold the bags of cash that lobbyists would give them.[48] And late into the twentieth century, they were taken on elaborate junkets as a way to "persuade" members of the wisdom in the lobbyists' clients' positions.[49] If the aim of the lobbyist, as Kenneth Crawford colorfully described it in 1939, was to "burn [the] bridges between the voter and what he voted for,"[50] for most of its history, there were no obvious limits on the means to that burning.

Including flat-out bribes (which were not even illegal in Congress until 1853).[51] Throughout the nineteenth century, and well into the twentieth, lobbyists paid "consulting fees" to members of Congress—directly.[52] In the early nineteenth century, Congressman Daniel Webster wrote to the Bank of the United States—while a member of Congress voting on the very existence of the Bank of the United States—"If it be wished that my relation to the Bank be continued, it may be well to send me the usual retainers."[53] That example was not unique. Members of Congress would expressly solicit personal payments from those they regulated.[54] Crawford quotes a letter from Pennsylvania Republican George Washington Edmonds to the official of a shipyard dependent upon government contracts:

> "As you undoubtedly know, a Congressman must derive some of his income from other sources than being a member of the House, and in this connection I would like to bring to your attention the fact that my secretary and myself have a company in Philadelphia. Please put us on your inquiry list for materials in connection with ships."[55]

Yet when lobbying was this corrupt, perhaps counterintuitively, its effect was self-limiting. Though these practices were not uncommon, they were still (at least after 1853) illegal. Lobbyists and members had to be discreet. There may have been duplicity, but there were limits. The payoffs could not be so obvious. And almost as a way to minimize the wrong, the policies bent by this corrupt practice had to be on the margins, or at least easily ignored. There are, of course, grotesque stories, especially as they touched land and railroads. But in the main, the practices were hidden, and therefore limited. They knew shame.

Today's lobbyist is not a rogue. It is an absurd simplification and an insult to the profession to suggest that the norms of the industry circa 1890 have anything to do with the norms of the profession today. The lobbyist today is ethical, and well educated. He or she works extremely hard to live within the letter of the law. More than ever before, most lobbyists are just well-paid policy wonks, expert in a field and able to advise and guide Congress well. Regulation is complex; regulators understand very little; the lobbyist is the essential link between what the regulator wants to do and how it can get done. Indeed, as we'll see more later, much of the lobbyist's work is simply a type of legislative subsidy.[56] Most of it is decent, aboveboard, the sort of stuff we would hope happens inside the Beltway. The ordinary lobbyist today is a Boy Scout compared with the criminal of the nineteenth century. He has as much in common with his nineteenth-century namesake as Mormons have with their nineteenth-century founders.

Yet as lobbying has become more respectable—and this is the key—it has also become more dangerous. The rent seeking that was careful and hidden before is now open and notorious. No one is embarrassed by what the profession does, because everything the profession does is out in the open for all to see. Indeed, almost literally: Since 1995, no profession has been required to disclose its activities more extensively and completely than lobbyists.

But as this practice has become more professional, its effect on our democracy has become more systemic. And the question we need to track is what that systemic effect is.

As I describe more below, in the classic understanding of the modern profession, the lobbyist is simply a "subsidy." Private interests subsidize Congress by helping congressmen do their job. Those subsidies are many—advice, research, support, guidance for issues the legislators already believe in. But on that list, one of those subsidies has the potential to corrupt the whole process. As Robert Kaiser describes best, in at least the last thirty-five years, the demand for campaign cash has turned the lobbyist into a supplier.[57] Not so much from the money that lobbyists give directly— though lobbyists (and their spouses and their kids), of course, give an endless amount of money directly. But instead from the funding they secure indirectly—from the very interests that hire them to produce the policy results that benefit those interests.

In a way that is hard to see, and certainly hard to model, lobbyists have become the center of *an economy of influence* that has changed the way Washington works. They feed a frantic dependency that has grown among members of Congress—the dependency on campaign cash—but they can feed that dependency only if they can provide something of value to their clients in return. The lobbyists are funding arbitrageurs. They stand at the center of an economy. We can draw that economy like this:

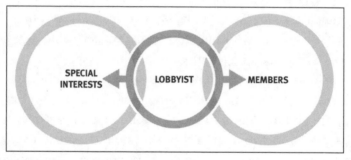

FIGURE 6

On the one side of this economy are the members, frantically searching for campaign cash. On the other side are interests that increasingly find themselves needing or wanting special favors from the government. As government grows, as it has, "its tentacles in every aspect of American life and commerce," then "no serious industry or interest can function without monitoring, and at least trying to manipulate, Washington's decision makers."[58] These manipulators make themselves essential to the extent that they provide a suite of essential services—including, for many, the channeling of campaign cash.

As Kaiser describes:

The more important money became to the politicians, the more important its donors became to them. This was a boon to [the lobbyists]. "The lobbyists are in the driver's seat," observed

Leon Panetta. "They basically know that the members have nowhere else to turn" for money.... Lobbyists had become indispensable to politicians.[59]

The rise of this funding economy was fueled by earmarks. Candidate Obama may have been right in 2008 when he said that earmarks are a very small portion of the overall federal budget—less than half a percent of 2007 outlays.[60] But Senator McCain was certainly right when he said that the percentage itself is beside the point. The important question about earmarks isn't their absolute size relative to the federal budget. The important question is how easily the value of those earmarks can be privatized, so that, in turn, they can benefit the (campaign cash) interest of the congressman: If a congresswoman could secure a $10 million earmark benefiting Company X, how easily can some of the value of that $10 million be channeled back to her campaign? Not directly, and not illegally, but if a congressman is going to make the president of Acme, Inc., $10 million happier, is there some way that some of that "happiness" can get returned? How sticky can the favor be made to seem? How fungible? And most important, once the dance gets learned, how easily can it be applied to other policy issues, not directly tied to earmarks?

The answer to these questions is obvious and critical: If the only actors involved in this dance are members of Congress and the special interest seeking favor, then it is difficult to keep this dance within the bounds of legality. But if there is an agent in the middle—someone who works not for the congressman but for many special interests seeking special favors from Congress—the dance becomes much, much easier, since there are obvious ways in which it can happen well within the boundaries of federal law.

To see how, we must first address an assumption that tends to limit imagination about how this economy of influence might work.

Too many assume that the only way that government power can be converted into campaign cash is through some sort of quid pro quo. Too many assume, that is, that influence *is* a series of deals. And because they imagine a transaction, too many are skeptical about how vast or extensive such an economy of influence could be—first, because there are laws against this sort of thing, and second, because almost every single member of Congress, Democrat and Republican alike, strikes any one of us as clearly above this sort of corruption.

There are laws against quid pro quo bribery. These laws are, in the main, respected. Of course there are exceptions. Consider this key bit of evidence in the prosecution of Randy "Duke" Cunningham (R-Calif.; 1991–2005), the Vietnam War Top Gun fighter pilot turned congressman who promised in his 1990s campaign a "congressman we can be proud of":

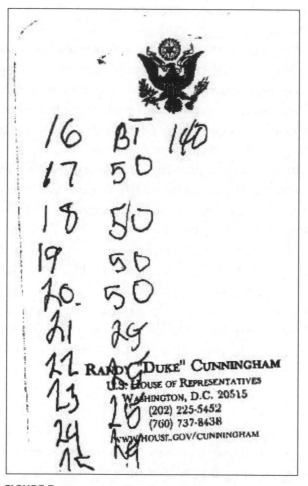

FIGURE 7

Look at the numbers: The first column represents the size of the government contract (in millions) the congressman was promising. The second column reports the size of the bribe (in thousands) necessary to get that contract. "BT" refers to a yacht. I'm no expert, but I know enough to say: This is not the work of a genius.

There are more Randy "Duke" Cunninghams in Congress, no doubt. But not more than a handful. I agree with Dennis Thompson that ours is among the cleanest Congresses in the history of Congress.[61] And if the only way that government power could be converted into campaign cash were by crossing the boundaries of criminal law, then there would be no book to write here. If the only possible "corruption" were the corruption regulated by bribery statutes, then I'd be the first to insist that ours is not a corrupt Congress.

Yet there is an obvious and overwhelming argument against the idea that corruption needs a transaction to work. Indeed, there is an argument—and it is the core argument of this book—that the most significant and powerful forms of corruption today are precisely those that thrive without depending upon quid pro quos for their effectiveness.

This argument can be proven in the sterile but powerful language of modern political science. Justin Fox and Lawrence Rothenberg, for example, have modeled how a campaign contribution "impacts incumbent policy choices," even if the candidates and funders can't enter into a quid pro quo arrangement.[62]

But the argument is much more compelling if we understand the point in terms of our own ordinary lives. Each of us understands how influence happens without an economy of transactions. All of us live such a life all the time.

Economies, Gift and Otherwise

Think about two economies, familiar to anyone, which we might call, taking a lead from Lewis Hyde, a gift economy and an exchange economy.[63]

A gift economy is a series of exchanges between two or more souls who never pretend to equate one exchange to another, but who also don't pretend that reciprocating is unimportant—an economy in the sense that it marks repeated interactions over time, but a gift economy in the sense that it doesn't liquidate the relationships in terms of cash. Indeed, relationships, not cash, are the currency within these economies. These relationships import obligations. And the exchanges that happen within gift economies try to hide their character as exchanges by tying so much of the exchange to the relationship. I give you a birthday present. It is a good present not so much because it is expensive, but because it expresses well my understanding of you. In that gift, I expect something in return. But I would be insulted if on my birthday, you gave me a cash voucher equivalent to the value of the gift I gave you, or even two times the amount I gave you. Gift giving in relationship-based economies is a way to express and build relationships. It's not a system to transfer wealth.

The gift economy is thus the relationship of friends, or family, or different people trying to build an alliance. It was the way of Native Americans completely misunderstood by their invading "friends." "An Indian gift," Thomas Hutchinson told his readers in 1764, "is a proverbial expression signifying a present for which an equivalent return is expected."[64] But the equivalence could never be demanded. And the equation could never be transparent.

An "exchange economy," by contrast, is clearer and in many ways simpler. It is the quid pro quo economy. The transactional economy. The this-for-that economy. It is the economy of a gas station, or a vending machine at a baseball park. In exchange for this bit of cash, you will give me that thing/service/promise. Cash is the currency in this economy, and as many of the terms of the relationship as possible get converted, or liquidated, into cash. It is the economy of commodification. It is an economy within which we live much of our lives.

As I've written elsewhere,[65] following the work of Yochai Benkler, Lewis Hyde, and others, there's nothing necessarily wrong with commodification. Indeed, there's lots that's great about it. As Lewis Hyde puts it:

> It is the cardinal difference between gift and commodity exchange that a gift establishes a feeling-bond between two people, while the sale of a commodity leaves no necessary connection. I go into a hardware store, pay the man for a hacksaw blade and walk out. I may never see him again. The disconnectedness is, in fact, a virtue of the commodity mode. We don't want to be bothered. If the clerk always wants to chat about the family, I'll shop elsewhere. I just want a hacksaw blade.[66]

There's plenty that's good about leaving important and large parts of your life simplified because they are left commodified. The more bits that are simplified, the more time you have for relationships within the gift economies in which we all (hopefully!) live.

For in both economies, then, reciprocity is the norm. The difference is the transparency of that reciprocity. Gifts in this sense are not selfless acts to another. Gifts are moves in a game; they oblige others. In the economies that Hyde describes, the game in part is to obscure the extent of that obligation, but without extinguishing it. No one is so crass as to say, "I gave you a box of pearls; you need to give me something of equal value in return." Yet everyone within such an economy is monitoring the gifts given and the gifts in return. And anytime a significant gap develops, the relationship evinced by the gifts gets strained.

Against this background, I suggest that we can understand Washington a bit better.

In the days of wine, women, and wealth, Washington may well have been an exchange economy. I doubt it, but it's possible. Whatever it was then, however, it has become a gift economy.[67] For as the city has professionalized, as reformers have controlled graft more effectively and forced "contributions" into the open, the economy of DC has changed. If the law forbade DC from being an exchange economy, it could not block its becoming a gift economy.

So long as the links are not expressed, so long as the obligations are not liquidated, so long as the timing is not too transparent, Washington can live a life of exchanges that oblige without living a life that violates Title 18 of the U.S. Code (the Criminal Code, regulating bribery). As Senator Paul Douglas (D-Ill.; 1949–1967) described it fifty years ago:

> Today the corruption of public officials by private interests takes a more subtle form. The enticer does not generally pay money directly to the public representative. He tries instead by a series of favors to put the public official under such a feeling of personal obligation that the latter gradually loses his sense of mission to the public and comes to feel that his first loyalties are to his private benefactors and patrons. What happens is a gradual shifting of a man's loyalties from the community to those who have been doing him favors. His final decisions are, therefore, made in response to his private friendships and loyalties rather than to the public good. Throughout this whole process, the official will claim—and may indeed believe—that there is no causal connection between the favors he has received and the decisions which he makes.[68]

This is a gift economy. As Jake Arvey, the man behind Adlai Stevenson's political career, defined politics: "Politics is the art of putting people under obligation to you."[69] Obligation, not expressed in legally enforceable contracts, but in the moral expectations that a system of gift exchange yields. This idea is confirmed in recent work by Thomas Groll and Maggie McKinley:

> What these data and model show is that the contract lobbying market has become a market for relationships, rather than a simple market that trades influence for policy, and that these relationships yield greater access to the lawmaking process for clients who can afford to leverage the lobbyist's relationships or afford to provide campaign contributions.[70]

A gift economy is grounded upon relationships, not quid pro quos.[71] Those relationships grow over time, as actors within that economy build their power by developing a rich set of obligations that they later draw upon to achieve the ends they seek. In this world, the campaign contribution does not "buy" a result. It cements a relationship. (Kaiser: It "reinforce[s] established connections."[72]) As one former lobbyist put it when asked why contributions are made: "Well, it isn't good government. It's to thank friends, and to make new friends. It opens up channels of communication."[73]

It is within this practice of reciprocity that obligation gets built.[74] And as economist Michele Dell'Era demonstrates, the gifts necessary to make this system of reciprocity work need not be large.[75] What is important is that they be repeated and appropriate within the norms of the context. What is critical is that they are depended upon.

Unlike traditional gift economies, however, Washington is a gift economy not because anyone wants it to be. It is a gift economy because it is regulated to be. Having banned the quid pro quo economy, the market makers have only one choice: to do the hard work necessary to build and support a gift economy. The insiders must learn a dance that never seems like an exchange. Demands or requests can be made. (Day one: "Congresswoman, our clients really need you to see how harmful H.R. 2322 will be to their interests.") But those demands are unconnected to the gifts that are given. (Day two: "Congresswoman, we'd love to hold a fund-raiser for you.") Even congressmen (or at least their staff) can put one and one together. And even when the one doesn't follow the other, everyone understands how to count chits. There's nothing cheap or insincere about it. Indeed, the lobbyist is providing something of value, and the member is getting something she needs. And so long as each part in this exchange remains allowed, the dance can continue—openly and notoriously—without anyone feeling wrong or used.

For this economy to survive, we need only assume a rich and repeated set of exchanges, among people who come to know and trust one another. There has to be opportunity to verify that com-mitments have been met—eventually. In the meantime, there must be the trust necessary to enable most of the exchange to happen based on trust alone. It must be the sort of place "where one never writes if one can call, never calls if one can speak, never speaks if one can nod, and never nods if one can wink"—precisely how Bar-ney Frank described DC, borrowing from the words of Boston pol Martin Lomasney.[76]

As I've already described, the seed for the current version of this economy was earmarks. The lobbying firm retainers that secured these earmarks paid for the infrastructure that now gets leveraged to much greater and more powerful ends. Think of earmarks as the pianist's scales. They taught technique. But the technique gets deployed far beyond scales.

It wasn't always so. The modern earmarks revolution was born recently, and in a rather unlikely place. Its inventor was a McGov-ern Democrat, Gerald S. J. Cassidy, and its first target was a grant to support a nutrition research center at Tufts University in 1976. Cas-sidy and Associates "brought something new to an old game," Kai-ser writes, "by stationing themselves at a key intersection between a supplicant for government assistance... and the people who could respond."[77] Once they did, the supplicants recognized they had tripped upon gold. There were thousands of organizations and individuals keen to get government money spent in a particu-lar way. And if the will of these organizations could be achieved through the camouflage of the earmarking process, they'd be more than eager to pay for it. To pay, that is, both Cassidy (directly) and members of Congress (indirectly).[78] By 1984, there were fifteen university clients paying large monthly retainers to Cassidy's firm, and about a dozen more clients—all seeking earmarks.[79]

Cassidy couldn't patent his brilliant insight (or at least he didn't—who knows what silliness the patent office would endorse). But as other lobbyists recognized just what was happening, other firms entered the market he originally staked out. Soon an industry was born to complement the practice (and profits) of the lobbyists of before: The product of that industry was a chance at channeling federal spending; the producers of that product were the lobbyists; the beneficiaries of that product were the lobbyists, the congressmen, and the interests who might benefit from the earmark. For a time, Cassidy and his colleagues "could truthfully tell clients that they had never failed to win an earmark for an institution that had retained them."[80] "Never" is a sexy word in the world of political power.

As this economy grew, the lobbyists' role in fund-raising grew as well. As one lobbyist put it expressly, "I spend a huge amount of my time fundraising...A huge amount."[81] That behavior has been confirmed to me by countless others, not so eager to be on the record. "The most vital people" in this economy, Jeff Birnbaum reports, "aren't the check writers but the check raisers."[82] "Washington has thousands of lobbyists who raise or give money to lawmakers."[83]

At first, some of the old-timers in DC worried about the monster that Cassidy had helped birth. As Senator Robert Byrd (D-W. Va.; 1959–2010) put it:

> The perception is growing that the merit of a project, grant or contract awarded by the government has fallen into a distant second place to the moxie and clout of lobbyists who help spring the money out of appropriation bills for a fat fee.... Inside the Beltway, everyone knows how the game is played.... Every Senator in this body ought to be repulsed by the perception that we will dole out the bucks if stroked by the right consultant.[84]

The concern was not just among Democrats. Members from the middle era of the twentieth-century Congress from both parties were unhappy as they watched Congress become the Fundraising Congress. Senator John Heinz (R-Pa.; 1977–1991) asked how he could explain to Pennsylvania universities that money was now handed out "not on the basis of quality, but on the basis of senatorial committee assignments."[85] Senator John Danforth (R-Mo.; 1976–1995) made a similar complaint.[86]

As the practice grew, the range and scale of the asks only increased, and the capacity of congressmen to decide on earmark requests based on the merits of the request declined substantially. My former congresswoman, Jackie Speier (D-Calif.; 2009–), asked me to chair a citizens' commission to review earmark requests. Almost a dozen civic leaders from the district and I spent hundreds of hours poring over almost sixty specific requests. The topics of these requests ranged from streetlights to sophisticated defense technologies. The size ranged from the tens of thousands to the many, many millions.

What struck all of us on this commission was just how impossibly difficult it would be for anyone to weigh one request against another in a rational way. Moreover, we all were unanimous in our view that there was something inappropriate about for-profit companies asking for government help to better market or produce their products. Yet there were many requests of exactly that form, and thus many, many opportunities in districts unlike ours for the beneficiaries of those potential grants to make their gratitude known.

"But isn't all this illegal?" you ask. Even if the exchange merely increases the probability of a payment in return, isn't that enough to show quid pro quo corruption?

The answer is no, and for a very good reason: Quid pro quo corruption requires intent. The guilty government official must intend to pay for the contribution made. That's the meaning of pro: this pro (for) that. But in the mechanism I'm describing, the repayment is attenuated, and there is no necessity that it even be intended. Indeed, as cognitive psychologists have now plausibly suggested using brain scan technology, it is quite plausible that "intent" to repay a gift happens completely subconsciously.[87] The member need not even recognize that she is acting to reciprocate for her action to be repayment for a previously recognized gift.

Indeed, the only way to clearly separate the gift to the member from the member's actions in return would be if such gifts were anonymous.[88] But of course, every contribution that matters today is as public as a pop star's latest affair. Without doubt, key staffers in every member's office know who supports their congressman and who doesn't. More likely than not, the key staffers have made sure of it.

The gifts within this economy go both ways. Sometimes it is the lobbyist who secures the gift. Sometimes it is the member who makes the gift, expecting the recipient will, as the moniker suggests, reciprocate.

How would this work?

A large proportion of earmarks went to nonprofit institutions. Nonprofit institutions have boards, and board members have an obligation to work for the interest of that institution. Sometimes that work includes fund-raising, especially fund-raising to support new buildings or new research ventures. Members of the board thus have an obligation to the institution to raise the funds to meet those objectives.

So imagine you're a board member of a small college in Virginia. Your board has decided to build a new science center. And just as you launch on this difficult task, your congresswoman secures an earmark to fund one building. You, as a board member, have now received a gift—from this congresswoman. A gift, not a bribe. You have no obligation toward that congresswoman. To the contrary, you have something better: You have gratitude toward her, for she has helped you and your institution.

That gratitude, in turn, can be quite lucrative—for the congresswoman. When you next receive a fund-raising solicitation from that congresswoman, it will be harder for you to say no and still feel good about yourself. She did a favor for you. You now should do a favor for her in return. The simplest way to return the favor is to send a check to her campaign committee. So you send a check— again, not necessarily even aware of how the desire to reciprocate has been induced by the congresswoman's gift. At no point in this process has any law been broken. The earmark was not a quo given in exchange for a quid. No promise of anything in return need have been made. The earmark is instead simply part of the economy.

Representative Peter Kostmayer (D-Pa.; 1977–1981, 1983–1993) described this dynamic precisely, and his own recognition of its stench:

> I was once asked by a member of Congress from Pennsylvania to raise some money for the Pennsylvania Democratic Party, and he gave me a list of universities that had gotten big federal grants—academic pork. And he asked me if I would make calls to the presidents of these universities across the state to get contributions. I decided I was uncomfortable doing it, and I didn't do it.[89]

My point just now is not to criticize what earmarks supported, though I'd be happy to do that as well. Whether you think the spending makes sense or not, my point is to get you to see the dynamic that earmarks support. Or better, the platform they help build. That platform enables a certain trade. The parties to that trade are lobbyists, their special-interest clients, and members of Congress. Because that platform supports a gift economy, the trade it enables does not cross the boundary of quid pro quo corruption. The lobbyists never need to make any link explicit. They're proud of their "professionalism" in respecting that line. Indeed, they are surprised when anyone expressly crosses it. (Kaiser reports one example that reveals the understanding: The National Association of Home Builders was upset at a change made to certain pending legislation. In response, they expressly declared that there would be no further campaign contributions until the change was undone. "The statement raised eyebrows all over Washington. The NAHB had broken one of the cardinal rules of the game.")[90]

The gains in this system that each of the three parties in the system—lobbyists, their clients, and members of Congress—realize should be obvious. (Indeed, there is valuable theoretical work suggesting just why the lobbying game proves to be more valuable than the bribery game, and why we should expect, over time, a democracy to move from bribery to lobbying.)[91]

But to make understandable the enormous growth in this "influence cash," now leveraged by the "influence peddlers," we should enumerate it just to be clear:

1. Members of Congress get access to desperately needed campaign cash—directly from the lobbyists, and indirectly, as facilitated by the lobbyists. They need that cash. That cash makes much simpler an otherwise insane existence, as it cuts back at least partially on the endless need for members to raise campaign funds elsewhere.

2. The clients of the lobbyists get a better chance at changing government policy. In a world of endless government spending and government regulation, that chance can be enormously lucrative. As researchers at the University of Kansas calculated, the return on lobbyists' investment to modify the American Jobs Creation Act of 2004 to create a tax benefit was 22,000 percent.[92] A paper published in 2009 calculates that, for every $1 that an average firm spends to lobby for targeted tax benefits, the return is between $6 and $20.[93] Looking at universities, John M. de Figueiredo and Brian S. Silverman found that universities with representation on the House or Senate Appropriations Committee see a 0.28 to 0.35 percent increase in earmarks for every 1 percent increase in lobbyist expenditures relative to universities without such representation.[94] Frank Yu and Xiaoyun Yu found that "compared to non-lobbying firms, firms that lobby on average have a significantly lower hazard rate of being detected for fraud, evade fraud detection 117 days longer, and are 38 percent less likely to be detected by regulators."[95] Hill, Kelly, Lockhart, and Van Ness have demonstrated how "lobbying firms significantly outperform non-lobbying firms."[96] All of these studies confirm what is otherwise intuitive: As the returns from lobbyists' investments increase, the willingness to invest in lobbyists will increase as well. Thus, as journalist Ken Silverstein puts it, while clients can pay retainers "easily reaching tens of millions of dollars...such retainers are undeniably savvy: The overall payout in pork is many times that, totaling into billions."[97]

3. Lobbyists get an ever-growing and increasingly profitable business. The lobbying industry has exploded over the past twenty-five years. Its growth and wealth match almost any in our economy. In 1971, Hacker and Pierson report, there were just 175 firms with registered lobbyists in DC. Eleven years later, there were almost 2,500.[98] In 2009, there were 13,700 registered lobbyists. They spent more than $3.5 billion—twice the amount spent in 2002,[99] representing about $6.5 million per elected representative in Congress. Current numbers are slightly less (11,800 lobbyists and $3.24 billion spent), but as Tim LaPira and Herschel Thomas argue, a significant reason for that decline is that more of the activities of lobbyists is moving outside the scope of reporting requirements. As they write, "We estimate that there are more professionals engaged in influencing public policy 'under the radar' than there are who are transparent about their clients and activities, implying that lobbying disclosure reports provide only a partial view of policy influence in Washington."[100]

And finally, as the lobbying industry grows, DC gets rich, too. As former labor secretary Robert Reich describes:

> When I first went to Washington in 1975, many of the restaurants along Pennsylvania Avenue featured linoleum floors and an abundance of cockroaches. But since then the city has become an increasingly dazzling place. Today, almost everywhere you look in downtown Washington you find polished facades, fancy restaurants, and trendy bistros. There are office complexes of glass, chrome and polished wood; well appointed condos with doormen who know the names and needs of each inhabitant; hotels with marble-floored lobbies, thick rugs, soft music, granite counters; restaurants with linen napkins, leather-bound menus, heavy silverware.[101]

There are many in the lobbying profession, of course, who deplore the state of the industry. They obviously don't want to return to the old days. They instead want the industry to evolve into the profession they dream it could be. As one lobbyist put it, "Money does make a difference—and it has changed the character of this town.... The truth is that money has replaced brains and hard work as the way for a lobbyist to get something done for his client."[102] And many, including the American Bar Association's Task Force on Federal Lobbying Laws, have recommended "so far as practicable, those who advocate to elected officials do not raise funds for them, and those who raise funds for them do not advocate to them."[103] As the ABA report states:

> The multiplier effect of a lobbyist's participation in fundraising for a member's campaign (or the member's leadership PAC) can be quite substantial, and the Task Force believes that this activity should be substantially curtailed.... [A] self-reinforcing cycle of *mutual financial dependency* has become a deeply troubling source of *corruption* in our government. (Emphasis added.)[104]

That follows the strong recommendation of President Bush's chief ethics lawyer, Professor Richard Painter:

> The best way to change the profession's reputation for abusing the system of campaign finance is to end lobbyists' involvement in campaign finance. When lobbyists bundle their own and clients' money to buy government officials' attention they undermine public confidence not only in government but also in the quality of lobbyists' advocacy and the merits of their cause. The bagman image erodes credibility even if credit is due for a lobbyist's intellectual ability, experience, and integrity.[105]

Until these reformers succeed in their reform, however, much of the value from the service of lobbyists will continue to derive not so much from the "bagman image" but from the fund-raising reality.

In this model of influence, campaign cash plays a complicated role. My claim is not that campaign cash buys any particular result directly. As Dan Clawson, Mark Weller, and Alan Neustadtl put it,

"Many critics of big money campaign finance seem to assume that a corporate donor summons a senator and says, 'Senator, I want you to vote against raising the minimum wage. Here's $5,000 to do so.' This view, in its crude form, is simply wrong."[106]

Where lobbying does buy votes directly, it's a crime, and I've already said I don't think (many) such crimes occur.

Instead, campaign cash has a distinctive role, depending upon which of three buckets it finds itself within:

1. In the first bucket are contributions that are effectively anonymous. These are gifts, typically small gifts, that a campaign receives but doesn't meaningfully track. That doesn't mean they don't keep tabs on the contributor—of course they do, for the purpose of asking the contributor for more. I mean instead that they don't keep tabs on the particular issue or interest that the contributor cares about. This is just money that the campaign attracts, but that it attracts democratically. It is the support inspired by the substance of the campaign.

2. The second bucket is the non-anonymous contributions. These are the large gifts from people or interests whose interests are fairly transparent. PAC contributions fit in here, as do contributions by very large and repeated givers. For these contributions, the candidate knows what he needs to do, or say, or believe. If campaign contributions are an investment, as many believe, then these investments are made with a clear signal about the return that is expected.

3. Finally, the third bucket is most important for the dynamic I am describing in this chapter: that part for which a lobbyist can claim responsibility. Again, some of this is direct: the money the lobbyist gives. But the more important cash is indirect: the part bundled, or effectively coordinated or inspired by the lobbyist, which, through channels, the beneficiaries learn of. Everyone who needs to be thanked is thanked, which means everyone who needs to know eventually does.

As we move from bucket one to three, risks to the system increase.

Bucket 1 is the most benign and pro-democratic of the three. This is the part that the candidate's campaign inspires directly. It's the direct echo of the policies he or she advances. If there is pandering here to raise more cash, it is democratic pandering. It's the kind the opponent can take advantage of. It is the part that feeds political debate. And as Robert Brooks put it more than a century ago, "It is highly improbable that the question of campaign funds would ever have been raised in American politics if party contributions were habitually made by a large number of persons each giving a relatively small amount."[107]

Bucket 2 is where the risks begin. For here begins the incentive to shape-shift, and not necessarily in a public way. The understandings that might inspire contributions to this bucket can be subtle or effectively invisible. As Daniel Lowenstein writes, "From the beginning of an issue's life, legislators know of past contributions and the possibility of future ones. . . . All of these combine in a manner no one fully understands to form an initial predisposition in the legislator."[108]

Again, it's not easy to achieve such understandings effectively and legally. To the extent they're expressed, they're crimes. To the extent they're implied, they can be misunderstood. The rules regulating quid pro quo corruption don't block this sort of distortion. But they certainly make it much harder to effect.

Bucket 3 is where the real risk to the system thrives, at least so long as lobbyists are at the center of campaign funding. For here the relationships are complicated and long-standing, and their thickness makes it relatively simple to embed understandings and expectations.

We don't have any good data about how big each bucket is. The data we do have is (predictably) misleading because of (predictable) loopholes in the rules. My colleague Joseph Mornin used the public records to try to calculate the size of bundled contributions.[109] He found large numbers overall. But even that careful analysis understates the influence, because the rules don't require a lobbyist to report a bundle if the event at which it occurs was jointly sponsored, and if each lobbyist was responsible for less than $16,000. So if ten lobbyists hold a fund-raiser at which they bring together $150,000, none of that need be reported.[110]

But critically, size is not necessarily the most important issue. Influence happens on the margin, and the most powerful are the contributors who stand there. Even if Bucket 3 were small compared to Buckets 1 and 2, if it provided a reliable and substantial source of funds, then its potential to distort policy would be huge.

This point is important, and often missed. As economists put it, price is set on the margin. The economic actor with the most power is the last one to trade. ("What do I need to do to get the next $10,000?") Thus, even if small, Bucket 3 is where the action is. The argument is parallel to one about technological innovation made by Judge Richard Posner:

> The level of output in a competitive market is determined by the intersection of price and marginal cost. This implies that the marginal purchaser—the purchaser willing to pay a price no higher than marginal cost—drives the market to a considerable extent. It follows that a technological innovation that is attractive to the marginal consumer may be introduced even though it lowers consumer welfare overall; this is a kind of negative externality.[111]

In the context of contributions to a campaign, the same dynamic is true. The bending necessary to secure sufficient funds from Bucket 3 may well make those giving to Bucket 1 less happy. That's just the nature of these markets on the margin.

Campaign contributions in this model are thus not the only or even the most significant expenditure that special interests make. Indeed, lobbying expenditures (2009–2010) were four times as large as campaign expenditures in 2010. But though "themselves... never enough to create or maintain a viable government relations operation," as Clawson, Alan Neustadtl, and Mark Weller describe, contributions are a "useful, perhaps even a necessary, part of the total strategy."[112]

And finally, there is one more "useful, perhaps even necessary, part of the total strategy" that we cannot ignore: the power that one's future has over one's behavior today. This part was made obvious to me by an extraordinary congressman from Tennessee, Democrat Jim Cooper (D-Tenn.; 1983–1995; 2003–).

First elected to Congress in 1982 (at the age of twenty-eight), Cooper has a longer perspective on the institution than all but twenty-nine of its members.[113] Early into my work, Cooper captured one part of it for me with a single brilliant distillation. As he told me one afternoon, while we were sitting in his office overlooking the Capitol: "Capitol Hill is a farm league for K Street."[114]

Cooper worries that too many now view Capitol Hill as a stepping-stone to life as a lobbyist—aka K Street. Too many have a business model much like my students at Harvard Law School: They expect to work for six to eight years making a salary just north of $160,000 a year. Then they want to graduate to a job making three to ten times that amount as lobbyists. Their focus is therefore not so much on the people who sent them to Washington. Their focus is instead on those who will make them rich in Washington.

This, too, is an important change. In the 1970s, 3 percent of retiring members became lobbyists. Thirty years later, that number has increased by an order of magnitude. Between 1998 and 2004, more than 50 percent of senators and 42 percent of House members made that career transition.[115] As of June 2011, 195 former members of Congress were registered lobbyists.[116] In 2009, the financial sector alone had 70 former members of Congress lobbying on its behalf.[117] Indeed, as Jeffrey Birnbaum reports, there are members who are explicit about the plan to become lobbyists.[118] Ken Silverstein reports on one particularly pathetic example:

> While still a senator, [Bob] Packwood had confided to his fatal diaries that he regarded the Senate, where he dwelled for

twenty-seven years, as but a stepping-stone to a more lucrative
career as an influence peddler. Perhaps someday, he mused, "I
can become a lobbyist at five or six or four hundred thousand"
dollars a year. Less than a year after he resigned in disgrace,
Packwood formed a firm called Sunrise Research and was making lavish fees representing timber firms and other corporate
clients seeking lower business taxes.[119]

The system thus feeds itself. It's not campaign contributions
that members care about, or not directly. It is also a future. A job. A
way to imagine paying for the life that other professionals feel entitled to. A nice house. Fancy cars. Private schools for the kids. This
system gives both members and their staff a way to have it all—at
least if they continue to support the system.[120]

What exactly is wrong in what they're doing, given the system
as it is? The wanna-be lobbyists get to do their wonky policy work.
They get to live among the most powerful people in the nation.
Their lives are interesting and well compensated. And they never
need to lie, cheat, or steal. What could possibly be bad about that?
Indeed, anyone who would resist this system would be a pariah
on the Hill. You can just hear the dialogue from any number of
Hollywood films: "We've got a good thing going here, Jimmy. Why
would you want to go and mess things up?"

CHAPTER 8

What So Damn Much Money *Does*

Consider two statements by two prominent Republicans. The first, by Senator Tom Coburn (R-Okla.; 2005–2015):

> Thousands of instances exist where appropriations are leveraged for fundraising dollars or political capital.[1]

The second by former Federal Elections Commission chairman Bradley Smith:

> The evidence is pretty overwhelming that the money does not play much of a role in what goes on in terms of legislative voting patterns and legislative behavior. The consensus about that, I think, among people who have studied it is roughly the same as the consensus among scientists that global warming is taking place.[2]

To be clear, Smith is a corruption denier, not a global warming denier. What he is saying is that the evidence from political science suggests—contrary to Senator Coburn and to the whole thrust of this book—that the money doesn't matter. Indeed, he says more than just that: He is saying that anyone who suggests that the money matters—to "legislative voting patterns and legislative behavior"—is as crazy as global warming deniers. That no honest scholar (let's put aside politicians) could maintain that we have any good evidence to suggest that there's a problem with the current system. That any honest scholar would therefore focus his work elsewhere.

I've found that people have two very different reactions to Chairman Smith's statement. The vast majority react in stunned disbelief: "Is he nuts?" is the most common retort. It is also among the kindest. Almost all of us react almost viscerally to corruption deniers, just as most (liberals, at least) react to global warming deniers.

A tiny minority, however, react differently. If they're careless in listening precisely to what Chairman Smith said ("money does not play much of a role in what goes on in terms of legislative voting patterns and legislative behavior"), they say something like this: "Yeah, it is surprising, but the data really don't support the claim that money is corrupting Congress." And if they're more on the activist side of the spectrum, and less on the academic side, they're likely to buttress this observation with something like "So you, Lessig, need to take this evidence seriously, and justify your campaign, since the facts don't support it."

I once confronted this latter demand in a bizarre Washington context. I had been invited to address a truly remarkable group called the Lib-Libertarians—a mix of liberal and libertarian DC souls who meet for dinner regularly to talk about common ideas. Most of them were lawyers. Some were journalists. And some were in various stages of the revolving and gilded door between government and the private sector.

I like liberals. (I am one.) I also like libertarians. (I still believe that if we understood that philosophy properly, I would be one of those, too.) So I carelessly assumed that my anti-money-in-politics argument would be embraced by the collected wise and virtuous souls in that DC dinner hall.

It wasn't, by at least a significant chunk. For when I tried to brush off a version of Chairman Smith's claim, I was practically scolded by my host. How could I "possibly," he asked, "ignore these data?" How could I "honestly," he charged, "make an argument that doesn't account for them?"

That scolding was fair. I can't honestly make an argument that demands we end the corruption that is our government without honestly addressing "these data."

The Republican senator from Oklahoma is right (not the global warming denier, Senator James Inhofe [R-Okla.; 1994–], but Coburn): There are thousands of "instances...where appropriations are leveraged for fundraising dollars or political capital." That defines the corruption that I have described in this book. Nothing in what I will say in this chapter will undermine that claim.

And Chairman Smith is also, in part at least, right. He is right that political scientists have not shown a strong connection between contributions to political campaigns and "legislative voting patterns." There is some contest about the question (much more than there is about global warming, I'd quibble), but it is fair to say that there is no consensus that the link has been shown.

Yet the aim of this chapter is to convince you that even if Smith is (partly) right—even if the political scientists can't see a connection between contributions and votes—that does not exonerate Congress. Why the political scientists can't see what the politicians do see is obvious enough. You can support the reform of Congress without denying the power of statistical regression. You can be a root-striker even if you can't directly see the root.

The Deviations That Money Inspires

It is my belief, contrary to Chairman Smith, that money *does* "play...a role in what goes on in terms of legislative voting patterns and legislative behavior." We can call that role "deviation." Because of money, Congress's legislative voting pattern and behavior deviate from what it otherwise would be. This is what money does.

That deviation is the *consequence* of the corruption that I described in Chapter 7. But it is important at the outset to make clear that deviation itself *is not the corruption*.

I am not saying that every gap between what the people want

and what Congress does constitutes corruption. As I've described it, the "corruption" in our system comes from the systemic disempowerment of a significant slice of voters (through what I've called for a shorthand, "tweedism"); it is not constituted by distortion, or deviation from some hypothetically preferred agenda. Deviation is the consequence of corruption. It is why we have practical reason to want to remedy corruption. But it is not the corruption itself.

A comparison might make this point more clearly. People with an infection typically have a fever. That fever is the consequence of the infection. But the fever is not the infection. And there are plenty of times that one has a fever (in the sense of a temperature above normal) that doesn't have anything to do with an infection. The fever is the consequence of the infection; it is not the cause of the infection, or the same thing as an infection.

In this analogy, deviation is the fever; corruption is the infection. In this chapter, I intend to describe the evidence we have for the deviation caused by corruption. But it is the improper dependence of Congress that creates the corruption, not this deviation.

Our current Congress is far from the Congress that our Framers imagined. In a million ways. It doesn't deliberate together, as a whole. Members don't listen to other members during debate. Each representative represents at least twenty times the number of citizens that representatives at the founding did. Almost half of the Congress returned home after each election cycle in the first century of the Republic. No more than 10 percent do so today.[3]

But the difference I want to focus on here is the economy of influence that defines the life of a member. How is the Republic altered because we have allowed this dependency to evolve? How would it be different if we found a way to remove it?

I've already suggested the beginnings of an answer to this question in Chapter 1: Imagine yourself in your congresswoman's shoes. Imagine the life she leads. She has a campaign manager who tells her she needs to raise hundreds of thousands, maybe millions, of dollars, preferably long before the next election, so that no one in his right mind would even think about running against her.

So each day she does her bit. A couple of hours here, a couple of hours there, on the phone with people she doesn't know, asking for money. The routine would be comical if it weren't so disturbing: A day on Capitol Hill consists of racing to vote on the floor of the House, to a quick drop-in on a committee meeting, and then off the Hill to a fund-raising office with a telephone and an operator's headset, where, until the vote buzzer rings again, she will call and call and call again.

This life puts enormous pressure on a member. It is pressure that comes in part from the member herself (she wants to win), and in part from her staff, from her supporters, and from her party. And then she meets with a dizzying array of lobbyists, many of whom are eager to help relieve that pressure. How would that offer of "help" change what she thought, or what she did? How would it matter?

We don't need Sigmund Freud here. As I described in Chapter 1, we all recognize the drive deep in our bones (or more accurately, our DNA) to reciprocate.[4] Some of it we see directly. Some of it we don't. The subconscious is guided by interactions of reciprocity as much as the conscious. We reciprocate without thinking. We are bent to those to whom we are obliged, even when we believe, honestly, that we are not. What Robert Brooks wrote over a century ago we can repeat today: "By far the worst evil of the present system is the ease with which it enables men otherwise incorruptible to be placed tactfully, subtly, and—as time goes on—always more completely under obligations incompatible with public duty."[5]

Sometimes the politicians admit as much. In 1905, an aging Senator Thomas Collier Platt of New York "acknowledged receiving cash contributions to his campaigns from the insurance companies, and in return for that money he admitted that he had 'a moral obligation to defend them.'"[6] Much more recently, former Congressman Tony Coelho (D-Calif.; 1979–1989) admitted to Robert Kaiser that "the need for this money 'does affect legislation' by convincing members to avoid angering moneyed interests."[7]

Most of the time, however, they deny it. They insist that their judgment is independent of campaign cash. They insist they haven't been affected. "It is insulting," I've been told, "to suggest that my actions have been influenced by my contributors. They have not, and never will be."

America doesn't believe the denials. The vast majority of Americans believe money buys results in Congress: 75 percent, according to a poll, believe "campaign contributions buy results in Congress."[8] Indeed, as John Hibbing and Elizabeth Theiss-Morse conclude, Americans also believe the contributions "enrich politicians."[9]And if this is a commonsense view, then it is confirmed, albeit more subtly, by some current members of Congress, and more frequently by former members of Congress.

In an excellent series, the Center for Responsive Politics has interviewed retired members of Congress about the influence of money in politics. Again and again, both Democrats and Republicans insist that, of course, the money matters. For example:

> Representative Joe Scarborough (R-Fla.; 1995–2001) (yes, that Joe Scarborough): "Across the spectrum, money changed votes. Money certainly drove policy at the White House during the Clinton administration, and I'm sure it has in every other administration too."[10]

> Senator Slade Gorton (R-Wash.; 1981–1987, 1989–2001) (Asked: Have you seen votes in the Senate where you just knew that certain votes were lining up certain ways because of the money?): "The answer to that question certainly has been yes."[11]

> Representative Tim Penny (D-Minn.; 1983–1995): "There's not tit for tat in business, no check for a vote. But nonetheless, the influence is there. Candidates know where their money is coming from."[12]

> Representative Mel Levine (D-Calif.; 1983–1993): "On the tax side, the appropriations side, the subsidy side, and the expenditure side, decisions are clearly weighted and influenced… by who has contributed to the candidates. The price that the

public pays for this process, whether it's in subsidies, taxes, or appropriations, is quite high."[13]

Representative Eric Fingerhut (D-Ohio; 1993–1995): "The completely frank and honest answer is that the method of campaign funding that we currently have...has a serious and profound impact on not only the issues that are considered in Congress, but also on the outcome of those issues."[14]

Senator Bill Bradley (D-N.J.; 1979–1997): "We've reached a point where nothing but money seems to matter. Political parties have lost their original purpose, which was to bring people together... and instead they become primarily conduits for cash."[15]

Others have reported the same:

Senator Tim Wirth (D-Colo.; 1987–1993): "It's basically corrupt. It is legalized corruption. And people aren't going to say that. They will recoil when you say it, but it is true."[16]

Senator Olympia Snowe (R-Me.; 1995–2013): "Congressional scheduling is now at the mercy of fundraising events...There used to be a time when we would separate politics and policy at least for the first year after the election, to attempt to synchronize our legislative agenda on issues crucial to the nation before the campaign season of the second year. Now we are experiencing a perpetual focus on campaigns and fundraising."

Representative Luis Gutiérrez (D-Ill.; 1993–): "I thought that there would just be this huge group of people all running to the same finish line,...all of us saying, 'We're going to do campaign finance reform. We're going to eliminate the parking [reserved for members of Congress] at National Airport. The chauffeurs are gone, the perks and the privileges, the things that make us different.' Well, people take that stuff pretty personal here. They take it as a personal affront to themselves....[Congress is] the belly of the beast....It's a monster."[17]

Even when members think they're denying an effect, their denial just confirms that the effect is real. Former Senator Slade Gorton (R-Wash., 1981–1987, 1989–2001), a supporter of the current system, commented, "It just seemed to me that those who were trying to buy influence on both sides were simply wasting their money."[18] Does that mean that those who bought on only one side were not wasting their money? Or as Representative Hamilton Fish IV (R-N.Y.; 1969–1995) commented: "I look at a contribution as a 'thank you' for the position I took, not as expecting that I would take a position in the future . . . .[It was] a reward, not a bribe."[19] But of course, we use rewards to induce people to do things they otherwise wouldn't do all the time. Why not here?

Most of us believe that the money has an influence. Former members from both political parties confirm it. That influence, we believe, bends the results of Congress from what they otherwise would have been. That constitutes, for the vast majority of Americans, proof enough of the corruption that is our government. This is the common view.

Yet as I said at the start of the chapter, our common view could be wrong. Indeed, as I describe in the section that follows, there is important scholarship that raises real questions about whether we can say that money in fact bends democracy in the way most of us feel it does. We need to confront that scholarship to see exactly what it sees, and exactly what it misses.

0. It Matters Not at All

Some believe that this dependence upon money does nothing. That it is harmless. Or at least, they insist, we have no good evidence that this dependence does anything, and since we've got no evidence, we've got no good reason to change it.

By "evidence," these conservatives (with a small *c*—they could well be politically liberal; my point is that they're scientifically conservative) mean numbers. Statistics. Regressions that show an input (campaign contributions) and an output (a change in votes).

There is no good evidence, these scholars insist, that campaign contributions are changing political results. There may be many such contributions. Securing them may well occupy a huge chunk of a congressman's life. But we don't have the data to support the claim that this money is buying results that otherwise would not have been obtained.[20] As Frank Baumgartner and his colleagues summarize the research, there is "no smoking gun, no systematic relationship between campaign contributions and policy success."[21]

The most prominent work making this claim is by political scientists Stephen Ansolabehere, John M. de Figueiredo, and James M. Snyder. In an important paper published in 2003, "Why Is There So Little Money in U.S. Politics?,"[22] these authors question just about every strand of the commonsense view that money is buying results in Congress.

The most important bit of their argument for our purposes questions whether campaign contributions actually affect legislative decisions. Ansolabehere and his colleagues first collected about forty articles that tried to measure the effect of PAC contributions on congressional voting behavior. Looking across this range of studies, they conclude, "PAC contributions show relatively few effects." "In three out of four instances, campaign contributions had no statistically significant effects on legislation or had the 'wrong' sign...."[23]

Ansolabehere and his colleagues then identified a number of statistical problems in some of the studies they collected. This led them to perform their own statistical analysis. That analysis used the voting score produced by the U.S. Chamber of Commerce as the dependent variable. They then estimated six models that mirrored the range of their original forty studies and that included campaign contributions among the independent variables.

Their conclusions are not good for the commonsense view (even if they sound promising for the republic). While they did find some evidence that contributions had an effect on voting patterns, that effect was small relative to other factors. Much of that effect, moreover, was eliminated once they controlled for voter

118   DEEPER

preference. And once they controlled for legislator-fixed effects
(such as the party of the legislator), they were able to "eliminate
the effects of contributions entirely."[24] As they conclude: "Indica-
tors of party, ideology and district preference account for most
of the systematic variation in legislators' roll call voting behavior.
Interest group contributions account for at most a small amount of
the variation. In fact, after controlling adequately for legislator ideology, these contributions have no detectable effects on legislator
behavior."[25]

In understanding the significance of this claim, we should first
be very careful about what exactly is being argued here. Ansolabehere and his colleagues are themselves careful to insist that they
are not saying that contributions have no effect. Indeed, as one version of their paper asserts, "It is still possible that campaign contributions have significant effects on economic policies."[26] How,
given the data they've studied?

To raise sufficient funds, candidates might skew policies in
ways preferred by donors. As they write:

> Campaign contributions might therefore act like weighted
> votes. And contributors, who are disproportionately wealthy,
> might have different policy preferences than the median
> voter.[27]

Aka *tweedism*: "Campaign contributions" are the "weighted
votes" in the Green Primary. Those voters do—not might—"have
different policy preferences than the median voter."[28] What Ansolabehere et al. are suggesting is that the distortion of money could
be the distortion through tweedism. As Brugman reminds us, this
was the system in Rome—where the rich had more votes than the
poor—as it fell.[29]

Even ignoring this important admission, by saying, "We can't
see a relationship between roll call votes and PAC contributions,"
these authors are not saying what the antireform think tank Center
for Competitive Politics reports them as saying—viz., "a substantial

majority of academic research on the subject has shown that there is little connection between contributions and legislative votes or actions."[30] "We don't see it" is not the same as "there is nothing to see."

Ansolabehere and his colleagues' conclusions, moreover, are not uncontested. Some political scientists do believe that there is a link between money and results that can be demonstrated by the numbers alone.[31]

Thomas Stratmann, for example, conducted a meta-analysis of the same forty studies that Ansolabehere and his colleagues reviewed. That analysis rejected the conclusion that money does not affect results.[32]

Sanford Gordon and his colleagues find that an executive's likelihood of contributing to political candidates is tied to how sensitive his or her salary is to firm profitability: the higher the sensitivity, the higher the likelihood of contributions, reinforcing the suggestion that the contribution is an investment rather than consumption.[33]

Justin Grimmer and Eleanor Neff Powell use the dynamic of "committee exile"—a member losing a committee assignment after a party's loss at an election—to track the plausible objective of PAC contributions. Their work provides "evidence that corporations and business PACs use donations to acquire immediate access and favor—suggesting they at least anticipate that the donations will influence policy."[34]

Douglas Roscoe and Shannon Jenkins did a careful meta-analysis of the existing literature. Using advanced techniques, as Clayton Peoples describes it, "they determine that contributions are significant, even when considering reverse causality (that 'friendly giving' is a consequence rather than a cause of lawmaker votes.)"[35] Instead, as they conclude, "a reasonable conclusion is that one in three roll call votes exhibits the impact of campaign contributions."[36]

Consistent with this result, in a study of PAC contributions related to the 1984 Deficit Reduction Act, Sanjay Gupta and Charles

Swenson found that firms whose managers' compensation included earnings-based bonuses made larger PAC contributions, and that contributions generally were "positively associated with firm tax benefits."[37]

Likewise, Atif Mian and his colleagues found that the voting patterns on the 2008 Emergency Economic Stabilization Act were strongly predicted by the amount of campaign contributions from the financial services industry.[38] Not exclusively, but partially, and certainly enough for us to wonder whether the money is queering results more generally.

At the state level, Lynda Powell has used powerful survey techniques to show "that campaign contributions to legislators do influence the content and passage of legislation in their chambers."[39] It would be bizarre if this were true at the state level but not at the level of Congress.

And finally, perhaps the most interesting research trying to explain Ansolabehere and his colleagues' work uses the metaphor of an iceberg: that only part of the influence provided by a contribution can be seen, and part is hidden. As Marcos Chamon and Ethan Kaplan explain, "A candidate may support a special interest not only in order to receive a contribution, but also in order to discourage that special interest from making a contribution to his or her opponent."[40] For example:

> Suppose a special interest group contributes $2,000 to the stronger of two candidates in exchange for its support, while threatening to contribute $10,000 to her opponent if that support is denied. This $2,000 equilibrium contribution...can induce the same level of support from that candidate that a $12,000 would in a traditional bilateral contracting setting.[41]

Plus the added advantage to the special-interest group: A threat to give $10,000 threat is cheaper than giving $10,000!

This work provides strong pushback against the theory that campaign contributions are mere consumption (and therefore don't affect results), and it explains how such investments could well, consistent with the data, provide a return.[42]

But let's assume for the moment that Ansolabehere and his colleagues are right. Let's assume the data won't show a clear link between contributions and results.

If that is true, does that fact exonerate Congress? Are the critics unfair, if Ansolabehere and his colleagues are correct?

The critics are not unfair. For even if the political science skeptics are right, there are three undeniable effects of this economy of influence, each of them a reason for concern, and all three together a demonstration of the urgency in solving it.

1. Extortion

By far, the cleverest response to these data comes from conservative author Peter Schweizer, in his book *Extortion* (2013). After reviewing the literature finding no clear connection between contributions and roll call votes, Schweizer asks the obvious question: What if the incentive for the fund-raising is the other way around? The assumption of scholars seeking to identify an effect from campaign money on congressional policy is that the funders seek something from Congress. But what if it is Congress seeking something from the funders? What if it isn't influence that funders are buying, but extortion that members of Congress are practicing? As Schweizer writes:

> Campaign contributions are not about buying votes, they are often about extortion. Legislators have the bargaining power, and they largely initiate solicitations of money. It isn't a bribe. In white-collar crime, the distinction between bribery and extortion is often based on the determination of "which party initiates the exchange." This also explains why many corporate executives and PACs largely give to incumbents regardless of party. A challenger can't do very much to them. But if they fund only the losing candidate, there might be hell to pay from the winner. If it's a close election, execs might hedge their bets and

give to both candidates to secure protection from both sides. Of course, once an election is over, there is only one extortionist left. Corporate PACs send money "disproportionately to incumbents, majority party members, and those serving in leadership positions, especially those on the most powerful committees."[43]

Schweizer's account is brilliant, and fantastically difficult to test empirically. It fits with the more sociological (or confessional) accounts of how Congress behaves today. Jack Abramoff's fantastic book, *Capitol Punishment* (2011), is filled with accounts that fit Schweizer's model directly.[44] When lobbyists sought to induce corporations to support certain bills or congressmen, there was a range of techniques that operated as effective threats. The most innocuous (or seemingly so) included a congressional hearing on a question that could easily cost a firm millions in legal and consulting fees to defend.[45] A firm would be quite eager to avoid those costs. A favorable relationship with a committee chairman would be an effective way to do that.

Schweizer's whole story of how the corruption of Washington works places heavy emphasis on this "extortion" game. "What if politics is really largely about fund-raising and making money?,"[46] he asks early in his book. "What if the greater culprits are inside the halls of power in Washington rather than on the outside?"[47]

From this perspective, he weaves a powerful and compelling account of how insiders leverage their incredible power both to fund their campaigns and, ultimately, to get rich.

But we don't need to embrace the most cynical view to see the power of this perspective for understanding the academic research. It is a fair criticism of the academic work that it assumes the donations are made voluntarily. Yet if the causation is the other way around, then the influence is corrupting even if it doesn't produce measurable correlations between the preferences of the victim of that extortion and the policies of Congress. Think about a more pedestrian version of this sort of extortion: We wouldn't look to the failure of a local mafia to give the victims of its extortion benefits as proof that there is no extortion. The victims are trying to avoid penalties; they're not seeking special favors.

The Internet houses a particularly revealing example of the dynamic that Schweizer describes. This is a transcript of a voice mail left for a lobbyist by Congresswoman Elinor Holmes Norton:

> This is Congresswoman Elinor Holmes Norton.
>
> I notice that you have given to other colleagues on the Transportation and Infrastructure Committee. I am a Senior Member—twenty-year veteran—and am Chair of the Subcommittee on Economic Development, Public Buildings and Emergency Management. I am handing the largest economic development project in the United States now, the Homeland Security Compound of three buildings being built on the Old St. Elizabeth's Hospital site in the District of Columbia, along with sixteen other sites here that are part of the stimulus.
>
> I was, frankly, surprised to see that we don't have a record, so far as I can tell, of your having given to me, despite my long and deep work. In fact, it has been my major work on the committee and subcommittee has been essentially in your sector.
>
> I am simply, candidly, calling to ask for a contribution. As the senior member of the committee and a subcommittee chair, we have obligations to raise funds and I think it must have been me who hasn't, frankly, done my homework to ask for a contribution earlier. So I'm trying to make up for it by asking for one now, when we particularly need contributions, particularly those of us who have the seniority and the chairmanships, and are in a position to raise the funds.
>
> I'm asking you to give to Citizens for [. . .]
>
> I'll send you a follow-up note with appreciation for having heard me out.[48]

The person posting this voice mail makes it seem as if this behavior is limited to Democrats. But as Schweizer quite fairly insists throughout his book, there is nothing partisan about this behavior. The pressures of fund-raising fall equally on both parties. (Though I do doubt whether a lobbyist would have leaked the

voice mail of a white male committee chairman, but that may just
reflect my own bias here.)

2. Distraction

So, first, the money might be producing a kind of political extortion. Second, and most obviously, like cell phones on the highway,
the money is producing a distracted Congress.

If members spend up to 30 to 70 percent of their time raising
money, that means they have less time to do the sort of things
members of Congress traditionally did. For example, deliberate. If
you compared our Congress in 1792 to the British House of Commons in 1792, we'd fare pretty well. Today, Congress compared to
today's Commons is an embarrassment. The British actually take
time to deliberate as a body (as our Framers intended us to do).
Our Congress does not. Or to read the bills: As Washington lobbyist Wright Andrews responded when asked about whether members read "most of the bills," "Most of the bills? [They read a]lmost
none of them! Any member that was honest will tell you that."[49] (In
a private session, Bill Gates reported that when he was a congressional page, he read "every bill." That may have been possible in
the 1960s, even for mere mortals [which Gates plainly is not], but
it is literally impossible today: The complexity of the bills Congress
considers is vastly greater than in the past. The Senate version of
the health care reform bill, for example, was more than two thousand pages long when introduced.)[50] Instead, the job of members
is increasingly that of raising campaign funds. As Fritz Hollings
(D-S.C.; 1966–2005) wrote after he retired from the Senate:

> I had to collect $30,000 a week, each and every week, for six
> years. I could have raised $3 million in South Carolina. But to
> get $8.5 million I had to travel to New York, Boston, Chicago,
> Florida, California, Texas and elsewhere. During every break
> Congress took, I had to be out hustling money. And when I was
> in Washington, or back home, my mind was still on money.[51]

Even twenty years ago, then–Senate majority leader Robert Byrd (D-W.Va.; 1959–2010) wanted reform for campaign finance because the Senate had become "full-time fundraisers instead of full-time legislators."[52] "Members," as Anthony Corrado of Brookings describes, "are essentially campaigning and raising money all the time."[53] This is an important change. "For most of American history," Norman Ornstein and Thomas Mann write, "campaigns generally were confined to the latter half of election years."[54] Now that the campaign is permanent, the other work that was customarily done during the balance of the term must, in some ways, suffer.

The numbers support what common sense predicts. Between 1983 and 1997, the total number of nonappropriations oversight committee meetings fell from 782 to 287 in the House, and 429 to 175 in the Senate.[55] Between 1975 and 2008, total subcommittee meetings tanked as well:[56]

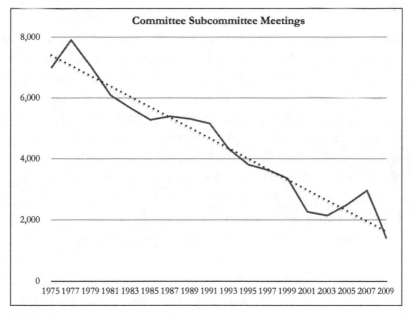

FIGURE 8

There has been a similar decline in the number of days in which Congress has been in session, at least in the House:[57]

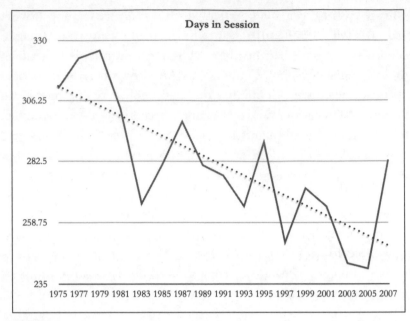

FIGURE 9

Maybe fewer days "in session" is a good thing, if it gives members more time in the district, and hence more time to understand their constituents. But even the idea of "in session" doesn't fully capture how the place has changed. As historian Gordon Wood describes, in the First Congress, when Congress was "in session," "nearly all" members sat at their desks in the Hall of Congress, listened to debates for five hours a day, and were "usually attentive to what their colleagues had to say on the floor of the House."[58] The "work" of a congressman was to deliberate—which means to debate, and listen, and argue, and then decide.

The "work" of members even "in session" today has no connection to that picture. Maybe a handful of times in a two-year period a majority of Congress will sit together in a single room listening to the debate about anything. The gathering of a majority of Congress today is almost exclusively ceremonial. It is practically never for the purpose the Framers envisioned: deliberation. Instead, bells, like those from elementary school announcing recess, ring; members race from wherever they are (which is most likely just off the Hill, making fund-raising telephone calls) to the floor; they are instructed by their staff as they enter the chamber what the vote is and how they are to vote. They vote, and then they leave. As political scientist Steven Smith describes:

> On only the rarest of occasions, such as the debate over the 1991 resolution on the Persian Gulf War, do senators engage in extended, thoughtful exchanges before a full chamber. Instead, under pressure to attend committee meetings, raise campaign funds, meet with lobbyists and constituents, and travel home, senators deliberately minimize the time they spend on the floor.[59]

One consequence of this change is that members are less responsible for legislation. Not formally responsible—that hasn't changed. But practically. Their legislative work declines, more of the product of legislative work gets done by others—lobbyists, staffers. And as a result, or at least, one correlation, is that laws become longer, and more complex. Here's the change in the average length of an enacted bill since 1975:

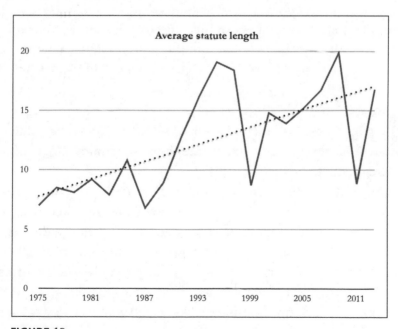

FIGURE 10

This is a change in the culture of Congress. It has produced an institution that is radically different from what it was. It is also radical when compared with Congress just thirty years ago. It has been criticized most by more-senior members. Republican Senator Trent Lott (R-Miss.; 1989–2007), for example, describes Congress as having "had a different feel to it—there was a respect for chain of command; there was a respect for the institution."[60] In the words of Representative Tim Roemer (D-Ind.; 1991–2003): members "spend too much of their time dialing for dollars rather than sitting in their committee room and protecting the dollars of their con-stituents."[61] Likewise with Representative Peter DeFazio (D-Ore.; 1987–): "You have to pretty much neglect your job.... You're spend-ing all this time on telephones, talking mostly to people you don't know, you've never met."[62] And again, Representative Lee Hamilton (D-Ind.; 1965–1999):

> The House has developed atrocious habits, [including] the fact that members only spend two or three days a week in Wash-ington, [a] breakdown in the deliberative process that guaran-tees that all legislation is carefully scrutinized, and all voices heard...the exclusion of the minority party, [and] failing to live up to its historic role of conducting oversight of the Execu-tive Branch.[63]

He concludes, "No one today could make a coherent argument that the Congress is the co-equal branch of government the Found-ers intended it to be."

No doubt it's too much to tie all of these failings to the rise of fund-raising. And no doubt, for some, anything that keeps Con-gress from regulating more must be a good thing. But at the very minimum, we can say with confidence that the fund-raising dis-tracts Congress from its work, and not surprisingly so. Any of us would be distracted if we had to spend even just 30 percent of our time raising campaign funds. If you hired a lawyer to work for you, and you saw that 30 percent of the time he billed you each month was actually time spent recruiting other clients, you'd be rightfully upset. If you learned that teachers at a public elementary school that your kids attended were spending 30 percent of their time running bake sales to fund their salaries rather than teaching your kids how to read, you'd be rightfully upset, too. So it doesn't seem crazy that we should be rightfully upset that the Congress we elect to represent us spends even just 30 percent of their time raising funds to get reelected rather than reading the bills they are passing, or attending committee meetings where those bills are discussed, or meeting with constituents with problems getting help from the Veterans Administration. At the very minimum, the Fund-raising Congress is flawed because the Fund-raising Congress is distracted.[64]

3. Distortion

Distraction produces an obvious effect. Less is done, and less is done well. But beyond the friction of mere distraction, we have powerful reasons to believe that the work of Congress is distorted.

At the end of a powerful and creative analysis of the effect of lobbying on policy outcomes, Frank Baumgartner and his colleagues present data that contrast the public's view of "the most important problem facing the country today" with data "reflecting the concerns of the Washington lobbying community."[65] The image is quite striking, as seen on the next page (see figure 11).

This is a picture of "disconnect," as Baumgartner and his colleagues describe it. It is a "consequence of who is represented in Washington." "It may be," as the authors write, "that political systems built around majoritarianism work better for lower-income citizens. It's certainly the case that in the United States...inequities...are sharply exacerbated by the organizational bias of interest-group politics."[67]

The division between "majoritarianism" and "interest-group politics," however, might be too simple here. For even among democracies driven by "interest-group politics" (as opposed to majoritarianism),

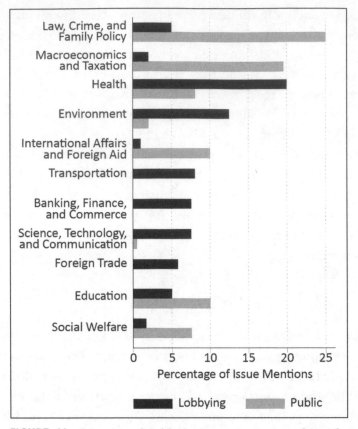

FIGURE 11. *Percent of lobbying cases compared to the average responses to the Gallup poll question "What is the most important problem facing the country today?"*[66]

"disconnects" may be different. How much of that disconnect comes from the way elections in Congress get funded? Would the disconnect be less if the elections were funded differently? Would the distortion be as clear? Or would there be, as Nicholas Stephanopoulos measures it, better alignment between the preferences of the median voter and what our Congress actually does?[68]

The most effective way to gauge this distortion is with perhaps the finest theoretical work in political science about lobbying in Congress over the past decade, and a work that seems at first at least to exonerate Congress of the cynic's charge.

In their 2006 paper, "Lobbying as Legislative Subsidy," Richard

Hall and Alan Deardorff provide a model to explain just what lobbying in Congress does.[69] Lobbying, they argue, is best understood
as a "legislative subsidy." Lobbyists don't try to flip their opponents.
They work instead to solidify and help their base. Most of the
work of lobbyists, they say, is directed toward getting people who
already agree (at least in principle) to better support what they
agree with. So lobbyists for unions, for example—and there are
some: 1.26 percent of the lobbying dollars spent in 2009 were from
labor spending[70]—don't waste their time trying to convert Mitch
McConnell (R-Ky.; 1985–) to the important role that unions have in
our economy. They instead spend their time with Representative
James Langevin (D-R.I.; 2001–), or Senator Richard Durbin (D-Ill.;
1997–), helping them to better advance their views that labor needs
support. Lobbyists, in other words, try to subsidize the work of the
members of Congress whom they like, by helping them do better
the sort of stuff they already want to do.

This picture makes the process seem almost benign. If lobbyists
are just supporting members, how could they be corrupting them?
What's the harm? How could a free gift of aid consistent with what
a member already wants to do hurt anything or anyone?

The answer is, in at least three ways—two of which (and the
most important of which) Hall and Deardorff explicitly recognize,
and the third of which follows directly from their model.

First, and as Hall and Deardorff acknowledge, "Representation
[can be] compromised without individual representatives being compromised."[71] It may well be that lobbyists do nothing more than help
a member do what the member already wants to do. But not every
issue the member wants to support has the same "subsidy" behind it.

If, for example, a member went to Washington after campaigning on two issues, the need to stop Internet "piracy" and the need
to help working mothers on welfare, on day one she'd find a line
of lobbyists around the block eager to help with the first issue, but
none there to help her with the second. That difference would be
for all the obvious reasons. And the consequence would be that her
work would get skewed relative to her desires going in. At the end of

two years, that member could well reflect that she supported only the issues she said she would support. But if she were only slightly more reflective, she'd recognize that the proportion of support she gave her issues was driven not by her own judgment about the relative importance of each, but instead by the weight of the subsidy, including, indirectly, of campaign funds.

Second, and related, the benign account underplays the way such a system of "subsidy" may in the end block effective access to representatives in government.

If there's one effect that money has that even supporters of the current system concede, it is on access to government.[72] As Larry Makinson puts it, "Virtually everyone…accept[s] that money buys access to members."[73] The reason is clear enough. As former Senator Paul Simon (D-Ill.; 1985–1997) describes it:

> If I got to a Chicago hotel at midnight, when I was in the Senate, and there were 20 phone calls waiting for me, 19 of them names I didn't recognize and the 20th someone I recognized as a $1,000 donor to my campaign, that is the one person I would call. You feel a sense of gratitude for their support. This is even more true with the prevalence of much larger donations, even if those donations go to party committees. Because few people can afford to give over $20,000 or $25,000 to a party committee, those people who can will receive substantially better access to elected federal leaders than people who can only afford smaller contributions or can not afford to make any contributions.[74]

Indeed, as Clawson and his colleagues argue, "The principal aim of most corporate campaign contributions is to help corporate executives gain 'access' to key members of Congress."[75] And that's certainly its effect. As Representative Romano Mazzoli (D-Ky.; 1971–1995) put it: "People who contribute get the ear of the member and the ear of the staff. They have the access—and access is it. Access is power."[76]

Hall and Deardorff argue persuasively that if their theory of subsidy is correct, then all access is doing is enabling like minds to work together better—a "greater legislative effort on behalf of a shared objective, not a disingenuous vote."[77]

This description may be too sanguine. If the model of reciprocity that I described in Chapter 7 is correct, then there is a shared interest among lobbyists, special interests, and members for the lobbyists to become a practically exclusive channel through which legislative change gets made (or blocked). We are nowhere close to this exclusivity now, but we need to recognize why everyone involved would like us to be. The more the lobbyist becomes central, the richer the lobbyist becomes. This benefits the lobbyist. And the more the lobbyist becomes central, the easier it is for candidates to secure funding. This benefits the candidates. And the more the lobbyist becomes central, the easier it is for (some) special interests to trigger legislative change. This benefits these (relatively dominant) interests. For this exclusivity benefits not every special interest. As Hall and Deardorff write:

> Subsidies help legislators to work harder primarily on behalf of the interests that can afford the high costs, not only of organizing and making campaign contributions, but of paying professional lobbyists and financing the organizations that support them. Such resources are not equally distributed across groups. Business interests exhibit "tremendous predominance" in federal lobbying....Hence, the hypothesis set forth here, that public interest groups without electoral assets can influence legislative behavior, does not imply that they countervail the influence of private interest groups and thereby correct the distortions.[78]

Or put more directly: "Lobbying distorts the representative's allocation of effort in favor of groups sufficiently resource-rich that they can finance an expensive lobbying operation."[79]

I saw this dynamic firsthand. For many years, the focus of my work was on issues relating to copyright and the Internet. Often I would have the opportunity to speak directly to members of Congress about these issues. The most striking feature of those exchanges was not that members disagreed with me. It was that members didn't understand that there was another side to the issue. They had never even heard it. They were baffled when it was described to them. To them, the world was divided into those who believed in copyright and those who didn't. To meet someone who believed in copyright but didn't think the Motion Picture Association of America or the Recording Industry Association of America channeled the word of God (that's me) was, to say the least, anathema.

This wasn't because these members were stupid. They weren't. It wasn't because they were lazy. Most members of Congress work much harder than the majority of people, if you count all the junk they have to do, including fund-raising. Instead, this was simply because this different side was nowhere on the radar screen of these members. They hadn't heard it, because it hadn't had access.

Consider the lobbying that led to the financial "reform" bill. In October 2009, there were 1,537 lobbyists representing financial institutions registered in DC, and lobbying to affect this critical legislation—twenty-five times the number registered to support consumer groups, unions, and other proponents of strong reform.[80] A system that makes lobbyists the ticket to influence is a system that wildly skews the issues that will get attention. This, in time, will distort results.

Finally, the third reason this "legislative subsidy" model doesn't exonerate the current system is a dynamic that Hall and Deardorff don't discuss but that is also consistent with their model. In describing "lobbying as legislative subsidy," Hall and Deardorff write: "The proximate objective of this strategy is not to change legislators' minds but to assist natural allies in achieving their own, coincident objectives."[81]

But what is this "nature"? How is it begot? How nourished?

When a Republican member of Congress votes to raise the sugar tariff (as 35 Republican senators and 102 Republican members in the House did with the 2008 Farm Bill),[82] is that because that member ran on the platform that eight domestic sugar manufacturers should be protected from the free market? The same question could be asked about tax expenditures benefitting America's most profitable corporations (the modern equivalent, as Jay Cost describes, of the corrupt giveaways of nineteenth-century tariff policy).[83] Or when frontline Democrats—meaning first-term members in closely fought districts, no more liberal or conservative than more-senior Democrats—on the House Committee on Financial Services voted to exempt car dealers from consumer protection legislation, while senior Democrats on the same committee did not, is that because those younger Democrats ran on a platform that consumers needed to be protected everywhere, except from used car dealers?[84]

What's missing here is an understanding of how "nature" gets made. For the relevant effect could be as much in anticipation as in response. And if it were in anticipation, then the methods that Ansolabehere and his colleagues deploy could not pick up the change. The money would not be buying a change in preferences; the change in preferences would be buying the money.

The best illustration of this dynamic is a comment by former Representative Leslie Byrne (D-Va.; 1993–1995), recounting what she was told by a colleague when she first came to Washington: "I remember the comment of a well-known, big money-raising state delegate from Virginia. He said, 'Lean to the green,' and he wasn't an environmentalist."[85]

This is shape-shifting. It may well be unlikely that a lobbyist would waste his time trying to get a member to flip. There's too much pride and self-respect in the system for that. There's too much of an opportunity to be punished.

But if a lobbyist is important, or influential over sources of campaign contributions, then the effect of her influence could well be felt ex ante: a member could take a position on a particular issue in anticipation of the need to secure that lobbyist's support. Representative Eric Fingerhut (D-Ohio; 1993–1995) says as much directly: "People consciously or subconsciously tailor their views to where they know the sources of campaign funding can be."[86] That "tailoring" isn't a flip, for it isn't a change. It is simply articulating more completely the views of a member, as that member grows into her job.

Now obviously this dynamic won't work for everything. Certain issues are too prominent, or too familiar. But for a vast range of issues that Congress deals with, shape-shifting is perfectly feasible because, for these issues, there's no visible change. As Representative Vin Weber (R-Minn.; 1981–1993) puts it, a representative keeps "a mental checklist of things [members] need to do to make sure their PAC contributors continue to support them."[87]

This dynamic is especially significant for smaller or more obscure issues. Again Vin Weber puts it: "If nobody else cares about it very much, the special interest will get its way."[88]

Likewise, Jeff Birnbaum: "It's the obscure and relatively minor issues that produce the most frenetic lobbying. And it is there, on the lucrative edges of legislation, that lobbyists work their ways. Lobbyists constantly obtain special exceptions or extra giveaways for their clients, and few other people ever notice."[89]

Again, Eric Fingerhut: "The public will often look for the big example; they want to find the grand-slam example of influence in these interests. [R]arely will you find it. But you can find a million singles."[90]

When the issue is genuinely uncertain, or just so obscure as not to be noticed, this lobbying can induce shape-shifting—away from the position the representative otherwise would have taken.

Such shape-shifting is perfectly consistent with Hall and Deardorff's model. Indeed, the conditions they identify where it does make sense for a lobbyist to try to persuade turn out to be precisely the sort of cases that Fingerhut, Birnbaum, and Weber are describing: obscure issues that a representative has no strong preference about, that are to be publicly voted upon, the results of which are uncertain.[91] As Martin and Susan Tolchin quote former congressman and governor James Blanchard (D-Mich.; 1983–1991), "In Congress, people feel strongly about two or three issues.... On almost all [other] issues, there's no moral high ground."[92]

Shape-shifting is thus one reason the effect of money on legislative voting would be invisible. It is distinct from another

dynamic that would also be invisible to the regressions. The ranking of members by groups such as the Chamber of Commerce is
based upon roll call votes. But roll call votes are the very end of
a very, very long legislative process. A bill gets introduced. It gets
referred to a committee. Very few of the bills referred to a committee get a hearing. Even fewer get referred to the floor for a vote.
On the floor, there are any number of ways in which the proposal
can be stopped. Or folded into something else. Or allowed to die.
There is only one way to pass a bill in Congress, and a million ways
to kill it.

But influence can be exercised—and hence a campaign contribution rewarded—in any of the stages of the potential life of a
bill. If it is, it is invisible to the regressions. If a senator puts an
anonymous hold on a bill, that doesn't enter anyone's ranking. If a
chairman decides not to assign a hearing to the bill, he doesn't get
tagged as a result. In a whole host of ways, legislative power can
be exercised without a trace. And where it is exercised without a
trace, the regressions cannot map cause and effect. As Lynda Powell puts the point:

> Examining only floor votes that determine the final passage or
> failure of a bill ignores all the decisions that determine the details
> of its substantive content, as well as those that determine whether
> or not a bill is ever written or comes to a vote. And it is in these
> less observable areas of legislative activity that legislators may
> most easily accommodate the interests of donors.[93]

The House Select Committee on Lobbying Activities makes a
similar point, linking back to the idea of "vetocracy":

> Complex government inevitably means government with bottle-
> necks at which pressure can be quietly and effectively applied....
> The prevention of governmental action, and this is the aim of
> many lobbies, is relatively easy under these circumstances.[94]

"Most issues," Baumgartner and his colleagues find, "do not reach those final stages and most are not highly publicized, even within the Beltway."[95] That means, again, the opportunity for invisible influence is great. Senator Larry Pressler (R-S.D.; 1979–1997) describes a particular example, drawn from the recent battle over health care:

> There should have been an up or down vote on [single-payer health insurance], or a vote at least on cloture. There was neither. For some reason, it just went away. Barack Obama abandoned it completely, although he had said he was for it. Some Republicans are for it—I was for it way back and Nixon was for it…on a much more significant basis. Bob Packwood had a plan for it. But the point is, when they really started doing the health care bill, everybody disappeared who was for a single payer system. I would suspect that is because of the insurance companies' contributions, especially to the Democrats.[96]

Pressler's example could be multiplied a million times over. Indeed, it is almost too obvious to remark.

Finally, Lynda Powell reports on an obvious dynamic that we weaken the ability to track contributions to roll call votes:

> A lobbyist from one of the largest firms in the capital approached him and told him that he knew what he was trying to do and he would not be successful. The lobbyist explained that if one client was interested in a piece of legislation, he did not have that client donate to advance the legislation's chances but had another disinterested client do so.[97]

"You say," the skeptic insists, "that this competing dependency upon money draws the members away from what they otherwise would have done. But is there any evidence for this? Do we have a way to calibrate the extent of this distortion, or even any measure to demonstrate that there is distortion?"

There are two ways we might measure distortion. One maps

the gap between what "the people" believe about an issue and what Congress does about that issue. Call this *substantive distortion*. The other way maps the gap between what Congress actually works on and what is important or, alternatively, what the people want them to work on. Call this *agenda distortion*.

The evidence for substantive distortion is compelling, at the level not of roll call votes—that's the fight we've just rehearsed—but of actual policy decisions. A wide range of important work in political science makes it possible to argue with confidence that, first, there is a wide gap in the policy preferences of "the funders" and "the people," and second, in the face of that gap, Congress tracks not "the people" but "the funders."

The first work to make this point powerfully and clearly was by Princeton professor Larry Bartels. In a study of the correlation between U.S. Senate roll call votes and an index by Poole and Rosenthal designed to measure the ideological position of members across multiple dimensions,[98] Bartels concludes that "in almost every instance, senators appear to be considerably more responsive to the opinions of affluent constituents than to the opinions of middle-class constituents, while the opinions of constituents in the bottom third of the income distribution have no apparent statistical effect on their senators' roll call votes."[99]

Martin Gilens extended Bartels's analysis substantially by examining about 1,781 national survey questions between 1981 and 2002.[100] These questions asked whether the respondent supported or opposed some particular change in U.S. policy, and then tracked whether in fact those changes occurred. Looking at all the survey questions, Gilens was able to demonstrate a significant difference between the likelihood that a measure would be enacted if the rich supported it and the likelihood when the middle class or poor supported it.

More striking was the comparison when looking at the subset of questions where the highest income group differed substantially in their views from the lowest ($n = 887$) and where the highest differed substantially in their views from the middle-income group ($n = 498$). What Gilens found here was amazing: While policymakers were responsive to the increasingly strong preferences of the highest-income groups (the more of whom supported a policy, the more likely it was to be passed), there was a "complete lack of government responsiveness to the preferences of the poor"[101] (meaning increasing support among the poor for a particular policy did not increase the likelihood of its passage). And middle-income voters "fare little better than the poor."[102]

Gilens's latest work (with Ben Page) builds on this earlier analysis, with even more depressing results. Gilens and Page conducted the largest empirical study of actual policy decision by our government in the history of political science. They related those actual decisions over the past thirty-five years to the attitudes of the economic elite, organized interest groups, and the average voter. In three graphs, their paper captures more powerfully than anything else in modern political science just what's wrong with America's democracy.

The first graph links the attitudes of the economic elite to the probability that a policy choice will be adopted. As the graph shows, as the percentage of the elite supporting a proposal goes up, the probability of that proposal being adopted rises.

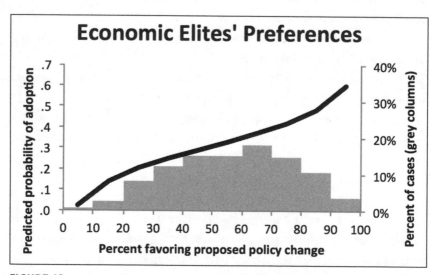

FIGURE 12

The same with organized interest groups. As the number of such groups supporting an idea goes up, the probability of that idea being enacted rises.

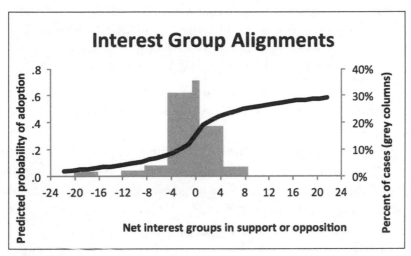

FIGURE 13

But the story is different for the average voter. As this graph shows, as the percentage of average voters who support an idea goes from 0 percent to 100 percent, the probability that idea will be adopted *doesn't change.*

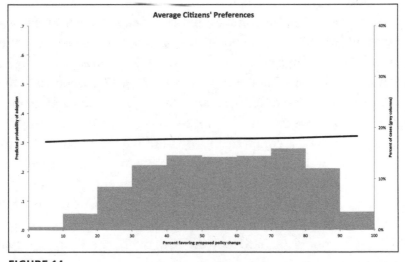

FIGURE 14

The average voter's influence is a flat line—both literally and figuratively. As Gilens and Page put it in English:

> When the preferences of economic elites and the stands of organized interest groups are controlled for, the preferences of the average American appear to have only a minuscule, near-zero, statistically non-significant impact upon public policy.[103]

In a democracy, the "average American" has "near zero" "impact upon public policy."

Gilens and Page have captured this point incredibly well. But they're not the first to demonstrate the responsiveness of our system to the economic elite[104]—a responsiveness (to the elite) that has only grown over time.[105]

Jacob Hacker and Paul Pierson's powerful book *Winner-Take-All Politics* (2010) in part tracks that growth. Hacker and Pierson frame their account by distinguishing between two kinds of societies, Broadland and Richistan. In Broadland, all income groups across some period of time are doing better, even if not necessarily at the same pace. In Richistan, only the very rich do better across that same period of time. The rest of society is either just holding on or falling behind.

Until about 1972, the United States, Hacker and Pierson argue, was Broadland. We then became Richistan. And not just in some slight or statistically meaningless sense, but instead, in as gross and extreme a sense as any comparable nation in the world. Between 1979 and 2009, as Darrell West describes, "after-tax income stagnated for most workers...but rose dramatically for the top 1 percent."[106]

Indeed, the best comparison to where we are today is not any other nation in the world, but rather to when we were on the cusp of the Depression. In 2007, the richest 1 percent of families was within a point of matching the share of income that the top 1 percent had in 1928.

These numbers are hard to make real, but here's a way to visualize them:

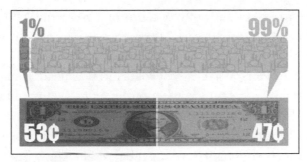

FIGURE 15

Between 2001 and 2006, the total income of all Americans added together grew. But it didn't grow proportionately. Not even close. For every dollar of added income, fifty-three cents of that dollar went to the top 1 percent of American households.[107] The figures for wealth (as opposed to income) are almost as stark: 1 percent of Americans "now own about one-third of the country's wealth."[108]

It's even worse if you think about the top one-tenth of 1 percent (0.1 percent): For income gains between 1979 and 2005, the top 0.1 percent received over 20 percent of all gains, while the bottom 60 percent received only 13.5 percent:

FIGURE 16[109]

In constant dollars, the average income of the top 0.1 percent (including capital gains) in 2007 was more than $7 million. In 1974, it was about $1 million. Their share of the pie grew from 2.7 percent to 12.3 percent—a 4.5x increase.[110]

For the top one-tenth of one-tenth of 1 percent (0.01 percent), it's even more extreme: The average after-tax income increased from about $4 million in 1979 to more than $24 million in 2005.[111] In Hacker and Pierson's terms, "Broadland was dead. Richistan was born."[112] Broadland is where most of the gains go to the bottom 90 percent of households; and Richistan is where most of the gains go to the top 1 percent. Indeed, were it not for the increase in hours worked over the past thirty years, the middle class would not have gained at all, and the lower class would have fallen behind, while the highest-income groups have exploded.[113] "The bottom went nowhere, the middle saw a modest gain, and the top ran away with the grand prize."[114]

Whenever anyone starts talking about inequality, the first reaction of many (at least on the Right but also in the middle) is to turn off. Our Constitution is not Soviet. We are not committed to the philosophy of Karl Marx, or even John Rawls. That there are rich and poor in America is a fact of American life. Some believe it explains the innovation in American life. And no set of clever graphs demonstrating "how the rich get richer" is going to move those who believe that the "unalienable right...[to] Life, Liberty, and the Pursuit of Happiness" includes the right to get rich faster than your neighbor.

Likewise, there are important differences between the wealth of the Gilded Age and the wealth today. The rich today are different. In 1929, as Rajan and Zingales put it, "70 percent of the income of the top .01 percent of income earners in the United States came from holdings of capital.... The rich were truly the idle rich. In 1998, wages and entrepreneurial income made up 80 percent of the income of the top .01 percent."[115] The rich are not idle anymore. Indeed, they work harder than most of us: "In the 1890s, the richest 10 percent of the population worked fewer hours than the poorest 10 percent. Today, the reverse is true."[116]

My point in introducing Hacker and Pierson is not to reinforce the arguments of egalitarians, or the socialist Left. For the critical insight that they add to this debate is not that inequality is growing.

It is instead the *reasons* that inequality is growing. Conservatives might well and consistently believe that there's nothing wrong with getting rich. But from the birth of conservative thought, conservatives have always objected to people getting rich because of the government. It's one thing to invent the lightbulb and thereby become a billionaire (though sadly, Edison wasn't so lucky). It's another thing to use your financial power to capture political power, and then use political power to change the laws to make you even richer. As Darrell West puts it:

> Wealth in and of itself is not problematic. It is how rich people convert financial might into political power for their own benefit that creates problems.[117]

So then what explains our move to Richistan? Is it geniuses producing endless wealth? Or is it government regulation that is protecting endless wealth?

Hacker and Pierson work hard to suss this out. Maybe the rich were better educated. Maybe that education produced this difference in rewards. But the rich in Hacker and Pierson's account are not what most people would call rich. The rich are the super-rich—the 0.1 percent or 0.01 percent. Those people are not better educated than the top 1 percent. Indeed, as Gilens finds, "Fewer than one-third of Americans in the top income decile are also in the top education decile, and vice versa."[118] If there's a reason that we became Richistan, it's not because of Harvard or Berkeley or MIT.

It isn't raw smarts, or native talent. So then what accounts for our leaving the happy world of Broadland and becoming Richistan?

According to Hacker and Pierson, and astonishingly: *changes in government policy.* A whole series of interventions by the government beginning in 1972 produced an enormously wealthy class of beneficiaries of those changes. This is not the neighborhoods of Desperate Housewives. Or even Hollywood or Silicon Valley. It is instead a kind of wealth that is almost unimaginable to the vast majority of Americans.

The biggest winners here are financial executives. As Nobel Prize–winning economist Joseph Stiglitz writes, "Those who have contributed great positive innovations to our society—from the pioneers of genetic understanding to the pioneers of the Information Age—have received a pittance compared with those responsible for the financial innovations that brought our global economy to the brink of ruin."[119] In 2004, "nonfinancial executives of publicly traded companies accounted for less than 6 percent of the top .01 percent of the income bracket. In that same year, the top 25 hedge fund managers combined appear to have earned more than all of the CEOs from the entire S&P 500."[120]

The next big winners were the top executives from the S&P 500 companies. In the 1970s, the executives at the S&P 500 made thirty times what their workers did, and today make three hundred times what their workers make.[121] Their average salary was more than $13.5 million in 2014, about 373 times the pay of the average American worker.[122] Likewise, as their salaries have skyrocketed, the position of the self-employed has collapsed. Between 1948 and 2003, "the self-employment rate in the United States fell from 18.5 percent to 7.5 percent"[123]—the second-lowest among twenty-two rich nations according to an OECD study.[124] The nation of our parents was defined by makers and innovators. We've become a nation defined not by the upwardly mobile entrepreneurs, but by Wall Street fat cats—the nation predicted by the apostle Matthew (13:12): "For whosoever hath, to him shall be given, and he shall have more abundance."[125]

So let's repeat the point in a single line, because it is critical to everything in this book: *Changes in government policy, Hacker and Pierson argue, account for the radical change in the distribution of American wealth.* This isn't the rich getting richer because the rich are smarter or working harder. This is the connected getting richer because their lobbyists are more effective. No political philosophy—liberal, libertarian, or conservative—should be okay with that.

To be fair, this last step in the argument—linking the rich to the connected (by which I mean the funders)—is not a step that Hacker and Pierson explicitly make. Indeed, and surprisingly, they don't place campaign finance anywhere near the top of their program of reform. And while Gilens clearly references it, he is quite insistent that the work he has done so far cannot establish, at least at the level of confidence that a political scientist requires, exactly why policymakers respond to the rich more clearly than they respond to the poor.

Yet as Gilens acknowledges:

> The most obvious source of influence over policy that distinguishes high-income Americans is money and the willingness to donate to parties, candidates, and interest organizations.... Since not only the propensity to donate but also the size of donations increases with income level, this figure understates—probably to a very large degree—the extent to which political donations come from the most affluent Americans.[126]

Senator Bob Dole (R-Kans.; 1969–1996) puts the point more simply and more directly: "Poor people don't make campaign contributions."[127]

We could add a critical and absolutely certain corollary to Senator Dole's point: The people who do make campaign contributions are very very different from the poor or even the average American. As Nicholas Stephanopoulos summarizes the data:

> Individuals who contribute at least $200 to federal candidates are "overwhelmingly wealthy, highly educated, male, and white." In 2004, for example, 58 percent of these donors were male, 69 percent were older than fifty, 78 percent had a family income above $100,000, and 91 percent had a college degree. In 2012, these donors amounted to just 0.4 percent of the population, but supplied 64 percent of the funds received by candidates from individuals.[128]

And that's just the demographics. The ideology of these donors—relative to the general public—is even more worrisome.

While as we've seen, the distribution of political values of Americans is normal, the values of donors is highly bimodal—with a peak at the far Right and a peak at the far Left.[129] And the very top givers are particularly sharply distinct. A recent study by Ben Page, Larry Bartels, and Jason Seawright summarized[130] the differences along a number of critical dimensions:

Views of the Wealthy and the General Public, Percent in Agreement

VIEW	THE TOP 1 PERCENT	THE GENERAL PUBLIC
I favor cuts in Medicare, education, and highways to reduce budget deficits.	58	27
Government has an essential role in regulating the market.	55	71
Government should spend what is necessary to ensure that all children have good public schools.	35	87
I'm willing to pay more taxes to provide health coverage for all.	41	59
Government should provide a decent standard of living for the unemployed.	23	50
Government should provide jobs for everyone willing to work who can't find a private sector job.	8	53

Maybe most depressing, since so clearly confirming of this most depressing truth, is the work of Michael Barber, tracking the alignment between the views of senators and the median voter in their state, the median voter in their own party, and their donors.[131] As Barber concludes, while there's no real alignment with the median voter, and substantially more alignment with the median voter of the senator's own party, "among both Republicans and Democrats, the ideological congruence between senators and the average *donor* is nearly perfect."[132]

This focus on alignment—which has been developed in the

academic literature most fully by Nicholas Stephanopoulos[133]—is just one way to measure the distortion that the campaign finance system introduces into our democracy. But whether one adopts that particular way of seeing the distortion or not, that there is an effect seems hard to escape. How we fund campaigns affects how our government governs. That conclusion isn't amazing; that it might be controversial is.

The question we must ask as citizens, not political scientists, is what we will make of the data we've gotten so far. It is clear that government bends in the direction that the funders prefer. It is plausible, more likely than not, that this differential bending is because of the influence of campaign funding. If you considered the matter in the way the Framers did, accounting for the structural and predictable ways in which dependency might express itself, it is almost irresistible, from their perspective, that these data show that Congress betrays a competing dependency "on the funders"—competing, that is, with a dependency "on the people alone." The Framers were proud that they had ensured a two-year cycle of punishment and reward for the House. Yet the cycle of punishment and reward for funders is every day, not every two years. For two or three or more hours every day, as a member fund-raises, she feels the effect of the "votes" of funders. That feeling must at least compete and, given the data, conflict with the effect felt every two years in an election.

This is how journalist Jeffrey Birnbaum puts it: "Moneyed constituents possess higher status than constituents who merely vote."[134]

And it is precisely the way that Ansolabehere and his colleagues—the scholars most skeptical about the effect of money on politics—suggested that money may still (despite them not finding the correlation) be buying results. Again, as I quoted them at the start of this chapter:

> To raise sufficient funds, candidates might skew policies in ways preferred by donors. Campaign contributions might therefore act like weighted votes. And contributors, who are

disproportionately wealthy, might have different policy preferences than the median voter.[135]

This again is how tweedism works. The evidence is pretty strong,
at least for us citizens, that this is precisely what is happening. [136] And
so, too, is the conclusion of Gilens and Page's paper again relevant:

> When the preferences of economic elites and the stands of
> organized interest groups are controlled for, the preferences of
> the average American appear to have only a minuscule, near-
> zero, statistically non-significant impact upon public policy.[137]

It may be that Gilens and Page are wrong. You might insist that
there are important times when Congress is responsive to the people.
So while Mian and his colleagues do find that mortgage campaign
contributions have a rising and significant effect on voting patterns,
they also demonstrate that members were also responsive both to
voter preferences and to special-interest campaign contributions.[138]
No doubt, if our Republic was meant to be dependent upon the people, there is much in the data to show that we are still, in important
ways, a Republic dependent upon the people. But not—and here is
the critical point—upon, as the Federalists put it, "the people alone."

The question is not whether Congress sometimes gets it right,
any more than the question with an alcoholic bus driver is whether
he sometimes drives sober. The question is why we allow Congress
so often to get it wrong. Even if you think the system is bent just
slightly—and ours is bent way more than slightly—it is still a bent
system.

"But," defenders of the status quo argue, "don't unions or the
AARP also have unequal influence? Is there something corrupt
about that?"

The answer depends on the source of the influence. No doubt,
there was a day when a union could reliably promise candidates
millions of votes. That power translated into important political
influence. But that is power that comes directly from votes. It is

precisely the power that the intended dependency of our democracy, upon the people alone, was meant to credit. My point isn't that democracy requires equal influence. It is that the influence that is to express itself, however unequally, is the influence of votes in an election.

The same point applies to political parties. Across our history, political parties have had an enormous influence in controlling the direction and the character of public life. That control has been a concern to many, especially liberals. " 'The system' is robust," Harvard professor Nancy Rosenblum has put it. "Candidates are dependent on parties, even apart from funding."[139] As she quotes Lincoln Steffens: " 'Isn't our corrupt government, after all, representative?' Steffens asked. He records a Philadelphia politician's puzzled confession: 'I'm loyal to my ward and to my—own, and yet—Well, there's something wrong with me, and I'd like to know: what is it?' "[140]

Parties, like unions, exercise their power in two ways. First, by mobilizing votes. Second, by concentrating economic power. The former is not troubling to the dependency theory of democracy. Power through votes is just what the doctor ordered. It is the power through money that raises the problem here. Avoiding "unequal influence" is not the objective. Preserving electoral influence is.

"Isn't that," the defenders continue, "just what money does? No one literally buys an election (anymore at least). The only thing money does is buy speech that helps persuade voters to one side in an election over another. If you don't object to unions driving members to the polls (literally, on buses), why would you object to spending money to try to persuade people to go to the polls (through television ads)?"

Great point. There's no doubt that the purpose of campaign funds is to persuade. And there's also no doubt that those funds persuade differently. Some of that persuasion comes from the television or radio ads a campaign is able to buy—getting a voter to support the candidate. Some of that persuasion comes from the ability to convince a challenger that the fight is just not worth it—"There's no way we could raise enough money to overcome his war chest of one million dollars." All of that persuasion is benign from the perspective of a democracy dependent upon the people alone. Seen in this way, in other words, money is just part of a campaign to get votes.

The word "just" in that sentence, however, shouldn't be passed over so quickly. For one thing, the current system plainly does filter out a wide range of people who might otherwise be plausible and powerful candidates for Congress.[141] Under the current system, the ability to raise money is a necessary condition to getting party support. As Hacker and Pierson report about the Democratic Congressional Campaign Committee, "If a candidate proved a good fundraiser, the DCCC would provide support....If not, the committee would shut him out."[142] The point was reportedly made quite clear by Rahm Emanuel when he was chairman of the DCCC: "The first third of your campaign is money, money, money. The second third is money, money, and press. And the last third is votes, press, and money."[143]

The more important point, however, is not about what the money does. It's about what has to be done to get the money. The effect of the spending of the money might be (democratically) benign. But what is done to secure that money is not necessarily benign.

To miss this point is to betray the Robin Hood fallacy: the fact that the loot was distributed justly doesn't excuse the means taken to secure it. Take an extreme case to make this critical point: Imagine a lobbyist signaled to a congressman that he could ensure $1 million in campaign funds so long as the congressman delivered a $10 million earmark for the lobbyist's client. Even if the $1 million is for the benign purpose of persuasion, there is an obvious problem in the deal made to secure it. The distortion is in the deal, not in the way the money is spent. The problem comes from the distortion necessary to secure the deal, not from the effect of the money spent in a campaign.

Of course, in this example, the deal is a crime. And I've already said I don't think such crime happens (much). But the same point is true even if we substitute the more benign (as in legal) dance of the gift economy I described in the previous chapter for the quid pro quo game. Here again: If we assume the congressman has

shape-shifted himself in all sorts of predictable ways for the purpose of ensuring funds for his campaign, even if that shape-shifting
dance is not illegal, and even though the money he secures gets
spent for the wholly positive purpose of persuading people in an
election, that doesn't acquit the shape-shifting. For again, the problem is not the money; the problem is the distortion created to produce the money. Senator Wyche Fowler (D-Ga.; 1987–1993) tells a
related story that makes the same point:

> The brutal fact that we all agonize over is that if you get two
> calls and one is from a constituent who wants to complain
> about the Veterans Administration mistreating her father, for
> the 10th time, and one is from somebody who is going to give
> you a party and raise $10,000, you call back the contributor.
> And nobody likes that. There's no way to justify it. Except that
> you rationalize that you have to have money or you can't cam-
> paign. You're not in the game.[144]

There's nothing wrong with the effect the $10,000 will have.
Nor is there anything wrong with the member calling back the
contributor. The wrong here—tiny in the scale of things but standing for the more general wrong—is the call not made.

Consider one final example: Birnbaum describes a congressman
in the mid-1980s who was undecided about whether to support
funding to build the B-1 bomber. Reagan was "frantic for support"
for the bomber, so the congressman was a "hot commodity." A
deal was struck to get the congressman's vote. What was his price?
A dam or some special funding for road construction in the district? No such luck (for his constituents). His price: "a VIP tour of
the White House for twenty or thirty of his largest and most loyal
campaign contributors."[145] Again, there's nothing wrong with the
White House giving VIP tours. But I suspect a constituent in this
congressman's district would be right to ask whether there wasn't
a better deal, for the district, that could have been made.

Once this distinction is made clear, the bigger point should be obvious. We don't excuse a bank robber if he donates the money he stole to an orphanage. Neither should we excuse a political system that bends itself because of its dependency upon funders just because it donates the proceeds it collects to funding political speech. It is the bending, the distortion, the distraction, that is the problem, and all that is produced by this competing dependency upon the funders rather than the people.

That's substantive distortion. The argument supporting it is long and complex. Length and complexity are certain to lose some souls on the way.

The argument for agenda distortion, however, is much simpler. Indeed, it can be made with a single case.

In the spring of 2011, the United States faced many public policy problems. We were in the middle of two wars. The economy was still in the tank: Thirteen million Americans were unemployed, almost 15 percent were on food stamps, and 20 percent of kids were living in poverty. There was an ongoing battle about health care, and the public debt. There was a continuing fight over taxes. Likewise over immigration policy. Many wanted tort reform. Legislation to address global warming had still not been passed. Nor had an appropriations bill, or a budget. And a fight between Tea Party Republicans and the rest of Congress was bringing America to the brink of a government shutdown.

So within that mix, what issue would you say was "the most consuming issue in Washington—according to members of Congress, Hill staffers, lobbyists and Treasury officials—"[146] at least as reported by the *Huffington Post*'s Ryan Grim and Zach Carter?

A bill to limit the amount banks could charge for the use of debit cards: so-called "swipe fees."

This bill, addressing the question of "interchange rates," meaning the amount banks can charge retailers for the use of a debit card, was the leading issue for lobbyists. And therefore for Congress, too. As Grim and Carter describe, "A full 118 ex-government officials and aides [were] registered to lobby on behalf of banks.... At least 124 revolving-door lobbyists" were lobbying on behalf of retailers. The issue dominated Congress's calendar. And beyond it, "a handful of other intra-corporate contests consume most of what remains on the Congressional calendar: a squabble over a jet engine, industry tussling over health-care spoils and the never-ending fight over the corporate tax code."

We all recognize that "Congress is zombified." Nothing gets done. Or at least, nothing relative to the issues that any objective measure would say were the most important issues for the nation to resolve. But "one of the least understood explanations," as Grim and Carter explain, "is also one of the simplest: The city is too busy refereeing disputes between major corporate interest groups." As Grim and Carter quote one anonymous moderate Democratic senator:

> I'm surprised at how much of our time is spent trying to divide up the spoils between various economic interests. I had no idea. I thought we'd be focused on civil liberties, on education policy, energy policy and so on.... The fights down here can be put in two or three categories: The big greedy bastards against the big greedy bastards; the big greedy bastards against the little greedy bastards; and some cases even the other little greedy bastards against the other little greedy bastards.

Why, you might ask, is Congress held hostage like this? Why can't it just focus on what it wants to focus on? I doubt there is a single member of the House or the Senate who thought, "I'm going to go to Congress so I can 'divide up the spoils between various economic interests.'" So why don't they simply do what they went to Congress to do? ("Oh poor, poor me, I hate CBS." "So change channels!")

The answer is almost hidden in Grim and Carter's brilliant essay. As they write, "The clock never ticks down to zero in Washington: one year's law is the next year's repeal target. Politicians, showered with cash from card companies and giant retailers alike, have been moving back and forth between camps, paid handsomely for their shifting allegiances."

Just to be sure you didn't miss the money point in this money quote: Congress, Grim and Carter claim, sets its agenda, at least in part, so as to induce funders to fund their campaigns. Who has time to deal with jobs, or poverty, or unemployment, or a simpler tax code? Where is the money in that? As Grim and Carter write, "Political action committees organized by members of the Electronic Payments Coalition, a cadre of banking trade groups, dumped more than $500,000 into campaign coffers during January and February [2011] alone."[147]

This dynamic is perfectly consistent with the analysis of Hall and Deardorff. There is plenty of persuading action on an issue not centrally salient to the public. It also follows directly from the excellent and extended analysis of Baumgartner and his colleagues of lobbying: "The bad news is that the wealthy seem to set the agenda," and "there's little overall correspondence between the congressional agenda and the public's agenda," and because of this "many issues never get raised in the first place."[148]

It is perfectly inconsistent, however, with Chairman Smith's claim that the money doesn't affect "legislative behavior." Setting Congress's agenda is quintessentially "legislative behavior," and if it isn't money that explains this particular mix, then it is pure insanity.

I chose the more charitable reading: It is the money. Money affects "legislative behavior."

4. Trust

But let's say you still don't buy it. Let's say you still believe (and I'm not going to hide it) *astonishingly* that the raising of the money within this lobbyist industrial complex, has no systematically distorting effect. That perhaps it distracts members of Congress, but so what? The less Congress does, you think, the better. The political scientists haven't proven that "money buys results," in your view. And my gift economy argument just doesn't persuade you either.

Even if you assume that everything I've described is completely benign—that the policy decisions that Congress enacted when subject to the dependency upon funders as well as the dependency upon the voters is precisely the same as the decisions it would make if dependent upon the voters alone—there is still an undeniable whopper of a fact that makes it impossible simply to ignore this competing dependency upon the funders: trust.[149]

The vast majority of Americans believe that it is money that is buying results. Whether or not that's true, that is what we believe.

This belief has an effect. Or better, it has a series of effects.

Its first effect is to undermine the trustworthiness of the system. A decline in trustworthiness correlates with a fall in trust. According to a 2014 Pew Research Center survey, "Just 24 percent [of American voters] say they can trust the government in Washington almost always or most of the time, among the lowest measures in half a century."[150] Forty years before, that number was 70 percent.[151] According to the American National Election Studies project at the University of Michigan, the public's perception of elected officials is near historic lows.[152] Whereas in 1964, 64 percent of respondents believed that government was run for the benefit of all and 29 percent believed that government was run for the benefit of a few big interests, in 2008, only 29 percent believed government was run for the benefit of all, and 69 percent believed it was run for the benefit of a few big interests. Similarly, whereas in 1958, only 24 percent of respondents believed that "quite a few" government officials were "crooked," in 2010, that percentage had increased to 55 percent.[153] A poll commissioned by Common Cause, Change Congress, and Public Campaign following the Citizens United decision found that 74 percent of respondents agreed that special interests have too much influence, and 79 percent agreed that members of Congress are "controlled" by the groups and people who finance their campaigns.[154] Only 18 percent believed that lawmakers listened to voters more than to their donors. Similarly, in 2008, 80 percent of Americans surveyed told the Program on International Policy Attitudes that they believed government was controlled by "a few big interests looking out for themselves."[155]

Correlation is not a model. My claim is not that the trust of Americans in their government is driven by the trustworthiness of the system for funding campaigns alone. Ezra Klein rightly maps the gap between any such single explanation for trust in America and the history of campaign finance practices and regulations.[156] Rightly, because no one could possibly believe that an idea as complex as trust could be explained by a single variable alone. We Americans have had a lot of shocks within the economy of trust over the past fifty years—from Johnson and Vietnam, to Nixon and Watergate, to Clinton and Lewinsky, and many others.

But the overlap of these different trust-weakening influences should not somehow excuse this central weakening of trustworthiness. As people understand more clearly the role of money in politics, they render politics less trustworthy.[157]

We know this from more than anecdotes or polls alone. In a psychological experiment I conducted with my colleagues Piercarlo Valdesolo, Steven Lehr, and Mahzarin Banaji, we tried to measure the effect of apparent conflicts of interest on attitudes of trust. Looking at three institutions—consumer products, medicine, and politics—we found:

> The mere suggestion of a financial interest in an outcome, absent any direct evidence of corrupt behavior, is enough to cause participants to see institutions and other unrelated actors as trading off social goods for financial gain, and thus corrodes their trust and confidence.[158]

The *New England Journal of Medicine* reports a similar effect with doctors evaluating hypothetical studies of new drugs: Trust of pharmaceutically funded studies was systematically lower than trust for studies by the government, or where the funding source was not mentioned *regardless of the rigor of the study*. "Credibility" as they put it, gets "downgraded" with industry-funded trials.[159]

Loss of trust induces a second effect. It leads any rational soul to spend less time exercising her democratic privileges.[160] We're all busy sorts. Some of us have families. Some hobbies. Some treat our families as hobbies. But whatever the mix that drives our day, the belief that money is buying results in Congress is a sufficient reason for us to spend less time worrying about what Congress does—at least, that is, if we don't have money. What reason is there to rally thousands of souls to the polls if, in the end, the polls can be distracted by the money? How would you explain it to your kid? ("Willem, I don't have time to play soccer, I've got to go waste my time electing a member to Congress who won't have time to listen or do what the voters want.") The politically engaged sorts are always quick to spread scorn on the vast majority of Americans who don't pay attention to politics. But maybe it's not they who deserve the scorn. How ridiculous to waste time on elections when there are soup kitchens, or churches, or schools that could use our volunteer time? As Jeffrey Birnbaum puts it, "Rather than get mad and try to change the system . . . most Americans have given up."[161]

My claim about the relationship between trust and participation might be challenged by some. A large empirical analysis done by Steven J. Rosenstone and John Mark Hansen looking at survey data concludes that distrust of government does not reduce voter turnout.[162] This conclusion has been relied upon by many to suggest that levels of trust are independent of levels of participation.[163]

But the trust that I am speaking of, however, is more accurately described as a view about efficacy: If one believes "money buys results in Congress," one is likely to believe that participation will be ineffective. And as Rosenstone and Hansen found, voters' feelings of "political efficacy" and "government responsiveness" have a large effect on voter participation.[164]

Thomas Patterson has developed this view, arguing that "political efficacy" and confidence in government are strongly linked. Looking at the 2000 election, Patterson also found that distrust is linked to lower participation rates. Moreover, "of all the reasons Americans give for their lack of election interest, the most troubling is their belief that candidates are not very worthy of respect: that they are beholden to their financiers."[165] "Skepticism about Congress," as Michael Golden puts it, "is one of the main deterrents to voting."[166]

One dramatic example confirms this point. One of the groups

most affected by the explosion in cynicism is the group that was
most benefited by the romance with Obama: Rock the Vote!, a non-
partisan nonprofit whose mission, according to *Wikipedia*, is to
"engage and build the political power of young people." Founded in
1990, it has developed a range of techniques and new technology
designed to register young voters, and turn them out "in every election." In 2008, the organization "ran the largest nonpartisan voter
registration drive in history"—more than 2.25 million new voters
registered, and there was a substantial increase in voter turnout
among the young.[167]

But when Rock the Vote! polled its members about their plans
for the 2010 election, the single largest reason that young people
offered for why they did not plan to vote was "because no matter
who wins, corporate interests will still have too much power and
prevent real change."[168] That echoes the response that Representative Glenn Poshard (D-Ill.; 1989–1999) got when he asked a group
of students why they do not trust government: "Congressman, just
follow the money. You will know why we do not trust you."[169]

The belief that money is buying results is consistent with the result
that fewer and fewer of us engage. Why would one rationally waste
one's time? In the Soviet Union, the party line was that the party was
to serve the workers. The workers knew better. In America, the party
line is that Congress is to serve the people. But you and I know better, too. And even if we don't actually know, our belief is producing
a world where the vast majority of us disengage. Or at least the vast
majority of you in the middle, the moderate core of America, disengage. Leaving the henhouse guarded by us polarized extremist foxes.

These are fair criticisms. I have tried throughout this book not
to punch above my weight. It takes real statistical skill to demonstrate social cause and effect. I don't have that skill and I don't
believe we have the data even if I did. At the most, I have tried to
suggest the correlation between the rise in the perceptions about
the role of money in politics, which produces a fall in trustworthiness, and with that fall, a fall in the trust.

But of course, none of this could establish that if we removed the corrupting influence, trust would return. At some point disappointment is fatal. It may be that the public's disappointment with the federal government has crossed that line.

Whether it has or not, however, at a minimum, if we're to rebuild trust, we should begin by restoring trustworthiness to the institutions of our government. If Congress were trustworthy—because no compromising interest could fairly be said to affect them—and the people still didn't trust, that would be the people's fault. But we should at least give them the chance to make that mistake.

"But then maybe you should write a book trying to convince America that money is not buying results," the defender objects. "I mean, if Americans believed the earth was flat, that wouldn't be a reason to ban airlines from flying across the horizon."

You can write that book. If you think you have the data to prove that the existing system is benign—that it doesn't distort democracy, that the idea that representatives would actually deliberate is silly, that this competing dependency is a good thing, or at least harmless—then make my day. Meanwhile, my view is that even if America's judgment wouldn't pass peer review in a political science journal, it's pretty damn insightful. We should listen to it and do something about it rather than sitting around waiting for the political scientists to deliver their gold-standard proofs.

The problem is trust—or is at the least trust. As Marc Hetherington put it, "Part of the public's antipathy toward government is born of concern that it is run for the benefit of special interests....Measures that can change this perception should increase political trust."[170] We need to deploy those measures. But we can't until we change what it is reasonable to believe—by removing the overwhelming dependency of members upon special-interest funding. As Dennis Thompson has written, "Citizens have a right to insist, as the price of trust in a democracy, that officials not give reason to doubt their trustworthiness."[171]

"Officials" in this democracy have given us reason to doubt.

So let's survey the field of battle again. I began this chapter by acknowledging two apparently conflicting Republican claims: On the one hand, Senator Coburn claiming that there were "thousands of instances...where appropriations are leveraged for fundraising dollars." On the other, Chairman Smith claiming that "the money does not play much of a role in what goes on in terms of legislative voting patterns and legislative behavior."

There can be no doubt that the chairman is wrong at least about "legislative behavior." Members spend between 30 and 70 percent of their time feeding this addiction. The majority of the attention of Congress gets devoted to the questions that matter most to their pushers (e.g., bank "swipe fees"). These two facts alone demonstrate the extraordinarily important way in which the money affects legislative behavior. No one could say that this effect is benign.

The harder question is whether the money affects "legislative voting patterns." Here, it is the testimony of another Republican, Senator Larry Pressler (R-S.D.; 1979–1997) that is most helpful. As he explained to me, whether or not the money matters in the very last moment in the life (or death) of a bill, there is no evidence that it does not matter in the million steps from the birth of a policy idea to the very last moments in the life (or death) of a bill. Instead, all the "evidence" here is to the contrary: People who live inside this system (e.g., former members) and people who study the life of this system (e.g., journalists such as Kaiser) and people who have modeled the system as having a more complex reality than a series of contracts (e.g., sociologists and former lobbyists) all affirm that money is mattering here a very great deal. How could it not?

In the end, this debate is not really a disagreement among scholars. It is a fight pressed by those defending a status quo. In that fight, there is an addict whose addiction is destroying his ability to do his job. The addict denies the addiction. But at some point the denial feels like the dialogue from any number of familiar works of fiction: "I can handle it." "It isn't affecting me or my work." "I

understand how it might affect others. But it doesn't affect me."
"I'm above it." "I can control it."

Right.

The corruption denier is in denial. It is time to move on.

Okay, But Is Money the Real Root?

There are a thousand hacking at the branches of evil to one who is striking at the root.

—Henry David Thoreau, *Walden* (1854)

We are now at a place where we can evaluate fairly some skepticism about the view I have offered about the corruption (and now equality-denying) character of money in our political system.

Because there are skeptics about the primacy that I've given to the role of money. Ezra Klein, in his review of the first edition of this book, argued that the "theory of general relativity" necessary "to explain the big stuff" was not money in politics, but instead "partisan polarization."[172] A review in *The Economist* thought the real problem was gerrymandering.[173]

Klein is right that polarization is a critical problem with American politics today. The data are staggering. Congress is more polarized today that at any point since the Civil War. We are indeed the house divided, as Lincoln warned, and that division is fundamentally debilitating.

But the cause of a problem is the thing you can affect. There are a lot of reasons America's Congress is more polarized. The most important of these is not because the average American has become more polarized, but because she has sorted herself into a geographically more polarized America.

Yet we're not going to ban moving to the suburbs as a way to reduce polarization.[174] Or we're not going to force politically diverse sorts to integrate. This is a constraint on polarization we're not going to change.

Likewise, politically active Americans have moved farther to the extremes—mainly on the Right, and a bit on the Left, too. But it's a free country: No one's going to ban falling for Fox News or Rachel Maddow.

These are the real reasons why politicians vote more extremely than they did in the past. But they are not the sorts of reasons that we could change. The reasons for polarization that we *could* change are few.

The most important of those reasons is the way we fund campaigns. The most important, not the only. "Safe seats" make it easier to be extreme. To the extent gerrymandering and single-member districts produce safe seats, eliminating gerrymandering and establishing multimember districts could go a long way to reducing the pressure to polarize.[175]

Changing the way we fund campaigns would also reduce the pressure to polarize. For one very effective technique to raising money is the vilification of the other side—a practice made even easier, as Kaiser notes, because members "never develop personal relationships with colleagues from the other party."[176] (One member told me that in the five years he had been in Congress, he had had lunch with a colleague no more than five times: "If you have time for lunch, you have time to fundraise."[177]) From Chris Dodd's perspective, "Pragmatic moderation was what 'made the place work'... but now 'everything works against' that moderation."[178]

Michael Golden cites one particularly illuminating example, described by Senator Joe Manchin (D-W.V.; 2010–) in a 2014 CNN interview:

> There's so much money involved... I go to work everyday, and I'm expected to raise money against the other side, if you will. So as a Democrat I go to work, I'm expected to raise money for the DSCC and my Republican counterparts and my colleagues are expected to raise money for the RSCC. That money is used against any Democrats or Republicans up for elections, and then we're even expected to go campaign against them.

Now that doesn't add for a good atmosphere, for us to start next week, come back after all this stuff happens the weeks prior to that and say, "OK, will you work with me now, can you co-sponsor a bill." That's what's happening. The money has infiltrated and has driven us apart.[179]

The business model of hate is an effective tool to driving supporters to give more generously. In this sense, polarization may well be the effect we should be most concerned about. But the way we fund campaigns is one cause of that polarization.

So why not address the gerrymandering first?

If we fixed gerrymandering, and created a democracy in which 50 percent of the seats were competitive, the only certain consequence of that change would be to radically increase the cost of campaigns. But if we haven't addressed the way we raise the money to fund campaigns, we would only exacerbate the problem, not fix it.

So my argument is not against the many other reforms that are also necessary to fix our democracy. We need those, too.

But we need reform in the right order, beginning with reform that is generative of other reform. Changing the way we fund elections is a generative reform in just this sense.

In the end, my claim is emphatically not that the only problem in American politics is money. It's not. I don't doubt the great harm done by polarization. I have no doubt that gerrymandering and winner-take-all districts exacerbate that polarization.

But my focus is on the practical changes that could begin a process to fix this long list of flaws that have defeated this democracy.

The way we fund campaigns is at the top of that list. If we fixed that, other fixes would come.

CHAPTER 9

How So Damn Much Money *Defeats the Left*

On November 4, 2008, America voted to change its government. With the highest voter turnout in forty years, sixty-nine million Americans elected the first African-American president, with twice as many electoral votes as his opponent, and almost ten million more of the total votes cast. House Democrats gained twenty-one seats, padding an already comfortable majority. And with the defection of one Republican, Senate Democrats gained enough seats to secure a filibuster-proof majority.

Obama's victory electrified the reform community. While no political liberal, his campaign had promised substantial change. Health care reformers were ecstatic to have a chance at real health care reform. Global warming activists thought they had elected a sexier version of Al Gore. And as Wall Street's collapse threw the economy over the cliff, America was very eager to hear Obama attack Wall Street. ("I will take on the corruption in Washington and on Wall Street to make sure a crisis like this can never, ever happen again"[1]; "We have to set up some rules of the road, some regulations that work to keep the system solvent, and prevent Wall Street from taking enormous risks with other people's money, figuring that, 'Tails I win, heads you lose,' where they don't have any risk on the downside."[2]) If ever there was the opportunity for progressive change, this election seemed to promise it.

I was a strong supporter of Obama. Indeed, long before you likely had ever even heard the name "Obama," I was a strong supporter of Obama. He was a colleague of mine at the University of Chicago. In 2000, he ran for Congress in the South Side of Chicago. The campaign was awful. Yet after his defeat, Obama was optimistic. "It was a good first try," he assured me. If that campaign was "a good first try," I thought, then he had even less political sense than me.

Despite that defeat, however, I have backed every Obama campaign since. In one sense, that's not surprising. We were friends. But it was more than that. Like many who know the man, I believed there was something more than the typical politician here. I was convinced by Obama. More than convinced: totally won over. It wasn't just that I agreed with his policies. Indeed, I didn't really agree with a bunch of his policies. It was instead because I believed that he had a vision of what was wrong with our government, with a passion and commitment to fix it.

That vision is the great orator's summary of the argument of this book. In speech after speech, from 2007 through the summer of 2008, Obama described the problem of Washington just as I have here. As he said, "The ways of Washington must change."

> If we do not change our politics—if we do not fundamentally change the way Washington works—then the problems we've been talking about for the last generation will be the same ones that haunt us for generations to come.[3]
>
> But let me be clear—this isn't just about ending the failed policies of the Bush years; it's about ending the failed system in Washington that produces those policies. For far too long, through both Democratic and Republican administrations, Washington has allowed Wall Street to use lobbyists and campaign contributions to rig the system and get its way, no matter what it costs ordinary Americans.[4]
>
> We are up against the belief that it's all right for lobbyists to dominate our government—that they are just part of the system in Washington. But we know that the undue influence of lobbyists is part of the problem, and this election is our chance to say that we're not going to let them stand in our way anymore.[5]
>
> Unless we're willing to challenge the broken system in Washington, and stop letting lobbyists use their clout to get their way, nothing else is going to change.[6]

The reason I'm running for President is to challenge that system.[7]

If we're not willing to take up that fight, then real change—change that will make a lasting difference in the lives of ordinary Americans—will keep getting blocked by the defenders of the status quo.[8]

It was this theme that distinguished Obama most clearly from the heir apparent to the Democratic nomination, Hillary Clinton. For in 2008, Clinton was not running to "change the way Washington works." She stood against John Edwards and Barack Obama in their attack on the system and on lobbyists in particular. As she told an audience at YearlyKos in August 2007: "A lot of those lobbyists, whether you like it or not, represent real Americans. They represent nurses, they represent social workers, yes, they represent corporations that employ a lot of people. I don't think, based on my 35 years of fighting for what I believe in, I don't think anybody seriously believes I'm going to be influenced by a lobbyist."[9]

The "anybody" here didn't include the thousand or so in the audience, who moaned in disbelief as Clinton lectured them about what they could and could not "seriously believe."

Instead, Clinton's vision of the presidency was much like her husband's (though, no doubt, without the pathetic scandals). She saw the job of president to be to take a political system and do as much with it as you can. It may be a lame horse. It may be an intoxicated horse. It may be a horse that can only run backward. But the job is not to fix the horse. The job is to run the horse as fast as you can. There was a raft of programs that Clinton promised to push through Congress. Nowhere on that list was fundamental reform in the way Washington worked.

I was therefore glad, not so much that Clinton had lost (she is an amazing politician and, as her time in the Senate and as Secretary of State has confirmed, an extraordinary stateswoman), but that Obama had won. For as this book should make clear, it was my view, too, that the critical problem for the next president was the corruption that we've been exploring here. Not because corruption is the most important problem, but because this corruption is the first problem. Corruption is the gateway problem: until we solve it, we won't solve any number of other critical problems facing this nation.

I thought Obama got this. That's what he promised, again and again. That was "the reason [he] was running for President[—]to challenge that system."[10]

Yet that was not the game that Obama played. Instead, the game he played was exactly the game that Hillary Clinton had promised and precisely the game that Bill Clinton executed: striking a bargain with the most powerful lobbyists as a way to get a bill through— and as it turns out, surprise, surprise, "the people" don't have the most powerful lobbyists. Obama became his Chief of Staff, Rahm Emanuel, who "agreed with Obama about the dysfunction of Washington," but "wasn't interest in trying to change the game."[11]

As I watched that strategy unfold, I could not believe it. The idealist in me certainly could not believe that Obama would run a campaign grounded in "change" yet execute an administration that changed nothing of the "way Washington works."

But the pragmatist in me also could not believe it. I could not begin to understand how this administration thought that it would take on the most important lobbying interests in America and win without a strategy to change the power of those most important lobbying interests. Nothing close to the reform that Obama promised is possible under the current system; so if that reform was really what Obama sought, changing the system was an essential first step.

The reason should have been obvious in 2009, because it has become unavoidably obvious since.

In the best of times, the Clinton model of governing will have but limited success, so long as (1) markets remain concentrated, and (2) the system for campaign funding remains unchanged.

Reform shifts wealth. Those it shifts wealth from resist. "Their bird is in the hand," as Kenneth Crawford put it during the New Deal, "they battle to keep it."[12,13]

But the effectiveness of their "battle" turns on their strength—both their raw power, and their ability to exercise that power.

The way we fund campaigns is the means by which that power is exercised. But the ability to exercise that power effectively turns on just how concentrated a particular interest is.

So, for example, imagine there were only one oil company in the nation: if the value of being allowed to ignore the cost of carbon in the products that oil company sold were $100 billion, in principle, that oil company should be willing to spend $100 billion to avoid being forced to internalize the cost of carbon in the products it sold. In a system where money can influence politics, that money gets spent effectively to influence this critical policy.

The story is more complicated if there is more than one entity that benefits from the status quo. Then each faces what economists call a "free-rider problem." It may be good for each that the status quo is preserved, but it is better for each if the status quo can be preserved without it having to pay to preserve it. Each, in other words, would like to "free-ride" on the spending of the others. To spend effectively, interests must coordinate.

This makes the case for reform much more promising (for the reformer at least) if markets are competitive. If there are a large number of entities comprising a special interest, it is much less likely that these entities could coordinate their fight to preserve the status quo. Thus in a competitive market, reform should be simpler, all things being equal, than in a concentrated market, if only because the targets of that reform have a harder time defending against it.

The problem for us, however, is that major markets in America have become heavily concentrated, and on key issues it has become much easier for allies to coordinate. Indeed, in the critical markets for reform—finance, for example—firms are more concentrated today than ever before. That concentration makes their coordination simpler, and any reform harder.[14]

Concentration doesn't necessarily translate into what lawyers call "market power," and it is market power that triggers the special limits of antitrust law. So by pointing to these concentrated markets, I'm not suggesting that the Antitrust Division of the Justice Department or the Federal Trade Commission is not doing its work.

But these concentrated markets do translate into a greater opportunity for coordinated political action: for the fewer corporations there are with interests at stake, the fewer it takes to persuade to support a campaign to defend those interests.[15]

This insight has led even free-market scholars such as Raghuram Rajan and Luigi Zingales to argue for a "political version of antitrust law—one that prevents a firm from growing big enough to have the clout in domestic politics to eventually suppress market forces."[16] We don't have that kind of antitrust today. Indeed, we have very few limits on the ability of the capitalists to protect themselves— from either reform or capitalism. Antitrust law (as interpreted in light of the First Amendment) exempts from review conspiracies to change the law, even if the change is simply to protect those conspirators.[17]

Thus, no matter what reform a new government might try, there is a well-funded and well-connected gaggle of lobbyists on the other side. Those lobbyists know that politicians will listen to their arguments quite intently, because their arguments about good policy carry with them (through the complicated dance that I described in Chapter 1) campaign cash. These lobbyists thus get to the front of the line. Their concerns get met first, long before the concerns of the voter.

No example better captures this dynamic than the fight over health care reform. The president made the reform of health care a priority in the campaign. He made it a priority in his administration. From his first days in office, Obama and his team strategized on how they could get reform passed. And how they got that reform passed shows plainly (if painfully) where the power in this system lies.

Obama had made promises about health care reform during his

campaign. The "public option" was one of those promises. Though
the details were never precisely set, the idea was simple enough:
The government would offer a competing health care plan that
anyone would have the freedom to buy. That option would thus
put competitive pressure on private insurance companies to keep
prices low. It may well have been that no one ever bought that public option plan. That doesn't matter. The aim wasn't to national-
ize health insurance. The aim was to create competitive pressure
to ensure that the (highly concentrated) health insurance market
didn't take advantage of a national health care program to extort
even greater profits from the public.

Again, how was never specified. Sometimes Obama spoke of the
health care plan that members of Congress received. Sometimes he
spoke of a "new public plan." As the campaign website described:

> The Obama-Biden plan will create a National Health Insur-
> ance Exchange to help individuals purchase new affordable
> health care options if they are uninsured or want new health
> insurance. Through the Exchange, any American will have the
> opportunity to enroll in the new public plan or an approved
> private plan, and income-based sliding scale tax credits will be
> provided for people and families who need it.[18]

Likewise, at a speech at the University of Iowa on March 29, 2007:

> "Everyone will be able to buy into a new health insurance plan
> that's similar to the one that every federal employee—from
> a postal worker in Iowa to a congressman in Washington—
> currently has for themselves."

Or again, three and a half months later, to the Planned Parent-
hood Action Fund on July 17, 2007:

> "We are going to set up a public plan that all persons, and all
> women, can access if they don't have health insurance."

Or again, five months later, to the Iowa Heartland Presidential Forum on December 1, 2007:

"We will set up a government program, as I've described, that everybody can buy into and you can't be excluded because of a pre-existing condition."

These promises continued after the campaign. During the president's weekly address on July 18, 2009:

"Any plan I sign must include an insurance exchange: a one-stop shopping marketplace where you can compare the benefits, cost and track records of a variety of plans—including a public option to increase competition and keep insurance companies honest—and choose what's best for your family."[19]

But whether that plan or another, the idea that there would be some backstop for all of us was a central plank in the campaign.

So, too, was doing something about the high cost of prescription drugs. The pharmaceutical industry is one of the most profitable industries in both America and Britain.[20] One reason it is so profitable is a monopoly that the government gives it in the form of drug patents. Those patents are necessary (so long as drug research is privately financed), but there has long been a debate about whether these patents get granted too easily, or whether "me-too" drugs get patent protection unnecessarily. (A me-too drug is a new drug that performs very similarly to a drug it is intended to replace. Patents for such drugs may be unnecessary since the cost to society of a patent is large [higher prices], and the added benefit from the me-too drug is small.)

Patents, however, are not the only government-granted protection from the effects of an otherwise free market. In addition to patents, the government sometimes promises not to use its own market power to "force" drug companies to offer lower prices to the government. I put that word in scare quotes, because of course, we're not talking about billy clubs, or tanks. This isn't force. Instead, it is just the workings of an ordinary market, where buyers with market power pay less than buyers without market power. Ordinary souls understand this to be the difference between wholesale and retail: The wholesaler pays less per unit than retail prices. But when the wholesaler is really, really big, that means it can leverage its power to get really, really good prices from the seller.

Thus talk of "market power" and "forcing" shouldn't lead you to think that anything bad is happening here. A seller is "forced" to sell to wholesalers at lower prices in just the sense that you are "forced" to pay $3.50 for a latte at Starbucks. If you don't like the price, you can go someplace else. If the seller doesn't like the price the wholesaler demands, the seller can just say no. People might not like what the market demands. But most of us don't get a special law passed by the government to exempt us from the market just because we don't like what it demands.

The drug companies, however, did. In 2003, Congress passed President Bush's biggest social legislation, the Medicare Prescription Drug, Improvement, and Modernization Act.[21] This massive government program—estimated to cost $490 billion between 2006 and 2015,[22] and not covered by any increase in taxes—was intended to benefit seniors by ensuring them access to high-price drugs. It also had the effect of benefiting the drug companies, however, by ensuring an almost endless pipeline of funds to pay for the high-cost drugs that doctors prescribe to seniors.

The best part of Bush's plan (for the drug companies, at least) was a section called Part D, which essentially guarantees drug companies retail prices for wholesale purchases.[23] The law bars the government from negotiating for better prices from the drug companies. Thus, while the government is not permitted to use its market power to get lower prices from the drug companies, the drug companies are permitted to use their (government-granted) market power (from patents) to demand whatever price they want from us.

This is not a simple issue. Sane and independent economists

will testify that it is very hard to determine exactly what price a government should be able to get its drugs for. For just as there is a problem with a monopoly (one seller), there is a problem with monopsony (one buyer). Permitting a monopsonist to exercise all of its market power can certainly cause social harm in just the way that permitting a monopolist to exercise all of its market power can cause social harm.

My point, however, is not to map an economically ideal compromise—even assuming there is one. It is instead to track the evolution of the president's position on these complicated policy questions.

For when Congress passed the Prescription Drug Act, there was no ambiguity in Barack Obama's view of Part D. He was outraged. As he said on the floor of the Senate, this was just another example of "the power and the profits of the pharmaceutical industry... trump[ing] good policy and the will of the American people." It was "a tremendous boon for the drug companies." And as he added, "When you look at the prices the Federal Government has negotiated for our veterans and military men and women, it is clear that the government can—and should—use its leverage to lower prices for our seniors as well. Drug negotiation is the smart thing to do and the right thing to do."[24]

Obama continued that criticism during his campaign. On the Obama-Biden website, the campaign stated:

> Barack Obama and Joe Biden will repeal the ban on direct negotiation with drug companies and use the resulting savings, which could be as high as $30 billion, to further invest in improving health care coverage and quality.

And the example was the subject of the campaign ad named "Billy":

> Narrator: "The pharmaceutical industry wrote into the prescription drug plan that Medicare could not negotiate with drug companies. And you know what, the chairman of the

committee, who pushed the law through, went to work for the pharmaceutical industry making $2 million a year."

The screen fades to black to inform the viewer that "Barack Obama is the only candidate who refuses Washington lobbyist money," while the candidate continues his lecture:

"Imagine that. That's an example of the same old game playing in Washington. You know, I don't want to learn how to play the game better, I want to put an end to the game playing."[25]

So just as clearly as the public was promised a public option, the public was also promised that Obama's reform would never include another "tremendous boon for the drug companies" in the form of a(nother) free pass from the forces of the market.

Obama broke both promises. Obamacare did not include a public option. It did include the drug companies' special protection from the forces of the market.

But that alone does not describe the problem. Governing is all about compromise. Promises made are part of that compromise. The question is not whether promises were broken. The question is: *Why* were they broken? What is the nature of the force that forced these compromises into the system?

As the story is told by Jonathan Cohn of the *New Republic*, Obama took on health care almost as "a test": "Could the country still solve its most vexing problems? If he abandoned comprehensive reform, he would be conceding that the United States was, on some level, ungovernable."[26]

But the question was *on what terms* would America be governed. As Cohn writes: "Obama had promised to change the way Washington does business. No more negotiating in the anterooms of Capitol Hill. No more crafting bills to please corporate interests. But Obama also wanted to pass monumental legislation. And it wasn't long before the tension between the two began to emerge."[27]

This statement is almost right, but not quite. Certainly Obama

had promised to end the practice of "crafting bills to please corporate interests." ("Unless we're willing to challenge the broken
system in Washington, and stop letting lobbyists use their clout to
get their way, nothing else is going to change."[28]) But that's different from a promise to give up politics. ("No more negotiating in
the anterooms of Capitol Hill.") There's nothing wrong with negotiating, and with compromise, so long as the driving force in that
compromise is the single dependency that this democracy is to
reveal: the people. Maybe voters in Nebraska need something from
California before they can support health care. There's no sin in
making that deal.

The sin, as Obama described it during the campaign, and as I
have described in this book, is when forces not reflecting the people force compromise into the system. It is the "undue influence
of lobbyists"[29]—undue because not tied to the proper metric for
power within a democracy. Undue when reflecting money, rather
than reflecting democratic power.

Yet the story that Cohn tells is the story of such "undue influence" again and again. The administration strikes a deal to get
PhRMA's support for the bill. The price? A promise to protect
PhRMA in just the way President Bush did with the Prescription
Drug Act: no bargaining to lower prices. The administration estimated that a health care bill would increase the revenue to the drug
companies by $100 billion. This deal struck by Obama with the
lobbyists from PhRMA assured PhRMA that it would keep much of
that increase.

The same with the "public option." The Congressional Budget
Office had estimated that a public option would "save the government around $150 billion,"[30] by putting competitive pressure on
insurance companies to keep their rates low. That competitive pressure seemed to many only fair, as insurance companies, like PhRMA,
were about to get a big boost from the bill: a requirement that everyone have insurance. But alas, as Cohn describes, "That money would
come out of the health care industry, which prevailed upon ideologically sympathetic (and campaign-donation-dependent) lawmakers

to intervene. They blocked a bill until Waxman [dropped the public option]."[31]

The lesson here is obvious. There are "institutional constraints" on change in America. Central to those "constraints" is, as Cohn lists it with others, "the nature of campaign finance."[32] And what is its "nature"?: that "corporate interests" (Cohn's words) "use lobbyists and campaign contributions to rig the system and get [their] way, no matter what it costs ordinary Americans"[33] (Obama's words). Here that "nature" "cost ordinary Americans" up to $250 billion: apparently the price we have to pay for reform to please these corporate masters, given the "nature of campaign finance."

After health care reform passed, Ezra Klein, then a columnist at the *Washington Post*, wrote with praise that Obama had "succeeded at neutralizing every single industry"[34]—insurance, PhRMA, the AMA, labor, and even large businesses. Klein meant that term "neutralizing" precisely: that Obama had succeeded in balancing the forces of each powerful interest against the other, with the result that his reform (however hobbled it was) would pass.

That meaning for the term "neutralizing" was made ambiguous, however, by the title that the editors gave to the essay ("Twilight of the Interest Groups"), a title that suggested that Klein was arguing that Obama had weakened the power of the interest groups. That he had, in fact, as he had promised during the campaign, "fundamentally change[d] the way Washington works."[35]

Pulitzer Prize-winning writer Glenn Greenwald picked up on this hint, and as is his style, picked on it mercilessly. As he wrote:

If, by "neutralizing," Ezra means "bribing and accommodating them to such an extreme degree that they ended up affirmatively supporting a bill that lavishes them with massive benefits," then he's absolutely right.

Being able to force the Government to bribe and accommodate you is not a reflection of your powerlessness; quite the opposite.

The way this bill has been shaped is the ultimate expression—and bolstering —of how Washington has long worked. One can find reasonable excuses for why it had to be done that way, but one cannot reasonably deny that it was.[36]

Greenwald's criticism of Klein's title may be unfair (columnists rarely pen the title of a column). The criticism of Obama, however, is completely fair.

Had President Hillary Clinton passed health care as Obama did, she would deserve great praise. That Obama passed health care the way Clinton would have does not earn him the same praise. Rather than "take up the fight" to "change the way Washington works," Obama has simply "bolstered" "how Washington has long worked." That bolstering, in turn, has made every other change that much harder.

The story is very much the same with just about every other area of major reform that Obama has tried to enact. Consider, for example, the reform of the banks.

Whole forests have been felled cataloging the reckless behavior of the banks that threw the economy over the cliff in 2008. "Reckless" from the perspective of society, not from the perspective of the banks. In my view, following Judge Richard Posner, there was nothing "reckless" about the behavior *from the perspective of the banks*. From their perspective, they were behaving perfectly rationally: if you know your losses are going to be covered, gambling is a pretty good business model.

Real reform needed to focus on the incentives to gamble. The government needed to ensure that it no longer paid for the banks to use other people's money to gamble with our economy. As almost everyone agreed, after spending an enormous amount of public funds to save the banks so as to save the financial system, at the very least, we should ensure that we don't have to save the system again.

From this perspective, the fundamental flaw in the system is one that conservatives often focus upon in the context of welfare: the system had created a "moral hazard problem." With welfare, the conservative's concern is that unemployment payments (intended to cushion the burden of losing a job) may encourage people not to seek a job. With the financial system, the conservative's concern should be that the promise of a government bailout will encourage the banks to behave more recklessly.

Indeed, the evidence of this moral hazard is quite compelling.

Banks in the United States have gotten huge in the past ten years. They've gotten only bigger after the crisis.[37] As the *LA Times* reported in the fall of 2013, "There is rare agreement among many Democrats and Republicans in Washington that those banks still are too big to fail, leaving the nation's economy even more at risk."[38] Before the crisis, each bank could reasonably hope that if it got into trouble, the government would help it. After the crisis (and as I'll explain below, reform notwithstanding), that hope is now a certainty.

Thus, the market as it is means large banks are still able to gamble with more confidence than small banks. It also means that these large banks are therefore a less risky borrower than small banks (since there's no risk they'll be allowed to go bankrupt), and can therefore borrow money on the open market for a discount relative to small banks. Again, as Simon Johnson and James Kwak calculated the advantage in 2009: "Large banks were able to borrow money at rates 0.78 percentage points more cheaply than smaller banks, up from an average of 0.29 percentage points from 2000 through 2007."[39]

"In the period since" the crisis, as Oliver Hart and Luigi Zingales summarized a study by economists Dean Baker and Travis McArthur in 2010: "The sprea[d] had grown to 0.49 percentage points. This increased spread is the market's estimate of the benefit of the implicit insurance offered to large banks by the 'too big to fail' policy. For the 18 American banks with more than $100 billion each in assets, this advantage corresponds to a roughly $34 billion total subsidy per year."[40]

A $34 billion subsidy per year: that's 500,000 elementary school teachers, or 600,000 firefighters, or 4.4 million slots for kids in Head

Start programs, or coverage for 4 million veterans in VA hospitals.[41] We don't spend that money on those worthy causes in America. We instead effectively give that money to institutions that continue to expose the economy to fundamental systemic risk while paying the highest bonuses to their most senior employees in American history.

As the system now works, when the banks' gambles blow up, we bail them out. The bailouts, plus an endless stream of (almost) zero-interest money (if one could call $9 trillion in loans from the Federal Reserve a "stream"), gave the banks the breathing room they needed to avoid bankruptcy, and the fuel they needed to earn the massive profits to pay back the bailout, and also pay their senior executives their bonuses. In 2009, investors and executives at the thirty-eight largest Wall Street firms earned $140 billion, "the highest number on record."[42]

This is a system of incentives crafted by government regulation— both the regulation to permit the gambling and the regulation to guarantee the losses. Together, it has created the dumbest form of socialism known to man: "socializ[ing] the losses while privatizing the gains"[43]—thus benefiting the privileged while taxing all the rest. And we should say, following Zingales, "If you have a sector... where losses are socialized but where gains are privatized, then you destroy the economic and moral supremacy of capitalism."[44]

Banks are rational actors. They would not expose our economy to fundamental systemic risk if it didn't pay—them. And it wouldn't pay them if they believed that they would go bankrupt when their gambles blew up. So the single most important reform here should have been to end this "moral hazard problem" for banks. And the one simple way to do that would have been to guarantee that banks wouldn't be bailed out in the future.

The reform bill that passed Congress in 2010 tried to make that guarantee. But that guarantee is not worth the PDF it is embedded within. If any of the largest banks in the United States today faced bankruptcy, the cost that bankruptcy would impose on America would clearly justify the government's intervening to save it. In the face of that collapse, it would be irrational for the government *not* to save it. "No matter how much we try to tie our hands," Zingales writes, "when a major crisis comes it is impossible to stop the politicians from intervening."[45] Real reform cannot depend upon irrational tough love. Real reform must depend upon making it possible to let the gamblers lose—so they know it makes sense for them to stop gambling.

The simplest way to achieve this real reform would be to force banks to a size that would make (their) failure possible.[46] Thus, as Simon Johnson and James Kwak recommended in 2010:

1. A hard cap on the size of financial institutions: "No financial institution would be allowed to control or have an ownership interest in assets worth more than a fixed percentage of U.S. GDP.... [T]he percentage should be low enough that banks below that threshold can be allowed to fail without entailing serious risk to the financial system. As a first proposal, this limit should be *no more than 4 percent of GDP*, or roughly $570 billion in assets today."

2. A lower hard cap on size for banks that take greater risks, including derivatives, off-balance-sheet positions, and other factors that increase the damage a failing institution could cause to other financial institutions: "As an initial guideline, an investment bank (such as Goldman Sachs) should be effectively limited in size to *2 percent of GDP*, or roughly $285 billion today."[47]

Yale professor Jon Macey makes a similar proposal.[48]

This reform has been questioned.[49] But it would have produced a market of banks that were not so big that the government would have to save them. These banks would therefore live life like any other entity in a competitive market, keen to make money, but careful not to take on unnecessary or extreme risk. The market would thus be the ultimate and efficient regulator, because the market would not forgive failure. Bankruptcy would be the remedy for failure, not a blank check from the Federal Reserve.

Yet the banks fought this obvious reform with fury—and succeeded. As Lowenstein describes it, "Wall Street institutions emerged from the crisis more protected than ever."[50] "For better or worse," as Tyler Cowen wrote after the reform bill was passed, "we're handing out free options on recovery, and that encourages banks to take more risk."[51] Hacker and Pierson quote "two New York Times reporters describing Wall Street executives as 'privately relieved that the bill [did] not do more to fundamentally change how the industry does business.' "[52] Sebastian Mallaby "put [it most] simply": "Government actions have decreased the cost of risk for too-big-to-fail players; the result will be more risk taking. The vicious cycle will go on until governments are bankrupt."[53]

How was this nonreform reform bill passed?

Well, we know a bit more about how it was passed since the first edition of this book was published in 2011. Robert Kaiser, the author of *So Damn Much Money* (2009), whose framing I have stolen throughout the heart of this book, has told the story in an incredible account of the passing of Dodd-Frank, *Act of Congress* (2014).

Given his earlier book, it's no surprise that Kaiser was sensitive to the role of money in the passing of Dodd-Frank. Never was its effect crude, in the way that insurance companies and pharmaceutical companies used their power to craft critical parts of Obamacare. (Though Kaiser does describe the truly astonishingly crude way that Republicans used the prospects of legislation to raise money on Wall Street. In one fund-raiser, he quotes an anonymous CEO who " 'was appalled' by [Senate Minority Leader McConnell's] remarks. 'It was all politics. 'We're going to beat this financial reform for you'—all of it politics, no policy.' "[54])

But neither was money's effect weak.

In part, its strength can be seen through the weakness of the reforms. As James Kwak has put it, a kind of "cultural capture" blocked anyone in Congress from really considering the kind of fundamental reform that fundamental collapse might merit.[55]

Neither Dodd nor Frank nor almost any of their colleagues wanted to "use the Great Crash of 2008 ... to seek the breakup of America's big banks or any other fundamental alteration of the final sector."

> Both agreed it would be enough to put the financial sector under stricter new rules, without trying to undo the two decades of growth and concentration that had transformed American finance, making it the most profitable sector of the American economy.[56]

This "moderation," as Kaiser describes it, "surely was influenced by the political money game"[57]—though certainly not directly, or illegally. It was more the indirect cultural game that made it implausible to imagine shaking things up too much—even though these now "traditional" institutions had pretty dramatically shaken the American economy up. That fact—that great harm had been caused by the (publicly) reckless behavior of an incredibly wealthy industry—didn't seem to matter much in DC. As Senator Tom Harkin (D-Ia., 1985–2015) put it, no doubt to the discomfort of many:

> I defy anyone here ... to show me one person, one trader, one whiz kid ... who lost their home, their money and everything and were put out on the street because of what happened [in the Great Crash] ... [But] we can show you hundreds of thousands of Americans who lost their homes, lost their businesses, are out on the street because of what Wall Street did.[58]

As Kaiser comments:

> Harkin captured a reality that was rarely mentioned in this final stage of the legislative process. Something truly awful had happened in the previous two years, victimizing millions of Americans but very few of the perpetrators. [Yet] those victims rarely made more than a cameo appearance.[59]

Many attributed this "reality" to the power of the banks—and again, remember, power here is measured in money. As Senator Dick Durbin told an Illinois radio station:

> The banks—hard to believe in a time when we're facing a banking crisis that many of the banks created—are still the most powerful lobby on Capitol Hill. And they frankly own the place.[60]

Barney Frank, at least, disagreed. "The big banks got nothing," Kaiser quotes Frank as saying, "with," as Kaiser describes, "evident satisfaction."[61]

But that literally cannot be right. What the banks got was moderate reform—reform that continues to be criticized as failing to address effectively the fundamental structural issues[62]—indeed as we could describe it, Brer Rabbit reform. Remember the rabbit who, once caught, pleads with his captor not to be thrown into the briar patch (but who secretly wants this of all the possible punishments because he knows this is the one that he can escape). That's exactly the "reform" that Dodd-Frank gave. Rather than the simple reform of Glass-Steagall, which in a single paragraph divided investment companies from traditional banks, Dodd-Frank launched an endless regulatory process to police the conflicting incentives produced by the modern industry of banking. In that process, the banks knew that they would be the only interest effectively represented. So years would pass before regulations would come into effect. And the regulations that did come to effect would be bent as much as possible to the interests of the banks. This was a system designed by lobbyists for lobbyists—indeed, a staffer for Barney Frank, who played a key role in writing portions of the law relating to credit default swaps, left just before it was passed to lobby for the word's largest credit default swap clearinghouse.[63] And in the five years since Dodd-Frank was passed, the industry has invested more than $2 billion in lobbying to produce the kinds of regulations the banks could live with.[64]

Of course, the banks wanted no reform, just as Brer Rabbit wanted not to have been caught. But once the biggest financial crisis since the Depression had thrown the economy over the cliff, the banks, like Brer Rabbit, were caught. The only question was what would happen to them.

Dodd-Frank, as Kaiser puts it, "was an anomaly—an accomplishment produced by a catastrophe, and by the fear engendered by that catastrophe."[65] It is story that "does demonstrate that Congress still *can* work...but only in extreme circumstances—so extreme that they are unlikely to recur for a long time."[66] And even then— even after the worst economic crisis that almost all of America had ever known—still, it was money that mattered. "Congress was complicit in the crash of 2008," Kaiser writes, "in ways no member stood up to announce, but a great many understood."[67] It will be complicit in the next crisis, too.

Former chairman of the SEC Arthur Levitt describes the dynamic perfectly:

> During my seven and a half years in Washington...nothing astonished me more than witnessing the powerful special interest groups in full swing when they thought a proposed rule or a piece of legislation might hurt them, giving nary a thought to how the [battles over corporate reform] might help the investing public. With laserlike precision, groups representing Wall Street firms... would quickly set about to defeat even minor threats. Individual investors, with no organized labor or trade association to represent their views in Washington, never knew what hit them.[68]

In the words of perhaps the twentieth century's greatest philosopher, David Byrne: "same as it ever was."

Finally, if the point isn't clear enough, consider one last example: climate change regulation.

The 2008 campaign happened against the background of a profound awakening of awareness about the dangers of climate change. Al Gore was behind much of this new awareness. His talks, amplified by the talent of a filmmaker such as Davis Guggenheim, became a recipe for a real change in awareness. The film won an Oscar. Gore won a Nobel Peace Prize. Both political parties, and both candidates, insisted that they were the candidate, and theirs was the party, to fight global warming. Senator McCain had long maintained, contrary to many Republicans, that he believed global warming was real, and something the government had to address. Senator Obama could say the same, and made climate change legislation a central plank of his campaign.

So when Obama won by a landslide, and with a majority in the House and a supermajority in the Senate, environmental activists were ecstatic: Here, finally, was a chance to get something done about arguably the most important public policy problem facing the globe.

In the first two years of the Obama administration, environmental groups did whatever they could to support the administration's efforts to get a bill. After they contributed close to $5.6 million in the 2008 elections, and spent $22.4 million lobbying Congress in 2009 (compared with $35.6 million spent by opponents of reform in the 2008 election, and $175 million spent lobbying Congress in 2009),[69] the House produced an extremely compromised "cap-and-trade" bill.[70]

Even that bill, however, couldn't survive the onslaught of special-interest money. On July 22, 2010, Senate Majority Leader Harry Reid (D-Nev., 1987–) announced that the cap-and-trade bill was dead. And thus, no global warming legislation would be passed during at least the first term of Obama's administration. Neither in the second. The reason? As NASA climate scientist Jim Hansen put it, "I believe the biggest obstacle to solving global warming is the role of money in politics."[71]

In each case, the story is the same. The interests that would be affected by the CHANGE that Obama promised lobbied and contributed enough to block real change. Not completely, but substantially. Twenty billion dollars have been spent lobbying Congress during the first six years of the Obama administration, almost $5 billion more than was spent in the last six years of the Bush administration.[72] That money blocks reform. It will always block reform, at least so long as the essential element to effecting reform, Congress, remains pathologically dependent upon the campaign cash that those who block reform can deliver. As Al Gore has described it, "The influence of special interests is now at an extremely unhealthy level....It's virtually impossible for participants in the current political system to enact any significant change without first seeking and gaining permission from the largest commercial interests who are most affected by the proposed change."[73]

Robert Reich makes the same point: "As a practical matter, this means that in order to enact any piece of legislation that may impose costs on the private sector, Congress and the administration must pay off enough industries and subsets of industries...to gain their support and therefore a fair shot at winning a majority."[74]

The president gets this. He waged a campaign committed to changing it. He promised us that changing it was "why [he was] running." He challenged us to "take up the fight"[75] with him.

We did. But he abandoned it.

And yet the Obama administration will be remembered as an enormous success. As well it should be. Given the constraints on governing today, he has done an extraordinary amount of good, across a wide range of contexts.

Despite the compromises, Obamacare is a foundational change. Tens of millions have protection who didn't before. The cost of health care insurance has fallen because of the incentives Obamacare created.[76]

Dodd-Frank, too, has done enormous good. Though it "may not prevent the next financial crisis," as sometime-critic Paul Krugman has written, "there's a good chance that it will at least make future crises less severe and easier to deal with."[77] That's because the Act gives the government more power to deal with risky institutions, by identifying and regulating "systemically important financial institutions"; it establishes clearer authority for the government to take over troubled banks; and of course, it created the most important new power for consumer protection in a generation—the Consumer Financial Protection Bureau.

On the environment, though Obama has not been able to enact legislation to address climate change, his administration has done everything it can *on its own* to deal with greenhouse gases, and to move America to renewable energy. The stimulus did a great deal to spur that change. For the first time in forever, the administration upped the fuel efficiency standards. It has imposed hugely valuable emission restrictions on power plants.

And the list of other lesser, though important, changes is very, very long. We have left the age of the social scold: Tolerance and the open embrace of difference are the new normal. Student loans have been saved from high-priced private processors. Immigration prosecutions have been rationalized to target real offenders, and to avoid innocent victims (kids).

These successes are enormously important. They have been accomplished despite militant opposition by Republicans, both while in the minority and in the majority, and despite endlessly unfair criticisms by a commercially partisan press. And while there are many examples of policies that I disagree with—none more than the surveillance policies—no fair weighing of the Obama administration could conclude that it was anything other than an enormous success—*given the constraints*.

Yet the whole point of Obama's early campaign was that *these very constraints* would make it impossible to achieve real and lasting reform.

In this, Obama was exactly right: "If we do not fundamentally change the way Washington works, then the problems we've been talking about for the last generation will be the same ones that haunt us for generations to come." That's still true, despite his enormous success.

And in this, Obama was clear—his campaign was about "ending the failed system in Washington that produces those policies."

Yet the "system" was not changed during the Obama administration. Obama didn't even propose a single reform that would have changed it (not to mention, his failure to act on his promise to introduce legislation to reform presidential public funding after becoming the first President since Nixon elected with private money only).

There is no doubt he did enormous good, given the flaws. But there is also no doubt that these flaws fatally weaken the possibility of doing the kind of good the nation needs.

It's not Obama's weakness that failed to pass climate change legislation. It is a failure baked into the current system.

It's not Obama's weakness that produced health care reform deeply compromised by its gifts to powerful interests. It is a weakness made inevitable by the current system.

It is not Obama's fault that key reforms built into the Dodd-Frank Act are being rolled back through bipartisan legislation. It is the fault of a system that holds national policy hostage to the financial interests of the most powerful contributors to political campaigns.

Obama did what he could, given the system, brilliantly. But what he didn't do is move us closer to a system that could address the fundamental problems that we continue to face. We cannot, as a nation, go on without addressing these fundamental problems that we continue to face. Doing the best you can with a broken system is an achievement worthy of praise. But not fixing the system is failure, regardless of that good.

If you brought your cancer-stricken mother to a hospital, because the doctor promised to remove the tumor, and months later, the tumor had not been touched, you might well be grateful to the hospital that they treated your mom so well. You might agree that the new diet has restored color to her cheeks. And that she's indeed comfortable and well quaffed.

But you wouldn't be wrong to observe that the tumor was still there. You'd be right to observe it, and to ask about it, and to insist they move quickly to remove it. Malignant tumors are fatal, and this is your mom.

They might stand there, the doctors, and tell you they're doing the most that they can. Maybe they are. But you would want them to try the one thing that might save her. Regardless of how difficult that was.

This is the way we have to think about the challenges facing this nation. As Thomas Mann and Norm Ornstein put it:

All of the boastful talk of American exceptionalism cannot obscure the growing sense that the country is squandering its economic future and putting itself at risk because of an inability to govern itself.[78]

As the deans of congressional studies, they should know. And we should respond.

CHAPTER 10

How So Damn Much Money *Defeats the Right*

You know from reading this far that I am not from the Right. Or actually, I am *from* the Right—I grew up a libertarian, chairman of the Pennsylvania Teen-Age Republicans, and the youngest member of a delegation in the 1980 GOP convention. But I no longer have the politics that I once did. I am now firmly a Democrat, even if my parents work hard to ignore that fact.

But by far, the happiest moment I had after writing the first edition of this book was in reading a review in the conservative magazine *The American Spectator*. A friend had e-mailed the review to me. I remember feeling a deep dread as I clicked the link. That dread only grew as I read the first paragraph of the review:

> Larry Lessig, a liberal at Harvard Law School, has written a book he thinks conservatives should read.[1]

But then as the reviewer, George Mason professor Frank Buckley, continued, "And he's right."

My happiness went way beyond the thought that I might finally have something to share with my (conservative) dad. It was instead this glimmer of hope about what I believe is the single most important fact that will determine whether we can win this Republic back—that both sides of our increasingly and fiercely divided political culture can at least identify with the problem, and agree that it is something that must be attacked.

And indeed, in the five years since I finished the first edition of this book, the most important hope for this movement has come from the seemingly endless stream of writing on the Right pointing to exactly the system of corruption that I have focused here. *Hope* not because only the Right wins in America—I know many on my side believe that, even while many on the other side believe the opposite. But hope because only if this issue is understood as an *American* issue first can we on the Left or those on the Right have any hope of fixing it.

In 2011, Peter Schweizer published *Throw Them All Out*, pointing to a pattern of stock sales by members of Congress suggesting the incredible corruption of them trading on inside information.[2] Shortly after, Schweizer published *Extortion*, which, as I've described in Chapter 8, tries to understand the money game in Washington from the perspective of the giver—pressured by regulators (aka Congressmen) into staying on the good side of the regulators (aka Congressmen) by keeping Congress happy (aka by giving money to their campaigns).

Jay Cost practically stole my title (though I'm a big believer in sharing, so I was very happy to see the book): *A Republic No More* (2015). The book is a powerful and historical account of the ways in which the government has become unhinged from the people. Hunter Lewis's *Crony Capitalism in America* (2013) likewise has a breathtakingly wide sweep of examples of the public interest bending to private power, as cronies wield the inevitable power that this system gives them, or that they must embrace in the face of the (Schweizer-like) extortion the system produces. Jack Abramoff's *Capitol Punishment* (2011) provides a rich catalog of examples of how this corruption—"legalized bribery"[3] as he describes it—works, not just in the criminal sense, which he openly confesses, but legally, too. And he also describes how not much has changed in the time since he was sent to a federal penitentiary. Chapter 4 of Charles Murray's latest book, *By the People* (2015), is "A Systematically Corrupt Political System," and in it he maps a picture of the "corruption" of Congress that tracks my own here. And Richard Painter's forthcoming book, *Taxation Only with Representation* (forthcoming, 2016), is the most comprehensive account of why conservatives should support radical reform in the way campaigns are funded. Painter was

the ethics czar in George W. Bush's White House. He is a conservative with the highest personal integrity, and joins many others from
the Right—including the former FEC Chair, Trevor Potter (who was
also Stephen Colbert's lawyer when he had a super PAC), and Mark
McKinnon, strategist for George Bush and John McCain—in pushing
for fundamental reform in the way campaigns are funded.

This issue is not a left-wing issue—and it has never really been a
left-wing issue. Indeed, read the words of the political father of the
modern conservative movement, Senator Barry Goldwater (R-Ariz.,
1953–1965, 1969–1987):

> When the power of determining the winners of elections
> is lodged in the hands of a few rich persons or groups, who
> are not accountable for their actions, no way is left to control
> them. This is the road to anarchy.... The survival of free elec-
> tions, the purity of our electoral process, and the effective per-
> formance of government duties are endangered by unlimited
> expenditures.... One very drastic change has occurred since
> the Supreme Court made its decision in early 1976. Campaign
> spending has skyrocketed. Total election spending in the nation
> has doubled and the end is nowhere in sight.... As vital as free
> speech is...the argument was not made forcefully enough to
> convince the Supreme Court that what is at stake is the integ-
> rity of the entire political process. The success of our national
> experiment with self-rule is on the line.[4]

And this "old school" conservative thinking is being matched
by new school conservatives as well. Here's Republican John Bohlinger, lieutenant governor of Montana:

> Republicans should leap to the forefront of this movement and
> embrace a true conservatism, one that preserves, protects and
> defends our system of government, rather than undermining it
> by pretending money is speech and corporations are people.
> Frankly, we could use an issue that reminds people we're on
> their side, not that of the special interests. There is nothing

more important or more sacred to our constitutional form of government than our ability to protect the rights of individual citizens to participate freely in the selection of their representatives. It is time for more Republicans to stand and be counted in this critical fight for the Republic.[5]

But the single political event that gives me most hope is the launch of the group Take Back Our Republic, headed by one of the campaign directors in David Brat's upset campaign. Brat ousted House Majority Leader Eric Cantor in a primary fight in 2014. His most powerful charge against Cantor was that Cantor had become a "crony capitalist," spending more time raising money on Wall Street than in his district in Virginia. (After his "retirement," Cantor took a position at an investment banking house, earning $3.4 million a year.[6]) One of the leaders in that campaign, John Pudner, now leads Take Back Our Republic, rallying Republicans across the country to the very same charge that defeated Cantor. At the very least we can say that even if the media thought of this as a left-wing issue in 2007, there is a growing and vibrant movement on the Right that has now claimed this issue, too.

I am not saying I agree with everything these authors have written (though I wish I could write as powerfully, and successfully, as they have). And I do think there is an unwillingness among some of these authors (though certainly not Painter, Potter, Pudner, or McKinnon) to confront the way we fund campaigns as the root cause of this disaster.

But the acknowledgment of this corruption by at least those who live outside the Beltway is spreading across the political divide. Republican state legislatures have passed resolutions calling for an amendment to overturn *Citizens United* (sixteen as of this writing); Republican state legislators have cosponsored successful calls for an Article V convention to address *Citizens United* (five as of this writing). Polls consistently find broad support for reform among Republicans as well as Democrats.[7] Even the lawyer who has done more to undermine campaign finance regulations—James

Bopp—has now acknowledged that he supports the public funding of elections.[8]

All this is enormous progress. And against this background, the
argument of this chapter seems almost quaint. But the arc of this
chapter still captures the essence of the conservative argument. It
is more colorfully made by Schweizer, Lewis, and Cost. It is more
comprehensively made by Painter. It is more authentically made by
Charles Murray. But in its core, it is this, now updated with the new
data provided by the past five years of experience.

The most important political movement in the second half of the
twentieth century began in 1964. A wildly popular Democratic
president, Lyndon Baines Johnson, was not going to be defeated.
The Republican Party therefore let the nomination go to the least
likely Republican to win, Arizona's Senator Barry Goldwater. Goldwater waged a campaign to mark out a new political movement.
His ideals resonated with just a few then. But they were the seeds
of a revolution for the Republican Party, at least when properly cul-
tivated by Ronald Reagan a decade later.

Reagan's first run for the presidency was also a defeat. On
November 20, 1975, he announced he would challenge a wildly
unpopular president of his own party, Gerald Ford. No one knows
for sure whether Reagan really thought he could win. But no one
expected that he would come so close to dislodging a sitting president. In 1980 he was the logical pick for his party's nomination. He
easily defeated the unpopular incumbent, Jimmy Carter.

People forget how important ideas were to Ronald Reagan. By
the end of his term, his opponents had painted him as little more
than an actor on a very important stage. But I doubt we have had a
president in the past fifty years who more carefully and completely
thought through a philosophy for governing and government.
Reagan was more an academic than even the professor president,
Barack Obama. Whether you like his ideas or not, they were ideas.

If you doubt my claim, then just listen to the extraordinary collection of radio lectures Reagan delivered between January 1975

and October 1979. Said to have been written completely by Reagan himself, scrawled on yellow legal pads in his office in Pacific Palisades, California, without the help of aides or clerks, these thousand-plus three-minute shows mapped a series of arguments about the major issues of the day. They were not cheap shots at current events. They were not fluffy rhetoric masking empty ideas. They were instead conclusive evidence of a president with a plan. Again, ideas.

At the core of these ideas was a suspicion of government. Again and again, Reagan returned to the theme of a government gone wild. His claim was not that bureaucracies were filled with evil souls or idiots. The problem, instead, was good intentions gone bad. And not because the bureaucrats didn't work hard enough (though Reagan didn't often predicate "energy" of government employees). It was instead because there was something inevitable about the failure of big government. We needed a world where people relied more on themselves, Reagan argued. A world where government helped too much was a world where people did too little. Liberty, like muscle, had to be exercised. The "Nanny State" would inevitably weaken liberty, good intentions notwithstanding.

Lost liberty, however, wasn't Reagan's only concern. He worried as well about an inevitable inertia within big government. Once we let government get too large, Reagan feared, we would inevitably lose control of a certain political, or public choice, dynamic. As Reagan described, quoting (who he said was) Alexander Fraser Tytler: "A democracy cannot exist as a permanent form of government. It can only exist until the voters discover that they can vote themselves largesse from the public treasury. From that moment on, the majority always votes for the candidate promising the most benefits from the public treasury with the result that a democracy always collapses over loose fiscal policy."[9]

As a prediction, I take it that most would agree with Reagan in at least this respect: We have driven our government to the brink of bankruptcy. Total debt held by the public today is greater than $13 trillion.[10] That number will increase by between $1 trillion and

$2 trillion each year until 2020 at least. If it does, then by 2020, half of federal tax revenue will go simply to servicing the debt.[11] "Prudence" is not our middle name.

Yet however strongly we can agree with where things went, with all due respect to the most important political figure in my lifetime, we should push a bit more to understand just why things went where they went.

Reagan spoke as if the engine driving our inevitable destruction were the rapaciousness of the masses and the bureaucrats—the masses, as they "vote themselves largesse out of the public treasury"; the bureaucrats, as they relentlessly pushed to regulate an ever greater scope of human activity.

When you look to the causes of the massive explosion in government debt, however, it's hard to see "the masses" as responsible for much of anything. Instead, the overwhelming dynamic in income in America over the past two decades has been rising inequality, which "government taxes and benefits have actually exacerbated[—]an outcome witnessed in virtually no other nation."[12] Sure, the Medicare Prescription Drug, Improvement, and Modernization Act was designed to help the middle class. But Part D was a $49.3 billion gift to big PhRMA.[13] Sure, health care reform will help millions of uninsured, but it was also a $250 billion gift to PhRMA and the insurance industry.[14] Sure, Obama pledged $700 billion to save Wall Street and another $800 billion to stimulate the economy. But it was the banks that received the vast majority of that bailout (and more important, the $9 trillion of effectively zero-interest loans from the Fed). Fewer than $75 billion was ever intended to go to homeowners, and in the end, just over half of that did.[15] The Home Affordable Modification Program was expected to aid 4 million owners avoid foreclosure. "By the end of [2014], only about 1.5 million owners had received a permanent modification."[16] Of the $1 billion committed to the FHA's refinancing program, less than $65 million was spent as of May 2015.[17] As TARP's special inspector general, Christy Romero, wondered in 2014: "The question becomes: Will Treasury help them get back on their feet in the same way it helped the banks get back on their feet?"[18] Is there any wonder about the answer?

The engine behind this spending, or at least the most horsepower, came not from the masses, but from the special interests. And these interests could leverage their power to achieve this rapaciousness because—in part at least—of the "self-reinforcing cycle of mutual financial dependency" between members of Congress and the lobbyists, as the American Bar Association's Lobbying Task Force put it.[19]

Reagan couldn't see this in the early 1970s when his philosophy was finally set. The dynamic hadn't quite taken hold. No doubt there was "rent seeking"—efforts by special interests to secure favors through the government that they couldn't get through the free market. But then, the level of this rent seeking was nothing close to the level that is now the new normal. It's not the game that has changed. It is the scale. Reagan can be forgiven for missing this scale.

Likewise with the alleged rapaciousness of bureaucrats: It's easy to see where Reagan's fear came from. In the early 1970s, it was a Republican, Richard Nixon, who had established the Environmental Protection Agency (EPA), the Occupational Safety and Health Administration (OSHA), the Consumer Product Safety Commission (CPSC), and the Mining Enforcement and Safety Administration (MESA). As these regulators got going, there was a wide range of new stuff regulated. That flurry of activity could well have seemed like a trend. As if the agencies would take off, regulating untethered to the mother ship.

But agencies can regulate only as far as Congress allows. And as it turns out, the reasons that Congress might have for allowing the reach of regulation to grow are more than a simple pro-regulatory bias.

We'll see this point more in the pages that follow. But for now, imagine a follower of Ronald Reagan who wants to achieve three core Reagan objectives. First, she wants to shrink the size of government. Second, she wants to simplify the U.S. tax system. Third, she wants to make sure that markets are allowed to be efficient.

What would block this Reaganite's work? What within the current economy of influence that is DC would make these changes practically impossible?

1. Making Government Small

When Al Gore was vice president, his policy team had a proposal to deregulate the Internet. As a "network of networks," the Internet lives atop other physical networks. In 1994, some of those networks were telephone networks; some were (promised to be) cable networks. The bits running on the telephone lines (both the dial-up connections and DSL) were governed by Title II of the Communications Act of 1934. The bits running on cable lines were regulated by Title VI.

Title II and Title VI are very different regulatory regimes. One has an extensive regulatory infrastructure (Title II); the other has a very light (with respect to access at least) regulatory infrastructure (Title VI). So Gore's idea was to put both kinds of Internet access under the same regulatory title, Title VII, and to give that title the smallest regulatory footprint it could have. Not no regulation, but much less regulation than is contemplated today by "network neutrality" advocates.

Gore's team took the idea to Capitol Hill. The Hill didn't like the idea. As his chief lobbyist for the idea recounted to me, "Hell no! If we deregulate these guys, how are we going to raise any money from them?"

As I said, Reagan often spoke as if it were the bureaucrats who were pushing to increase the size of government. These bureaucrats would push and push and push until they regulated absolutely everything they could.

What Reagan didn't think about was how members of Congress—even Reagan Republicans—might themselves become the problem. How Republicans and Democrats alike have an interest in extending the reach of regulation, because by increasing the range of regulated interests, you increase the number who have an interest in trying to influence federal regulation. For how is that influence exercised? Through the gift economy enabled by Santa, the lobbyist. And through, as Peter Schweizer puts it, the extortion lobby of campaign funding.

Now, of course no one would say that Congress regulates simply for the purpose of creating fund-raising targets—though that
was the clear implication of Ryan Grim and Zach Carter's story
about the perennial battles among potentially large funders that
get waged in Congress.[20] But souls on the Right—especially those
enamored of incentive theories of human behavior—should recognize that the cause of growing government is more likely tied to
Congress's thinking about the targets of fund-raising than bureaucrats angling to increase the scope of their work. Conservatives
should see that having lots of targets of regulation is actually a good
way to have lots of targets for fund-raising. And thus, so long as
fund-raising is a central obligation of members of Congress, there is
a conflict between the interests of small government activists and
the interests of the fund-raising-dependent congressmen.

This point is even clearer when you think about it from the
perspective of the targets of this fund-raising. According to one
survey, almost 60 percent of Americans believe that when members of Congress meet with regulators and other government
officials, "they do so to help their friends and hurt their political
opponents."[21] This was Schweizer's point in *Extortion*. That fact
produces "fear," his study concludes, in the minds of business leaders. That "fear . . . drives most business leaders to contribute to campaigns. It's also why most say donors get more than their money's
worth back for their political 'investments.' "[22]

Martin Schram asked former members about that fear. As he
describes it:

> I asked: "Just what do you suppose the lobbyist is thinking
> when he or she gets a telephone call from a senator or repre-
> sentative serving on a committee that oversees the lobbyist's
> special interest—and the member asks for a large contribu-
> tion?" . . . . When . . . pressed . . . the members pondered it, and
> then often voiced the same basic, obvious conclusion: "The
> lobbyist must figure that he or she has no choice but to
> contribute—or risk being shut out."[23]

This dynamic is common. One Joyce Foundation study found that "four fifths of [individual donors] said that office holders regularly pressured them for contributions."[24] Almost 84 percent of corporations reported that candidates pressured them for contributions at least occasionally; 18.8 percent said this happened frequently.[25] Even the reformers reportedly practice this extortion. As Clawson, Alan Neustadtl, and Mark Weller describe, one "PAC officer reported that though John Kerry (Democrat–Massachusetts) makes a public issue of not accepting PAC contributions, his staff had nonetheless called the corporation to say that Kerry expected $5,000 in personal contributions from the company's executives."[26] It is for this reason that my colleague Rob Sitkoff concludes that the best justification for bans on corporate giving in politics is to avoid the extortion by politicians of corporate wealth.[27]

"The longer I stay in Washington," reporter Jeff Birnbaum writes, "the more I believe the protection-money racket is a good metaphor for what a lot of campaign giving is about."[28] A protection racket, or a gift economy—you pick, but each of which depends upon the other side's having something to give. And the key for reformers on the Right to see is that the more the government's fingers are in your business, the more the politicians have to "give." "Donors coerce politicians," as Clawson, Alan Neustadtl, and Mark Weller put it, "and politicians coerce donors."[29]

The same dynamic explains the organization of Congress. Newt Gingrich "believed that the more committees and subcommittees a person can be on, the more attractions they can acquire to present to contributors."[30] Of course, as I've already reported, the attendance at hearings of those committees has also fallen off dramatically. But that's consistent with an account of the growth of committees that looks more to the influence of committee membership on potential funders than to the importance of the actual work of the committees. As Martin Schram reported after interviewing former members of Congress, "Lawmakers freely acknowledged that they and their colleagues often sought assignments to certain 'cash cow' committees primarily because members of those committees are able to raise large amounts of campaign money with little effort."[31] Here is the purest example of regulating to raise money, open and notorious in the current context of Congress.

The lesson is simple: Getting a smaller government is difficult enough. Getting a smaller government when members have a direct financial interest in a bigger one might well be impossible.

2. Simple Taxes

It has been a central plank of the Republican Party since before Ronald Reagan that our system taxes too much, and too complexly. Simpler, "lower taxes" has been the common and consistent refrain. Of course, sometimes that refrain has been translated into lower taxes, at least for some. But the aspirations of many on the Right (and sometimes even on the Left, such as Jerry Brown in the 1992 presidential election) that we move to a flat tax, so simple it could be completed on a postcard, have not been realized.

Why? Who benefits from complex taxes? And how could that benefit possibly outweigh a universal push for simplicity?

To understand the nature of tax law in America, you have to understand one simple point: Complexity is a feature, not a bug. From the perspective of those closest to crafting the code, complexity offers a host of opportunities that simplicity simply can't. Some of those opportunities are legitimate: the chance to better target taxing to achieve economic goals. But many are completely illegitimate. And for the illegitimate, when simplicity is pushed, complexity pushes back harder.

The most obvious, if most trivial, example of this is the very system for collecting taxes. In 2005, the State of California started experimenting with a system they called "ReadyReturn" (now called "CalFile"). The ReadyReturn system treated taxes the way Visa treats your credit card bill. Rather than demanding that you fill out a form listing all the times you used your Visa over the prior month, and then sending a check to Visa for the total, Visa sends you a bill that lists all the charges you made, and the amount Visa thinks you owe it. Of course, you're free to challenge any charge on the bill. Credit card companies are pretty good about removing them. But obviously, given that Visa knows every charge you've made, it makes more sense for them to fill out your bill than for you.

Advocates for the ReadyReturn asked, "Why aren't taxes the same?" For the vast majority of taxpayers, the government, like Visa, knows exactly how much the taxpayer owes. Wages are reported to the government by employers. Interest and dividend payments are reported by banks. For most Americans, that's all there is to the annual tax ritual. So why not a system that sent the taxpayer a draft tax form that was already filled out? As with the Visa statement, the taxpayer would be free to challenge it. But for the vast majority of taxpayers, no change would ever be needed.

Not necessarily a postcard, but just as simple.

In 2005, following a plan sketched by Stanford law professor Joe Bankman, California implemented an experimental system like this for taxpayers with just one employer and no complicated deductions. The reviews were raves. As one report put it: "Most of the taxpayers who voluntarily participated in a test run of the state's ReadyReturn program said it alleviated anxiety, saved time and was something government ought to do routinely. More than 96 percent said they would participate again."[32]

So the following year, the state taxing authorities decided to expand the experiment. But very quickly, they hit a wall. Strong legislative opposition was growing to oppose this effort at tax simplification.

Why? From whom? Well, not surprisingly, from those who benefit most from a world where taxes are complex: consumer tax software makers, who sell programs to consumers to make completing complex taxes easier.[33] Leaders in the California legislature blocked a broad-based rollout of this immensely popular improvement in the efficiency of the California tax system because it would hurt the profits of businesses who sold software to make California's existing and inefficient tax system more efficient.

Now, again, this is small potatoes. And it has nothing directly to do with Congress (though a similar program at the federal level has been stalled at the IRS for similar reasons). But it illustrates the discipline we need to adopt if we're to understand why obvious problems don't get fixed. Sometimes problems pay. When they pay enough, those who benefit will work to block their being fixed. Such is how a vetocracy works.

This is a lesson we've seen before. But the more invidious story about complex taxes is actually quite a bit different, and much more significant.

The taxes that most of us think about are quite general. Most pay the same sales tax. And while the rates for income taxes are different depending upon your income, the impression the system gives is that broad classes of taxpayers pay the same basic rates. The tax code, to the uninformed, is a set of rules. Rules are meant to apply generally.

In fact, our tax code is riddled with the most absurd exceptions. Special rates that apply to "all corporations incorporated on January 12, 1953, in Plymouth, Massachusetts, with a principal place of business in Plymouth, employing at least 300 employees as of 2006"—that is, a case where "all" means "one." Special exceptions to depreciation rules, or to deduction limitations.

These exceptions are proposed and secured by lobbyists. Indeed, lobbyist firms specialize in providing the "service" of securing these special benefits. The firm Williams and Jensen, for example, advertises that it has "the primary mission of advancing the tax policy interests of clients" and claims to have a "results-oriented approach," including "enacting legislative proposals to achieve a tax purpose, or alternatively revising or opposing existing proposals that would harm clients," and "securing transition rules or appropriate relief when Congress adopts tax law changes."[34] A paper by Brian Richter and his colleagues demonstrates convincingly one clear example of such a special tax benefit that gave one (and only one) NASCAR facilities firm accelerated tax depreciation for their racetrack construction projects. The company secured that benefit through about $400,000 in fees paid to the lobbyist firm.[35] Richter's paper then provides an incredible empirical analysis of lobbying disclosure data to show that "firms that lobby are able to accelerate their tax depreciation at faster rates than firms that do not lobby."[36]

In light of this finding, it is not "surprising that [corporations] spend...money on lobbying since it has a quantifiable payoff in at least one important area, taxes."[37] For firms spending an average of $779,945 on lobbying a year, "an increase of lobbying expenditures by 1% only costs the mean firm $7,799 over its prior year lobbying expenditures; the tax benefits it receives range from $4.8M to $16M."[38] That's a 600 percent to 2,000 percent return—not bad for government work!

This, too, is something we've seen before. Yet it is just the first step in a two-part dance that, unless stopped, will drive our taxing system into bankruptcy.

The key to the dance is this: When you get a targeted tax benefit, you don't get to keep it forever. Instead, because of the rules governing how our budget gets drafted (so-called "PAYGO rules"),[39] each of these special benefits "sunsets" after a limited period. Because of these sunsets, each must be reconsidered every time a budget gets drafted.

Sunsets sound like a good idea. Indeed, some seem to treat them as a panacea for all the ills of a government. But when you begin to think more carefully about the obvious incentives, or political economy, that sun-setting creates, the virtues become a bit more ambiguous. For every time a "targeted tax benefit" is about to expire, those who receive the benefit have an extraordinarily strong incentive to fight to keep it. Indeed, we can say precisely how much they should be willing to pay to keep it. If the tax benefit is worth $10 million to the company, they should be willing to spend up to $10 million to keep it.

Professor Rebecca Kysar has framed the point most effectively in the context of "tax extenders"—the term used for temporary tax provisions. In a paper published in 2006 in the *Georgia Law Review*, she described the obvious (though apparently missed by those who created these sunsets) incentives a system of sunsets produces. As she wrote, "The continual termination of certain tax benefits and burdens creates occasions for politicians to more easily extract votes and campaign contributions from parties affected by the threatened provision."[40]

They do this by "increas[ing] the amount of rent available for extortion."[41] (Remember, "rent" refers to the surplus produced by government regulation, which different interests fight over—with the interest at issue here including the politician.) Increasing "extortion"-inducing "rents" produces only one thing: more extortion!

That wasn't exactly the purpose of these sunsets, either when pressed generally (as they were, most importantly, by President Carter) or specifically in the context of taxes. Indeed, the first tax extenders were created as a genuine compromise to test whether a controversial predication about tax revenue was true. In 1981, Congress enacted Reagan's idea of a credit for research and development. Some on the Left doubted the credit would produce the revenue the Reaganites predicted. As a compromise, the credit was made temporary, so that the actual effect could be measured.[42]

Harmless enough—as were other original sunsets for tax provisions, all either experiments or addressing a temporary problem (such as the benefits granted to employees working in or near the World Trade Center affected by the attack on 9/11).[43] But if the road to hell is paved with good intentions, then the paving here has certainly worked. For the numbers should give us a clue as to why these intended sunsets were never actually going to happen. In the first twenty-five years of the life of tax sunsets, only two were allowed to expire—and one of those was renewed in the next session of Congress, with a retroactive gift given to cover the lapse.[44]

The lie to this game becomes clear, Kysar argues, when you look again at the very first "tax extender." For whatever skepticism there was at the beginning, most economists agree that this Reagan idea was a brilliant one. The tax credit really did produce more growth and revenues than it cost. It was perfectly tuned to induce growth and investment—precisely the purpose any such benefit would have.

So once that point had been proven, why didn't Congress just make it permanent? We had run the experiment. The data showed that the benefit made good economic sense. Why go through the game of renewing a good idea every two years?

The answer, Kysar suggests, has lots to do with the nature of the beneficiaries.[45] "The principal recipients of the research credit," Kysar writes, "are large U.S. manufacturing corporations." In many cases, the credit "cuts millions of dollars from the tax returns of a single corporation." So, obviously "these business entities are more than willing to invest in lobbying activities and campaign donations to ensure the continuance of this large tax savings."[46]

And they do. And the politicians they make these donations to have recognized this. And the lobbyists with clients eager to ensure that these extenders are extended have recognized this. As the Institute for Policy Innovation, a libertarian think tank, put it, describing the research and development tax credit:

Congress allows the credit to lapse until another short extension is given, preceded of course by a series of fund-raisers and speeches about the importance of nurturing innovation. Congress essentially uses this cycle to raise money for re-election, promising industry more predictability the next time around.[47]

These flashes of recognition have now produced one of the most efficient machines for printing money for politicians that Washington has ever created—by focusing and practicing and concentrating the money to inspire ever more tax burdens on those who don't organize well (you and me) so as to fund ever-lessening tax burdens on those who organize perfectly well (the largest corporations and the very rich). Mancur Olson would not have been happy that he was so right.[48]

The pattern is obvious. As Kysar quotes one lobbyist:

With the extenders, you know you always have someone who will help pay the mortgage. You go to the client, tell them you're going to fight like hell for permanent extension, but tell them it's a real long shot and that we'll really be lucky just to get a six-month extension. Then you go to the Hill and strike a deal for a one-year extension. In the end, your client thinks you're a hero and they sign on for another year.[49]

The cost of this game is only growing. In December 2010, the *Wall Street Journal* reported on "extender mania." As they described, in the 1990s there were "fewer than a dozen" tax extenders in the U.S. tax code.[50] As of 2010, there were more than 140. The *Journal*, however, didn't even notice the dynamic at the core of Kysar's argument. But to you, it should be obvious. The system is learning. It is evolving, and developing an ever-more-efficient way to create the incentive for people to contribute to campaigns, by creating a mechanism that threatens a tax increase unless a reprieve can be bought. At least among those who can afford the reprieve (meaning the lobbyists and the funders), you can be certain that that reprieve will be bought. December 2010 saw the huge battle over whether "Bush tax cuts" would be extended for the very rich. But that was just a small part of the struggle that was actually going on. It was instead a gaggle of special benefits that got magically extended, through a dance that included billions spent on campaigns and lobbyists by those who got the special benefit.

This "extender mania" was not cured by Kysar's insightful article. As Howard Gleckman wrote for *Forbes*, after describing the history of particular extensions:

> If you are a lobbyist, this history represents scalps on your belt (and client fees in your pocket). If you are a member of Congress, it is the gift that keeps on giving—countless Washington reps and their clients attending endless fundraisers, all filling your campaign coffers, election after election.[51]

And thus have we produced the inverse of the world that Reagan predicted when "quoting" Tytler. But with us, at least in the context of taxes, the problem is not the voters' voting themselves "largesse out of the public treasury." The problem is Congress's learning how it can threaten the richest in our society with higher taxes, so as to get them to give the endless campaign cash Congress needs. So, modifying Tytler just a bit, we could say:

> A democracy cannot exist as a permanent form of government. It can only exist until the voters [congressmen] discover they can vote themselves largesse out of the public treasury [by playing around with the tax code]. From that moment on, the majority [in Congress] always votes [to sunset the tax benefits of] the candidate [the citizens and corporations] promising the most benefits from [to] the[ir campaign] treasury—with the result that democracy always collapses over loose [tax] policy.

New York real estate mogul Leona Helmsley famously said, "We don't pay taxes. Only the little people pay taxes."[52] Now you have a sense just why.

"But what about Reagan's 1986 tax reform?" you ask (at least if you're fifty-plus and remember that reform). "You've already called it his most important tax legislation. Didn't it radically simplify that tax code? Doesn't that prove your theory wrong?"

Would that it did.

Reagan's 1986 reform was brilliant. It was bipartisan, and real reform. It eliminated a world of tax breaks and special deals. It seemed to signal (to the hopelessly naive at least) that the special interests had lost. Reagan the reformer (with the help of key Democrats in Congress) had radically transformed the mother of all special-interest legislation: the tax code.

Almost overnight, however, everything undone by the 1986 reform was replaced. As Hacker and Pierson describe, "If you take a good look at the tax code now, you'll see that it is chock-full of new tax breaks, far more expensive than the ones eliminated with such fan fare."[53]

I once was on a conservative talk show, talking about just these issues. "You're wrong," the Glenn Beck wanna-be scolded me, "all our problems would be solved if we had a flat tax."

"Maybe," I responded. "But how are you going to get a flat tax? What congressmen are going to give up the benefits they get from having a bunch of rich people and corporations coming to them each year begging for more tax benefits?"

The tax system is many things. It is first a revenue system for our government. But it is also, if only indirectly, a revenue system for congressional campaigns. The critical insight here is to see just how complexity in the system is an enabler of the latter, even if it is intended to be the former. It is because no one understands the system that targeted benefits are relatively cost-free to those who give them. No one has the time even to recognize how this dynamic shifts the tax burden to those who can least defend against it. And more important for those who want a simpler tax system: Too few see how this dynamic ensures that simplicity is never achieved. One tax rate for everyone would give no one a special reason to write a check to their congressman. That's all you need to know to understand why we're never going to get one tax rate for everyone. So long as tax favors can inspire campaign funds, the game of tax favors will continue.

This same insight points to the most egregious feature of the current tax system: its incredible tilt to the tax interests of the wealthiest. The Congressional Budget Office calculated that the top 1 percent of earners got 17 percent of the tax benefits "from credits and deductions"; the top 20 percent got 50 percent "of the benefits overall."[54] The "top tax deductions" cost the Treasury close to $1 trillion each year.[55] That's a lot of potential lobbying money to protect the existing benefits!

Thus again we could say: Getting a system of simpler taxes is difficult enough. Getting a system of simpler taxes when Congress has a direct financial interest in complexity might well be impossible.

3. Keeping Markets Efficient

Theorists and principled souls on the Right are free-market advocates. They are convinced by Hayek and his followers that markets aggregate the will of the public better than governments do. This

doesn't mean that governments are unnecessary. As Rajan and
Zingales put it in their very strong pro-free-market book, *Saving
Capitalism from the Capitalists* (2003), "Markets cannot flourish
without the very visible hand of the government, which is needed
to set up and maintain the infrastructure that enables participants
to trade freely and with confidence."[56] But it does mean that a society should try to protect free markets, within that essential infrastructure, and ensure that those who would achieve their wealth
by corrupting free markets don't.

Yet often the biggest danger to free markets comes not so much
from antimarket advocates (the Communists and worse!) as from
strong and successful market players eager to protect themselves
from the next round of strong and successful market players. As
Rajan and Zingales describe:

> Capitalism's biggest political enemies are not the firebrand
> trade unionists spewing vitriol against the system but the
> executives in pin-striped suits extolling the virtues of competi-
> tive markets with every breath while attempting to extinguish
> them with every action.[57]

The perpetual danger is that this competition will be "distorted
by incumbents,"[58] because of an obvious fact not about markets,
but about humans: "Those in power...prefer to stay in power.
They feel threatened by free markets"[59]—even if it was free markets that gave them their power!

This is not a new point. Adam Smith, founding father of the
modern free-market movement (even if, like most founding fathers,
his work is only indirectly and partially understood by those who
follow him most vigorously), famously condemned the very heroes
of free-market wealth:

> People of the same trade seldom meet together, even for merri-
> ment and diversion, but the conversation ends in a conspiracy
> against the public, or in some contrivance to raise prices.[60]

It was from this recognition that Smith offered his rule for interpreting any proposal by successful incumbents for regulating the
market. Such proposals, Smith said, "ought never to be adopted, till
after having been long and carefully examined, not only with the
most scrupulous, but with the most suspicious attention."[61]

For such proposals "come...from an order of men, whose interest is never exactly the same with that of the public, who generally have an interest to deceive and even oppress the public, and
who accordingly have, upon many occasions, both deceived and
oppressed it."[62]

Thus, as an example, Rajan and Zingales point to Congress's aid
for the tourism industry after 9/11: "The terrorist attacks affected the
entire tourism industry. But the first legislation was not relief for the
hundreds of thousands of taxi drivers or restaurant and hotel workers, but for the airlines, which conducted an organized lobbying
effort for taxpayer subsidies."[63]

Principled souls on the Right thus worry about how to protect,
as Rajan and Zingales put it, capitalism from the capitalists. As Rajan
writes in his own work, "The central problem of free-enterprise
capitalism in a modern democracy has always been how to balance
the role of the government and that of the market. While much
intellectual energy has been focused on defining the appropriate
activities of each, it is the interaction between the two that is a central source of fragility."[64]

This is a worry because there are only two things we can be certain of when talking of free markets: first, that new innovation will
challenge old; and second, that old innovation will try to protect
itself against the new. Again and again, across history and nations,
the successful defend their success in whatever way they can.
Principles—such as "I got here because of a free market; I shouldn't
interfere with others challenging me by interfering with a free
market"—are good so long as they don't actually constrain. Once
they constrain, the principles disappear. And once they disappear,
the previously successful use whatever means, including government, to protect against the new. This was one of the problems the

Progressives fought against: "To destroy this invisible government, to dissolve the unholy alliance between corrupt business and corrupt politics is the first task of the statesmanship of the day."[65] This is one of the battles that should join progressives of the Left and free-market advocates on the Right.

James Bessen makes a similar point about how the way we fund campaigns affects innovation. In an essay published in *Foreign Affairs*,[66] Bessen writes:

> Government policies have, across the board, increasingly favored powerful interest groups at the expense of promising young start-ups, stifling technological innovation.

"The root of the problem," Bessen writes:

> is the corrosive influence of money in politics. As more intense lobbying and ever-greater campaign contributions become the norm, special interests are more able to sway public officials.

Bessen's examples are many (followed up with even more evidence in a book published in 2015, *Learning by Doing*[67]).

Defense Department procurement, for example, used to favor "a diverse group of private firms, including start-ups and university spinoffs." Over the past few years, however, that has changed as "procurement has strayed from this successful formula. Instead of awarding contracts to start-ups and spinoffs, the Pentagon has favored traditional defense contractors." The reason? "Large defense contractors have the money and influence to secure lucrative government contracts."

Likewise, with patents. Start-ups have suffered, Bessen writes, because of the "proliferation of patent litigation." That growth began after Congress ("after persistent lobbying by patent lawyers") created a special patent court to enforce patent claims. Since that change, patent litigation has surged: "A 2013 study by the Government Accountability Office found that the number of defendants in patent lawsuits more than doubled between 2007 and 2011; software patents accounted for 89 percent of the increase."

Some of these suits defend appropriate rights appropriately. But many are the work of "patent trolls." Bessen offers this extreme example:

> In the early 1980s, for example, one inventor developed a kiosk for retail stores that could produce music tapes from digital downloads, filing a patent for an "information-manufacturing machine" at "a point of sale location." A patent troll named E-Data later acquired the patent and interpreted it to cover all sorts of digital e-commerce, making millions of dollars from suits against more than 100 companies.

These lawsuits are expensive. Bessen calculates that in 2011, the roughly 5,000 "firms named as defendants...paid more than $29 billion out of pocket."

That burden, in turn, led many to press for reform to the patent system. The culmination of that push was the America Invents Act of 2011. But despite high hopes, as Bessen describes, "The new law did little to deter patent trolls or to discourage the vague software patents that allow trolls to abuse the system. In fact, the law granted relief to only one industry: finance." It's no surprise that of the "more than 1,000 lobbyists [who] worked on the bill, including ten former members of Congress, 280 former congressional staffers, and more than 50 former government officials," Wall Street had enough to get the one special favor of the law: relief!

"Politics," Bessen concludes, "is about balancing competing interests. Opposing factions battle one another but ultimately compromise, each getting something it wants." But in the lobbyist-driven battle that defines DC now, quoting Jim Cooper (D-Tenn.; 1983–1995; 2003–), Bessen writes, "The future has no lobbyists." And so the future will have less innovation.

One of the most striking examples—because so blatant—of this protectionism is the story of "Internet Radio."

If you've spent any time on the Net, you've experienced the magic of Internet Radio. Almost every terrestrial radio station has a mirror on the Internet. From your computer or iPhone you can "tune" into literally thousands of stations around the world.

But in the beginning of Internet Radio, it wasn't just existing radio stations that had mirrors on the Net. It was literally hundreds of thousands of music enthusiasts who had launched their own "radio station." These were wanna-be DJs, or experts in some remote domain of music—jazz from 1910 to 1915; the best baroque in Italy. You think of a theme, there was likely to be an Internet Radio station, and hobbyists and amateurs competed with the professional radio stations to serve a growing audience an amazing diversity of creative work.

Until the lawyers showed up. Because of course, broadcasting music triggers copyright law. And copyright law is a favorite tool of protectionists. So in 1995, Congress enacted a special copyright levy on Internet Radio that didn't apply to ordinary radio. And then the government launched a royalty proceeding to determine how much money Internet Radio stations would have to pay.

No one should oppose fair rates for creative work. But the striking part of the Internet Radio story is that, at least for some, the whole purpose of the setting the rates was not to get a "fair" royalty for copyright owners. It was instead to shrink the competition in radio. As I described in my book *Free Culture* (2004), recounting an interview with Alex Alben, vice president for Public Policy at Real Networks:

> The RIAA, which was representing the record labels, presented some testimony about what they thought a willing buyer would pay to a willing seller, and it was much higher. It was ten times higher than what radio stations pay to perform the same songs for the same period of time. And so the attorneys representing the webcasters asked the RIAA, . . . "How do you come up with a rate that's so much higher? Why is it worth more than radio? Because here we have hundreds of thousands of webcasters

who want to pay, and that should establish the market rate, and if you set the rate so high, you're going to drive the small web-casters out of business...."

And the RIAA experts said, "Well, we don't really model this as an industry with thousands of webcasters, we think it should be an industry with, you know, five or seven big players who can pay a high rate and it's a stable, predictable market."[68]

Translation: We want to use the law to knife the baby, so the future of radio (and hence music) is much like the past.

This is the dynamic that Zingales and Rajan were writing about: the incumbents protecting themselves against the challenger. Recognizing the threat of this dynamic is nothing new. Neither is it partisan. As Dean Post writes:

As early as 1894, the irreproachable Elihu Root, a "conservative of conservatives" [and Republican], had proposed amending the New York State Constitution to prohibit corporate campaign contributions and expenditures. "The idea," Root said, "is to prevent the great moneyed corporations from furnishing the money with which to elect members of the legislature of this state, in order that those members of the legislature 5may vote to protect the corporations. It is to prevent the great railroad companies, the great insurance companies, the great telephone companies, the great aggregations of wealth, from using their corporate funds, directly or indirectly to send members of the legislature to these halls, in order to vote for their protection and the advancement of their interests as against those of the public."[69]

Rajan and Zingales offer a range of remedies to secure a free society from this type of market protection. The most interesting I've described: the notion of a political antitrust doctrine, a doctrine that aims at blocking not only inefficient economic behavior, but also concentrations in economic power that could too easily translate into political power. In this, their work echoes Louis Brandeis, who opposed "bigness" not just for (mistaken) economic reasons, but more important, because of the view that "in a democratic society the existence of large centers of private power is dangerous to the continuing vitality of a free people."[70] It also echoes the battles by Presidents Jefferson and Jackson centuries ago, who both fought the first Bank of the United States, because both "saw a powerful bank as a corrupting influence that could undermine the proper functioning of a democratic government."[71]

But the one point that Rajan and Zingales strangely leave aside is the role of money in politics on the capacity for capitalists to corrupt capitalism. So long as wealth can be used to leverage political power, wealth will be used to leverage political power to protect itself. This was Teddy Roosevelt's view: "Corporate expenditures for political purposes... have supplied one of the principal sources of corruption in our political affairs."[72]

But however clever political antitrust might be, a more fundamental response would be to weaken the ability of wealth to leverage political power. Never completely. That would not be possible. But at least enough to weaken the return from rent seeking, perhaps enough to make ordinary innovation seem more profitable.

Any reform that would seek to weaken the ability of wealth to rent-seek would itself be resisted by wealth. So long as private money drives public elections, public officials will work hard to protect that private money. And if you doubt this, look to Wall Street: Never has an industry been filled with more rabid libertarians; but never has an industry more successfully engineered government handouts when the gambling of those libertarians went south. When threatened with our existence, none of us—including principled libertarians—will stand on principle. The Right needs to recognize this as well as the Left.

All three examples point to a step in arguments from the Right that too many too often overlook. I've been in the middle of hundreds of arguments in which someone on the Right (and I was that person for many years) invoked a common meme: something like, "This problem, too, would be solved if we simply didn't have such a big/invasive/expensive government."

Maybe. But the point these three examples emphasize is that you can't simply assume the problem away. If you believe big or expensive government is the problem, then what are you going to do to change it? How are you going to shrink it? What political steps will you take toward the end that you seek?

My sense is that too many on the Right make the same mistake as too many on the Left. They assume that change happens when you win enough votes in Congress. Elect a strong Republican majority, many in the Tea Party believe, and you will elect a government that will deliver the promise of smaller government and simpler taxes—just as activists on the Left thought that they could elect a strong Democratic majority and deliver on the promise of meaningful health care reform, or global warming legislation, or whatever other reform the Left thought it would get.

What both sides miss is that the machine we've evolved systematically thwarts the objectives of each side. The reason for the thwart is different on each side. Change on the Left gets stopped because a strong, powerful private interest uses its leverage to block changes in the status quo. Change on the Right gets stopped because strong, powerful public interests, Congress, work to block any change that would weaken their fund-raising machine.

The point is not that the Right agrees with the Left. They don't. The ends that both sides aim for are different.

But even if the Left and the Right don't share common ends, they do share a common enemy. The current system of campaign funding radically benefits the status quo—the status quo for private interests and the status quo of the Fund-raising Congress.

The same dynamic will thus work against both types of reform. Private interests will flood DC with dollars to block change that affects them. And government interests, as in congressmen, will keep the grip tight on large, intrusive, complicated government, in part because it makes it easier to suck campaign dollars from the targets of regulation.

The existing system will always block the changes that both sides campaign for. Both sides should, therefore, have the same interest in changing this system.

This is not a new point, though it is strange how completely it gets forgotten. In 1999, Charles Kolb, a Republican and former George H. W. Bush administration official, led the Committee for Economic Development (CED) to take a major role in pushing for campaign finance reform. The CED describes itself as "a non-profit, non-partisan business led public policy organization." Since 1942, the CED has pushed for "sustained economic growth." It has been well known for pushing for that growth from a relatively conservative position.

Central to its mission since 1999 has been the argument that the existing system of campaign funding is broken. As it wrote in its first campaign financing report:

> The vast majority of citizens feel that money threatens the basic fairness and integrity of our political system. Two out of three Americans think that money has an "excessive influence" on elections and government policy. Substantial majorities in poll after poll agree that "Congress is largely owned by the special interest groups," or that special interests have "too much influence over elected officials." Fully two-thirds of the public think that "their own representative in Congress would listen to the views of outsiders who made large political contributions before a constituent's views."
>
> These findings, typical of the results of public opinion surveys conducted in recent years, indicate a deep cynicism regarding the role of money in politics. Many citizens have lost faith in the political process and doubt their ability as individuals to make a difference in our nation's political life. Americans see rising campaign expenditures, highly publicized scandals and allegations regarding fundraising practices, and a dramatic growth in unregulated money flowing into elections.[73]

The CED was "deeply concerned about these negative public attitudes toward government and the role of money in the political process." It was "also concerned about the effects of the campaign finance system on the economy and business." For "if public policy decisions are made—or appear to be made—on the basis of political contributions, not only will policy be suspect, but its uncertain and arbitrary character will make business planning less effective and the economy less productive."

The solution, the CED argues, is for business to be less tied to campaign fund-raising. "We wish," as the report states, "to compete in the marketplace, not in the political arena."[74] Because, again, that competition doesn't create wealth or produce new jobs. It just fuels the very rent seeking that all good conservatives should oppose.

The CED has continued its work in this field since the first edition of this book. The organization runs a "Money in Politics Project."[75] In 2013, it commissioned a bipartisan-run nationwide survey of 302 business leaders on money in politics.[76] Here are its key findings—none surprising in light of everything we've seen so far:

- 85 percent say that the campaign finance system is in poor shape or broken;
- 87 percent say that the campaign finance system needs major reforms or a complete overhaul;
- 71 percent believe that major contributors have too much influence on politicians;
- 75 percent say that the U.S. campaign finance system is pay-to-play.

These are business leaders—the people most familiar with what Peter Schweizer calls the "extortion" of the system.[77] Why is there any debate about the need for reform here at all?

CHAPTER 11

How So [Damn Little] Money *Makes Things Worse*

At the start of the Soviet Union, the average salary of members of the Politburo was said to be not far from the salary of the average worker.[1] This equality expressed an ideal within the Soviet system—the ideal that the USSR was a workers' state and that state employees, even leaders, were no better than other workers.

That expression was a lie. While the formal salary of members of the Politburo was close to the average salary for Soviet workers, the effective salary was much, much higher. Members of the Politburo got vacation homes (dachas), access to Western stores, government-issued cars with drivers, foreign publications, better health care, and better opportunities for their kids. Meaning government employees were in effect actually highly paid relative to the average worker, or anyone else in Soviet life. The only way to make more in the Soviet system was to be a criminal (assuming there was a sharp distinction between members of the Politburo and criminals).

America isn't the Soviet Union. But in a weird way, our Congress is quickly becoming a kind of Politburo. Tenure for members of Congress now rivals the average tenure of members of the Politburo. (House: 8.8 years. Senate: 9.7 years[2]; average tenure for Politburo: just over 9 years.[3]) And more troubling is the way that Congress effectively inflates its salary. Through games quite Soviet, many members of Congress live like millionaires, even though their take-home salary is the same as the very best students who graduate from Harvard Law School in their first year practicing law.

Now let me be clear about the criticism I intend this chapter to make. The salaries of key officials in our government strike many as high. Some believe them too high. The last amendment to our Constitution was for the very purpose of blocking any salary increase for members of Congress until after an election. It is a common populist refrain among critics of government that the "bureaucrats" are paid too much. Even worse, members of Congress.

This populist view is wrong. What we know from economics, and from experience with governments across the world, is that if you underpay government officials relative to their talents or their peers, they will find ways to supplement their income. Those supplements are not cost-free, even if they cost the Treasury nothing. They sometimes involve outright bribes. (Norman Ornstein explains the "inexplicable petty corruption of powerhouses like Dan Rostenkowski...by their belief that they were making such immense sacrifices to stay in public service.")[4] But in America, at least with members of Congress and senior members of the administration, that sort of bribery is not the problem. The real danger is that policy gets bent, through the unavoidable influence spread by those who need the favor of government. If, as Congressman Jim Cooper (D-Tenn.; 1983–1995; 2003–) told me, "Capitol Hill has become a farm league for K Street," then no one should doubt that players on a farm league do everything they can to get to the majors.

Yet the purpose of this chapter is not to argue that we should increase the salaries of government officials. We should. But so, too, should people stop smoking and stop "breakfasting" at Dunkin' Donuts. There's a limit to what's possible. I recognize that limit here. I'm not going to fell trees on the fool's errand of trying to persuade you to rally with me to increase Mitch McConnell's pay.

Instead, the point of this chapter is to underline why the fact that we underpay government officials will make it much harder to change how Congress now works. The very mechanisms that we have evolved to compensate for our undercompensated government workers make change through ordinary political means enormously difficult, and, just maybe, impossible.[5]

The Ways We Pay Congress

Some in Congress don't give a squat about how much they're paid. Some don't care because they're millionaires. (Indeed, more than 50 percent of the members of Congress are millionaires, compared with 5 percent of the American public.[6]) Some of them spent millions to get to Congress in the first place. To them, government service is a luxury good. They are proud to serve. They'd be proud to serve even if the salary were zero (or negative—which it is for most who self-fund their campaigns).

Others don't care about how much they're paid because they're married to wealthy spouses. That spousal income is sometimes completely benign. (Senator Ron Wyden's [D-Ore.; 1981–] wife owns the Strand Bookstore in New York City. There are not many policies that get bent by the influence of used-book store owners.) Sometimes it is much less benign. (When Indiana senator Evan Bayh [D-Ind.; 1999–2011] was elected to the U.S. Senate, his thirty-eight-year-old wife, a junior law professor at Butler University and a mid-level attorney at Eli Lilly, got appointed to the board of the insurance company that would become WellPoint. No doubt Susan Bayh is a talented soul. But as the website *TheStreet* commented when the appointment was made, "Her work background at the time she was appointed...would have been surprising, given that she had no insurance experience and was relatively young and inexperienced to serve as a director on a multibillion-dollar board."[7] One can't help wondering whether that appointment would have been made but for the marriage, or whether the policies of the senator weren't affected by the affiliations of the spouse.[8]) But in most cases, these members with wealthy spouses are not likely looking for ways to make things easier financially for themselves.

Finally, some members don't care about the size of their salaries because they come from inexpensive districts, they don't have kids, and they learn to live on the salary that Congress provides. They share an apartment in DC. They come home as frequently as they can.

Put all of these three types of congressmen aside. In what follows, I'm not talking about them.

Instead, think about those who aren't rich, who don't have a high-income-earning spouse, and who don't come from rural West Virginia. Think about a member from Seattle, or Boston, or San Francisco. Imagine that member needs to keep a home in the district, but brings her family to DC. Imagine her spouse is a school-teacher, and they've got three kids. Think about what a member like that does.

There are a number of ways that members like these can cope with the salary they get. Some cut costs by living in their office—literally, sleeping on a couch and showering in the gym. Some simply suck it up, and serve for a relatively short time before returning to private life. And some do something more—by securing a future for themselves that compensates for the (relatively) low pay of their present.

The motives of the members in this group need not be questioned. Many just simply can't afford perpetual service to a low-paying government, at least if they're going to afford to raise a family. Or at least, if they're going to raise a family the way their family might reasonably expect, given their talents and the comparable opportunities. Whatever the pressure, the question I mean to raise is about the work these members do after their life in Congress. Because if their plan is to enter the influence market that DC has become, then they can't help developing a dependency upon that market doing well. It's not just the need to keep future employers happy. That's a possible but, I think, distant concern that would rarely extend its reach into the day-to-day work of the job.

Instead, the real problem is imagining a soul like this voting to destroy a significant chunk of the value of this influence industry—which fundamental reform of the type that I discuss in Chapter 15 would do. For if lobbyists weren't able to channel funds to campaigns, and hence, if congressmen didn't depend upon lobbyists to get them the resources they need to run, then the value of lobbying services would decline. Lobbyists' market power would decline.

And hence the ability of lobbying firms to pay former members of Congress millions would disappear. If "Capitol Hill is a farm league for K Street," then imagine asking players on a minor league baseball team whether salaries for professional baseball players should be capped, and you will quickly get the point.

Of course there are members who would ignore that consequence. Of course there are some who would do the right thing, regardless of how it affected them personally. But fortunately or not, members of Congress are humans. They are much more likely to develop all sorts of rationalizations for keeping alive the system that will keep them millionaires. You think you wouldn't? You think they are so different from you?

Life after Congress is thus one reason why members would be reluctant to think about fundamentally changing the economy of influence that governs DC today.

A second reason is much more contemporary (with a member's tenure), and much more disgusting.

Members of Congress are not members of the Politburo. Unlike with members of the Politburo, the salary of a member of Congress is basically it. They don't get a housing stipend. For most of them there are no fancy government limos driving them from one place to another. There's no summer dacha. There are no free flights on government planes. As for most of us, their salary is their salary.

But unlike for most of us, their salary is not all they get to live on. Rather, members of Congress have perfected a system that allows them to live a life a bit more luxurious than a first-year associate at a law firm. And the way they do this ties directly to the need to raise campaign cash.

Many members of Congress (at least 436, up from 397 in first edition of this book, according to the Center for Responsive Politics)[9] have leadership PACs. A leadership PAC is a political action committee that raises money from individuals, and other PACs, and then spends it to support candidates for office. Members of our Congress stand in the well of the House handing one another checks for up to $5,000. Such checks are the glue that keeps the system together.

Raising money, however, costs money. These costs are the expenses that a leadership PAC incurs. A member of Congress might want to take a potential contributor to dinner. That costs money—especially today in DC, which now has some of the most expensive restaurants in the United States. Or if the member really wants to impress the potential contributor, she might take him on a golfing trip, or to a "retreat" in a work-inducing location such as Oahu. These things cost money, too. So the leadership PAC must raise money to spend money to raise money.

But much of the way the leadership PAC spends its money benefits, in a perverse sort of way, the member of Congress. A member from California, not independently wealthy, with a spouse who doesn't work, and who is trying to raise three kids, doesn't have much money for fancy dinners if the family lives near DC. Even less if the family stays in the district and the member has to maintain two residences.

So how does that member get to go to fancy restaurants?

He sets up a leadership PAC, and all doors are open. As Jeff Birnbaum reports, "More than one lawmaker...was willing to declare almost any lobbyist-paid meal a fund-raiser as long as the host of the dinner didn't just pick up the check but also provided one as well—eventually."[10]

The numbers here are really quite amazing. In the 2010 election cycle, leadership PACs collected more than $44 million in contributions.[11] In 2014, that number climbed above $50 million.[12] But there's no actual obligation that members spend this PAC money on other members. So here are just some of the delicious/disgusting (you pick) tidbits that public records reveal:

"[Thirty] Democrats and 17 Republicans...collected $1.07 million without spending a dime on other candidates."

"A committee created by Rep. Rodney Alexander (R-La.) [2003–2013], called Restore Our Democracy, collected nearly $100,000 this [2010] cycle and spent nearly two-thirds to finance his participation with donors or friends in two Mardi Gras balls....Alexander's committee has not used any funds directly for an election campaign."

Two thirds of the expenditures of then–House minority leader John Boehner (R-Ohio; 1991–) have gone toward fund-raising costs, which included "fine meals and trips to luxurious resorts,"..."including $70,403 at the Ritz-Carlton in Naples [, Florida,] and more than $30,000 at Disney" resorts.

Representative Steny Hoyer (D-Md.; 1981–) spent more than $50,000 on "travel with donors to resorts" in the 2010 election cycle, and $9,800 on entertainment tickets and limousines.

House minority whip Eric Cantor (R-Va.; 2001–2014) raised $2.1 million for his leadership PAC, and spent $136,000 on golf events, baseball games, skiing, resorts, and restaurants. In November 2009 his leadership PAC spent $30,000 on a "Beverly Hills fundraising event."[13]

Representative Charlie Rangel (D-N.Y.; 1971–) used funds from his leadership PAC to commission a portrait of himself.[14]

All this luxury would go away if Congress were to end special-interest fund-raising as the means to getting reelected. Members would have to live on the salary they got. They would have to pay for their own dinners. Holidays would be at Ocean City (New Jersey), not Oahu or the south of Florida.

Now, again, I'm sure there are members of Congress who'd be okay with this. I'm sure many would be happy to make do with the salaries they got.

But I'm equally sure that there are many who recognize that a congressional pay raise is not in the offing, and that living life on $174,000 is not what they bargained for. Some who recognize this might well decide to leave office. But many more would fight the reform of this system to its death.

There's no easy way to figure out if a candidate for Congress is either (a) the sort who's going to be happy living frugally, or (b) the sort who's going to pretend he'll be happy, but then live life taking every advantage he can. Other countries get this, and rather than risk it, they pay their representatives a high, but competitive rate. Ministers in Singapore, for example, rated seventh least corrupt country in the world in 2014 by Transparency International, make about $750,000 a year.[15]

But this problem is not likely to be fixed anytime soon. (And raising salaries without also fixing the way we fund elections would certainly be no solution.) If we're not going to decide that members of Congress make too little, if we're not going to recognize that underpaying people only gets us bad people, or turns good people bad, then the prospect that we're going to get members of Congress to vote to support a new system of campaign finance just got much, much worse. For the choice to make Washington clean is now a choice to make a member poor.

The Benefits of Working for Members

The bigger challenge, however, may not be with the 535 members, or more precisely, the proportion of the 535 who are not rich or who didn't marry rich or who don't live in West Virginia. The bigger challenge may be with their staff, and with the staff of every major regulatory bureaucracy.

Here, again, we've opted for government on the cheap. Staffers on Capitol Hill get paid on average between $30,000, for a staff assistant, and $116,424, for a chief of staff. The maximum salary earned by any staffer is $177,680. (Only one staffer earned this level of pay as of August 2015.)[16] The chairman of the SEC earned $165,300 in 2013.[17] The average starting salary for an attorney at the SEC is slightly over $81,000.[18] By contrast, the starting salary for an analyst working in investment banking on Wall Street with just a bachelor's degree is from $100,000 to $150,000 after bonus.[19] As study after study has concluded, we pay government employees too little.[20] The same is true for state and local governments.[21]

So why, then, do government officials choose to work for so little?

No doubt some of them do it because they believe in public service. They could get a job anywhere, but they work for the government because they want to do something that does something for America. David Walker, the former (and fantastic) comptroller general of the United States is not wanting for employment options. These are people who serve because public service is in their DNA.

There are many souls like this throughout American society. They are soldiers who work for less because they believe they are working for something more. They are teachers who work for less because they believe they are working for something more. Doctors at NIH, lawyers at the Justice Department, federal judges—the government is filled with people who do what they do for reasons other than money. We are fortunate to have such people among us. We should think hard about how to have more.

Not every staffer working on Capitol Hill, however, is working for nothing because she believes in something. And not every regulator at the SEC is earning less than his equal on Wall Street because he believes his work will make society a better place.

Instead, living in the "farm league," some of those people see their time on the Hill, or within major regulatory agencies, as an investment. They work for six or eight years as a staffer to a major committee, then they cash out and become a lobbyist. An experienced staffer leaving Capitol Hill can expect a starting salary of about $300,000 per year. Some senior staff members have been known to secure salary and bonus packages of $500,000 or more. If the senator whom a staffer worked for is still in office, the staffer can receive as much as $740,000.[22] Heads of agencies do much better: In 2011, Michael Powell, former chairman of the FCC, became chief lobbyist for Comcast, and was reported to be making more than $2.2 million per year. In the same year, FCC commissioner

Meredith Attwell Baker left the commission to join Comcast after voting to approve Comcast's merger with NBC Universal.

This gap in salaries is an enormous change. In 1969, a "newly minted lobbyist with solid Capitol Hill experience could count on making a touch more than the $10,000 they earned as congressional staff. Today, the congressional staffer making $50,000 can look at a peer making five or six times that much as a lobbyist."[23]

The prospects are even better if you enter the revolving door. Start your career as an associate at a law firm, leave to spend a few years as a staffer on the Senate Committee on Banking, Housing and Urban Affairs, and return to that law firm as a principal making hundreds of thousands if not millions a year, where you will represent numerous financial institutions before the Senate.[24] "As of 1987, most of the administrative assistants or top congressional staffers in the House spent five and a half years working in Congress." A decade later, the average tenure had fallen by more than 25 percent.[25] In total, 3,600 former congressional aides have "passed through the revolving door."[26]

In both of these types of cases, the government employee traded her experience for cash. And as the amount of cash that gets traded goes up, more and more will enter government service with that trade in mind.

Again, sometimes this trade is completely benign. After World War II, fighter pilots became commercial pilots. They were paid (practically) nothing to risk their lives to protect America. Then they were paid lots more because of the experience they'd earned while serving to protect America. No one thinks that the prospect of becoming a commercial pilot somehow compromised the service of the military pilot. Indeed, to the contrary: the lucrative post-service salary made it easier to get great pilots to serve in the war.

Sometimes, however, that trade is not at all benign.

Consider, for example, the lobbying firm PMA Group, Inc., created and run by staff alumni of Representative John Murtha (D-Pa.; 1974–2010). In 2008, that firm persuaded 104 different House members to add separate earmarks into the defense appropriations bill worth $300 million to PMA Group clients. These same lawmakers have received $1.8 million in campaign donations from the lobbying firm since 2001. When these deals came to light in 2009, the PMA Group closed shop. Its founder, former Murtha aide Paul Magliocchetti, pled guilty to illegally laundering political contributions, and was sentenced to twenty-seven months.[27]

Or consider a second example: When an artist records an album, the artist gets the copyright. For many years, the recording industry has wanted that rule changed, so that the company making the recording, by default, gets the copyright. This is no small matter: For many artists, and their heirs, the copyright to the recording is the most important right they get. In 1999, Mitch Glazier, the chief counsel to the Subcommittee on Courts and Intellectual Property in the House of Representatives, is said to have inserted into a bill of technical corrections to the Copyright Act a fairly fundamental change: an amendment that classified many recordings as "work made for hire" (meaning the record company, not the artist, would by default get the copyright). Immediately after he allegedly did this, Glazier left Capitol Hill and became senior vice president of governmental relations and legislative counsel for the Recording Industry Association of America.[28]

Our government is shot through with examples like this, far beyond the problems with Congress. A huge proportion of the "staffers" who support the military move seamlessly from private defense contractors to the government and back again, keeping their security clearance, doing the same sort of work, but sometimes at a high salary (when private) and sometimes at a low salary (when for the government). The rotation balances out to a very nice salary on average, but many would not be in this service if the private part didn't complement the public.

Again, maybe sometimes this accommodation is completely harmless. Much more often, these relationships earn the insiders something special, whether it is special access to members of Congress that a lobbyist firm then sells to clients, or a special relationship that an ex-staffer can use to influence an enforcement decision, or simple friendship so that their arguments will be given greater credibility than those of others, and can be used to delay action on an issue.[29]

The best evidence of this influence is a paper that studied the effects on a staffer turned lobbyist when the member that former staffer worked for left Congress. Drawing upon the extensive data provided by the lobbying disclosure reports, political scientist Jordi Blanes i Vidal and his colleagues were able to calculate that a lobbyist with experience in the office of a senator sees a 24 percent drop in lobbying revenues immediately after that senator retires.[30]

When you look at these numbers, it is hard to understand them as anything except direct evidence of the channels of influence that the current system buys. In other words, the value of these lobbyists was to a significant extent a function of their connections. But why? Why was the connection so valuable to the firm, if the connection itself wouldn't translate into significant legislative benefit to the clients of the lobbying firm?

There's nothing evil in the story of these staffers turned lobbyists. Or at least, there need be nothing evil. These are not people securing bribes; they are not even necessarily working against the ideals they believe in. Indeed, most of them are doing jobs they love. In this sense, they're living an American dream, honorably and honestly, in the vast majority of cases.

The issue here is not whether these people are good. The issue is whether the system they work within is corrupt. Does it tend to distract members from their constituents? Does it build a dependency that conflicts with the dependency intended?

Of course it does. Or at least, most Americans would be justified in believing it did. This is just another example of how the current system differs fundamentally from the system our Framers intended. It is another example of a difference that matters.

In 2011, when Republicans took control of the House, they purported to "ban earmarks."[31] That ban continued into the next Congress. But despite the formal rule restricting the ability of members to direct federal spending, the rule has apparent leaks. Members still take credit for federal spending, even if the mechanism by which that spending commitment is made has become more obscure.[32]

Eliminating earmarks has certainly not reduced federal spending. But for our purposes, that's not the question. The real issue is whether it undermines the economy of influence that leads to corruption. Jack Abramoff believes it has:

> Eliminating earmarks did almost nothing to reduce out of control federal spending, but it was an important step in the direction of controlling the special interests.[33]

Maybe. Important, no doubt. Effective is something only time will tell.

CHAPTER 12

Two Conceptions of "Corruption"

As I argued in Part I, tweedism is corruption because tweedism systematically denies citizens equal political rights. The remedy for that corruption is to restore equal political rights. And the particular remedy that I have pressed most strongly would restore those rights by publicly funding public elections.

Yet public funding may well not be enough. We have entered the age of the super PAC, and if Congress has no power to limit the super PAC, then all the clean money in the world won't neutralize the incredibly powerful and interested money that is flowing into our politics through super PACs.

I believe Congress does have the power to regulate the super PAC, whether or not it has the power to limit the ability of individuals, corporations, or unions to spend money in elections. And I believe that nothing in the Supreme Court's jurisprudence would stop it from recognizing this power in Congress, even while upholding its decision in *Citizens United*.

The key is the word "corruption." Congress's power over political speech turns on the meaning of the word "corruption." As the Court has held again and again, if a law is targeting "corruption," that law is permissible under the First Amendment, even if it otherwise "abridges speech."

So far, the Court has limited its conception of "corruption" to individual, quid pro quo corruption. But there is a second conception of "corruption" that the Court should also be able to see. Indeed, a conception that especially the conservatives on the Supreme Court should be able to see. That conception does not necessarily reverse *Citizens United*. But it does show why Congress should have the power to limit super PACs. My aim is to make the argument why here.

Among constitutional lawyers and scholars, most will reject the argument I'm about to make. But when I listen to their reasons, I hear more cynicism than reason. We don't believe that the reason the Court does what it does is actually principle or reason anymore. We, or most of us, believe the reason the Court does what it does is simple politics. There are conservative judges and liberal judges, and to know how a case will be decided, these judicial cynics believe, you just have to know how many of each will sit on the panel. We are "like a priesthood," as Roberto Unger wrote more than thirty years ago, "that had lost their faith and kept their jobs." Most of us stand "in tedious embarrassment before cold altars."[1]

I want to be the last naive law professor. And in the argument that follows, I will display that naive faith, by offering an argument to show why the Court could reject super PACs even while embracing *Citizens United*—on the assumption that reason and consistency matter to the Supreme Court, for the conservatives and liberal alike.

Not as a pose, but as a belief, and as an act of respect. The Supreme Court is not, in the sense I have described, corrupt. Quibble as we might about its sensitivity to politics, the Court is a gem of institutional integrity. Trust in the federal courts in America is consistently high, though trust in the Supreme Court has recently fallen.[2] If the Court just reflected a bit on why it had that integrity, it would understand a bit more why it must give Congress the opportunity to secure the same for itself.

"Corruption"

The ordinary meaning of "corruption"—at least when we're speaking of government officials, or public institutions—is clear enough. Corruption means bribery. Taking this (money) in exchange for that (special favor or privilege from the government). Corruption means "quid pro quo," this for that.

In this sense, as I described, Congressman Randy "Duke" Cunningham (R-Calif.; 1991–2005) was corrupt. The government charged that he took over $2.4 million in exchange for securing contracts from the Defense Department. Duke was convicted, and sentenced to eight years and four months in prison.[3]

In this sense, Congressman William J. Jefferson (D-La.; 1991–2009) was corrupt. In a raid on Mr. Jefferson's home, federal agents found $90,000 wrapped in aluminum foil in his freezer. He was charged with receiving up to $400,000 in bribes and alleged to have sought much more.[4] In 2009, he received the largest prison sentence for corruption in the history of the United States Congress: thirteen years. (In the same year, an eighteen-year sentence for conspiracy to possess cocaine was upheld by the 11th Circuit Court of Appeals[5]).

These are both classic instances of bent and bad souls. They are the stuff the U.S. Criminal Code was written for.

And not just the Criminal Code. Since *Buckley v. Valeo* (1976), it has been clear that Congress has the power to do more than just criminalize quid pro quo bribery. It also has the power to ban contributions that might raise the suspicion of quid pro quo bribery. *Buckley* held, and no decision has ever doubted, that Congress has the power to ban large contributions to campaigns, at least when it is reasonable for people to wonder whether those large contributions are really just disguised bribes. As the Court said almost forty years ago:

> Of almost equal concern as the danger of actual quid pro quo arrangements is the impact of the appearance of corruption stemming from public awareness of the opportunities for abuse inherent in a regime of large individual financial contributions. In *CSC* v. *Letter Carriers*, the Court found that the danger to "fair and effective government" posed by partisan political conduct on the part of federal employees charged with administering the law was a sufficiently important concern to justify broad restrictions on the employees' right of

partisan political association. Here, as there, Congress could legitimately conclude that the avoidance of the appearance of improper influence "is also critical...if confidence in the system of representative Government is not to be eroded to a disastrous extent."[6]

Thus, even to avoid just the public's perception that members may be selling their office, Congress has the power to limit the extent to which one person can signal his support (through contributions) for a political candidate.

This is not an insignificant power, because the liberty to contribute to the campaign of another is an important free speech liberty. To be able to say, "I support Mr. Smith," not only in words, but in deeds, by being able to show just how much you support Mr. Smith, is important. That liberty is the freedom to signal intensity, in a way that's credible and real. No government should have the power to remove that liberty. At least not completely.

Yet despite its importance, the Supreme Court has upheld Congress's power to limit that liberty so as to avoid the mere impression that something more than simple praise is going on. So important is it to our political system that the people not reasonably believe corruption is the game that Congress has the power to restrict political speech to avoid this kind of corruption.

Call this type 1 corruption. Type 1 corruption is a *corruption by individuals*. It involves an individual crossing a moral or legal line. It is corruption only if the individual *knows* he is crossing a moral or legal line. It is doing wrong. The Constitution permits the law to regulate type 1 corruption, by permitting Congress to block it (through bribery and illegal influence statutes), or to block contributions that raise a reasonable suspicion of it.

But if there is a type 1, there is a type 2. If corruption can predicate of an individual ("Cunningham is corrupt."), it can predicate of an institution, too ("Parliament is corrupt."). And when it predicates of an institution, its meaning is different. A corrupt institution is not just an institution with a bunch of corrupt individuals.

Indeed, whether an institution is corrupt or not is not directly tied to the corruption of individuals with it. An institution could be corrupt even if no individual within it was corrupt. And an institution could be not corrupt even if it is filled with corrupt individuals. The two ideas are distinct, and it just a confusion to try to reduce the one to the other.

Call this second type of corruption "institutional corruption." And though there is now a field exploring "institutional corruption," in at least a few different flavors, there is one particular type of institutional corruption that is the focus of this book. Let's call it "dependence corruption."[7]

Here's an example: The job of a judge is to follow the law. Some say that in Japan, judges follow more than the law.[8] Japanese judges, these scholars argue, are sensitive not only to what the law says, but also to whether a particular decision is likely to upset the government. They pay attention to this extrajudicial concern because (at least these scholars claim) the government controls the promotion of judges on the basis of their behavior. And so, if you're a Japanese judge and don't want to end up in some regional court in the countryside, you need to be certain not to disappoint those who decide where you'll serve by deciding a case in a way that goes against what they want.

I don't know whether these charges are correct—Japanese judges to me seem to have the highest integrity, though given the integrity of the source of this scholarship there must be something to it.

But imagine the charges are correct. Because if they are, they are a perfect example of the one type of "institutional corruption" that I want to focus on here. A judiciary is to be "dependent on the law." But if this story about judges in Japan is correct, then these judges are dependent not just on the law. They are dependent on the favor of the government, too. That second dependence conflicts with the first. Because of that conflict, the independence of the judges, the freedom to decide cases dependent only upon the law, is weakened.

We could make the same point without picking on the Japanese. Think about the system that many states use to select their judges: contested elections. Certainly one of the dumbest ideas of the Progressives' (and President Jackson before them), this system has now spiraled into the most extreme example of campaign cash weakening the public's trust of a crucial arm of government. In the 2008 cycle, state Supreme Court candidates from across the nation raised $45.6 million, seven times the amount raised in the 1990 cycle.[9] In the 2012 cycle, the first after the Supreme Court's decision in *Citizens United*, that spending climbed to $56.4 million, with $24 million coming from outside spending, more than two times the rate from 2010.[10] This money produced "unprecedented pressure from interest groups [on judges] to make decisions that are based on politics,"[11] not law, as former Supreme Court Justice Sandra Day O'Connor writes. (Remember, O'Connor is no commie: Appointed by Ronald Reagan, she was one of the most important conservative justices on the Rehnquist Court.) With "so much money go[ing] into influencing the outcome of a judicial election," she continues, "it is hard to have faith that we are selecting judges who are fair and impartial."[12]

And indeed, we don't "have faith." In a survey conducted in 2002, 76 percent of Americans said they thought "campaign contributions influence judicial decisions."[13] Seventy percent of surveyed judges expressed concern that "in some states, nearly half of all supreme court cases involve someone who has given money to one or more of the judges hearing the case."[14] Indeed, almost half (46 percent) of the state court judges surveyed in that 2002 survey said they believe "contributions have at least a little influence."[15] Seventy-nine percent of Texas attorneys believe that "campaign contributions significantly influence a judge's decision."[16]

That number in particular makes sense to me: One of my students reported on a study he had conducted that included one Texas judge who begins each hearing by asking the lawyers to identify their firm, and then, in front of everyone present, opens his contribution book to check whether that firm had contributed to his reelection.[17]

The suspicions of 76 percent of Americans, 70 percent of surveyed judges, 46 percent of state judges, and 79 percent of Texas attorneys are borne out by the empirical studies of judicial voting behavior and contributions. Professor Stephen Ware, for example, studied Alabama Supreme Court decisions from 1995 to 1999 and found "the remarkably close correlation between a justice's votes on arbitration cases and his or her source of campaign funds."[18] A 2006 study by *New York Times* reporters Adam Liptak and Janet Roberts found that over a twelve-year period, Ohio justices voted in favor of their contributors 70 percent of the time, with one justice voting with his contributors 91 percent of the time.[19] One example from Louisiana is particularly amazing:

> Justice John L. Weimer, for instance, was slightly pro-defendant in cases where neither side had given him contributions, voting for plaintiffs 47 percent of the time. But in cases where he received money from the defense side (or more money from the defense when both sides gave money), he voted for the plaintiffs only 25 percent of the time. In cases where the money from the plaintiffs' side dominated, on the other hand, he voted for the plaintiffs 90 percent of the time.[20]

"That's quite a swing," note the reporters.

Yeah. No kidding.

In both the Japanese and the American cases of tarnished judicial independence, the system that queers independence is a system of corruption. Like a compass that deviates because of an interfering magnetic field, because of the influence of the government (Japan), or the influence of campaign funders (state courts in America), the institution of the judiciary is corrupted by a second dependence that weakens its commitment to its primary or intended dependence. That corruption in turn weakens the fairness of that system. Over time it weakens public trust.

This is "dependence corruption." It is a corruption of an institution, not necessarily of individuals within that institution. And as applied to the institution of Congress, the concept of "dependence corruption" should be obvious:

As with every other branch of our government, the Framers intended Congress to be "independent." But as with the judiciary, "independent" didn't mean free to do whatever it wanted. Instead, as I described in Chapter 12, an "independent Congress" was to be one that was properly "dependent upon the people alone."[21]

That exclusive dependence was to be practiced by rapid and regular elections (every two years for the House). It was to be protected by blocking the executive from making appointments to Congress, and blocking foreign princes from giving gifts to Congress. And more. As Zephyr Teachout has cataloged in her incredible account of this bit of constitutional history, *Corruption in America,* the Constitution is filled with devices designed to ensure that Congress is protected from dependence-corrupting influences, and stays focused on the task of tracking the truth it is intended it to track: the people.

That independence gets corrupted when a conflicting dependence develops within Congress—a dependence that draws Congress away from the dependence that was intended; a dependence that makes Congress less responsive to the people. This is type 2 corruption; it is not individuals who are corrupted within a well-functioning institution. It is instead an institution that has been corrupted, because the pattern of influence operating upon individuals within that institution draws them away from the influence intended.[22]

Tweedism throws this second dependence into clear relief.

No one would doubt that a primary creates a dependence for an elected representative. A congressman is dependent on the vote in a general election as well as dependent on the vote in a primary.

That second dependence, however, is not a conflicting dependence because the primary is as much "the people" as is the general election. When it is not "the people"—when, for example, as Texas did, blacks are excluded from the primary—then the primary is a second dependence that conflicts with the intended, or primary dependence: on the people alone. But as primaries have evolved, they are not, in general, a dependence that conflicts with a dependence "on the people alone."

As I argued in Chapter 1, however, America doesn't have one primary anymore. America has two primaries. There is a voting primary, and there is a money primary, or a "Green Primary." To be able to compete in the general election, a candidate must do well in both of these primaries. In this sense, a candidate is dependent on those who decide each primary.

Yet as I argued in Chapter 1, there is no way to believe that voters in the Green Primary represent "the people." They don't. They represent the rich, both Republican and Democratic versions of the rich. Or not even the rich. They represent people with resources who want to influence government. They don't represent "the people."

That dependence on the Green Primary is thus a conflicting dependence within the system of exclusive dependence imagined by our Framers. In the terms that I've described, it therefore is a corrupting dependence, too. As we have allowed the funding of campaigns to evolve, we have permitted the institution of our representative democracy to be corrupted. Institutionally corrupted, whether or not individuals within it are individually corrupted, too.

With what consequence? one might ask. Does this corruption actually do any harm?

I've already described the particular harms in Chapter 8. And in light of that data, it is hard for me to believe that any but the most obtuse would conclude that the flaw in our system is harmless.

But why is the burden on me to establish that there's any harm at all? Why isn't the burden the other way around? Once we see how the system of dependence intended by our Framers has been corrupted, why isn't it the defenders of this system who should have to show that it doesn't matter? That, in the words of the law, why doesn't the other side have the burden to show that if there's error (which this corruption is), it is harmless error.

It is my view that the error is not harmless. That the corruption of the Green Primary is devastating to the notion of representative democracy. And that the consequence for self-government in America is profound.

But is it a "corruption" that the Supreme Court could see? Is it the sort of corruption that should entitle Congress to "abridge" the "freedom of speech" in order to remedy it? Is it the kind of corruption that would justify regulations designed to end it, if those regulations happen to restrict the expressive activity of some?

This is not an easy question. And it is not an easy question to get right. My friends in the progressive movement have moved too quickly, I believe, to embrace remedies that involve rejecting an important tradition of "free speech." We forget that it was Ralph Nader's organization, Public Citizen Litigation Group, that argued the first case to recognize the free speech rights of corporations— and not because Ralph Nader is a corporate tool.[23] Instead, his motive was one that we should celebrate and respect—the effort to force the government to justify its restrictions on the liberty to express oneself *whoever or whatever you are.*

Thus I do not support the simple slogans that have been offered as "remedies" to the corruption of our government. I do think that money is speech, in the sense that the government should have to justify restrictions on my ability to spend my money to advance my political ideas. I agree with Dean Robert Post that "the argument [that they don't is] untenable."[24]And I don't think declaring "corporations are not persons" will actually solve anything. As Kent Greenfield puts it, "Saying corporations are not persons is as irrelevant to constitutional analysis as saying that Tom Brady does not putt well."[25] As Justice Kennedy explained in *Citizens United*,[26] whether or not corporations are persons, Congress has no power to "abridge the freedom of speech" (in the context of campaign finance regulation)—unless that "abridge[ment]" is for the purpose of reducing "corruption."

Instead, I believe that the Court's framework for analyzing these questions—asking, "Is the regulation a regulation of 'corruption'?"—is just fine. And while I would support constitutional reforms that would better enable Congress to rationalize the election process (see Chapter 13 for more), until that day comes, we should do more to make sense of the Court's framework. For it is the template of what is possible now.

So within that framework, what can the Congress do?

I will answer this question in two steps. First, I will argue that especially the conservatives on the Supreme Court should recognize "dependence corruption" as a kind of corruption that Congress should be able to remedy. Second, I will describe the specific reforms that Congress should be able to enact, consistent with the conception of corruption.

My conclusion isn't likely to make anyone completely happy. Against the current reading of the Supreme Court's rule, I argue that in fact Congress has the power to regulate more than is thought. *SpeechNow*, on this view, was wrongly decided. But I also argue that on the record so far, *on the terms the Court has given us, Citizens United* is not clearly wrong. And that while *McCutcheon* is likely wrongly decided, the jury is still out. It's possible that with the public funding of elections, any dependence corruption induced by *McCutcheon* would be eliminated. On the record so far, we can't see.

"Dependence Corruption" Is "Corruption"

There are many theories of what "corruption" is, as Deborah Hellman has so powerfully demonstrated. "What constitutes political corruption in a democracy," as she writes, "depends on a theory of democracy. To put the point in a more grounded fashion, what constitutes corruption of legislators depends on a view about the proper basis for decision-making by elected officials."[27]

So as these "theories" change, the meaning of "corruption" changes.

This fact about "corruption" isn't limited to "corruption." Any number of fundamental principles within the law or philosophy or politics admit of many different conceptions. John Rawls didn't write "the theory of justice." He wrote "A Theory of Justice," because since time immemorial, philosophers and theorists have been sharing their theory of what justice is, and why one is better than another.

This is the nature of rich concepts. It's the nature of derivative concepts (as Hellman argues corruption is). And these natures create a particularly difficult problem for a court interpreting a written Constitution.

For as conceptions of fundamental ideals evolve, how is a Court supposed to respond to that evolution? Or even ignoring evolution, if there are ten difference conceptions of "equality," is a Court allowed to just pick the conception it likes? As Attorney General Edwin Meese put it, pretty soon constitutional interpretation would become "like a picnic to which the framers bring the words and the judges the meaning."[28]

It is this problem that animated the work of one of the most interesting movements in constitutional theory in the past forty years—"originalism." Originalism is the idea that in interpreting the Constitution, a judge should return to the founding, and read the text as the Framers would. Not because their conception is necessarily the best, and not because their conception should never be changed. But simply and primarily because judges have no other basis for selecting among the many possible meanings that any complex text might present. If the people don't like the original meaning, then they can change it by amending the Constitution. But better the people change it than unelected judges—or so the originalists believe. The role of the courts, on this view, is to avoid injecting into the Constitution anything that lacks a democratic pedigree.

This is not the book to evaluate or endorse originalism. There have been legions of critics, and lots of great work to make the theory make sense.

But whether one endorses originalism or not, it is a fact that at least a significant minority on the Supreme Court calls themselves "originalists." And that fact should matter as to whether "dependence corruption" is a kind of corruption that the Supreme Court sees Congress as having the power to remedy.

Because when the Supreme Court says that the First Amendment only permits the regulation of political speech when that regulation is design to address "corruption," it is a completely fair question to ask of the originalists at least, "From where do you derive the meaning of the word 'corruption'?" The whole justification for originalism is the notion that it should not be the judges who get to make up the meaning. The whole aim of the procedure of originalism was to bind the judges to a meaning they didn't themselves select, by tying them to a procedure that locked the meaning of contested concepts to the meaning the Framers would have given them.

This is not a constraint for the nonoriginalists on the Supreme Court. Justice Breyer is not an originalist. In his dissent in *McCutcheon v. FEC* (2014), a case that struck aggregate limits on contributions to political campaigns, Breyer offers a rich theory of the meaning of the term "corruption," deriving from his best understanding of the idea a conception of how a court, today, should read that term.

Breyer's conception is compelling. But against it, what a consistent originalist would ask is this: Where do you get the authority to make up the meaning that the Constitution should have? Breyer has no problem answering that question, because Breyer is not an originalist.

But the same question asked of an originalist should have some bite. So when an originalist says that the "hallmark of corruption is the financial quid pro quo: dollars for political favors," it is a perfectly fair question to ask that originalist, "From where do you derive that meaning?"

The answer for the originalist should be clear: The meaning of the word is the meaning the Framers would have given the word.[29] But then what's striking about the many Supreme Court opinions describing the scope of the term "corruption"—from *Buckley* to *Citizens United* to *McCutcheon*—is that not one tries to explicate the meaning of the term for our Framers.

Scholars have. Zephyr Teachout's book, *Corruption in America: From Benjamin Franklin's Snuff Box to Citizens United* (2014), is an extraordinary effort to explicate the meaning and role of the concept of "corruption" at the founding. More than any other modern legal scholar, she has brought to life the Framers' obsession with building structures that would avoid "corruption."

In Madison's notebook, Teachout writes, the word "corruption" is scrawled fifty-four times, and was discussed more than "factions, violence, or instability."[30] In their world, "corruption" was not limited to "unlawful abuses or usurpations." "Gouverneur Morris explicitly said that the corruption concern encompassed lawful abuses of power" as well.[31]

But what is that "corruption" that they were working so hard to avoid?

As Gordon Wood, perhaps the foremost historian on the ideas of the founding period, puts it:

> When the American Whigs described the English nation and government as eaten away by "corruption," they were in fact using a technical term of political science, rooted in the writings of classical antiquity, made famous by Machiavelli, developed by the classical republicans of seventeenth-century England, and carried into the eighteenth century by nearly everyone who laid claim to knowing anything about politics.
>
>   . . .
>
> The corruption of the constitution's internal principles was the more obvious and the more superficial danger.
>
> . . . the Crown had been able to evade the restrictions of the revolutionary settlement of 1688 and had "found means to corrupt the other branches of the legislature," upsetting the delicately maintained balance of the constitution from within.[32]

This is not the corruption of quid pro quo. Wood is not describing an elaborate system of bribery or influence peddling. He is describing the corruption of an institution, by one institution—the Crown—finding ways to "evade the restrictions" that the English Constitution intended, thereby "upsetting the delicately maintained balance of the constitution from within."

Here is the simplest but clearest example: The Framers repeatedly referred to Parliament as a "corrupt institution." But when they said that, they were not alleging that individuals within Parliament accepted bribes. They may or may not have accepted bribes (no doubt they likely did). But the corruption that the Framers were charging turned not on those bribes. It turned instead on the role of the king in the British Parliament.

The House of Commons was to represent the people—virtually, but it was the people that the House was to virtually represent. It represented the people through elections conducted in boroughs throughout Britain. Those boroughs were not evenly or equally crafted. Some were big, some were small, and the electors in those boroughs were not always or only the people. But in a "good enough for government" sense, the idea was that the people would be represented in the Commons, while the aristocracy would be represented in the House of Lords.

But the king corrupted this balance. In a bunch of boroughs—so called "rotten boroughs"—the king effectively controlled who was elected to Parliament. Those members were therefore not independent of the king. Those members were directly dependent on the king. They were therefore a corruption of an institution meant to represent not the king, but the people. They constituted a corruption of the intended dependence that the House of Commons was meant to have. As Alexander Hamilton put it, the "dependence" on "the king" by representatives from "rotten boroughs... is the true source of the corruption which has so long excited the severe animadversion of zealous politicians and patriots."[33] Historian J. G. A. Pocock, describes it in a similar way:

> The King's ministers were not attacked for sitting in Parliament, but they were attacked for allegedly filling Parliament with the recipients of government patronage. For what was universally acknowledged was that if the members of the legislature became dependent upon patronage, the legislature would cease to be independent and the balance of the constitution would become corrupt. Corruption on an eighteenth-century tongue—where it was an exceedingly common term—meant not only venality, but disturbance of the political conditions necessary to human virtue and freedom.[34]

This is precisely how the Framers spoke generally. Working with the Constitutional Accountability Center,[35] two researchers at Harvard collected 325 usages of the term "corruption" by the Framers in the time surrounding the framing of the Constitution. Of those, in more than half of the cases—57 percent—the Framers were discussing corruption of institutions, not individuals. By contrast, discussion of quid pro quo corruption was rare—only six instances, and all of them focused on corruption of individuals. No doubt these two types of corruption are related. "By eliminating systematic corruption," as John Joseph Wallis has written, "they hoped to mitigate the problems of venal corruption as well."[36] But whether or not related, they were still distinct.

More important, while the Framers understood that corruption could arise from acts of quid pro quo corruption by officeholders, they also saw that it could arise *when government institutions had an improper dependence.* In at least twenty-nine instances, the Framers spoke of corruption in exactly this way—five times the frequency of discussion of quid pro quo corruption.

So if corruption means anything, at least for an originalist, then it should mean improper dependence.

That concept can be applied by understanding, first, what dependencies now exist, and second, what dependencies were intended.

As applied to our tweedist nation, that's not a difficult standard to apply. We have Congress dependent on tweeds who are not the people, when we were to have a Congress "dependent on the people alone."

From the Framers' perspective, there could be no doubt that we have corrupted their system.

The question now is what the consequence of this recognition should be.

What Follows

Okay the argument so far is like this: *For an originalist,* "corruption" should mean at least "improper dependence." It should also mean quid pro quo, of course, but consistent with the principles of originalism, it cannot mean quid pro quo alone.

It follows that *for an originalist*, legislation that targets improper dependence should be upheld, at least if any restriction on speech is the least restrictive means to that legitimate end.

What this would mean for the existing jurisprudence of campaign finance law is limited, but critically important.

On the one hand, recognizing "dependence corruption" as a kind of corruption that Congress could remedy would give the Court a clear way to see why Congress should have the power to limit super PACs.

Here's why:

Remember, a super PAC is a political action committee that can take unlimited contributions, so long as it does not coordinate with any candidate or coordinating committee. The Supreme Court didn't create super PACs directly. Instead, it was a lower court that thought that *Citizens United* entailed that super PACs were protected by the First Amendment. As Chief Judge Sentelle reasoned in *SpeechNow v. FEC*,[37] if an individual or a corporation is *free to spend* unlimited amounts independent of a political campaign, an individual or a corporation must be *free to contribute* unlimited amounts to a political action committee that will spend its money independently of a political campaign.

As a matter of logic, Sentelle's argument is seductive. But the experience since *SpeechNow* should provide ample evidence of why this inference simply does not follow. And in November 2011, the link was drawn as clearly as it could have been, in perhaps the most illuminating exchange that I have ever seen about the effect of super PACs on our democracy.

The context was a television studio. Former Senator Evan Bayh (D-Ind., 1999–2011) was being interviewed by the late Senator Arlen Specter (R/D-Pa., 1981–2011), for a pilot that PBS was considering about the effects of money in politics. John Samples, vice president of the Cato Institute, a libertarian think tank headquartered in Washington, DC, had just suggested that there was no clear evidence that money affected results in Washington. If there was an effect, Samples said, it was a best uncertain.

Bayh was asked whether, based on his twelve years of experience in the Senate, he, too, was uncertain about money's effect.

He was not. To the contrary, based on his experience, Bayh was perfectly confident that he understood its effect.

Super PACs, Bayh said, have produced a very distinct dynamic in Washington—a dynamic generated by fear. The single greatest fear of any incumbent is that thirty days before an election, some anonymously funded super PAC will drop $1,000,000 against him. When that happens, there's little the incumbent can do. He can't then turn to his largest contributors—by definition, they have all maxed out and can't, under the law, give any more. So in anticipation, the incumbent must line up support far in advance. Or let's call this support "protection." In anticipation of the risk that the incumbent will be targeted, the incumbent needs a kind of assurance: that if she needs a defense, there will be the resources to defend her.

Bayh didn't use these words, but let's call this assurance "super PAC insurance." It's not technically "insurance"—it's not issued by an insurance company, and there's no cash premium collected in advance. But it functions like insurance, and indeed, like any insurance, there certainly is a premium of some sort that is collected in advance. Because if you're going to convince a super PAC to be there when you need them, you need to signal pretty convincingly that you're the sort of incumbent they would want to protect. "They'd love to support you, Senator, but they have a rule that they can't support anyone who doesn't get a 95 percent on their score card." And so the rational representative has a clear goal to work toward—95 percent or better—long before he actually needs anyone's money.

And thus, without a single dollar changing hands, the super PAC achieves its objective: bending congressmen to its program, through the expectation of a defense if a defense is necessary.[38] It's a dynamic that would be obvious to Tony Soprano or Michael Corleone—even if it was missed by some of the best federal judges in America, and by a big chunk of the reform community (including me!).

And thus the obvious point: As this process matures, members of Congress become dependent on a smaller and smaller number of super PAC funders. It's not just the tiny number of "relevant funders" of campaigns directly. It's the even smaller number of the super-rich who are funding the super PACs. In 2014, the top 1 percent of donors funded 69 percent of the super PAC money raised.[39] That number of funders may go up in 2016. Imagine it goes up by a factor of 250. Even then, the funders of these super PACs will represent no more than .01 percent of America.

So what super PACs are doing is further concentrating the number of relevant funders. They are reducing the number of tweeds as they represent an ever growing percentage of campaign expenditures. A single graph captures the dynamic beautifully[40]:

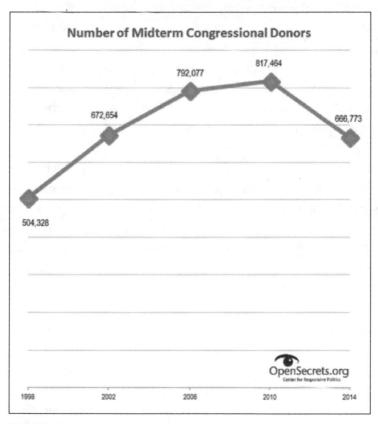

Number of Midterm Congressional Donors

792,077

817,464

672,654

666,773

504,328

OpenSecrets.org
Center for Responsive Politics

1998   2002   2006   2010   2014

FIGURE 17

This just reinforces a trend that predates the super Pac. As Martin Gilens writes:

> One clear trend in congressional elections is a shift in the source of individual donations toward larger gifts. Between the 2000 and 2008 election cycles, the proportion of all individual contributions that came from people who donated at least $1,000 to House candidates grew from 24 to 35 percent, while the proportion from people who donated less than $200 fell from 15 to 8 percent.[41]

All this is at the congressional level. At the presidential level, the story is even more extreme. As Senator Lindsay Graham said at the start of the 2016 presidential primary season:

> I would like to control the money in politics to the extent it will destroy the political process....There are probably 50 people in the country you've got to go to and see if they'd support you, because there's unlimited giving...if we don't have some control over the money, the most influential people in the country are going to be the ones with the most money.[42]

And indeed quickly, it became clear that even 50 was too high a number. The Republican candidates suffered the indignity of competing in the "Sheldon Adelson primary"—for a prize of hundreds of millions of dollars in campaign spending. Marco Rubio was even driven to say that "billionaires didn't have enough influence" in our political system while competing in the Koch brothers' primary (they promised to spend close to $1 billion in 2016).

This spending is meant to be "independent" of the campaign. But no one watching a half-dozen politicians vie for this "independent" spending could believe that the politicians didn't believe themselves *dependent* upon it. The quaint image of independent spending that doesn't create any dependence—the random ad in a newspaper, or billboards on someone's front lawn—is wholly unrelated to the reality that has emerged in American politics today. Not just from the perspective of the candidate, but also from the perspective of the donor. When asked what he expected to get in return for his $93 million in contributions to super PACs in 2012, including $30 million to the one supporting Romney in 2012, Adelson signaled that the top reason for his political support was "self-defense," referring to ongoing criminal investigations by the Justice Department.[43]

When *Citizens United* was decided, there were many who criticized the Court for its lack of political experience. There was not a single justice who had ever been a politician. None of them had any practical experience with how campaigns actually work.

From that perspective, removed from the actual experience of politics, it could well have seemed plausible that large independent expenditures would create gratitude, but no obligation.

But six years into this experiment in how money affects politics, it would take a studied blindness to believe that the system that has evolved creates just gratitude, and no obligation. The dance of the super PAC is now mature and well understood. Its whole purpose is to oblige—to create in a politician the real sense of obligation, to vote in a particular way, to exercise prosecutorial discretion in a particular way, to appoint in a particular way. That obligation, of course, is not enforceable in court. But neither is a bribe enforceable in court. Both rely on extrajudicial means to enforce the obligation that both create. And in the well-functioning relationship market of K Street, those extrajudicial means are better than anything any court could ever give.

So the question now becomes whether the kind of dependence evinced by the super PAC becomes the sort of "corruption" that Congress should be permitted to address.

In my view, the answer is *obviously* yes. The super PAC has exacerbated "dependence corruption" within Congress. However bad it was, it is now much worse. So at a minimum, regulations designed to address that corruption should be allowed. At a minimum, Congress should be permitted to limit the contributions to super PACs, even if Congress can't limit the expenditures of super PACs.

At a minimum, *SpeechNow* should be reversed.

But what about *Citizens United*? If *SpeechNow* goes, must *Citizens United* go, too?

Within the framework established by the Court so far, it is possible for the Court to insist that we don't yet have the data to support the claim that *Citizens United* is "corrupting." That's because we don't actually have much "Citizens United speech" *independent* of super PAC speech.[44]

If Congress eliminated the super PAC, and the Court upheld that limit, these facts could change. We could well see the same dynamic develop with corporate spending that we saw develop with super PAC contributions.

But I doubt it. The right of rich people to spend unlimited amounts to influence political campaigns has been the law since 1976. Not many rich people, however, have taken advantage of their rights.[45] There are a few. They are famous. But most rich people hesitate before putting their name on the line pushing one politician over another. Most seem to feel that that's one entitlement too far.

That pressure is even greater with corporations. Very quickly after *Citizens United*, corporations discovered the high cost of free speech. Target, for example, became its own name—a target—when it supported an antigay candidate for governor in Minnesota. Very quickly, it found its stores being picketed all across the country. Very quickly it decided to back down.[46]

I expect that if the super PAC option wasn't an option, and if elections were otherwise publicly funded, there would be a very small return to a corporation spending money in an election, which means—because remember, if there isn't a return, there's little reason to expect them to act—there would be very few which would actually do it. Not none, but just some. And maybe actually a *tolerable* amount—enough to let those voices be heard, without risking an improper dependence within Congress developing.

So it seems certain that *SpeechNow* must go, and possible that *Citizens United* would stay. What about the most recent of these critical campaign finance decisions—*McCutcheon v. FEC*?

The issue in *McCutcheon* was whether Congress could limit the *aggregate* campaign contributions from any one individual to any number of campaigns. Federal law limits the contributions to one candidate in one cycle at $2,600. The law at issue in *McCutcheon* limited the total amount of contributions that could be given in one cycle to any number of candidates. That limit was $123,200 to candidate and noncandidate committees during each two-year cycle.[47]

From the perspective of quid pro quo corruption, it seems hard to see how an aggregate limit could make sense. If giving $1,000 to one candidate isn't viewed as quid pro quo corruption, then how is giving $1,000 to 435 candidates quid pro quo corruption? Quid pro quo requires a deal. If there's no deal with one, then multiplying that zero by any number should still yield a zero.

But from the perspective of dependence corruption, these limits make perfect sense. If candidates (and parties) are able to milk rich donors for the maximum amount for every candidate and committee (estimated in total to be $3.6 million by Justice Breyer[48]), then the number of donors they need to identify falls. And if the number falls, then the gap between "the funders" and "the people" would only increase. Congress could well have the objective of closing that gap, by steering fund-raising to the many rather than to the few. Congress could, in other words, properly aim to reduce the "dependence corruption" of Congress by limiting the aggregate contributions that any one individual could make.

Thus to adopt "dependence corruption" as one of the legitimate forms of "corruption" that Congress might attack could well draw *McCutcheon* into doubt. The Court would have to be willing to overturn that case, even if it did not need to overturn any other of its cases.

That's a difficult ask, of course. In its defense, the Court was not presented this argument by the government. I had tried to persuade the Solicitor General to make that argument; he had conceded to me that, without it, the government "had no argument"; yet "dependence corruption" was nowhere in the government's brief. And hence the Court was perfectly justified in deciding the case on the basis of the only "corruption" that it had to that date recognized.

Or alternatively, the Court could wait and see. How much further did the pool of direct contributors concentrate after *McCutcheon*. We know the total number of $200+ contributors is falling (even as the total amount contributed is rising).[49] The Court could well wait to see whether the dynamic is as campaign finance geeks predicted—fewer and fewer giving more and more—or not. If it is as the geeks predicted, then the Court could well say that based on the facts as they developed, this is a compelling justification for restricting aggregate contributions. It's perfectly reasonable for the Court to say that it won't restrict speech on the basis of speculation; but it is willing to restrict speech when the proper form of "corruption" has been made manifest.

And then there is the strange case of *Yulee*. As I was finishing the revisions to this book, the Supreme Court surprised practically everyone by declaring that the First Amendment was not violated by a rule that forbids judges from soliciting campaign contributions. Florida has a system for electing judges. The campaigns for those elections cost money. But while Florida allowed the campaigns for judges to solicit contributions, judges themselves were protected. They were not allowed to do what members of Congress are forced to do—dial for dollars from the rich in Florida (and elsewhere).

The Supreme Court has long had a special place for judges in its campaign finance jurisprudence. In 2009, in an opinion written by the author of *Citizens United*, Justice Anthony Kennedy, the Court held that the Constitution forced a judge to recuse himself when independent expenditures created a "serious risk of bias" in the judge. In that case, a litigant had funded a huge independent expenditure campaign to defeat a judge. The judge who replaced him then cast the deciding vote in favor of the funder. Even though the money was independent of the judges' campaign, Justice Kennedy, in the words of Justice Holmes, "puked."[50]

But in *Yulee*, Justice Kennedy saw no problem with judges raising money directly. He voted with the dissent. And the real surprise in the case came from a justice who had dissented in the *Caperton* case, the chief justice, John Roberts.

Because now Roberts was the author of an opinion upholding a restriction on the speech of judges, in the name of preserving the integrity of the judiciary. Florida had, Roberts wrote, a "compelling interest in preserving public confidence in the integrity of the judiciary." But judges, charged with exercising strict neutrality and independence, cannot supplicate campaign donors without diminishing public confidence in judicial integrity.

As he concluded, perfectly reasonably, from my perspective:

> Simply put, Florida and most other States have concluded that the public may lack confidence in a judge's ability to administer justice without fear or favor if he comes to office by asking for favors.

That much is certainly true. But what's more difficult is to understand just why "judicial integrity" justifies speech restrictions while "legislative or presidential integrity" would not.

And here begins the most curious bit of the Court's opinion. The reason is the difference in the nature of judges. We are informed, by the Court, that:

> The role of judges differs from the role of politicians. Politicians are expected to be appropriately responsive to the preferences of their supporters. Indeed, such "responsiveness is key to the very concept of self-governance through elected officials." . . . The same is not true of judges. In deciding cases, a judge is not to follow the preferences of his supporters, or provide any special consideration to his campaign donors. A judge instead must "observe the utmost fairness," striving to be "perfectly

and completely independent, with nothing to influence or controul [sic] him but God and his conscience."[51]

Roberts is exactly right about judges. That sense of independence is at the core of our conception of judicial integrity. An "independent judiciary" is to be "dependent on the law"—not dependent upon politics or her funders.

But Roberts repeats a mistake that Justice Kennedy made in *Citizens United* when he suggests that "Politicians are expected to be appropriately responsive to the preferences of their supporters." Because the word "supporters" is ambiguous between those who vote for a politician, and those who fund an election.

Consider two versions of that sentence:

1. "Politicians are expected to be appropriately responsive to the preferences of the voters in their district."
2. "Politicians are expected to be appropriately responsive to the preferences of the funders of their campaign."

I submit (a) is uncontroversial, at least today. Some of the Framers would have been outraged by the idea, but as the concept has evolved, there is nothing wrong—certainly nothing corrupt—in the idea of a member of Congress voting as she does because of the views of her constituents. This statement by a member of Congress is not corrupt: "I do not personally agree with them, but my constituents overwhelmingly support blah blah blah, so I am voting in favor of bill XYZ."

But the same is not true about the funders of a campaign. Because the intended integrity of this system was tied to Congress being "dependent on the people alone." And as I've argued again and again, "the funders" are not "the people." And so clear is this denial of integrity that I doubt even Justice Kennedy would have no problem with a member of Congress saying this on the floor of the House:

"My constituents do not agree with this. They overwhelmingly oppose bill XYZ. And I, too, oppose bill XYZ. But the funders of my campaign overwhelmingly support blah blah blah, so, because, as the Supreme Court has written, my job is to be "responsive to the preferences of my supporters," I am going to vote in favor of bill XYZ."

I am not saying that such a statement is inconceivable. But I do think that the Supreme Court has not begun to establish that this conception of democracy is either our Framers' or ours. Any representative who said this publicly would be ridiculed—by Republicans and Democrats alike. And that is because we believe that the integrity of a legislature is constituted by its responsiveness "to the people alone," just as we believe the integrity of a court is constituted by its responsiveness "to the law alone."[52]

Representative Tony Coelho (D-Calif.; 1979–1989) is one of the men who changed Congress. In 1981, he became chairman of the Democratic Congressional Campaign Committee. Throughout the 1980s, as Kaiser writes:

Coelho would make a historic contribution in the 1980s by persuading corporate interests of many kinds to show their respect for—by giving campaign contributions to—the Democrats, who controlled the House and wrote important legislation that affected American business.[53]

Reflecting on what he had built, Coelho said this to Robert Kaiser:

The press always tries...to say that you've been bought out. I don't buy that....I think that the process buys you out. But I don't think that you individually have been bought out, or that you sell out. I think there's a big difference there.[54]

There is a big difference. Individuals live within a system that demands certain attentions. Certain sensibilities. As those sensibilities are perfected, the representative begins to function on automatic pilot. And when she bends, she's not bending because of a particular interest. She's bending because of a process she has learned, and perfected. As Kaiser puts it, these are "ordinary people responding logically to powerful incentives." There's nothing else to do. It isn't selling out. It is surviving.

It is also "corruption." It is not the corruption of the village idiot—Duke Cunningham or William Jefferson. It is not the corruption of crime. It is the "corruption" of an institution that has lost touch with the exclusivity of the influence that was to be driving it. It is dependence corruption, and Congress ought to have the power to regulate it just as it has the power to regulate the idiots.

This institutional sense of corruption is as old as the Republic. And it is as new as geeks groking politics. Here's the testimony of a thirty-something-year-old coder, Zach Phillips, at a Delaware state legislative hearing:

> I want to make a brief point about "corruption." I come from a software development background. When I use the word corruption, it isn't a moral judgment. It is a design judgment. When a file or application becomes corrupted, it isn't because the developer is bad or evil. It's because there's a mistake in the design and architecture. The fact that the job description of a politician in the US has become primarily fundraiser is a design problem. It's broken and must be fixed—before it's too late.[55]

There is no reason not to permit our democratic legislatures from protecting the system against this kind of corruption. There is no sanction for such a limit in the words of the Constitution, or in the meaning as interpreted by the most fidelity-focused of interpretive schools, originalism. It is time for the Court to correct the mistakes made in its name, and to give back to the people the right to protect their democracy against the most obvious forms of corruption. Not the crimes of Boss Tweed, but the system of tweedism.

PART III

★

UNCONVENTIONAL
THOUGHTS

On the horizon of reform, there is the short term, and there is everything else.

In the short term, there is an election just about a year after this book appears. As I finish its writing, months before that, there is much that I hope will happen in that election. But I won't predict that or describe that election here. Trees (and bits) were made for better things than that.

What should happen in that election is clear. We need a majority in Congress committed to fundamental reform, we need a president to lead that majority, and we need a public to demand that the president leads. Fundamental reform begins with changing the way elections are funded. It needs a leader, in the form of a president, who will make that chance central to her campaign. We will get nothing, she needs to say again and again, until we get this. Fixing this equality-destroying corruption is the necessary first step to getting a democracy that can work.

This campaign in the short term is crucial. The window for reform will close quickly. Complain as everyone does about the current system, eventually, the incumbents will accept the current system. If we don't change today soon, "today" will quickly become "for as long as we can see."

So you should join the current fight, and in the notes, I point to the most vital organizations waging that fight.[1] There is a wide range of them, so there's something for everyone, from libertarians and conservatives, to the most progressive of liberals.

But regardless of what happens in that short term, there is a longer-term struggle for reform. We can't tell the timing of this longer struggle, nor precisely what it will require. But in this final part, I want to describe two bits that may well prove essential.

I've said that I believe that 90 percent of the problem with the corrupting influence of money in politics could be solved through conventional means: a statute changing the way elections are funded, plus a Supreme Court convinced to trim back the extreme lower court extension of its own decision in *Citizens United*, which created the super PAC.

Yet even if that change happens, there will likely be more constitutional reform that will be necessary. How we get that reform is a critical question that is not well understood among the public or our leaders. I described this process in the first edition of this book. In the first chapter of this part, I extend that argument, and explain why I believe it will be crucial to getting the democracy we need.

In the final chapter, I return to an even crazier idea that I first sketched in the first edition. If the conventional means to fundamental reform fail, and if the one unconventional constitutional path to reform stalls, then we need to think seriously about a tame form of a revolution. Not one that overthrows a government, but one that inserts into the mix an alien catalyst for reform: a citizen, who with perfect analogy, we could call *Fodor*.

CHAPTER 13

A Proposing *Convention*

When our grandchildren look back at our time, they will be taught about something that too few of us even see: that we were living in the middle of a constitutional moment.

On the Left and the Right, there are vibrant and growing movements demanding fundamental change to our fundamental law. Movements demanding *amendments* to the Constitution.

These movements are in the background of politics just now. But literally millions have joined them in their different forms—some by signing a petition, others by organizing meet-ups, others still by supporting organizations that are pushing for constitutional change. In some form or another, a growing slice of America is now convinced that something in our fundamental law must change—even if they don't yet agree about what that change actually is.

These different movements have different strategies. But as currently deployed, I fear these strategies are destined to fail. Not because they must fail. I am not someone who believes that it is impossible to amend our Constitution. But instead because the leaders of these different movements are trapped on a partisan field. They believe that they can achieve constitutional change without questioning the logic of that partisan field. And so they do their work of constitutional politics while accepting the frame of partisan politics.

But here is the fundamental truth about constitutional change: With just one exception, it has always been cross-partisan. Constitutional reform is never about the Democrats beating the Republicans, or never about the Republicans beating the Democrats. With one exception, it has always been about us, as citizens, rising above the partisan fray to demand fundamental reform. Indeed, after this one exception, there is not a single amendment that was passed when one of the two parties opposed it.[1]

That one exception was the bloodiest war in American history: the Civil War. Following that war, the victors were (rightly) impatient. They insisted on their reforms before peace would be allowed. Today we recognize their changes as among the most important ideals inscribed within our Constitution. But except for the Thirteenth Amendment (abolishing slavery), we should remember that it was a century before those ideals had any of their intended effects on American law or society. The Civil War Amendments are the one exception to the cross-partisan rule of constitutional change. But unless we're willing to launch another civil war, that exception should prove the rule: We change the Constitution through amendment only when we approach that change as citizens, not as partisans.[2]

To say that the leaders of these movements have not yet left a partisan field is not to criticize them. Good leadership is all about recognizing just how far you can move your followers. And the truth is that we, the followers, are as trapped by the partisanship of today as are our leaders. We increasingly live within partisan bubbles. We reject those who question those bubbles. Patriotism has morphed into love of party, not country. "Traitor" predicates not of those who violate the Constitution (and there are plenty of those), but of those who question their tribe's partisan truths.

So I get the urge to partisanship. But unless we can get beyond it, no constitutional change will be possible. And then the lesson our grandkids will be taught is not just that we lived in a constitutional moment, but that we failed in our constitutional moment. That we failed to rise above the pettiest within us; that we failed to inspire leaders to inspire us to be citizens.

Don't get me wrong: To argue against partisanship in constitutional law is not to argue against partisanship. Political parties are an important part of a healthy democracy. On this issue, George Washington was wrong. And I don't think the differences between the two major parties are tiny or insignificant. To the contrary, they are real and substantial, and depending upon your values, inescapable. To argue against partisanship is not to imagine a grand kumbaya, or to insist that it turns out, we all agree.

But it is to say that these differences notwithstanding, we must find a way to craft an understanding beyond partisanship. Or maybe, before partisanship. Before we were Republicans, or before we were Democrats, or before we were committed Independents, we were citizens. And it is as citizens that we must approach the question of whether there are parts of our Constitution that must change.

The Movement on the Left

The movement on the Left ties to the subject of this book—the corrupting influence of money in politics. It gets born in its modern form with a gift from the Supreme Court: *Citizens United v. FEC* (2010).

Citizens United was hated at its birth, by citizens from across the political spectrum. The *Washington Post* reported opposition to the decision ranging from 76 percent among Republicans to 85 percent among Democrats.[3] But the movement against *Citizens United* has been distinctly from the Left. Groups such as People for the American Way and MoveToAmend.org started pushing hard to build support for a constitutional amendment to overturn the decision. Very quickly, an umbrella group called United4ThePeople .org formed to coordinate these reform efforts. United4thePeople .org now lists more than 155 cooperating organizations. At a Senate Hearing about *Citizens United* in 2012, it delivered almost 2 million signatures of Americans demanding constitutional reform.

But though many in this movement think of themselves as radical, the constitutional strategy of the anti–*Citizens United* movement is actually quite conservative.

The Constitution outlines two modes by which our fundamental law might be changed. One is for Congress to propose amendments to the Constitution; the other is for the states to call on

Congress to convene a "Convention for proposing Amendments" to the Constitution.

In the 226 years since the Constitution was adopted, we have only ever ratified an amendment proposed in the first way—by Congress. Thus the conservative path to amending the Constitution: getting Congress to do the proposing, which the states then ratify.

And this is the path that practically all of the organizations within this movement have followed as well. [There is just one critical exception—Wolf-PAC—which I will discuss (and effusively praise) below.] Thousands of volunteers from scores of affiliated groups have worked incredibly hard to get resolutions passed— by state legislatures, by local governments, by civic organizations across the country—that call on Congress to propose an amendment to deal with the corruption induced by *Citizens United*.

What precisely that amendment should say is a source of controversy. Some want an amendment to declare that corporations are not persons, and that money is not speech. Others want an amendment simply to secure to Congress the power that *Citizens United* seemed to deny. But regardless of the details—a question we'll return to later—the strategy is to rely upon Congress. The strategy is to hope that Congress will save us—at least if we demand it loudly and powerfully and politely enough.

But the sense of "demand" here is very specific. If every state legislature passed a resolution "demanding" that Congress propose an amendment, legally speaking, that would do nothing. Those resolutions would impose absolutely no legal obligation on Congress. Resolutions by the states are requests. They are the equivalent of a fancy "please, sir." But "please" has no legal force. Congress is free to ignore both "please" and "thank you."

That's not to say that a resolution strategy could never make sense for constitutional reformers. State resolutions are a valuable strategy to get Congress to do something that it is able to do or that it wants to do. But for the strategy to make sense, we have to have a reason to believe that Congress can actually act upon it. We have to believe, in other words, that the institution of Congress is capable of taking such a step—both politically, and institutionally.

Yet this is precisely what no reasonable person could possibly believe. *There is exactly zero chance that the United States Congress is going to pass by a two-thirds vote an amendment to effectively reverse* Citizens United.

Zero.

And this is absolutely clear for one obvious and undeniable reason: The Democrats have rendered this issue essentially partisan, and unless we invade Canada (and thereby gain a bunch more liberals in the Senate), there is zero chance that the Democrats will hold sufficient super-majorities in both Houses of Congress to propose an amendment anytime soon.

The Democrats have made this partisan in a thousand ways, but no example is clearer than what Harry Reid, the former Majority Leader of the Senate, did in the fall of 2014. Eight weeks before the election, Reid brought to the floor of the Senate a resolution for an amendment to overturn *Citizens United*. That particular proposal is flawed in a hundred ways—which is why even the liberal ACLU opposes it. But even if it were perfect, Reid's action is just the latest in a series guaranteed to assure that no Republican *in Washington* will ever support such an amendment. Reid's purpose was not to pass the amendment. His purpose was to embarrass the Republicans, and thereby raise desperately needed campaign funds for the Democrats. *Citizens United* is catnip to the Democratic base. And so millions flowed to Democratic candidates because of a resolution designed to end the influence of money in politics. (Talk about embracing the irony.)

I don't blame Harry Reid. Neither do I blame a lion for slaughtering a gazelle. It is in the nature of DC politics that every issue must be framed in a partisan way. And so obviously a strategy that depends upon DC is a strategy that depends upon a partisan spin.

But as I've said, constitutional reform cannot survive the partisan spin. And thus in its current form, this movement from the Left is ultimately sterile. It has enormous energy and endless good faith; it has called into life a kind of progressive activism that has been absent from the Left for too much of the past century—an activism focused on an equality of citizens as well as an equality of persons.

Yet as it is currently constituted, it is a movement that will produce no real constitutional change. Scores of reform organizations will be funded by the passion that this movement has engendered. E-mail lists will grow. But not a single comma of the Constitution will be altered.

The Movement on the Right

The constitutional movement on the Right is different. Its focus is different. And more important, its method is very different.

Its focus is more substance, and less process. The constitutional activists on the Right believe the federal government regulates too much. They believe it taxes too much. They believe it spends too much. These beliefs have led some on the Right to push for a balanced budget amendment, some to push to shift regulatory power from DC to the states, and some to give back to the states (either the state legislatures or the state governors) the power to select senators in the United States Senate.

But the Right is not pushing these proposals through the same process embraced by the Left. They've tried—for many years—to get Congress to propose their most fundamental change—a balanced budget amendment. They've learned that Congress is not going to pass any such thing.

So the Right has embraced the Framers' second mode by which amendments to the Constitution can be proposed to the states for ratification—"a convention." If thirty-four states make applications demanding that Congress call a convention, then by (constitutional) law, Congress is required to call a convention.

It has never happened before (though we've come close), and the rules for how it would happen in the future are notoriously vague (like much within the Constitution), but many on the Right believe that a convention is the best chance they have to get their ideas before the states, and to give the states the chance (*finally*) to vote them up or vote them down.

Thus the Right is pushing for conservative constitutional reform through historically innovative constitutional means. And thus the oddness of our age: The (substantive) liberals are the (procedural) conservatives; and the (substantive) conservatives, the (procedural) liberals.

But so what's the problem, then, with conservatives being innovative? And why is a convention a "dead end"?

Depending on how you count, there are between twenty and thirty active and recent resolutions by state legislatures calling on Congress to call an Article V convention. Almost all of those would limit the convention to considering topics pushed from the Right. If you talk to the leaders of these conservative movements, they're quite confident that within a year or two at the most, they'll have thirty-four states in their column. And then they'll start pressing Congress to respond to that call, by convening a convention limited to the issues that were identified by those thirty-four states.

Thus will the Right win the battle. Thus will they get their convention. And thus will we all lose the war.

For if the Right succeeds in getting Congress to call for an Article V convention limited to issues that the Right cares about alone, that will be the biggest fund-raising gift to the Democratic Party since the Iraq War.

Indeed, you can almost see the finance chairmen of the Democratic Party licking their collective chops. "The Tea Party Convention" will give FUD a new meaning. Thousands will be rallied to raise the money needed to "stop this assault on our Constitution." Women will be told they're going to lose the rights that *Roe v. Wade* secured to them. Gays will be told that the equal right to marry will be abolished. The right to bear arms will become an obligation to bear arms. Unions will be deemed unconstitutional.

The fear mongering will be vast—and absurd. False and absurd. As I'll explain below, there's exactly *zero* chance that any amendment would ever be ratified that is not squarely in the center of

American political thought—and obviously, none of those hypothetical amendments are.

But who could blame the fund-raisers for doing their job well? If it were the other way around—if there were a convention called for liberal purposes, you can be sure the same game would be played by the other side. And anyway, the fund-raisers would be quite right to reason that since there is zero chance of passing any amendment coming out of a partisan convention, there's little harm in milking the opportunity for all the money it will yield.

As a Democrat, I get this. Integrity has never been what the "i" in politics has stood for.

But as an American who believes that we need a way to address our fundamental problems, this all has the feelings of a tragedy. We are in the middle of an incredibly important constitutional moment. There is an urgency from both the Left and the Right to deliberate at least about how our Constitution could be improved. But the strategy of the Left is stillborn, and the strategy of the Right is self-defeating. Neither side will get what they want—which will make the defenders of the status quo quite happy.

What's needed is a way to bridge the gap between these two movements. The Left has got to move beyond its Oliver Twist–like "please, sir, more" strategy. It's got to embrace the only mechanism that has a chance to evade the control of Washington—a convention.

But the Right has got to lighten up on its restrictions for the scope of a convention. It needs to at least tolerate a convention—or a series of conventions—where ideas from the Left can be addressed as well.

If that's going to happen, the Right and the Left both need a good reason not to fear—each other, and the convention.

We need, in other words, a conception of the convention that no one has any reason to fear, and that no one can credibly say has been hijacked for the partisan views of any one side.

To get such a creature, we need to step back and understand a bit more the nature of this thing—"a convention." We need to rescue this most critical clause of our Constitution from the confusions imposed upon it by generations of ignorance (or worse).

"A Convention"

After the Revolutionary War, America formed itself into a nation under a Constitution. That Constitution is not the one that governs us today. The "Articles of Confederation" purported to be "perpetual." They were not. They were also much stricter about modifications than the ones that govern us today—they required that any amendment be unanimous:

> And the Articles of this Confederation shall be inviolably observed by every State, and the Union shall be perpetual; nor shall any alteration at any time hereafter be made in any of them; unless such alteration be agreed to in a Congress of the United States, and be afterwards confirmed by the legislatures of every State.

But that's not how the Articles of Confederation were, in fact, amended. In 1787, delegates from twelve states met in Philadelphia (Rhode Island stayed home). They drafted our Constitution. They then proposed that Congress send the draft to state *conventions* to be ratified—not, as the Articles of Confederation required, "state legislatures." And they stated, in the Constitution itself, that it would be "sufficient for the Establishment" of the Constitution that nine state conventions ratify it.

Even for lawyers, this is pretty clear: "Conventions" are not "legislatures"; "nine" is not "thirteen."

Thus the "convention" that gave us our Constitution contradicted the plain terms of the Constitution it was purporting to amend. The Constitution (of 1787) was thus adopted by violating the Constitution (of 1781).

These facts are not in controversy. How they should be interpreted is.

Some say there was nothing wrong with what our Framers did, since their "convention" was a "constitutional convention," which, as we know from constitutional theory, has the power to alter or abolish any Constitution at will. This was the theory of many about constitutions at the framing. Remember the words of the Declaration of Independence, announcing to the world "self-evident" "truths":

> that whenever any Form of Government becomes destructive of these Ends, it is the Right of the People to alter or to abolish it.

The Framers, under this theory, were actually being quite restrained. They had effectively abolished the old Constitution, but they sought ratification for the new from the people (represented in conventions) directly.

Others are less sanguine about the history of the 1787 convention. In their view, what this history proves is the danger of "a convention." The 1787 convention was conceived, the argument goes, within certain limits. The delegates to that convention exceeded those limits. In the language of this field, the 1787 convention thus "ran away." And this single precedent shows us exactly why we should fight like hell today, these skeptics insist, to avoid another "convention." For it, too, they warn, could "run away." And before you know it, we'd have the constitution of Soviet Russia. (The sounds like hyperbole, I understand, but in fact, it is precisely the argument advanced by the John Birch Society.[4])

Endless ink has been spilled by academics and activists arguing over what the 1787 convention was. Was it a runaway convention? Or was it a constitutional convention? Did it have the authority it exercised? Or did it exceed its authority?

But here's the critical bit that these arguments miss: The convention referred to in Article V of our Constitution *has nothing to do with* the convention of 1787. Whatever that convention was, an Article V convention is not that.

It doesn't take a law degree to see this. Nor does it require a PhD in history. This point is obvious to anyone who can read English. The only puzzle is why so many have fought this conclusion for so long.

In the language of the Framers, a "convention" was "a meeting, an act of coming together, used to refer to all sorts of assemblies, especially formal assemblies, convened for deliberation on important matters, whether ecclesiastical, political, or social."[5] These "meetings" were many—there are "records of about twenty conventions among colonies before Independence in 1776 and of eleven additional ones among states through 1787"[6]—and could have different purposes. Those purposes set the scope of the meeting's power. And while any particular convention might try to grab power beyond its scope, such power grabs fail.

For example, we all understand what a convention of the Democratic Party is. That means as well that we all understand what it is not. A Democratic convention has the power to adopt a platform for the Democratic Party. It obviously has no power to adopt a platform for the Republican Party. Sure, the convention might "run away." After completing its work on its own platform, it might well decide to draft one for the Republicans, too. And it might even adopt that Republican platform—as the platform of the Republican Party—in a final vote of the convention. But I doubt that anyone—certainly no Republican—has any fear about this possibility coming to fruition. Or if it did, any fear about its having any effect. A Democratic convention is for Democrats. In its very conception, that restricts the scope of its (increasingly modest) power.

The same is true about the "convention" spoken of in our Constitution.

Our Constitution sets out the power to convene a convention in Article V. Here is what it says:

> The Congress, whenever two thirds of both Houses shall deem it necessary, shall propose Amendments to this Constitution, or, on the Application of the Legislatures of two thirds of the several States, shall call a Convention for proposing Amendments, which, in either Case, shall be valid to all Intents and Purposes, as Part of this Constitution, when ratified by the Legislatures of three fourths of the several States, or by Conventions in three fourths thereof, as the one or the other Mode of Ratification may be proposed by the Congress....[7]

Notice first the words that are *not* in that text. Congress is *not* given the power to convene "a constitutional convention," or a "plenipotentiary convention."[8] It is given the power to convene "a Convention *for proposing Amendments*." This is a *proposing convention*, not a constitutional convention.[9] And to make it crystal clear, Article V goes on to say "which, in either Case, shall be valid to all Intents and Purposes, as Part of this Constitution, when ratified by the Legislatures of three fourths of the several States, or by Conventions in three fourths thereof." Which means, by implication, that they are *not valid for any intent or purpose until they are so ratified*. The product of a convention—if indeed it has any product—is a set of *proposed* amendments to the Constitution. It is not an amended Constitution. The products are then to be sent to the states for ratification. Only if three fourths of the states—thirty-eight—ratify those proposals will they have any effect on the Constitution.

If the English language has any meaning, then the convention spoken of in Article V has no power to change the Constitution. Its only power would be to *propose changes* to the Constitution. It likewise would have no power to change the mode by which amendments to the Constitution are ratified, since the mode by which amendments are ratified is itself part of the Constitution. All the convention of Article V can do is to give to the states proposals which the states then have the power to approve—or not. It is just a different path by which the states can be given a chance to change the structure of our Constitution.

But if this is all the convention can do, why is it there? What purpose did it have? Why not just leave the amending process to Congress, rather than this elaborate (and underspecified) "convention"?

That indeed was the original plan. As the Constitution approached its final draft, the amending clause within that draft gave Congress the exclusive power to propose amendments. But on September 15, George Mason of Virginia rose to a raise a pretty obvious question: *What if Congress is the problem?* As he put it: "No amendments of the proper kind would ever be obtained by the people, if the Government should become oppressive."[10]

Had *The Simpsons* been a part of late-eighteen-century American culture, we can imagine someone sputtering "D'oh!" at this point. Mason's objection led the convention of 1787 to add "a convention" to the Constitution's amending clause. If Congress was the problem, there would be a way of amending the Constitution that Congress couldn't control—the convention. No doubt, they were hopeful that such a remedy would never be needed. But if it were needed, the Constitution now had this safety valve: If Congress was the problem, then state legislatures, and hence state legislators, were the solution. If Congress went nuts, if it failed to propose the kind of constitutional reforms that (at least the legislatures deemed) necessary, then the Framers gave state legislatures a way to step in.

And not a way, but an obligation. State legislators have a duty under our Constitution to step up, and to act—at least if, as Mason put it, you believe that Congress has "abuse[d] their power, and refuse[s] their consent on that very account."[11] No other regular body of government has this power. Only state legislatures can force an amendment that Congress doesn't support onto the constitutional stage. And so if such an amendment is necessary, it is state legislators who must act to make it happen. It is their duty. It is their responsibility. They are the safety net for our constitutional tradition.

Okay, so the Constitution has a safety valve. If Congress goes nuts, the states are to step up. Through the procedure outlined in Article V, they are to make applications to Congress to call a convention. By the logic of "a convention," and by historical practice of hundreds of conventions, both at the founding, and at the state level throughout our history, we know that those applications can specify the convention's purpose, or the topics the convention can consider. *That's all an Article V convention can do*—to consider proposals within the scope of those topics, and recommend to the states specific amendments within that scope that the states might then ratify.

"But what if," the skeptic insists, "the convention exceeds those limits? What if it acted beyond the scope of its mandate? And indeed, what if it didn't get this memo, and acted as if it were a constitutional convention? What if, these promises grounded in reason notwithstanding, it exercised constitutive power?"

The Risk in the "Runaway"

Here is the answer: If the convention clause of Article V is a safety valve, then there is a safety valve within this safety valve. When you do the math, an obvious safety valve. But we need to work through some alternatives before we will see the protective potential of this safety value.

Safety Valve 1: Limits on the Convention

There are proponents of a convention who argue that there's nothing to fear, because Congress can constrain the convention. Congress can specify precisely the topics that the convention can consider. And any effort to reach beyond what Congress specifies would thus be illegitimate.

There's something to this argument—something that's true, conceptually, legally, and practically.

Conceptually, because again, the very idea of "a convention" is "a meeting, an act of coming together, used to refer to all sorts of assemblies, especially formal assemblies, convened for deliberation on important matters, whether ecclesiastical, political, or social"[12]—so that purpose certainly can constrain what the convention can do. There is no such thing as a convention *unrelated* to a particular purpose. There are only and always bodies convened to serve some purpose, and then to terminate. An Article V convention *could be* no different.

Legally, if you look at the long history of state conventions— conventions called to modify or rewrite state constitutions—all of those conventions were limited in precisely this sense. Those limits were generally effective. As a recent analysis of state conventions over the past fifty years concludes:

The state conventions show (as does the 1787 national convention) that a runaway convention is not impossible. But a runaway convention in most cases seems to produce either results that people like anyway (as with the 1787 national convention and the 1973 Rhode Island convention) or fails to result in constitutional change (as with the 1975 Arkansas convention, the 1963–68 Rhode Island convention, and the 1967 New York convention).[13]

Limits were respected. The conventions proved trustworthy in carrying out their charge, and only their charge. None of them "ran away" in the fundamental sense feared by convention opponents.

"But what about our founding convention? The one that gave us our Constitution? Didn't that convention 'run away'?"

In the words of Ronald Reagan, "There you go again. . . ." As I've already argued, the convention that gave us our Constitution was not convened pursuant to a clause that gave Congress the power to "call a Convention to propose Amendments." *It was not called pursuant to any power in the Articles of Confederation at all*. It was a convention exercising a latent power then generally acknowledged to be part of any free government—the power of the people to summon representatives to "alter or abolish" a Constitution. Whether or not that power continues to exist in America today— and I doubt that it does—that is *not* what a proposing convention under Article V could do.

"Yes, but the point is that Congress specified the scope for that convention, and the convention ignored that specification. Isn't that a precedent for the next federal convention, constitutional or not, ignoring Congress again?"

It isn't a *precedent* unless the convention you're talking about is the same sort of convention—a constitutional convention. And the reason is made clear by a pretty obscure bit of the history that gave rise to our own constitutional convention, the convention of 1787.

At the time our Framers began thinking about forming a new government, it was clear to almost all of them that the existing government had failed. Congress couldn't pay its bills because it had no power to tax. Congress could barely even meet, because it couldn't get a quorum to show up. The ship of state was sinking. And the leaders who gave us our Constitution stepped up to do something to save it.

What they did was to begin to organize the meeting that would eventually produce our Constitution. Virginia and New Jersey started the process.[14] Fairly quickly, a critical number of leaders agreed in principle with the idea of gathering to map out what would be next.

They did all this prearranging without the authority of Congress. They did it as citizens beginning to think through precisely how one exercised the "unalienable right" to "alter or abolish" their government.

When Congress got word of this effort, it moved quickly to respond. As Natelson describes:

> After most of the states already had accepted the invitation to participate, Congress passed a weak resolution expressing the "opinion" that the convention be limited to amending the Articles. All but two states disregarded this "opinion," but many writers have confused it with the convention call.[15]

Congress wasn't acting to give the group forming the meeting any authority it didn't already have. Its purpose was to avoid its own irrelevance. Congress could see that men convinced of its own impotence were mobilizing to think about what's next. It didn't want that conversation to happen independently of it. So it quickly passed a resolution, effectively endorsing the meeting, but defining it in a way that would limit its potential or significance.

How exactly should we think about that resolution?

Well, consider a hypothetical but historically grounded parallel. In 1912, there was a deep rift in the Republican Party between supporters of Teddy Roosevelt and supporters of the incumbent, William Howard Taft. When things broke down at the Republican Convention, Roosevelt's supporters left to hold a meeting to discuss whether they should leave the party and form a party of their own. They did eventually leave. A month later, they met as the "Bull Moose Party." But despite their passion, their move split the Republicans, and led to the election of neither Roosevelt nor Taft, but instead, Woodrow Wilson.

Now imagine just as the Roosevelt supporters were organizing to leave and to meet to discuss whether to form a new party, the Republican leadership passed a resolution that said:

> We approve of the decision by the supporters of Roosevelt to meet to discuss their future within the party, and we endorse and support that conversation. But we forbid those participating from discussing the idea of leaving the Republican Party. They are free to propose changes to our platform; they are not free to form a new party.

What would the significance of that resolution have been? Would it have bound TR's supporters? Would it be right to say that they had "ignored their instructions" when they subsequently created the Bull Moose Party?

The answer to those questions depends upon the loyalty one swears by being a member of a political party. I would think it is obvious that one is free at any point to leave a party if one disagrees with it. And if one is so free, then obviously the hypothetical resolution of the Republicans is irrelevant. The Republicans cannot bind members of the party to stay. So its resolution purporting to bind members of the party to stay is irrelevant. And if irrelevant, then it would be just wrong to say that the Republicans who formed the Bull Moose Party "acted outside the scope of their authority." They did not. They acted within their authority—to form whatever party they thought best.

The same analysis applies to the men who formed the convention that gave us the Constitution. If you believe, as they did, that it was an "unalienable right" of the people to "alter or abolish" their government, then they were free to meet to do that whenever they wished.

Remember, this was a "right." It was a right they thought "unalienable." And if they had begun the process of meeting to discuss precisely how, Congress could no more bind them than the Republican Party could bind TR's supporters. The Congress of 1787 was free to jump on the bandwagon. But they had no right to steer. That right—that "unalienable right"—was the people's, and the leaders who crafted our Constitution were stepping up to help guide the People.

So the constitutional convention that gave us our Constitution did not "run away" from anything. Or more precisely, it did not "run away" from any *legitimate* restriction that had been imposed upon it. Congress's wish for its own self-preservation was just that—a wish. Good for us that its wish was ignored.

The framing convention is thus again not a precedent for a proposing convention under Article V. Instead, I submit, the precedent for a proposing convention is all the state conventions that have been convened pursuant to their own constitutional provisions.

Because again: A proposing convention draws its authority from Article V. The framing convention drew its authority from the Creator, who Jefferson said, "endowed us with certain unalienable rights." The rules and structure of Article V constrain the proposing convention; only the Creator can constrain a constitutional convention. Under the rules and structure of Article V, Congress can specify the scope of the convention. If it does, the convention is bound to respect those limits, regardless of 1787.

This argument, however, excites opponents from the other direction. "Really? In setting the terms of an Article V convention, is there no limit on what Congress can do?"

There *is* a limit to what Congress can do. Congress's power under Article V is specified—it has the power to "call a Convention" and the power to then specify how any amendments proposed by that convention get ratified. And pursuant to what's called the "Necessary and Proper Clause," Congress also has the power to "make all Laws which shall be necessary and proper for carrying into Execution . . . all other Powers vested by this Constitution"—including the powers of Article V.

But that power is limited to laws "which shall be necessary and proper." And what that should mean is that Congress is not free to do whatever it wants, but instead is free to do only what is "proper." It would be "proper" for Congress to restrict the scope of a convention to the issues identified by the states calling for a convention. It would not be proper for Congress to ignore those restrictions, or to add restrictions, or topics, that are outside the scope of the applications. Congress is to act like a good lawyer, carrying into effect the will of its client—the Constitution, and the state legislatures. The whole purpose of this clause was to remove Congress from the driver's seat.

So Congress is empowered, but its power is limited. It can enact limits on the scope of the convention, but those limits must be "proper" in light of what the state legislatures have done. If they are proper, then those limits must be respected by the convention. The convention has no power to exceed proper limits imposed on it by Congress.

In this sense, then, these "limits" are a first safety valve on the safety valve of the proposing convention clause.

Safety Valve 2: The Courts

But now every lawyer reading what I've said so far is chafing at the bit. "Sure," they want to scream, "the Constitution says that Congress can only impose 'proper' limits. And sure, in theory, those limits must be respected. *But what happens if those limits are ignored?* [Lawyers get emotional about this sort of thing.] Who's going to stop Congress from imposing 'improper' limits? And who's going to discipline a convention to stick to the script?"

The answer, unfortunately, is no one. Though the Supreme Court is increasingly unpredictable about this—see, e.g., *Bush v. Gore* (2001)—in my view, there is exactly zero chance the Court would step in to invalidate a limit imposed by Congress and zero chance that the Court would step in to discipline a convention that exceeded proper limits. Indeed, the Supreme Court has almost said as much, as it has repeatedly insisted that the amending process is a "political question," meaning that it, the Court, will stay out of it.[16] So as much I regret a fact that makes my argument harder to make, I believe it is true. We can't count on the Supreme Court to save us, or to save the convention. Whatever is right or wrong, right and wrong won't be judicially determined or enforced.

But so what?

Imagine Congress imposes an improper restriction on a convention. No one will force the convention to respect it. If thirty-four states had passed applications calling on Congress to convene an Article V convention "to consider proposals to reduce the power of the federal government," it would be completely inappropriate for Congress to forbid that convention to consider "proposals to reduce the power of the federal government." A convention would therefore be free to consider such proposals, Congress's instruction notwithstanding. And whether it passed any proposal to reduce the power of the federal government or not, it would, in my view, be perfectly legitimate for the convention to consider them.

But this fact seriously undermines the significance of Safety Valve 1. Because if Congress could get away with exceeding its power, the convention could get away with exceeding its power, too. For example, if Congress had properly restricted the convention to three issues only, the convention could ignore that restriction, and consider five issues instead. The "limits" would be worth no more than the paper they were printed on. And so again, those fearful of the convention can fairly ask, "What's to stop the convention from doing something insane? What's the guarantee it won't wreck the Constitution?"

Safety Valve 3: The Safety Valve Itself

So here's where we are:

The power to demand a convention was intended by the Framers as a safety value—a way around a corrupted Congress; a way to fix what Congress itself wouldn't.

But that safety valve is uncertain: What's to guarantee it won't blow up? How can we protect the Constitution from crazy changes? What's to assure some minimal stability in the face of a "runaway" convention?

The answers to these questions depend first on being clear about just what's at stake. If—and there really is *no* "if" about it—"a convention" called pursuant to Article V is not a "constitutional convention," then if it "runs away," *the most it can do* is propose some crazy change. It can't change the Constitution itself; it can't change the way the Constitution gets amended. All it can do is to put on the table something that it wasn't supposed to address. Or put differently, the only risk a so-called runaway creates is the risk of a proposal to amend the Constitution that obviously—given the mix of interests in the United States—is insane.

To minimize this risk, the safety valve itself needs a safety valve. But so far, we've not found one that's slam-dunk certain. Congress can certainly limit the scope of a convention—either properly or not. That should be a strong guarantee, since practically every state convention called pursuant to a state constitution in the past fifty years has obeyed its limits.[17] But as I've said, I don't believe the Courts will second-guess Congress, and neither do I believe that any Court is going to regulate a convention. So in principle, there's a right and a wrong here. But in practice, there's no cop on the beat who will enforce what's right by stopping what's wrong.

Which leaves us in need of an ultimate safety valve: What can guarantee, or come as close to guaranteeing, that craziness won't happen?

Leave the Lawyers, Return to Real Politics

To answer this question, we need to approach it in the right way. This debate has been too much dominated by lawyers and theoreticians. It needs the splash of reality—of political reality, a practical political understanding of what the risks here actually are.[18]

For let's first remember the next bit of Article V—after it

establishes the ability of two thirds of the state legislatures to call on Congress to convene "a convention for proposing Amendments." After defining how amendments are to be proposed, the Constitution then describes *specifically* how they are to be adopted. As Article V states:

> [The proposals] shall be valid to all Intents and Purposes, as Part of this Constitution, when ratified by the Legislatures of three fourths of the several States, or by Conventions in three fourths thereof, as the one or the other Mode of Ratification may be proposed by the Congress;

Let's make this very simple: The only way a proposed amendment gets to be part of the Constitution is if three fourths of the states—either legislatures or state conventions, as Congress may choose—ratify it.[19]

Three fourths. Or thirty-eight states. To become part of our Constitution, an amendment needs the affirmative vote of thirty-eight states—which means that the vote of one house in thirteen states could block it.

So this becomes the crucial safety valve question: Is there any "crazy amendment"—an amendment that one side views as fundamentally repugnant to their values or beliefs—that could be ratified under our Constitution, if the vote of *one* house in *thirteen* states is enough to block it?

The answer to that question depends upon how America is divided—specifically, which political parties control which state governments, and how that division relates to the magic number 13.

As of this writing, there are thirty-one double-red states in America—meaning states where the Republican Party controls both houses in the state legislature.

And as of this writing, there are eleven double-blue states in America—meaning states where the Democratic Party controls both houses in the state legislatures.

And as of this writing, there are eight states with one house controlled by each party.

Adding these three categories of states together, this means that there are thirty-nine potential Republican vetoes on any proposed amendment to the Constitution (since an amendment can be stopped in a state with the vote of one house only). There are nineteen potential Democratic vetoes on any amendment to the Constitution.

And again all it takes to stop an amendment is the negative vote of thirteen houses.

So the precise political question becomes whether there is any amendment that would outrage Republicans that could not muster the opposition of thirteen houses in the thirty-nine Republican houses.

And likewise, the precise political question is whether there is any amendment that would outrage Democrats that could not muster the opposition of thirteen of nineteen Democratic houses.

Let's think about this practically: Republicans (and many Democrats but let's make this as hard for my argument as it can be) support the Second Amendment. Imagine a runaway convention that proposed abolishing the Second Amendment. Is it even remotely possible that thirteen houses in the thirty-nine Republican houses would not vote to block that repeal? Is it even conceivable, *politically conceivable*, that even if you got all eleven double-blue states to vote for the repeal of the Second Amendment, you'd also get *twenty-seven GOP states*—whether from the thirty-one double-red, or the remaining eight where the GOP controls at least one house?

Or think about it the other way round. Democrats (and many Republicans, but again, let's make this as hard for my argument as we can) believe in marriage equality. They believe the Constitution should ban discrimination on the basis of sexual orientation. Imagine a runaway convention proposed an amendment to forbid gay marriage, and to forbid the Constitution protecting the GLBT community against discrimination. Is it even remotely possible that thirteen of the nineteen Democratic houses would not vote to block that change? Is it even conceivable, *politically conceivable*, that even if you got all thirty-one double-red states to vote for it, you'd also get seventeen Democratic states—whether from the nineteen double-blue, or the remaining eight where the Democratic Party controls at least one house?

The answer to these questions should be obvious. There is no chance that thirty-eight states would ratify what I've called a "crazy" amendment. Because it is precisely when an amendment becomes "crazy"—meaning, precisely when an amendment triggers some strong partisan reaction—that it becomes impossible for such an amendment to be ratified. To be "crazy" means to be not long for the amending world.

The same argument applies for a proposal that's not crazy, but just unauthorized.

Imagine thirty-four states applied to Congress to call a convention to consider a balanced budget amendment. Imagine Congress called such a convention, "limited to considering proposals for amending the Constitution to require a balanced budget." And imagine finally, a convention were held, but that the convention exceeded its mandate, and proposed an amendment to abolish the Electoral College as well. That proposal isn't crazy. Indeed, it might even make good sense. So what would happen to that proposed amendment?

Well, first, Congress might decide not to send the amendment to the states to be ratified. Following the applications, Congress would have properly restricted the scope of the convention. If the convention exceeded its authority, Congress could well decide not to send the ultra vires amendment to the states. The proposal would get lots of attention. It might even persuade Congress to propose such an amendment itself. But under this scenario, it would die in Congress, because it was produced beyond the scope of the convention's power.

That outcome assumes a Congress with a backbone. Imagine we didn't have such a Congress. (It's possible.) Imagine instead that Congress felt bound to send to the states whatever amendment the convention proposed. So that indeed Congress did permit the states to consider the amendment abolishing the Electoral College.

But so how would such an amendment fare in the states? Because, of course, the states would have a very strong incentive to reject that amendment, solely because it was passed in contravention to the states' own directives. Or at least, contrary to the directive of thirty-four states. At least among those thirty-four, there would be a very strong reason for at least thirteen to discipline the convention for violating its orders. Without such a discipline, the convention becomes less reliable. With such a discipline, the convention becomes a more reliably usable device for the states to put on the constitutional table proposals for constitutional reform.

This alone should be incentive to enough for states to block the ultra vires amendment.

But imagine it isn't. Imagine the limits of the convention are ignored, and an amendment beyond those limits is proposed; imagine Congress sends that amendment to the states; and imagine thirteen states don't block it. Instead, imagine thirty-eight states ratify that amendment, its shameful and dishonorable birth notwithstanding.

Here then is the real question: *So what?* What would the real harm be, if an idea was good enough to earn ratification by thirty-eight states? We have a system where the states representing 5 percent of population have the ability to block constitutional change.[20] If that power notwithstanding, thirty-eight states expressed their desire for constitutional change, what *democratic reason* is there to resist it? Or put differently, in a democracy, what really is the harm when a supermajority ratifies a constitutional change, even if that constitutional change was born in sin?

In the end, this is the Framers' true safety valve. It isn't fancy. It doesn't require high theory. And it is built right into the Constitution's text.

The reason not to fear a runaway convention (meaning a convention that proposed amendments beyond its mandate, not a runaway in the sense of a convention that changed the rules, because that is not on the table) is not because we could stop a convention from running away. It is instead because it wouldn't matter if it did run away.

If a convention ran away, and proposed a series of crazy amendments, that would be a waste. But it wouldn't be a tragedy.

If a convention ran away, and proposed a sensible change, so sensible that thirty-eight states ratified it, the original sin notwithstanding, that would be a good thing. It would represent a consensus of political values practically never seen in American politics today.

The worst that could happen is that we ratify an amendment. What possible bad could come from that?

Risks

Every day, we take risks. World-changing (for us at least) risks. Rather than walk, we bundle our kids into a car and drive them to school. Or to get ice cream. When we do that, we expose them to a risk—the probability that we'll have an accident, and that our children will be killed. Nothing in the world could be worse for a parent. I know. I've seen it. Yet we take the risk that the worst possible thing will happen, to avoid the extra ten minutes it would take to walk.

That is a case of risk. I'm not saying the risk is worth it. Or that the risk is not worth it. My point in rehearsing what is familiar is that we don't—fortunately—live life the way a lawyer would recommend. We don't—fortunately—live life so as to eliminate all risk. The question we ask in life—in everyday life, every day of our lives—is not whether there's a risk. It's whether the risk outweighs the benefit. Or more dramatically, whether the risk outweighs the certain harm.

So imagine you're in a house. The fire alarm goes off. You determine the fire is in the kitchen—the room just below you. And you determine you could likely leave your room, run down the hall, and escape through the back stairs.

In that calculation, certainly, one could point out risks. It's certainly possible that the floor of the hall will collapse because the fire has spread to the beams. It's certainly possible that smoke will have escaped into the hall, making it impossible for you to breathe. And it's certainly possible that as you race down the back stairs, the fire in the kitchen will come through the wall and trap you. It's certainly possible, in other words, that your escape will fail.

But it takes a certain kind of craziness to leap from that possibility—that your escape might fail—to the conclusion that you should stay in your room. Because whether or not you are harmed while trying to escape, you are certainly going to be harmed if you stay in the room above a raging fire. There is no risk-free option in this hypothetical. Either way, you face risks.

The same in life: Doing anything—including doing nothing—has a risk. And the calculation we all make all the time weighs the risk of doing nothing against the risk of doing something. Or again, all the time, we recognize that even if there is a risk from doing something, that could easily be outweighed by the risk from doing nothing.

All this applies in an obvious way to the debate about whether the state legislatures should petition Congress to call "a convention."

The single argument most frequently made by state legislators opposing an Article V convention is the risk that "the convention will run away."

I've spent many pages trying to show that risk is small. But let's assume, contrary to my genuine belief, that small is not zero. Let's assume there's a risk that if we do something, something bad might happen.

What is the risk if we do nothing?

If you're drawn to the idea of a convention to allow the states to consider a balanced budget amendment, you have a clear sense of the risk if we do nothing. You think our nation is fiscally bankrupt, and you believe that there is nothing in politics today that can stop our slide to an even greater bankruptcy. And because you think about the costs of that bankruptcy for our kids, and for our economy, you believe those costs are high. Incredibly high. And so when a state legislator says she's doesn't want to take the "risk" of the Second Amendment being repealed, you need to say to her: What of the certainty of fiscal bankruptcy?

Or if you're drawn to the Article V convention because you believe the federal government has gotten too big, and has displaced self-government by the states in all those contexts in which that makes sense, then you also believe there's little in the current structure of federal government incentives to block this road to centralism. Neither Congress nor the president has enough incentive to disempower the federal government. The costs of that, you believe, are enormous. And so when a state legislator tells you he doesn't want to take the "risk" of the Second Amendment being repealed, you need to say to him: What about the certainty of all the other liberties that the federal government has or will take from us? You're worried about the one that seems to have an effective posse. What about the others without a posse that will certainly disappear as the federal government becomes more and more dominant?

Or if you're drawn to the Article V convention—as I am—because you believe our Congress has become fundamentally corrupted, not through bribery or criminality, but through a corruption of a system we use to fund campaigns; and if you believe—as I do—that that corruption has made governing impossible; that it has incentivized the business model of hate and polarization, and made it absolutely impossible for Congress to address any important issue sensibly—whether that is climate change, or Wall Street regulation, or health care, or the tax system, or food safety, or education, or the debt, or even copyright regulation—then the costs of this problem are, you believe with me, astronomical. If you believe, as I do, like this, the issue isn't the "risk" that something will go wrong. The issue is the certainty. And so when a state legislator tells you she doesn't want to take the "risk" of gay marriage being abolished, you need to say to her: What about the practical certainty that our government will fail? What about climate change?

And health care? And unemployment? And inequality? What about all the issues our government is certainly incapable of addressing sensibly now, given the current system of corruption that is our political system?

The point in all three cases should be obvious, and we need to make it more strongly than we have: The question isn't, "What is the risk?" The question is, "What are the risk*s*?" There may be a tiny risk—really tiny—of constitutional craziness. But against that tiny risk, again depending on your perspective, there is almost certainty of a calamity of much greater proportions.

And so to talk about the "risk" is not to justify doing nothing. To the contrary: For a state legislator to point to the risk as a reason to do nothing is like an ambulance driver who refuses to rescue a drowning child because she fears she "might" get in an car accident along the way. We don't call that "prudence." We call it cowardice. Talk of risk in this context is simply a way to obscure a more fundamental duty. Yes, there is a risk. But there is also a duty.

It is the duty of state legislators to step up and rescue this nation, if Congress itself has become the problem. That was the Framers' plan. Congress has become the problem. So it the duty of state legislators to step up to the constitutional obligation.

I get that this idea is unfamiliar to state legislators. I understand they like to think about local matters—water regulation, or how to get great schools in their state. But in the design of our Constitution, state legislators were given a critically fundamental duty: to be the ultimate safety value for a corrupted government. This is their job, even if this fact has become buried in 225 years of history.

To many, this is a scary thought. Congress is bad enough. We're supposed to rely on state legislators? Congressmen-wanna-be's?

But as I've watched states, and seen their governments up close, I've come to have enormous respect for state governments, at least in small(er) and less corrupted states. To watch the Delaware or Vermont legislature sit through committee meetings is an inspiration. To see the full 400 representatives in the New Hampshire legislature sit through debates, and deliberate about legislation, is to see what our forebears imagined representative democracy could be. The truth is, the vast majority of state legislators do what they do for the best possible reason. There's no K Street to cash out to. There's no limousine waiting to take them to work. They serve because they believe good government is needed. And indeed, if you compare the work they do to the "work" that Congress does, they are a credit to our Republic, at least as compared to an institution—Congress—that is essentially bankrupt.

I am genuinely glad that the Framers gave these citizens the obligation to backstop our democracy. Better them than unelected judges. But whether you like it or not—or more important, whether they like it or not—it is their job. The Framers chose them to rescue us from a corrupted and failed Congress.

That is where we are. They need to step up.

And if they don't step up, you need to hold them responsible. You need to say to each of them: If you don't get this, then study it. And if after you've studied it, you're still not ready to do the duty George Mason gave you, then step aside, and give your seat to someone who will. There is no more important obligation given to state legislators within our constitutional design. It's time they live up to it.

One Way Forward

Our government is broken. It may well take constitutional reform to fix it. This much many on the Right and many on the Left have come to believe. Let's call these two "many's" "constitutional reformers."

What constitutional reformers don't agree upon—yet, at least—is *how*. How are we going to achieve constitutional change?

Practically everyone in this movement believes that the essential step will involve thirty-eight states ratifying one or more amendments to the Constitution.

The only disagreement is how best to get those amendments before the states. How, in other words, to get those amendments "proposed." Should Congress do the proposing, or should a proposing convention?

I say *"practically* everyone" believes this, because not everyone does. Some in this movement want revolutionary reform. A new Constitution. Or a constitutional convention with constituent power. Or a process that at least invokes Jefferson's promise— that we retain the "unalienable right" to "alter or abolish" our Constitution—so that the process remains unconstrained by the eighteenth-century limits of Article V.

I am a constitutional reformer. I am not a revolutionary. I believe our existing Constitution gives us precisely the power to solve the problems that we face, precisely because it was intentionally crafted in light of the kinds of problems that we face.

The Proposing Convention Clause of Article V was written for us. And if we could get leaders from both sides to recognize the potential that Article V offers, we might actually get to a place where real change is possible.

Neither side can get there alone. A convention called for conservative causes alone will be a boon for liberal fund-raisers. A convention called for liberal causes alone would be a boon for conservative fund-raisers. Each side, in a sense, must take the other side hostage, if this process is to avoid the inevitable buzz saw of partisan politics.

So how could that be done? What would a plan look like? What precisely should state legislators be calling for, if they're to succeed in securing a convention with the political capacity to actually achieve something? What should the deal be? How could it be crafted?

The key is a simple compromise: We get to consider our proposals if you get to consider yours. A convention, that is, or a series of conventions, considering the core topics now being seriously pressed, covering both the Right and the Left politically.

Fair Deals

If you survey the range of plausible constitutional reforms now being pressed by activists on all sides, they fall, roughly, into three buckets: fiscal responsibility, electoral integrity, and states rights.

The fiscal responsibility proposals try to craft constitutional restrictions on a perceived inability of Congress to behave responsibly fiscally. These include balanced budget amendments, but could include ideas such as a line-item veto (giving the president the power to enforce fiscal discipline). Some even include monetary reform, to drive the Federal Reserve to behave (as they perceive it) more responsibly—or at least, not as "politicians."[21]

The electoral integrity proposals respond to the issues described in this book. The primary political motivator for these proposals is *Citizens United*. But they include all the ideas described here to assure equal citizens, by establishing a representative democracy.

States rights proposals strive to carve back on federal power. These include proposals for restricting the scope of federal regulatory power, by returning regulatory power to the states now held by the federal government.

While there is support for each of these topics from the Left and the Right, the first and the third are understood to come from the Right. The fiscal responsibility movement has had long ties to conservative Republicans; the (modern) states rights movement (as distinct from the racist states rights movement of the pre–civil rights era) is the creation of some of the founders of the Tea Party. The second, electoral integrity, comes primarily from the Left.

As I've said, any of the three on its own would excite fatal political opposition—fatal to the product of the convention, if not the convention itself. The solution to this obvious political problem is to bundle the topics, so a convention, or a series of conventions, could fairly cover the full range.

But the challenge for that idea is that practically none of the recent applications for a convention are tolerant of different topics. Practically all of them make the mistake of forcing the convention to consider just its topic—again ignoring the partisan danger a single-topic convention would raise.

This problem, however, could be cured. Each of the states that have made an application for a convention could cure this partisan problem by passing a resolution that fit their application to the idea of multitopic convention, limited to these three domains. Not an unlimited convention, but one fitting within the scope of these three topics. Thus a state having already passed a call for a convention would pass another resolution, similar to this:

> RESOLVED, that any prior restriction notwithstanding, the State of _____ hereby reaffirms its application for a convention pursuant to Article V of the Constitution to address the topic of _____, as well as topics _____ and _____.

If there were thirty-four such resolutions ratified, then the convention that was thereby convened could consider these three topics, either in a single convention, or in a series convened one after the other.

If states began to do this, then no doubt, there would still be opposition to a proposing convention. But it would more difficult for that opposition to be purely partisan. And by shifting the debate from a partisan field, we would have a chance to address it with sense.

And then to this cross-partisan mix, I would add one more part: the people.

The convention is an ad-hoc legal body. Its only power is the power to recommend.

But still, it is unprecedented at the national level; it raises serious anxiety among sensible people. I've tried to allay that anxiety in the many pages of this incredibly long chapter. But fear doesn't yield to an argument. To battle fear, we must show, not tell.

So to this mix, I would add one more recommendation: a series of shadow conventions, each with advisory, not legal, authority, and each populated by a random and representative mix of ordinary Americans. In the language of political science, this would be a series of deliberative polls, drawn from America as a whole, spread out over a year at least, considering the topics that might populate a convention.

I realize that, to most, this idea of bringing "the people" into the mix won't allay any anxiety about a convention. An ad hoc political body is bad enough; but a body of ordinary Americans?

I understand the anxiety. But ironically enough, the fear about the ignorance of ordinary Americans is itself grounded in ignorance. We fear "the people" because we have not seen "the people" adequately informed and fairly represented. Activists and public opinion polls are scary to most, but each suffers from each of these flaws. The most prominent activists on both the Left and the Right don't represent America; and the flash survey asking difficult questions asks those questions of a public that hasn't had the opportunity to understand the issues, or discuss them.

Deliberative polls solve both problems.[22] The participants in a deliberative poll are randomly selected; the body they join is thus representative of the public. There are just as many moderates as in the public generally. There are just as many women, etc.

More important, once the body is selected, it meets together, and is given the material necessary to understand and deliberate about the questions at issue. These are not ignorant people; they are informed people. They are not the fringes of the people; they are representative of the public.

These deliberative polls would be conducted over an extended period. Their results would be published, as would their deliberations. And if they succeeded as they have in many radically different contexts over the past twenty years, they would provide one final safety valve on the convention process. For whatever else a convention does, it must ultimately produce results that America, properly informed and represented, could embrace. There is no other way to understand what that America believes. Nor is there a better way to capture and represent it.

Because in the end, this is my bias. I love the idea of a representative Congress. I've not known one in my lifetime. I am enormously impressed by the integrity of at least small state governments. Yet even they must too often yield to politics. I work among scholars and academics. But professors are the last people in the world I would turn to to govern.

None of these ordinary entities of authority inspire. But the pcople, properly constituted, would. Not always: Juries can make terrible mistakes. And not every deliberative poll produces a result that makes sense.

But if I had to trust one entity to at least frame the issues that should govern a convention, I would without doubt trust the wisdom that could be inspired from ordinary citizens, properly constituted. Since I am a tenured professor at an elite university, that may make me a traitor to my kind. But if education teaches us anything—even an "elite education"—it is the dangers of any system that trusts to an elite the power over the rest.

In a sense, that has always been reality. But history does not yet give us an example of elites doing good, even if elites do well. We should try something different. Not direct democracy—none of us has the time for that.[23] But a system that at least admits the ideas of a reflective public, constituted in a way that guarantees representativeness, and practiced in a way that assures understanding. It is not rocket science. Or if it's made to seem like it is, someone is lying.

CHAPTER 14

Referendum Politicians

A "proposing convention" is an unconventional device for reset-ting the direction of our democracy. It was created with the hope that it might never be used. But it was created with the recognition that sometimes an institution can't cure itself. The Framers gave state legislators the power, and hence, the duty to intervene if the federal government had failed. On any honest view, they should intervene now.

But we're not limited to the strategies that seemed sensible two and a quarter centuries ago. There have been a few changes since then. Some. Those changes create new opportunities for hosting the intervention that our federal government needs. They give us new ways to reboot the Republic.

In this chapter, I describe a hybrid of two ideas from the first edition of this book.[1] The core idea is to imagine politicians elected for a single purpose—to bring about the change the nation needs to enable representative democracy to function. Call them *referendum politicians*: Their only job is to force a process that would reset the way the democracy functions, to establish a representative democracy (finally).

The referendum politician holds her office for a single purpose—to enact a package of fundamental reform. Once that package is enacted, the trusteeship ends, and the politician presumptively steps aside. As I'll describe more below, when it comes to the president, "presumptively" means certainly. For members of Congress, not necessarily. But to make the idea clear, let's begin with the president.

The Referendum President

It is the reality of American politics today that reform needs a president. It wasn't always that way, but the twentieth century has made it that way, and we're not far enough from that bizarre hundred years to know anything different.

But there's a structural problem with any ordinary president making this the central issue for her administration. Because to lead on this issue would almost certainly mean to fail on every other issue. And for the business model of the modern American president, such a strategy is a nonstarter.

The reason is obvious (and it makes me feel quite stupid that I didn't see it before): To take up the issue of reforming Congress is to take on Congress itself. All of Congress. Both parties included.

But for a president to take on Congress is for that president to practically guarantee that nothing that president wants will get passed by Congress. Even if she succeeds in forcing Congress to ratify the kind of changes described in Chapter 4—because those changes will require Congress to ratify them—depending on the battle that has been fought, that could be the last thing she gets Congress to pass. And if it is, then that president, however important she has been to the history of our democracy, will be a one-term president.

It used to be that there was no stigma associated with being a one-term president. Two thirds of the presidents between Washington and Lincoln were single-term presidents (ignoring the two who died in office). But today, it is a mark of failure. Even a man as great as Jimmy Carter has found it difficult to escape the loser box. George Bush Sr. has only been saved by a string of family successors. Even then, he has not achieved the post-presidential love that his son did.

I'm not saying it's impossible. I'm saying that it's possible it's impossible. And that possibility should lead us to think about a different model for presidential leadership: of a president with the sanction to demand reform, but who does not suffer the political costs from a bloody political conflict.

So consider the *referendum president*. Imagine a prominent, trusted, and well-liked national figure—ideally, not a politician, or if a politician, clearly an ex-politician. Warren Buffet, Michelle Obama, Bill Gates, or Jerry Brown on the Left. James Baker, Colin Powell, (former comptroller) David Walker, or Christy Todd Whitman on the Right.

Imagine that person announces that he or she would run for president in the Democratic or Republican Primary.

Imagine that candidate makes one pledge: If elected, he or she will do one thing, and then resign.

That one thing is passing a package of fundamental reform. Once Congress enacts that package, and the president resigns, the vice president becomes president.

The aim of the reform would be to establish political equality—the equality of citizens that I have described throughout this book. At a minimum, that requires a statute. It could as well include Congress proposing an amendment to secure fundamental reform. But the core focus of the change would be to end the Green Primary in America, and give members of Congress a chance to focus on what their constituents want.

The politics of this idea are quite specific. If the idea gets traction—if the campaign can be launched in a prominent enough way, such that the public can understand and respond to it, and if indeed, the public begins to support the idea—then the other candidates have an important choice. They can either resist the plan and argue against the referendum president, or they can endorse it. And if they endorse it, then the focus of the primaries can shift to who will replace the referendum candidate—really, just a trustee—once she steps down—who, in other words, will be the vice president. If they resist it, they risk losing a shot at becoming the president by being the vice president first.

A similar dynamic would evolve between the parties, too. The first person to announce would announce in one party. If the idea got traction, that party would quickly be seen as the best hope for reform. The other party would then face a choice similar to the one faced by the candidates in that party—does the party follow the lead, and promote their own referendum candidate, or does the party fight reform? If the movement for reform grows quickly enough, the other party might have no choice. They, too, will be pressed to lead with a candidate who promises the same sort of fundamental change. They, too, would quickly shift their focus to the person who will replace the trustee, once reform is enacted.

If both parties advance a referendum candidate, then reform is almost certain to happen. Inauguration Day will be a day of quick transition. The referendum president will be sworn in. He or she will give a speech, travel to the White House, and sign the legislation for reform that Congress has just enacted. There may be fights about the details, but there can be little doubt about the meaning of the election, and the mandate of the president. The best move for Congress would be to clear the deck as quickly as possible, so the nation can move on.

But if just one party advanced a referendum candidate, and that candidate won, the fight would depend on the *referendum representatives* that I describe in the section that follows. In the worst case, the referendum president would identify the resisters and wage a fight in the next election two years hence. In the best case, enough referendum representatives will have been elected to guarantee that the legislation moves.

Either way, the referendum president would have a mandate. The powers of the presidency—focused on a single goal—would push toward answering that mandate. And the probability of that reform being passed would be high. Here is a path to change that if successful in the first step—enacting the referendum candidate— seems almost certain to be successful in the second step—enacting fundamental reform.

Referendum Representatives

We can't, however, rely on a president alone. The president can't directly control Congress. And Congress has lots of ways to hide from the check of the American people.

So in addition to getting a president committed to fundamental reform, we need to assure a *sufficiently large fraction* in Congress committed to fundamental reform as well. Not necessarily a majority. But enough to hold Congress hostage until it enacts the reform that America needs.

So imagine in addition to a referendum president we add the idea of a referendum representative.

In its cleanest form, the referendum representative is a nonpolitician, who announces that she will run for Congress in a particular district for one purpose—to support the referendum president. Once the work of reform is done, this representative would resign and go home. But while the fight continues, she will stay in Washington to make certain the president can get the responsiveness from Congress that the president needs.

The nonpolitician bit is valuable and important, but not necessary here. For if the idea took off, there's no reason why regular members of Congress couldn't commit to being a member of the referendum caucus. Those members would commit to voting to advance reform, and securing its passage. Once the reform was passed, the caucus would disband and they would remain as members of the reformed Congress, committed to protecting the change they helped bring about.

In either case, the total number of referendum representatives needed is not necessarily large. It depends on the size of the majority party's majority. If the Republicans would otherwise have a twenty-seat majority in the House, then the reform caucus would only need to include at least twenty Republicans and whatever number of Democrats in addition. But the key to making this feasible is to remember that these reform representatives would not necessarily need to come from the (small number of) swing districts. They could come from the most Republican districts in the nation—so long as those Republicans voters could be convinced to support a reform candidate.

Both the referendum president and the referendum representatives aim at a single goal—making reform feasible. As I have described, the single most difficult barrier to reform is the belief of most of us that reform isn't possible.

But the referendum candidates show us how reform *is* possible. Like a bankruptcy judge, or a referee in a boxing match, the referendum candidate is different from an ordinary politician. She has political power, but her power is properly executed only if it remains directed to the end of reform. Success for a referendum president is simple to describe. So, too, is failure. And that clarity gives hope. *Whatever else* might happen in the next election, that clarity at least gives us the sense that fundamental reform would happen first. That possibility is precisely the hope that this movement needs.

Of course, it needs more than hope. It needs as well a journalism that reaches beyond the lazy cynic. It needs people willing to think beyond what has "always" happened before (in scare quotes, because of course, "always" never means always). And it needs, most of all, people unafraid to fail.

These are not simple needs—the last one especially. The pressure to hew to the status quo is overwhelming, and fear of failing only grows with experience.

But if you're here in this book, you know we have no other choice. You know that fundamental reform is essential. And if we think about the incredible strength that great people show us in so many different contexts—the brilliance of a film director, the courage of first responders, the genius of a Bill Gates or Steve Jobs, the wisdom of a Warren Buffet, the thousands of nameless health workers who fly to Liberia because there is a raging epidemic, the soldiers who without hesitation step in harm's way—it cannot be that this strength is so difficult. To take this risk is not to risk one's life. It is not a commitment to fifteen years of struggle. It is at most a risk of failure. And failure is the only lesson that has ever taught any of us.

Conclusion

The idea of a representative democracy is that it represent its citizens—equally.

Ours does not. In a host of ways, none more dramatic than the way we fund campaigns, we have allowed inequality to creep into our Republic. I don't mean the inequality of wealth, or the inequality of speech. We have those, too, but that has not been my focus here. Instead, we have allowed to evolve within our system a fundamental inequality in the commitment to represent equal citizens equally.

No system could ever achieve perfect political equality. Ours doesn't even try. Instead, we have allowed the basic commitment to an equality of citizens, one built into our framing design, to be corrupted. The mechanisms of accountability that our Framers intended for our Republic have been rewired. The forces that were meant to guide the democracy have been changed.

Our choice now is how to respond.

There are many who believe we cannot respond. That it is hopeless. In a national poll conducted at the end of 2013, while 96 percent said it was "important" to reduce the influence of money in politics, 91 percent said they didn't believe it possible.[1] So deep is our skepticism that even "reforms" are viewed as corruption. Eighty percent of us, according to a different poll, believe that every reform to fix the system so far was actually just a way to entrench the incumbents.[2]

This is the politics of resignation. We haven't "accepted" the system in the sense that we like it. We've "accepted" it, in the sense that we don't see what we can do about it. We don't believe the politicians will change it. We don't see anyone else who could. So we add "and a corrupt government" to Franklin's aphorism ("the only things that are certain are death and taxes"), and most of us then just stay home.

We must thaw that resignation. And that will require (1) a plan that seems possible, (2) a clearer sense of who this campaign is ultimately for, and (3) a better recollection of what fighting for equality means.

Let's start with the last. Because when you conceive of this fight as a fight for equality, there is an obvious history to draw upon, both for lessons and inspiration.

As I complete this book, the president is in Charleston, South Carolina, at a memorial for nine African-Americans murdered as a way to say, "Black lives don't matter." This was not money as speech, but murder as speech. But that statement, by a pathological racist, inspired an incredible response across America. Finally, 150 years after the end of the Civil War, the flag associated with the Confederate cause is coming down across the South. And those nine lives may well be the final deaths of that most bloody war—a war begun to save a nation, but ended with a rededication of that nation to the "proposition" that "all men are created equal."

On the same day that President Obama spoke, four liberal justices on the Supreme Court joined one conservative to declare that the right to marry could not be denied on the basis of whom one happened to love. Laws forbidding same-sex marriage, Justice Kennedy wrote, "denied the equal dignity of men and women."[3] That denial was finally reversed.

This day, June 26, 2015, when these two critically important movements for equality converged, will likely be remembered in American history. But what should certainly be remembered is the long struggle that got us to this day. The fight for equality regardless of sexual orientation is not complete. But it has made extraordinary progress in an incredibly short time, through the struggles of many in many different contexts of social and political life. By contrast, no one could say that the fight for racial equality is complete, or that it has made extraordinary progress in a short time. But when four black girls were killed in the bombing of the 16th Street Baptist Church in 1963, that murder-as-speech meant something different from nine souls being murdered today. In 1963, everyone feared the silent many who stood with the murderers. Today, it is only lunatics who believe or behave as Dylann Roof did. This is unacceptably slow progress. But it is progress.

That progress was earned. It took thousands to take to the streets to demand equality. It took the sacrifices of many more to force America to her better side. Jefferson's "promissory note," as Martin Luther King Jr. described it, that "all men are created equal," is still being paid off. But because of the fight of people like King, and Jimmie Lee Jackson, and the people brutalized on the Pettus Bridge, and the nine victims of the Charleston murder, we are closer today than we were fifty years ago.

In that struggle, African-Americans had a certain advantage. There was no doubt about the inequality that they suffered. It took many years and many significant victories to convince most African-Americans that there was a reason to protest against that inequality. For many years after the betrayal following Reconstruction, that fight seemed hopeless, or suicidal. But when victory seemed possible, African-Americans, and many white Americans, stepped up to fight because the injustice was clear. No one could miss it.

That's not the same for the fight that this book has been about. While we start with the same sense of hopelessness, we don't start with the same recognition. Unlike African-Americans suffering Jim Crow, those most affected by this inequality don't even yet see just how devastating it is for them. The most important challenge for this movement is to get them to see.

Because for many of us, though the problems we as a nation face are huge, they are not problems that will affect us directly, or immediately. Catastrophe is not going to happen tomorrow. Indeed, it's unlikely to happen anytime soon. Climate change is real, but for those of us over fifty, how will it really matter to us?

The fiscal debt is huge, yet it is in the nature of debt that it is some-thing that will be suffered most by someone other than us. Health care is expensive, and not, for most, terribly good. For those of us with privilege, it'll be just fine, at least for the rest of our lives.

In every single area needing critical reform, those with the most political power are also those who will suffer least if reform never comes. It's a terrible system. But it's not a terrible system for us. We who do politics well—we who vote, who fund campaigns—we'll be okay even if reform never comes.

But those who don't do politics well will not. And who are they? Our kids.

And so I return to the story of the protests in Hong Kong that began this book. Because the most striking feature of those pro-tests is that they were started by kids. Literally, students in high school, and college, and even some from elementary school took to the streets. Eventually their parents, and others from Hong Kong's society, felt obligated to step up and support their kids. But at first, those who showed up were the least experienced, and the most idealistic—and those with the most to lose if change didn't happen.

As I watched those protests develop, I was struck by two differ-ent, but related, thoughts. First, I was struck by my own deep skep-ticism that even with the energy those students had made manifest, they would never push the Chinese government to change. China is not a nation of democratic accommodation. Governments rise and fall, but not because the people demand it.

But second, I thought with envy about the effect of that same level of protest here. For if even a fraction of the proportion of stu-dents in America took to the streets as they did in Hong Kong, it seems impossible to imagine that that would not have a dramatic effect on our political system. Here, governments do rise and fall, and massive political mobilization is a rare but effective tool to bring about change. The Tea Party has done more to change the face of American politics than any other political movement in a generation, yet with a fraction of the mobilized support that the Hong Kong students deployed. And the Occupy Movement changed the very nature of our political discourse, even while self-consciously resisting the idea of engaging in electoral politics.

America has the potential for change through political action—still. But the only part of America with a real interest to care about change is the one part of America most pathetically apathetic about electoral politics: the youth.

That's not to say that the young are not engaged politically. The past decade has seen an incredible number of surprising and important political victories, fueled by the creative passion of the young, through the Internet.[4] From the campaign to stop the SOPA/PIPA legislation, to the fight for Net Neutrality, to the massive efforts to slow the TPP, to the efforts to force surveillance reform by stopping the Senate from renewing Patriot Act: These are all examples of political power, manifesting itself in ways that K Street does not control. And they are having a dramatic effect on important corners of regulatory policy.

The young *are* engaged. They are just not yet engaged on the issue of reform. Our challenge now is how to build on that energy. To encourage these leaders to take on this more fundamental battle. To show them a way, and to help them along.

And this then falls back on us—those of us not young, those of us without a direct interest in solving this problem, those of us who have stood by as our democracy was sold.

Tom Brokaw wrote about "the greatest generation"—my grandparents' generation, the people who suffered the depression and then defeated fascism across the world. What marked them was a willingness to give of themselves, to benefit us. Not for recognition or glory, but simply because it was the right thing to do.[5]

For all the reasons that generation was "the greatest," I fear ours may be the worst. Because the need for us to step up could not be greater. And yet compared to our parents and grandparents, the sacrifice that we would have to make is trivial. There is no war we'd have to fight. There are no German shepherds that will lunge at our necks. Bull Connor won't aim his fire hoses on our marches. No one is going to bomb the churches where our children worship. Nothing of the sacrifices that any of the people who fought to achieve the progress that the twentieth century saw would be required of us. All that we need to do is to organize, politically. To express our demand for equal citizenship, politically. And to use the power of this incredible democracy to finally deliver on a different promissory note, this one penned by Madison, not Jefferson—the promise of a government "dependent on the people alone," to be one in which "the people" mean "not the rich more than the poor."

It is time for us to do our part, if not for us, then for them. Let our revolution—peaceful, political, and with real, lasting power—be, unlike Hong Kong's, begun by us. Let us step up first. And when our kids see that we believe in the potential of this democracy again, they will join us. And when they join, we all will win.

Afterword

This book tracks the evolution of my own understanding of the problems of our democracy. In that evolution, I have been helped most powerfully by the passion of the people I've had the chance to meet when talking about this issue, and by the scholarship and encouragement of many, but especially Guy-Uriel E. Charles and Rick Hasen. Charles framed the puzzle of my "dependence corruption" argument powerfully and effectively in a review essay in 2014.[1] That framing pushed me to recognize both the need to reframe my focus on corruption alone, and the opportunity to see the link with equality. Hasen has consistently pressed an understanding of the flaw of our current system of campaign finance as tied to equality. As I understood that argument initially, it seemed to me too tied to a conception of speech equality. I did not, and do not, believe that our Republic requires an equality of speech. It requires an equality of citizenship. This more fundamental political equality is at the core of Hasen's latest powerful book, *Plutocrats United* (2016), and as I see our differences now, there is little that separates us on the equality argument, even if there remains disagreement about "corruption." Hasen thinks America's democracy is not corrupt, but unequal. I believe America's democracy is corrupt *because* unequal.

But the real motivation to dig deeper than "corruption" came from a friend and friendly critic. Someone just as committed to reform as I, but not convinced that the way I described the problem could inspire the energy it would take to fix it. I am grateful to Katie for this nagging skepticism, because it was right, and where it has led feels even more right.

This book is in significant part a reworking of the first edition of *Republic, Lost*. I am grateful again to those who made that possible. I especially grateful to those who helped with the part that's new. James Kwak, James Sample, Nicholas Stephanopoulos, Robert Van Houweling, and Luigi Zingals gave needed advice at critical points. I am thankful for their generosity. Ciara Torres-Spelliscy's questions pressed me to this way to framing the argument, and an event she conceived crystalized the understanding.

The infrastructure of this movement is provided—for free—by great organizations. I've had the honor of serving on the Sunlight Foundation's Advisory Board. I've learned tons from the extraordinary writings of Demos.org. And I've benefited greatly from the resources of the Center for Responsive Politics (aka *OpenSecrets.org*). Its director, Sheila Krumholz, has been a patient correspondent, answering many more questions than was fair. I'm grateful to her for that help, and to Doug Weber for helping to calculate the .02 percent statistic.

Han Ding and Greg Muren did an extraordinary job helping me to pull together the final draft of this book. There is no way it could have been done on time without their careful reading and critical writing. Ari Borensztein was immensely helpful in corralling the work necessary to draft this new edition. I am grateful to him, as well to the many researchers he organized, especially Aysha Bagchi, Matthew Ryan, Matthew Skurnik, and Joseph Posimato. I am thankful as well for the work of Susan Cox, and for her tireless determination. Recovering an old book and bringing it back to life is not easy. Without her patience, it would not have been possible.

I am grateful to Jin Suk for contributing figures 4, 6, 15, and 16, and helping me see how to show my words. Open Secrets provided the data for figures 3 and 17.

I am especially grateful to my agent, Amanda Urban, who responded to my fierce urgency for publishing these ideas now by crafting a very quick and perfect plan with my publisher. I am thankful to them as well.

But I could not be more thankful or more grateful than I am to my love. Since this work began, I have traveled to hundreds of places to speak about these ideas. That translates into at least a thousand nights when she was a single parent of three. I can't begin to know whether any of this will be worth the sacrifice in the end. But she never wondered, or doubted. That love is everything to me.

Notes

The Internet references linked in this book have been permanently archived using the *perma.cc* system. All the links referenced in these notes can be found at http://republicv2.lessig.org. If the originally referenced source is no longer available at the original link, *perma.cc* will provide an archived copy. The link for that link is http://republicv2.lessig.org.

Introduction

1. See Francis Fukuyama, *Political Order and Political Decay: From the Industrial Revolution to the Globalization of Democracy* (New York: Farrar, Straus and Giroux, Kindle Edition, 2014). Fukuyama draws on the work of George Tsebelis, who "coined the term 'veto players' as a means of comparing diverse political systems" (Kindle Location 8714).
2. Gallup, "Confidence in Institutions," June 2-7, 2015, available at link #1.
3. See, e.g., Cass Sunstein, "Political Equality and Unintended Consequences," *Columbia Law Review* 94 (1994): 1390-1414; Daniel R. Ortiz, "The Democratic Paradox of Campaign Finance Reform," *Stanford Law Review* 50 (1998): 893-914; Dennis F. Thompson, *Just Elections: Creating a Fair Electoral Process in the United States* (Chicago: University of Chicago Press, 2002); Yoav Dotan, "Campaign Finance Reform and the Social Inequality Paradox," *Michigan Journal of Law Reform* 37 (2004): 955-1015; Frank Pasquale, "Reclaiming Egalitarianism in the Political Theory of Campaign Finance Reform," *University of Illinois Law Review* 2008 (2008): 599-660. Yasmin Dawood has a fantastic summary of the field. See generally, "Campaign Finance and American Democracy," *Annual Review of Political Science* 18 (2015): 329-48, available at link #2.
4. Walter Shapiro, "The PAC to End All PACs Is a Farce," *Politico*, Aug. 24, 2014, available at link #3.

Chapter 1. Tweedism

1. The Basic Law of the Hong Kong Special Administrative Region of the People's Republic of China, available at link #4.
2. Hong Kong first holds "subsector" elections among its functional constituencies, which range from agriculture to finance to religion. Each subsector's population votes for its allocated number of members of the Election Committee, which

is then tasked with the ultimate responsibility of electing Hong Kong's Chief Executive. These initial subsector elections proceed by the block vote method, whereby fewer but more cohesive voters can influence an election disproportionately more than many but more diffuse voters. See "Election Committee," *Wikipedia*, last accessed July 1, 2015, available at link #5.

3. Tania Branigan, "Hong Kong Activists Vow to Take Over Financial Centre in Election Protest," *The Guardian*, Aug. 31, 2014, available at link #6.

4. Keith Bradsher and Chris Buckley, "Hong Kong Leader Reaffirms Unbending Stance on Elections," *New York Times*, Oct. 21, 2014, A10, available at link #7.

5. Texas was not the only state. As Charles Zelden describes, "Every Southern state adopted some form of the All White Primary between 1896 and 1915." Charles L. Zelden, *The Battle for the Black Ballot: Smith v. Allwright and the Defeat of the Texas All White Primary* (Lawrence, KS: University Press of Kansas, 2004), 2. Other techniques for achieving this discrimination included the literacy test, complex registration laws, the poll tax, and the grandfather clause. Darlene Clark Hine, *Black Victory: The Rise and Fall of the White Primary in Texas* (Columbia, MO: University of Missouri Press, 2003), 66.

6. Zelden, *Black Ballot*, 2.

7. "Guardian Council," *Wikipedia*, last accessed Aug. 8, 2015, available at link #8.

8. Others have understood this first stage of our election system in a similar way. I discuss John Bonifaz and Jamin Raskin. For other academic work describing a wealth primary, see Stephen Ansolabehere, "The Scope of Corruption: Lessons from Comparative Campaign Finance Disclosure," *Election Law Journal* 6 (2007): 163–83; Timothy Werner and Kenneth R. Mayer, "Public Campaign Finance and the Incumbency Advantage," working paper (2012), available at link #9; Jeffrey A. Winters and Benjamin I. Page, "Oligarchy in the United States?" *Perspectives on Politics* 7 (2009): 731–51, available at link #10; Valerie Rose El`Ghaouti, *The Changing Role of Soft Money on Campaign Finance Reform: The Birth of the 527 and Its Consequences*, master's thesis (Atlanta: Georgia State University, 2007), available at link #11.

9. For an account of the race, see Gina Bellafante, "A Cuomo Opponent Tilting at Corruption," *New York Times*, Aug. 3, 2014, MB1, available at link #12.

10. Cuomo's reason for refusing to debate was that some debates are "a disservice to democracy." He didn't explain why debating Teachout would have been a disservice. Thomas Kaplan, "Cuomo Is Running but Isn't One to Talk About It," *New York Times*, Sept. 3, 2014, A19, available at link #13.

11. Phillip Bump, "Andrew Cuomo Spent Almost 40 Times as Much for His Votes as Zephyr Teachout," *Washington Post*, Sept. 10, 2014, available at link #14; New York State Board of Elections, "Campaign Financial Disclosure," available at link #15; Bill Mahoney, "Cuomo Raised Millions Extra Due to Primary," *Capital*, Dec. 5, 2014, available at link #16.

12. There is no reliable measure of how much time the average member spends raising money. This is partly because members are not required to account for their time, an obvious problem that has led Brent Ferguson to call for rules mandating disclosure. See "Congressional Disclosure of Time Spent Fundraising," *Cornell Journal of Law & Public Policy* 23 (2013): 1, 4, available at link #17.

Many members claim it is large—very large. "As one Republican senator said: '[Fund-raising] devours one's time—you spend two or three years before your re-election fund-raising. The other years, you're helping others.'" Peter Lindstrom, "Congressional Operations: Congress Speaks—A Survey of the 100th Congress," Center for Responsive Politics (1988): 80, quoting unnamed Republican congressman.

Senator Robert Byrd, former majority leader, similarly observed: "To raise the money, Senators start hosting fundraisers years before they next will be in an election. They all too often become fundraisers first, and legislators second." 133 Cong. Rec. 115 (daily ed. Jan. 6, 1987).

Former Senate majority leader George Mitchell explained that senators constantly wanted him to reschedule votes because "they [were] either holding or attending a fund-raising event that evening." Martin Schram, *Speaking Freely: Former Members of Congress Talk About Money in Politics* (Washington, DC: Center for Responsive Politics, 1995), 37–38.

Representative Jim Bacchus (D-Fla.; 1991–1995) explained that he chose not to run for reelection because he would have had to abandon the job he had "been elected to do in order to raise a million dollars and be a virtual full-time candidate." Schram, *Speaking Freely*, 43.

Some estimate the number is two thirds or more. Philip M. Stern, *Still the Best Congress Money Can Buy* (Washington, DC: Regnery Publishing 1992): 130. "As I spoke to political consultants, they all said I should not even consider running for the Senate if I weren't prepared to spend 80 or 90 percent of my time raising money. It turned out that they were absolutely correct" [Representative Mike Barnes (D-Md.; 1979–1987)]; Shane Goldmacher, "Former Senate Leader Says Senators Spend Two-Thirds of Time Asking for Money," *NationalJournal*, Jan. 16, 2014, available at link #18. "Another former majority leader of the Senate, Senator Tom Daschle, agrees: 'A typical United States senator spends two-thirds of the last two years of their term raising money.'"

Some estimate the time is about 50 percent. Tracy Jan, "For Freshman [sic] in Congress, Focus Is on Raising Money," *Boston Globe*, May 12, 2013, available at link #19. "Democrat and Republican freshmen in targeted districts say they often spend up to half their days raising money, whether through dreaded 'call times' at a party-run phone bank near the Capitol, or attending fund-raisers." See also Ezra Klein, "The Most Depressing Graphic for Members of Congress," *Washington Post*, Jan. 14, 2013, available at link #20.

Some estimate the time is only about 25 percent. Paul S. Hernson and Ronald A. Faucheux, "Candidates Devote Substantial Time and Effort to Fundraising" (2000), available at link #21. "The high costs of running for office at the congressional and statewide level has [sic] forced 55 percent of statewide and more than 43 percent of U.S. House candidates to devote at least one-quarter of their time to fund-raising."

Some are skeptical of these numbers. See Ezra Klein, "Congress Spends Too Much Time Fundraising. But It's Less Time Than You Think," *Washington Post*, July 29, 2013, available at link #22, arguing that while the DCCC does in fact encourage new members to allot half their time to fund-raising, such an allotment is probably unrealistic.

A survey of members puts the number at about 20 percent. Congressional Management Foundation and The Society for Human Resource Management, "Life in Congress: The Member Perspective," 2013, available at link #23.

Perhaps the best introduction to the process is an episode of *This American Life*. See "461: Take the Money and Run for Office," narrated by Alex Blumberg and Andrea Seabrook, *This American Life*, WBEZ, Mar. 23, 2012, available at link #24.

13. Karla James, "Congressman Ashford Criticized for Lack of Fundraising," *Nebraska Radio Network*, Mar. 20, 2015, available at link #25.

14. *The Federalist Papers*, No. 52. Zachary Seth Brugman, "The Bipartisan Promise of 1776: The Republican Form and Its Manner of Election" (2012) (unpublished), 30, 43, available at link #26.

15. Except where indicated, these data were prepared for me by *OpenSecrets.org* on January 7, 2015, based on the data from their site. E-mail on file with author.

16. Kenneth Vogel, "Big Money Breaks Out," *Politico*, Dec. 19, 2014, available at link #27.

17. Center for Responsive Politics, *OpenSecrets.org*, "2014 Super PACs: How Many Donors Give?" available at link #28. That compares with 57 percent in 2012. Ibid.

18. U.S. Department of Labor: Bureau of Labor Statistics, Consumer Expenditures in 2013 (Feb. 2015), available at link #29.

19. Tania Branigan, "Hong Kong Activists," available at link #30.

20. The Sunlight Foundation and the Center for Responsive Politics calculate the influence a bit differently. Since 2010, they've looked at the influence of the "1 percent of the 1 percent." In the 2014 cycle, the 1 percent of the 1 percent was about 32,000 donors. Those 32,000 gave $1.2 billion—the largest amount and largest percentage given since the study began, accounting for 29 percent of all funds raised. To qualify as one of the 32,000, a member had to give at least $8,800. The median contribution was $14,750, and the maximum was $73 million (from a Democrat). Wall Street was the most important sector, giving $175 million. 135 members of this group gave more than $500,000; 63 gave $1 million or more. (In 2010, those numbers were 17 and 9.) 75 percent of the members of this group were men. Goldman Sachs was the "most prolific" group of members. And super PACs, candidates, and parties divided basically equal shares of the money (roughly 30 percent), with ordinary PACs receiving the balance. Every current member of Congress received money from the 1 percent of the 1 percent. Center for Responsive Politics, *OpenSecrets.org*, "The Political One Percent of the One Percent in 2014: Mega Donors Fuel Rising Cost of Elections," available at link #31.

Chapter 2. Corrupt *Because* Unequal

1. Senator William W. Bradley (D-N.J.; 1979–1997), "Government and Public Behavior," *C-Span video*, Dec. 8, 1997, available at link #32.

2. *The Federalist Papers*, No. 57.

3. Zachary Seth Brugman, "Bipartisan Promise" at 30, 33, available at link #33.

4. Ibid.

5. It is this that leads me to resist the direct reframing offered by Guy-Uriel E. Charles in "Corruption Temptation," *California Law Review* 102 (2014): 25–36.

Wealth inequality is certainly a product of the political inequality I describe here. "Dependence corruption" (which I define in Chapter 12) is an expression of that political equality. And while I certainly agree that inequality drives us to question the system of private funding of public campaigns, I don't go as far as Jamin B. Raskin and John Bonifaz in *The Wealth Primary* (Washington, DC: Center for Responsive Politics, 1994), to argue that private funding is unconstitutional. The constitutional concerns it raises certainly justify legislative responses, but ultimately, this needs to be a problem democracy solves, not judges.

6. Quoted in Michael Golden, *Unlock Congress: Reform the Rules; Restore the System* (Pacific Grove, CA: Why Not Books, 2015), 143.

7. *The Federalist Papers*, No. 52.

8. *The Federalist Papers*, No. 57.

9. Brugman, "Bipartisan Promise," 40.

10. Ibid., 41.

11. Ibid.

12. Danielle Allen, *Our Declaration: A Reading of the Declaration of Independence in Defense of Equality* (New York: Liveright, 2014), 107.

13. Ibid., 122.

14. Ibid., 34.

15. *Citizens United v. Fed. Election Comm'n*, 538 U.S. 310, 380 (2010).

16. Robert C. Post, *Citizens Divided: Campaign Finance Reform and the Constitution*, The Tanner Lectures on Human Values (Cambridge, MA: Harvard University Press, Kindle Edition, 2014), Kindle Location 1158. This is not true in Canada, where speech equality is a constitutional norm (Kindle Locations 1089–92).

17. *United States v. Classic*, 313 U.S. 299 (1941).

18. *Citizens United v. Fed. Election Comm'n*, 538 U.S. 310 (2010).

19. Demetri Sevastopulo and Julie Zhu, "Hong Kong Democracy Activists Vent Their Anger Against Beijing," *Financial Times*, Sept. 1, 2014, available at link #34.

20. Wendy Underhill, "Voter Identification Requirements: Voter ID Laws," *National Conference of State Legislatures*, Mar. 24, 2015, available at link #35.

21. "How to Rig an Election," *The Economist*, Apr. 25, 2002, available at link #36.

22. Sarah John, "Inequitable British Elections Provide Lessons for US Reformers," *FairVote*, May 12, 2015, available at link #37.

23. Golden, *Unlock Congress*, 143.

24. Ibid., 139.

25. Ibid., 151.

26. Ibid., 139–40; see Lani Guinier, *Tyranny of the Majority* (New York: Free Press, 1996).

27. Bruce Cain, *Democracy More or Less: America's Political Reform Quandary* (New York: Cambridge University Press, 2014). Cain rightly emphasizes the critical need for intermediary institutions of governance within a representative democracy. These institutions strengthen the representative function of a democracy. Cain is convincing that these are an essential part of a modern representative democracy, and absolutely convincing that direct democracy alternatives weaken effective rule.

28. Golden, *Unlock Congress*, 231.

Chapter 3. Consequences: Vetocracy

1. Fukuyama, *Political Order and Political Decay*.

2. Thomas E. Mann and Norman Ornstein, *It's Even Worse Than It Looks: How the American Constitutional System Collided with the New Politics of Extremism* (New York: Basic Books, Kindle Edition, 2012), Kindle Location 129. "Parliamentary-style parties in a separation of powers government are a formula for willful obstruction and policy irresolution."

3. Golden, *Unlock Congress*, 158; Mann and Ornstein, *It's Even Worse*, Kindle Locations 1367, 1417.

4. Darrell M. West, *Billionaires: Reflections on the Upper Crust* (Washington, DC: Brookings Institution Press, Kindle Edition, 2014), Kindle Locations 235–39.

5. Richard W. Painter, *Taxation Only with Representation: The Conservative Conscience and Campaign Finance Reform* (forthcoming, 2016).

6. Milton Friedman, "The Social Responsibility of Business Is to Increase Its Profits," *New York Times Magazine*, Sept. 13, 1970, available at link #38.

7. "Crony capitalism is good for those on the inside. And it is lousy for everyone else." Peter Schweizer, *Throw Them All Out* (New York: Houghton Mifflin Harcourt, 2011), 103.

8. Luigi Zingales, *A Capitalism for the People: Recapturing the Lost Genius of American Prosperity* (New York: Basic Books, 2012), 138.

9. Barry Lynn, *Cornered: The New Monopoly Capitalism and the Economics of Destruction* (Hoboken, NJ: Wiley, Kindle Edition, 2011), Kindle Location 3752. The "middle-level bureaucrats" of Thurmond Arnold's antitrust division, he wrote, were nothing less than "gods" of creation.

10. See, e.g., Gregory Wallace, "Elizabeth Warren Is Really Angry About Dodd-Frank Change," *CNN Money*, Dec. 10, 2014, available at money.cnn.com/2014/12/10/news/economy/elizabeth-warren/. Quoting Senator Warren's opposition to reinstating federal insurance of swaps: "That would let derivative traders on Wall Street gamble with taxpayer money and get bailed out by the government when their risky bets threaten to blow up our financial system."

11. "Too Big Not to Fail," *The Economist*, Feb. 18, 2012, available at link #39.

12. Center for Responsive Politics, *OpenSecrets.org*, "Finance/Insurance/Real Estate," available at link #40.

13. Center for Responsive Politics, *OpenSecrets.org*, "Interest Groups," available at link #41.

14. Consolidated and Further Continuing Appropriations Act, 2015, Public Law 113-235 (2014), available at link #42.

15. Robert G. Kaiser, *Act of Congress: How America's Essential Institution Works, and How It Doesn't* (New York: Knopf Doubleday Publishing Group, Kindle Edition, 2014), 129–30.

16. Ibid., 130.

17. Fukuyama makes a similar point: "Neither political party has an incentive to cut itself off from access to interest group money, and the interest groups don't want a system where money no longer buys influence." Fukuyama, *Political Order and Political Decay*, Kindle Location 8918.

Chapter 4. The Fix

1. Golden, *Unlock Congress*, 139.

2. Ibid. Of course, many others have called for reforms to achieve equal representational influence for all citizens. The non-profit "FairVote" has pushed most strongly for reforms that would achieve proportional representation. FairVote, "Fair Voting/Proportional Representation," available at link #43. The project also presses for ranked choice voting systems, where voters could indicate their order of preferences for candidates, national popular vote for president, a right to vote being expressed in the Constitution, and "instant run-off voting." FairVote, "Reforms," available at link #44. San Francisco has adopted instant run-off voting. FairVote, "Where Ranked Choice Voting Is Used," available at link #45. Justice Thomas has noted that the decision to establish single-member districts is purely statutory, and "one that we might be reconsidered in the future." *Holder v. Hall*, 512 U.S. 874, 909 (1994) (Thomas dissenting).

   The United States is relatively unique in its nonproportional system. Professor Mark Jones summarizes systems around the world at "Proportional Representation in Most Robust Democracies," FairVote, available at link #46.

3. On the public's dislike for presidential public funding, just such a centralized system, see Andrew Flowers, "A Checkbox on Your Tax Return Helped Kill Public Campaign Funding," *FiveThirtyEight*, Apr. 9, 2015, available at link #47.

4. This debate harkens back to a fight that divided progressives at the start of the last century. Progressives in the mold of Teddy Roosevelt saw the problem of private power remedied though stronger federal power. He accepted bigness; he wanted big government to match it. Woodrow Wilson (mainly because of his mentor in this, Louis Brandeis) saw the problem of private power remedied by breaking private power up. He rejected bigness; he wanted reforms to break it up.

   Similarly, so-called "campaign finance reformers" of all kinds see the problem of big money in politics. Some want to reform it through big government answers (top down public funding) or through big government limits (restrictions on speech). Others (and I am in this Wilson-Brandeis camp) want to reform it by diluting it, through bottom-up public funding that disables the power of concentrated funders.

   For an account of the Roosevelt-Brandeis difference, see Melvin Urofsky, *Louis D. Brandeis: A Life* (New York: Pantheon, 2009), Chap. 13.

5. As Theda Skocpol describes:

   > The postal system was the biggest enterprise of any kind in the pre-industrial United States, and for most citizens it "was the central government." In the 1830s and 1840s, the system accounted for more than three-quarters of U.S. federal employees, and most of the 8,764 postal employees in 1831 and the 14,290 in 1841 were "part-time postmasters in villages and towns scattered throughout the countryside." The federal army employed fewer men, and they were mostly "located at isolated army posts in the trans-appalachian West."

   Theda Skocpol, "The Tocqueville Problem: Civic Engagement in American Democracy," *Social Science History* 21 (1997): 455, 461–62.

6. As McChesney and Nichols describe, no one doubted that postal rates should be heavily subsidized. The real debate was whether they should be free. Congress never embraced free. See Robert W. McChesney and John Nichols, *The Death and Life of American Journalism: The Media Revolution That Will Begin the World Again* (New York: Nation Books, 2010), 124–25. But as Culver Smith estimates, while the maximum charge for a newspaper was 1.5¢, the minimum cost was 6¢ to 25¢, depending on the distance. Culver H. Smith, *The Press, Politics, and Patronage: The American Government's Use of Newspapers, 1789–1875* (Athens: University of Georgia Press, 1977), 6.

7. Paul Starr, *The Creation of the Media: Political Origins of Modern Communications* (New York: Basic Books, 2004), 89.

8. Theda Skocpol, "The Tocqueville Problem," 455, 461.

9. See Benjamin Rush, *Address to the People of the United States* (1787), available at link #48, quoted in McChesney and Nichols, *American Journalism*, 122.

10. McChesney and Nichols, *American Journalism*, 126–28. See also Starr, *Creation of the Media*, 92–93.

11. The system for the president could be added to this voucher system, or it could be completely separate. But in my view, the most important change that we need is to change the way congressional elections are funded. Legislation still needs Congress. Congress is still the easiest place to corrupt the process of legislation.

12. The idea of using vouchers to fund campaigns is not new. Senators Russell Long (D-La.; 1948–1987) and Lee Metcalf (D-Mont.; 1961–1978) proposed an early and modest version in 1967. See Thomas Cmar, "Toward a Small Donor Democracy: The Past and Future of Incentives for Small Political Contributions," *Fordham Urban Law Journal* 32 (2005): 443, available at link #49. David Adamany and George Agree built on the Metcalf plan to propose their own voucher program in *Political Money: A Strategy for Campaign Financing in America* (Baltimore: The Johns Hopkins University Press, 1975), 189–99.

    The more recent debate pushing vouchers as a small-dollar public funding system begins with Ed Foley's work, "Equal-Dollars-Per-Voter: A Constitutional Principle of Campaign Finance," *Columbia Law Review* 94 (1994): 1204, arguing for public funding proposals such as vouchers as a matter of constitutional obligation, and then more extensively by Richard L. Hasen, "Clipping Coupons for Democracy: An Egalitarian/Public Choice Defense of Campaign Finance Vouchers," *California Law Review* 84 (1996): 1, available at link #50. Bruce Ackerman and Ian Ayres build on that work in *Voting with Dollars: A New Paradigm for Campaign Finance* (New Haven: Yale University Press, Kindle Edition, 2002), which proposes a voucher system tied to an "anonymous donation booth"—a device that permits anonymous contributions beyond the contributions funded by vouchers. Pam Karlan separates out again the voucher proposal, and adds important support in "Elections and Change Under Voting with Dollars," *California Law Review* 91 (2003): 705.

    I advanced a voucher proposal in the first edition of this book, *Republic, Lost* (2011), which conditioned receipt of vouchers on a candidate's giving up contributions beyond $100. For an informed and experienced view of that proposal, see Michael J. Malbin, "Small Donors: Incentives, Economy of Scale, and Effects," *The Forum* 11 (2011): 385, 400–4.

Gans makes the important point that vouchers are equivalent to a tax credit (if simpler to use). David H. Gans, "Participation and Campaign Finance: The Case for a Federal Tax Credit," *Constitutional Accountability Center*, available at link #51.

Dylan Matthews discusses political prospects for vouchers—including its inclusion in the Government by the People Act, in "Can Vouchers Fix Campaign Finance?" *Washington Post Wonkblog*, July 22, 2012, available at link #52.

13. Ackerman and Ayres, *Voting with Dollars*, Kindle Locations 291-92.
14. See Susan C. Stokes, et al., *Brokers, Voters, and Clientelism: The Puzzle of Distributive Politics* (New York: Cambridge University Press, 2013), 317.
15. Ackerman and Ayres, *Voting with Dollars*, Kindle Location 67.
16. This was Goldwater's aim as well. Chris Myers, "Conservatism and Campaign Finance Reform: The Two Aren't Mutually Exclusive," *RedState*, Apr. 24, 2013, available at link #53. Goldwater: "In order to achieve the widest possible distribution of political power, financial contributions to political campaigns should be made by individuals alone."
17. Government by the People Act of 2014, H.R. 20, 113th Congress, available at link #54.
18. See Ezra Klein, "Big Money Corrupts Washington. Small Donors Polarize It," *Washington Post Wonkblog*, May 10, 2013, available at link #55; Adam Bonica, "Small Donors and Polarization," *The Boston Review*, July 22, 2011, available at link #56.
19. Michael J. Malbin, "Small Donors: Incentives, Economy of Scale, and Effects," *The Forum* 11 (2011): 385, 395-97.

See also Michael J. Malbin, Peter W. Brusoe, and Brendan Glavin, "Small Donors, Big Democracy: New York City's Matching Funds as a Model for the Nation and States," *Election Law Journal* 11 (2012): 3-20, available at link #57; Neil Malhotra, "The Impact of Public Financing on Electoral Competition: Evidence from Arizona and Maine," *State Politics and Policy Quarterly* 8 (2008): 263 (systems had helped competitors); A Look at H.R. 1826, and the Public Financing of Congressional Campaigns: Hearing on H.R. 1826 Before the H. Comm. on House Admin., 111th Cong. 206 (2009), statement of Jeffrey Garfield, Exec. Dir., Conn. State Elections Enforcement Comm'n, stating that in the 2008 Connecticut state elections more women had run for office than ever had previously, available at link #58; Steven M. Levin, "Keeping It Clean: Public Financing and American Elections," Center for Governmental Studies (2006), 46-47 (increased women's participation in Maine), available at link #59; Mimi Murray Digby Marziani and Adam Skaggs, "More Than Combating Corruption: The Other Benefits of Public Financing," Brennan Center for Justice at New York University School of Law, Oct. 7, 2011, available at link #60.

Keith M. Phaneuf, "The Clean-Election State," *American Prospect*, Jan. 5, 2012, available at link #61, found grassroots influence increased in Connecticut after public funding, while lobbying influence waned.

Wesley Joe, Michael J. Malbin, Clyde Wilcox, Peter W. Brusoe, and Henrik M. Schatzinger, "Individual Donors in Connecticut's Public Financing Program: A Look at the First Election Under the New System," paper presented at the Annual Meeting of the American Political Science Association, Toronto, Ontario, Sept.

3-6, 2009, available at link #62, found in the first election, donors to incumbents were essentially the same as before.

Seth E. Masket and Michael G. Miller, "Does Public Election Funding Create More Extreme Legislators? Evidence from Arizona and Maine," *State Politics and Policy Quarterly* 15 (2015): 24–40, available at link #63, could find no measurable difference in ideological extremity between publicly funded and non-publicly funded candidates.

See also Raymond J. La Raja, "Campaign Finance and Partisan Polarization in the United States Congress," *Duke Journal of Constitutional Law and Public Policy* 9 (2014): 223–58, available at link #64.

20. A distinct but related point responds to the important work of Raymond La Raja and Brian F. Schaffner. In a book published in the fall of 2015, *Campaign Finance and Political Polarization: When Purists Prevail*, La Raja and Schaffner find that "states that allow parties to raise and spend unlimited amounts of money tend to have less polarized legislatures." Raymond J. La Raja and Brian F. Schaffner, "Unlimited Party Fundraising and Spending Gives You Less Polarized Legislatures? Discuss." *Washington Post Monkey Cage Blog*, July 8, 2015, available at link #65. The mechanism for this effect is fairly clear. Party funding is more balanced than issue, or faction, funding. And if more money comes through parties than through individuals, the idiosyncratic, and typically polarized, influence of individuals can be reduced.

This is a great argument for assuring well-funded political parties. It is not a great argument for ignoring how that funding happens. If we imagine a system in which 1,000 families give both parties the money they need, no doubt the resulting system could be less "polarizing." It would also be more corrupt—since Congress, through the parties, would be "dependent" on an even tinier faction of the public to fund their campaigns. We could achieve the desired polarization effect without compromising on a commitment to a government "dependent on the people alone." For example, in a well-funded voucher system, Congress could make the default beneficiary of an unused voucher the political party the voter was a member of. That would assure a huge influx of money into political parties without concentrating funding in the very few.

21. Tad DeHaven, "Corporate Welfare in the Federal Budget," *Policy Analysis* 703 (2012): 1, 2.

22. This is the point passed too quickly in Lee Drutman's monumental *The Business of America Is Lobbying* (New York: Oxford University Press, 2015). Drutman rightly resists the idea that we could somehow banish corporate interests—at least so long as they are "determined" to remain (227). Nonetheless, he believes there are key reforms that could improve the influence that lobbyists might have. These include (1) balancing lobbying resources, (2) ending policy particularism, and (3) strengthening the independent informational capacity of Congress (223–36). These reforms, as he notes, would not address the problems created by how we currently fund campaigns. But changing the way we fund campaigns would radically change the power of lobbyists in the economy of influence with members of Congress.

Chapter 5. Distractions

1. Keith Olbermann, "Olbermann: U.S. Government for Sale," *Countdown on NBC*, Jan. 21, 2010, available at link #66.
2. Associated Press, "John McCain Blasts Citizens United Ruling," *Huffington Post*, Jan. 12, 2012, available at link #67.
3. See Center for Responsive Politics, *OpenSecrets.org*, "Estimated Cost of Election 2014," available at link #68.
4. The term "super PAC" was coined by Eliza Newlin Carney, who first used the term in a 2010 *National Journal* article. She had intended it to be mere shorthand for the clumsier "independent-expenditure only political action committee," but it quickly caught on as an "official" word. See Dave Levinthal, "How Super PACs Got Their Name," *Politico*, Jan. 10, 2012, available at link #69.
5. *Citizens United*, 558 US 50, 55 (2010).
6. "Estimated Cost of Election 2014," available at link #70.
7. Which is why Jeff Faux is correct that public funding alone won't be enough. See Jeff Faux, "Big Dollar, Little Democracy," *Dissent* 59 (2012): 89–95, available at link #71.
8. For a fantastic (and updated) account of that fight, see Jeffrey D. Clements, *Corporations Are Not People: Reclaiming Democracy from Big Money and Global Corporations*, 2d ed. (San Francisco, CA: Berrett-Koehler Publishers, 2014).

Chapter 6. What About "Free Speech"?

1. Of course, this line isn't sharp. Washington, DC, for example, is filled with ads purportedly directed at "the People" but really directed at government officials. It may be that to operationalize this distinction, speech really intended to influence government officials is rendered immune from any regulatory force. But the objective here is change the economy of influence. It isn't to control speech. If we succeed at changing that economy, the bleed from one type of speech to another won't alter the essential reform.
2. Mich. Comp. Laws § 169.254(1) (1979) codified § 54(1) of the Michigan Campaign Finance Act of 1976, Mich. Pub. Acts 388.
3. *Randall v. Sorrell*, 548 U.S. 230 (2006).
4. Post, *Citizens Divided*.
5. *Bell v. Hill*, 123 Tex. 531, 534 (1934).
6. *Nixon v. Herndon*, 273 U.S. 536 (1927).
7. *Nixon v. Condon*, 286 U.S. 73 (1932).
8. *United States v. Classic*, 313 U.S. 299 (1941).
9. David A. Stockman, *The Great Deformation* (New York: PublicAffairs, 2013), 316.
10. Ibid., 316–17.
11. Ibid., 318.
12. Ibid.
13. This is the point Justice Kagan makes in *Arizona Free Enterprise v. Bennett*, 131 S. Ct. 2806, 2845 (2011), Kagan dissenting:

     This Court, after all, has never said that a law restricting speech (or any other constitutional right) demands two compelling interests. One is enough.

And this statute has one: preventing corruption. So it does not matter that equalizing campaign speech is an insufficient interest. The statute could violate the First Amendment only if "equalizing" qualified as a forbidden motive—a motive that itself could annul an otherwise constitutional law. But we have never held that to be so. . . . When a law is otherwise constitutional—when it either does not restrict speech or rests on an interest sufficient to justify any such restriction—that is the end of the story.

That proposition disposes of this case, even if Arizona had an adjunct interest here in equalizing electoral opportunities. No special rule of automatic invalidation applies to statutes having some connection to equality; like any other laws, they pass muster when supported by an important enough government interest.

Chapter 7. Why *So Damn Much Money*

1. Robert G. Kaiser, *So Damn Much Money* (New York: Knopf Books, 2009), 356.
2. Norman J. Ornstein, Thomas E. Mann, and Michael J. Malbin, *Vital Statistics on Congress 2008* (Washington, DC: Brookings Institution Press, 2008), 19.
3. Arianna Huffington, *Third World America* (New York: Crown Publishers, 2010), 130.
4. "2014 Election Overview," Center for Responsive Politics, *OpenSecrets.org*, available at link #72.
5. Kaiser, *So Damn Much Money*, 115.
6. R. Sam Garrett, "The State of Campaign Finance Policy: Recent Developments and Issues for Congress," Cong. Res. Serv. (Apr. 29, 2011), available at link #73. "House and Senate campaigns' fundraising and spending have generally increased steadily since the early 1990s. Specifically, receipts more than doubled, from $654.1 million in 1992 to approximately $1.8 billion in 2010. Disbursements rose similarly, from $675.1 million to approximately $1.8 billion." In my view, the relevant question is much more pragmatic: Does the demand force members to spend more time raising money than before? Whether spending is constant relative to income or not, its nominal amount has increased, forcing more time to be spent on fund-raising. See Stephen Ansolabehere, John M. de Figueiredo, and James M. Snyder, "Why Is There So Little Money in U.S. Politics?" *Journal of Economic Perspectives* 17 (2003): 105.
7. Robert A. Caro, *Master of the Senate: The Years of Lyndon Johnson* (New York: Alfred A. Knopf, 2002), 483.
8. Randall Bennett Woods, *LBJ: Architect of American Ambition* (New York: Simon and Schuster, 2006), 434.
9. History buffs are always fascinated by the strange coincidences between Lincoln and Kennedy (described and dismantled at Barbara Mikkelson and David P. Mikkelson, "Linkin' Kennedy," *Snopes.com*, Sept. 28, 2007, available at link #74. The more interesting historical intertwining, in my view, is between the two presidents Johnson. Andrew Johnson, a Southern Democrat, was the most important force blocking the Radical Republicans from achieving their objectives for Reconstruction. Lyndon Johnson, a Southern Democrat, was, in my view, the most important political force correcting that deep injustice.

10. House: Federal Election Commission, Financial Activity of All U.S. House of Representatives Candidates: 1988–2000, available at link #75; Senate: Federal Election Commission, Financial Activity of All U.S. Senate Candidates: 1988–2000, available at link #76; Political Party Committees: Campaign Finance Institute, Hard and Soft Money Raised by National Party Committees: 1992–2010, available at link #77.

11. Kaiser, *So Damn Much Money*, 272.

12. Thomas Stratmann, "Some Talk: Money in Politics: A (Partial) Review of the Literature," *Public Choice* 124 (2005): 135, 148.

13. See John C. Coates IV, " 'Fair Value' as an Avoidable Rule of Corporate Law: Minority Discounts in Conflict Transactions," *University of Pennsylvania Law Review* 147 (1999): 1251, 1273–77, reviewing the idea of a "control premium."

14. Kaiser, *So Damn Much Money*, 201.

15. See Gary C. Jacobson, "Modern Campaigns and Representation," in Paul J. Quirk and Sarah A. Binder, eds., *The Legislative Branch* (New York: Oxford University Press, 2005), 118.

16. Federal Election Campaign Act of 1971, as amended in 1974, 2 U.S.C. § 431 (1974).

17. James J. Sample, "Democracy at the Corner of First and Fourteenth: Judicial Campaign Spending and Equality," *NYU Annual Survey of American Law* 66 (2011):727, 736, available at link #78.

18. Samuel Issacharoff, "On Political Corruption," *Harvard Law Review* 124 (2010): 119–20.

19. Sample, "Democracy at the Corner," 736.

20. Huffington, *Third World America*, 127.

21. Dan Clawson, Alan Neustadtl, and Mark Weller, *Dollars and Votes: How Business Campaign Contributions Subvert Democracy* (Philadelphia, PA: Temple University Press, 1998), 91.

22. Jacob S. Hacker and Paul Pierson, *Winner-Take-All Politics: How Washington Made the Rich Richer—And Turned Its Back on the Middle Class* (New York: Simon & Schuster, 2011), 224.

23. Ibid., 160.

24. Bertram Johnson, "Individual Contributions: A Fundraising Advantage for the Ideologically Extreme?" *American Politics Research* 38 (2010): 890, 906.

25. Shigeo Hirano, James M. Snyder Jr., Stephen Ansolabehere, and John Mark Hansen, "Primary Competition and Partisan Polarization in the U.S. Senate," *National Science Foundation* (2008), 4, finds that primaries don't contribute to polarization in the Senate, but this is not inconsistent with the claim about gerrymandered safe seats in the House. Unlike the House, the boundaries of the Senate are set by state lines.

26. Morris P. Fiorina and Samuel J. Abrams, *Disconnect: The Breakdown of Representation in American Politics* (Norman, OK: University of Oklahoma Press, 2009), 47.

27. Hacker and Pierson, *Winner-Take-All Politics*, 159.

28. Ibid.

29. Christopher Hare et al., "Polarization in Congress Has Risen Sharply. Where Is It Going Next?" *Washington Post*, Feb. 13, 2014, available at link #79.

30. Mann and Ornstein, *Even Worse*, Kindle Location 756.

31. Fiorina and Abrams, *Disconnect*, 87.
32. Jeffrey H. Birnbaum, *The Money Men: The Real Story of Fundraising's Influence on Political Power in America* (New York: Crown Publishers, 2000), 11.
33. Fiorina and Abrams, *Disconnect*, 168.
34. Sunlight Foundation Blog, June 26, 2013, available at link #80.
35. West, *Billionaires*, Kindle Location 359.
36. Mann and Ornstein, *Even Worse*, Kindle Location 2439.
37. Center for Responsive Politics, *OpenSecrets.org*, "Top Industries: Senator Max Baucus 2003–2008," Center for Responsive Politics, *OpenSecrets.org*, available at link #81. Between 2009 and 2014, the Campaign Committee raised an additional $1.1 million from finance, insurance, and real estate, and $990.2K from health. Center for Responsive Politics, *OpenSecrets.org*, "Top Industries, Senator Max Baucus 2009–2014," available at link #82.
38. Hacker and Pierson, *Winner-Take-All Politics*, 238.
39. Kaiser, *So Damn Much Money*, 151.
40. Schram, *Speaking Freely*, 15.
41. Kaiser, *So Damn Much Money*, 19.
42. Sheila Kaplan, "Lobbyist's Progress: An Interview with Jeff Connaughton," Harvard Edmond J. Safra Center for Ethics Lab Blog, Mar. 26, 2013, available at link #83.
43. Richard W. Painter, *Getting the Government America Deserves* (New York: Oxford University Press, 2009), 181.
44. This theory has received new support from Google's Ngram Viewer. See link #84.
45. William N. Eskridge Jr., "Federal Lobbying Regulation: History Through 1954," in *The Lobbying Manual*, ed. William J. Luneburg et al., 4th ed. (2009), 7, n. 7.
46. *Trist v. Child*, 88 U.S. 451 (1874).
47. Ken Silverstein, *Turkmeniscam: How Washington Lobbyists Fought to Flack for a Stalinist Dictatorship* (New York: Random House, 2008), 56.
48. Ibid., 57.
49. Ibid., 57–58.
50. Kenneth G. Crawford, *The Pressure Boys: The Inside Story of Lobbying in America* (New York: Julian Messner, Inc., 1939), 3.
51. Dennis F. Thompson, *Ethics in Congress: From Individual to Institutional Corruption* (Washington, DC: Brookings Institution, 1995), 2.
52. Crawford, *The Pressure Boys*, 25–26.
53. Thompson, *Ethics in Congress*, 2.
54. Painter, *Getting the Government America Deserves*, 27.
55. Crawford, *The Pressure Boys*, 27. Crawford states this letter is from "Edwards," but there was no "G. W. Edwards" who served in Congress. George Washington Edmonds served from 1913 to 1934. See Edmonds, George Washington (1864–1939), in Biographical Directory of the United States Congress, available at link #85.
56. This idea is framed in Richard L. Hall and Alan V. Deardorff, "Lobbying as Legislative Subsidy," *American Political Science Review* 100, no. 1 (Feb. 2006): 69, and described later.
57. Kaiser, *So Damn Much Money*, 291.

58. Silverstein, *Turkmeniscam*, 55.
59. Kaiser, *So Damn Much Money*, 291.
60. See Rob Porter and Sam Walsh, "Earmarks in the Federal Budget Process," Harvard Law School Federal Budget Policy Seminar, Briefing Paper No. 16 (May 1, 2014), 30, available at link #86.
61. Thompson, *Ethics in Congress*, 3. See also Fiorina and Abrams, *Disconnect*, 90. "Politics today is much 'cleaner.'"
62. Justin Fox and Lawrence Rothenberg, "Influence Without Bribes: A Noncontracting Model of Campaign Giving and Policymaking," *Political Analysis* 19 (2011): 325–41, available at link #87.

There are others who have developed models that might explain influence without assuming quid pro quo bribes. See, e.g., Brendan Daley and Erik Snowberg, "Even if It Is Not Bribery: The Case for Campaign Finance Reform," *Journal of Law, Economics, and Organization* 27 (2011): 324, 324, available at link #88. "We develop a dynamic multi-dimensional signaling model of campaign finance in which candidates can signal their ability by enacting policy and/or by raising and spending campaign funds, both of which are costly. Our model departs from the existing literature in that candidates do not exchange policy influence for campaign contributions, rather, they must decide how to allocate their efforts between policy-making and fundraising. If high-ability candidates are better policymakers and better fundraisers then they will raise and spend campaign funds even if voters care only about legislation. Voters' inability to reward or punish politicians based on past policy allows fundraising to be used to signal ability at the expense of voter welfare. Campaign finance reform alleviates this phenomenon and improves voter welfare at the expense of politicians. Thus, we expect successful politicians to oppose true campaign finance reform. We also show our model is consistent with findings in the empirical and theoretical campaign finance literature"; Filipe R. Campante, "Redistribution in a Model of Voting and Campaign Contributions," *Journal of Public Economics* 95 (2011): 646, 646, available at link #89. "Even though each contribution has a negligible impact, the interaction between contributions and voting leads to an endogenous wealth bias in the political process, as the advantage of wealthier individuals in providing contributions encourages parties to move their platforms closer to those individuals' preferred positions."

Insofar as Fox and Rosenberg "develop a model in which groups learn about the ideological preferences of politicians and donate to ones whose ideology seems congruent with their own," others have expressed concerns about groups' ability to accurately screen politicians for their ideologies. That is, a politician can pose as a true believer to secure the donation, then about-face. See Michael Tomaz and Robert P. Van Houweling, "Political Pledges as Credible Commitments," working paper (2012), available at link #90.

A randomized field experiment found that congressional officials (senior policymakers) made themselves three to four times more available when the organization seeking a meeting was one that contributed. This may undermine Fox and Rosenberg's model insofar as it's based not on a contract but on congruent ideologies. See Joshua L. Kalla and David E. Broockman, "Campaign Contributions Facilitate Access to Congressional Officials: A Randomized Field

Experiment," Apr. 2, 2015 (forthcoming in *American Journal of Political Science*), available at link #91.

63. I am not aware of any other work drawing upon Hyde, to model the lobbying behavior of Congress, but Phebe Lowell Bowditch does use it to understand the patronage system in Ancient Rome. See *Horace and the Gift Economy of Patronage* (Berkeley: University of California Press, 2001).

64. Lewis Hyde, *The Gift: Creativity and the Artist in the Modern World* (New York: Vintage, 1983), 3.

65. Lawrence Lessig, *Remix: Making Art and Commerce Thrive in the Hybrid Economy* (New York: Penguin, 2008), 117–76.

66. Hyde, *The Gift*, 56.

67. Dan Clawson and his colleagues made this point similarly:

> Campaign contributions are best understood as gifts, not bribes. They are given to establish a personal connection, open an avenue for access, and create a generalized sense of obligation. Only rarely—when the normal system breaks down—does a contributor expect an immediate reciprocal action by a politician. Even then, the donor would normally use circuitous language to communicate this expectation.

Clawson, Neustadtl, and Weller, *Dollars and Votes*, 61–62.
Sociologist Clayton Peoples has picked up on their analysis:

> A true relationship can build between contributors and legislators, and this starts with the initial contribution. Clawson et al. (1998) note that PAC officers tend to deliver contributions in person so that they can start building a relationship (p. 33). The relationships begun with initial contributing grow stronger with subsequent interactions. Part of this stems from the overlapping activities of PAC associates and legislators, or the "focused organization" of their ties to use Feld's (1981) terminology. PAC personnel "inhabit the same social world as [lawmakers] and their staffs…" and therefore contact occurs frequently since they "live in the same neighborhoods, belong to the same clubs, share friends and contacts, [etc.]" (Clawson et al. 1998: 85–86). This leads to genuine social relationships described by some as "friendship" and characterized by mutual trust. One PAC officer Clawson et al. (1998) interviewed said, "It's hard to quantify what is social and what is business…. Some of those [legislators] are my best friends on the Hill. I see them personally, socially…they always help me with issues" (pp. 86–87). Other PAC officers provide similar statements. For instance, one officer contends, "The [legislator] that is your friend, you are going to be his primary concern. The PAC certainly is an important part of that…" (p. 85). This leads Clawson et al. to conclude, "What matters is…a relationship of trust: a reputation for taking care of your friends, for being someone whom others can count on, and knowing that if you scratch my back, I'll scratch yours" (p. 88).

Clayton D. Peoples, "Contributor Influence in Congress: Social Ties and PAC Effects on U.S. House Policymaking," *Sociology Quarterly* 51 (2010): 649, 653–54.

Tolchin and Tolchin made a similar point in their powerful book *Pinstripe Patronage*:

> Lobbyists and members of Congress often become tied to each other through relationships based on mutual favors. These ties have become much stronger in recent years as election "reform" necessitates more and more fund-raising interdependence.

Martin Tolchin and Susan J. Tolchin, *Pinstripe Patronage: Political Favoritism from the Clubhouse to the White House and Beyond* (Boulder, CO: Paradigm Publishers, 2010), 89.

Among the best current ethnographies as well as theoretical models of how modern American lobbying works is Lee Drutman's *The Business of America Is Lobbying*. His account complements the understanding of lobbying as a gift economy.

68. Thomas M. Susman, "Private Ethics, Public Conduct: An Essay on Ethical Lobbying, Campaign Contributions, Reciprocity, and the Public Good," *Stanford Law and Policy Review* 19 (2008): 10, 15, quoting Paul H. Douglas, *Ethics in Government* (1952), 44.

69. Tolchin and Tolchin, *Pinstripe Patronage*, 2.

70. Maggie McKinley and Thomas Groll, "The Relationship Market: How Modern Lobbying Gets Done," Harvard Edmond J. Safra Center for Ethics Lab Blog, Feb. 13, 2015, available at link #92. Groll has formalized this analysis with Christopher Ellis. In "A Simple Model of the Commercial Lobbying Industry," *European Economic Review* 70 (2014): 299–316, they show how the growing constraint on members' time makes commercial lobbying firms more valuable. In "Repeated Lobbying by Commercial Lobbyists and Special Interests," working paper (June 2015), available at link #93, they link the increasing time that members spend fund-raising to the rise in commercial lobbying. Because members' time becomes so scarce, they depend increasingly on the expertise and support channeled through the lobbyist.

71. See also Clayton D. Peoples, "Campaign Finance and Policymaking: PACs, Campaign Contributions, and Interest Group Influence in Congress," *Sociology Compass* 7 (2013), 906. "A sociological view of contributing is that contributions may be best understood as "gifts" rather than "purchases".... In other words, contributing involves back-and-forth exchange of gifts (contributions)/favors with lawmakers, often over many years."

72. Kaiser, *So Damn Much Money*, 297.

73. Ibid.

74. Susman, "Private Ethics, Public Conduct," 10, 15–17.

75. Michele Dell'Era, "Lobbying and Reciprocity," working paper (Nov. 2009), 19.

76. Lawrence Lessig, "Democracy After Citizens United," *Boston Review*, Sept. 4, 2010, 15.

77. Kaiser, *So Damn Much Money*, 72.

78. Painter, *Getting the Government America Deserves*, 155. "Campaign contributions are involved in earmarks, sometimes from lobbyists and sometimes from other persons and entities that benefit from earmarks."

79. Kaiser, *So Damn Much Money*, 124.
80. Silverstein, *Turkmeniscam*, 137.
81. Birnbaum, *The Money Men*, 169–70.
82. Ibid., 50.
83. Ibid., 169.
84. Kaiser, *So Damn Much Money*, 193–94.
85. Ibid., 172.
86. Ibid., 167.
87. Association of American Medical Colleges, "The Scientific Basis of Influence and Reciprocity: A Symposium" (2007), 10–12, available at link #94.
88. This idea is developed in Ackerman and Ayres, *Voting with Dollars*, Kindle Locations 300–564.
89. Schram, *Speaking Freely*, 94.
90. Kaiser, *So Damn Much Money*, 353.
91. See Bård Harstad and Jakob Svensson, "Bribes, Lobbying and Development," *American Political Science Review* 46 (2011): 105.
92. Raquel M. Alexander, Stephen W. Mazza, and Susan Scholz, "Measuring Rates of Return on Lobbying Expenditures: An Empirical Case Study of Tax Breaks for Multinational Corporations," *Journal of Law and Policy* 25 (2009): 401, 404.
93. Brian Kelleher Richter, Krislert Samphantharak, and Jeffrey F. Timmons, "Lobbying and Taxes," *American Journal of Political Science* 53 (2009): 893, 907.
94. John M. de Figueiredo and Brian S. Silverman, "Academic Earmarks and the Returns to Lobbying," *Journal of Law and Economics* 49 (2006): 597, 598.
95. Frank Yu and Xiaoyun Yu, "Corporate Lobbying and Fraud Detection," *Journal of Financial and Quantitative Analysis* 46 (2011): 1865–91.
96. Matthew D. Hill, G. W. Kelly, G. Brandon Lockhart, and Robert A. Van Ness, "Determinants and Effects of Corporate Lobbying," *Financial Management* 42 (2013): 931, 946, available at link #95.
97. Silverstein, *Turkmeniscam*, 74.
98. Hacker and Pierson, *Winner-Take-All Politics*, 118.
99. Huffington, *Third World America*, 129.
100. Timothy M. LaPira and Herschel F. Thomas III, "Just How Many Newt Gingrich's Are There on K Street? Estimating the True Size and Shape of Washington's Revolving Door," SSRN Scholarly Paper (Apr. 2, 2013), available at link #96. See also Timothy M. LaPira, "Lobbying in the Shadows: How Private Interests Hide from Public Scrutiny, and Why That Matters," in Allan J. Cigler, Burdett Loomis, and Anthony Nownes, eds., *Interest Group Politics*, 9th ed. (Washington, DC: CQ Press, 2015), Chap. 11, available at link #97.
101. Robert Reich, "Everyday Corruption," lecture given at the Harvard Edmond J. Safra Center for Ethics (Apr. 5, 2010), on file with author.
102. Kaiser, *So Damn Much Money*, 20.
103. American Bar Association, "Lobbying Law in the Spotlight: Challenges and Proposed Improvements," Task Force on Federal Lobbying Laws Section of Administrative Law and Regulatory Practice (Jan. 3, 2011), vi, available at link #98.
104. Ibid., 20 (emphasis added). The ABA acknowledged that it drew on Susman, "Private Ethics, Public Conduct," 10.

105. Painter, *Getting the Government America Deserves*, 202.
106. Clawson, Neustadtl, and Weller, *Dollars and Votes*, 64.
107. Brooks, *Corruption in American Politics and Life* (New York: Dodd, Mead and Company, 1910), 228.
108. Daniel Hays Lowenstein, "On Campaign Finance Reform: The Root of All Evil Is Deeply Rooted," *Hofstra Law Review* 18 (1989): 325.
109. Joseph Mornin, "Lobbyist Money: Analyzing Lobbyist Political Contributions and Disclosure Regimes" (June 25, 2011), available at link #99.
110. The FEC has likewise radically narrowed the range of contributions that must be reported, by requiring a specific record indicating a bundle was intended. See Kevin Bogardus, "Bundling Rule Doesn't Capture All the Fundraising by Lobbyists," *The Hill* (2009), available at link #100.
111. Richard A. Posner, "Orwell Versus Huxley: Economics, Technology, Privacy, and Satire," in *Philosophy and Literature* 24 (2000): 1, 3.
112. Clawson, Neustadtl, and Weller, *Dollars and Votes*, 84.
113. List of Current Members of the United States House of Representatives by Seniority, available at link #101.
114. This theory has been brilliantly tested by Simon Weschle. See "Bribes, Campaign Contributions, and Revolving Doors: Mechanisms of Special Interest Influence," working paper (2014), available at link #102. Looking internationally, Weschle finds the revolving door technique of compensating legislators to be more common where compensation in office (through bribes or campaign contributions) is restricted.
115. Jeffrey Birnbaum, "Hill a Stepping Stone to K Street for Some," *Washington Post*, July 27, 2005, available at link #103.
116. Ryan J. Reilly, "Shadow Congress: Nearly 200 Ex-Lawmakers Work for Lobbying Shops," *Talking Points Memo* (June 14, 2011), available at link #104.
117. See Public Citizen, "Ca$hing In: More Than 900 Ex-Government Officials, Including 70 Former Members of Congress, Have Lobbied for the Financial Services Sector in 2009" (2009), available at link #105.
118. Birnbaum, *The Money Men*, 190–91.
119. Silverstein, *Turkmeniscam*, 68.
120. Brendan Daley and Erik Snowberg model the incentives of successful incumbents to support campaign finance reform—and even without assuming the endgame that Cooper imagines, find "successful politicians [will] oppose true campaign finance reform." Daley and Snowberg, "Even If It Is Not Bribery," 324.

Chapter 8. What *So Damn Much Money* Does

1. Tom Coburn, "Just Say No to Earmarks," *Wall Street Journal*, Feb. 10, 2006.
2. Brad Smith on *The Sound of Ideas*, WCPN, March 29, 2011, 8:20, available at link #106.
3. See John Armor, "Congress for Life," *Inner Self*, available at link #107.
4. Robert L. Trivers, "The Evolution of Reciprocal Altruism," *Quarterly Review of Biology* 46 (1971): 35.
5. Brooks, *Corruption in American Politics and Life*, 274.
6. Urofsky, *Brandeis*, 159.

7. Robert G. Kaiser, *Act of Congress*, 130.
8. Survey, Global Strategy Group (Jan. 11, 2011), on file with author. See also Hart Research Associates, "Protecting Democracy from Unlimited Corporate Spending: Results from a National Survey Among 1,000 Voters on the Citizens United Decision" (2010), finding that 95 percent strongly agree or somewhat agree that "corporations spend money on politics to buy influence/elect people favorable to their financial interests," 7. See also Eric Zimmermann, "Poll: 70 Percent Believe Congress Is Corrupt," The Hill's blog *Briefing Room* (Aug. 10, 2010), available at link #108, reporting the results of a Rasmussen poll that "voters are more likely to trust the integrity of their own representative, but not by much. A majority, 56 percent, think their own lawmakers can be bought." See also "Poll: Half of Americans Think Congress Is Corrupt," CNN (Oct. 19, 2006), available at link #109, finding that, four years before the Rasmussen poll, 49 percent of Americans said "most members of Congress are corrupt" and 22 percent said their individual legislator was corrupt; "Distrust, Discontent, Anger and Partisan Rancor: The People and Their Government," Pew Research Center (2010), 51, available at link #110.
9. John R. Hibbing and Elizabeth Theiss-Morse, *Stealth Democracy: Americans' Beliefs About How Government Should Work*, Cambridge Studies in Public Opinion and Political Psychology (New York: Cambridge University Press, 2002), 123.
10. Schram, *Speaking Freely*, 89.
11. Ibid., 31.
12. Ibid., 16.
13. Ibid., 23.
14. Ibid., 31.
15. Bill Bradley, "Government and Public Behavior," *Public Talk: Online Journal of Discourse Leadership*, available at link #111.
16. Golden, *Unlock Congress*, 10-11.
17. Kaiser, *Act of Congress*, 102.
18. Larry Makinson, *Speaking Freely: Washington Insiders Talk About Money in Politics* (Washington, DC: Center for Responsive Politics, 2003), 44.
19. Ibid.
20. For a review, see Frank R. Baumgartner and Beth L. Leech, *Basic Interests* (Princeton, NJ: Princeton University Press, 1998). Frank R. Baumgartner, Jeffrey M. Berry, Marie Hojnacki, David C. Kimball, and Beth L. Leech, *Lobbying and Policy Change: Who Wins, Who Loses, And Why* (Chicago: University of Chicago Press, 2009), 320. See also Lowenstein, "On Campaign Finance Reform," 307-8, summarizing skeptics' view.
21. Baumgartner et al., *Lobbying and Policy Change*, 194.
22. Stephen Ansolabehere, John M. de Figueiredo, and James M. Snyder, "Why Is There So Little Money in U.S. Politics?" *Journal of Economic Perspectives* 17 (2003): 105.
23. Ibid., 114.
24. Ibid., 105.
25. Ibid., 116. See also Douglas D. Roscoe and Shannon Jenkins, "A Meta-Analysis of Campaign Contributions' Impact on Roll Call Voting," *Social Science Quarterly* 86 (2005): 52-68.

26. Ansolabehere et al., "Why Is There So Little Money," 116.

27. Ibid.

28. Ibid., 126.

29. Brugman, "Bipartisan Promise," 37.

30. Center for Competitive Politics, "Fairly Flawed: Analysis of the 2009 Fair Elections Now Act (H.R. 1826 and S. 752)," Policy Briefing 2 (2009): 4.

31. As Richter and his colleagues write:

> The inordinate attention given to PAC contributions is essentially an exercise in "looking under the lamppost" since PAC data have been readily available since the 1970s, whereas lobbying data have only become available recently.... While focusing on contentious bills has its merits, crafty politicians have a variety of tools at their disposal to deliver favors, including attaching riders to mundane bills and exercising their power to steer bills in the congressional committee process. By not considering outcomes more broadly defined than roll-call votes on specific bills, existing research has arguably failed to detect some important benefits firms receive." Brian Kelleher Richter, Krislert Samphantharak, and Jeffrey F. Timmons, "Lobbying and Taxes," *American Journal of Political Science* 53 (2009): 894 (citations omitted).

32. Stratmann, "Some Talk: Money in Politics," 135, 146.

33. Sanford C. Gordon, Catherine Hafer, and Dimitri Landa, "Consumption or Investment? On Motivations for Political Giving," *Journal of Politics* 69 (2007): 1057.

34. Justin Grimmer and Eleanor Neff Powell, "Money in Exile: Campaign Contributions and Committee Access," working paper (2014), available at link #112.

35. Clayton D. Peoples, "Campaign Finance and Policymaking: PACs, Campaign Contributions, and Interest Group Influence in Congress," *Sociology Compass* 7 (2013): 904.

36. Douglas D. Roscoe and Shannon Jenkins, "A Meta-Analysis of Campaign Contributions' Impact on Roll Call Voting," *Social Science Quarterly* 86 (2005): 52–68.

37. Sanjay Gupta and Charles W. Swenson, "Rent Seeking by Agents of the Firm," *Journal of Law and Economics* 46 (2003): 253.

38. Atif Mian, Amir Sufi, and Francesco Trebbi, "The Political Economy of the US Mortgage Default Crisis," *American Economic Review* 100 (2010): 1967, 1969, available at link #113.

39. Lynda W. Powell, *The Influence of Campaign Contributions in State Legislatures: The Effects of Institutions and Politics* (Ann Arbor, MI: University of Michigan Press, Kindle Edition, 2012), Kindle Location 244.

40. Marcos Chamon and Ethan Kaplan, "The Iceberg Theory of Campaign Contributions: Political Threats and Interest Group Behavior," *American Economic Journal: Economic Policy* 5 (2013): 1, 2, available at link #114.

41. Ibid., 3.

42. As Lowenstein summarizes the skepticism:

> When one takes into account all the defects and difficulties inherent in these studies, it becomes increasingly difficult to regard their mixed results as a clean bill of health for the campaign finance system.
> Lowenstein, "On Campaign Finance Reform," 322.

43. Peter Schweizer, *Extortion: How Politicians Extract Your Money, Buy Votes, and Line Their Own Pockets* (Boston: Houghton Mifflin Harcourt, Kindle Edition, 2013), Kindle Locations 907–15.

   Bertram Johnson and Robert Van Houweling have made a complementing argument, predating Schweizer's. In *The Best Money Congress Can Buy: Legislative Fundraising and the Donor Collective Action Problem* (unpublished, 2009), they model and then empirically test a dynamic that assumes first that supporters of a legislator face a collective action problem (since they all have a collective interest in electing her but don't have an individual interest in funding her campaign), and that legislators would then have an incentive to encourage their supporters to solve their collective action problem. While they don't describe those incentives as "extortion," the same dynamic could be at play.

44. In the first edition of this book, I was dismissively critical of Jack Abramoff. My judgment was unfair. After reading his book, *Capitol Punishment* (2011), and spending some time getting to know him, I am convinced that while Abramoff crossed the criminal line, he is, or at least has become, a man of great decency. Abramoff has devoted a significant proportion of his energy since being released from jail to reforming the very institution that inspired him to behave in a way that sent him to jail. One need not make light of the wrongs that he committed to see the virtue in the acts he has since done.

45. Jack Abramoff, *Capitol Punishment: The Hard Truth About Washington Corruption from America's Most Notorious Lobbyist* (Portland, OR: BookBaby, Kindle Edition, 2011), Kindle Location 2309.

46. Schweizer, *Extortion*, Kindle Location 51.

47. Schweizer, *Extortion*, Kindle Locations 58–59.

48. "Eleanor Holmes Norton Tries to Strongarm Lobbyist and Demands Donations," YouTube video. Posted by "Stop Illegal Immigration!" Sept. 15, 2010, available at link #115.

49. Makinson, *Speaking Freely*, 86.

50. Carrie Budoff Brown, "Senate Bill Weighs in at 2,074 Pages," *Politico*, Nov. 18, 2009, available at link #116.

51. Ernest Hollings, "Stop the Money Chase," *Washington Post*, Feb. 19, 2006, available at link #117.

52. Andy Plattner, "Nobody Likes the Way Campaigns Are Financed, but Nobody's Likely to Change It, Either," *U.S. News & World Report*, June 22, 1987, 30.

53. Anthony Corrado, "Running Backward: The Congressional Money Chase," in Norman J. Ornstein and Thomas E. Mann, eds., *The Permanent Campaign and Its Future* (Washington, DC: American Enterprise Institute; Brookings Institution, 2000), 75.

54. Norman J. Ornstein and Thomas E. Mann, "Conclusion," in Ornstein and Mann, eds., *The Permanent Campaign*, 221–22.

55. Norman J. Ornstein and Thomas E. Mann, "When Congress Checks Out," *Foreign Affairs* (Nov.–Dec. 2006), 67, 70; see also Paul J. Quirk, "Deliberation and Decision Making," in Paul J. Quirk and Sarah A. Binder, eds., *The Legislative Branch* (New York: Oxford University Press, 2005), 314, 336 (effect on oversight panels).

56. Numbers drawn from Ornstein, Mann, and Malbin, *Vital Statistics*. See also Thomas E. Mann and Norman J. Ornstein, *The Broken Branch* (New York: Oxford University Press, 2006), 18. "In the 1960s and 1970s, the average Congress had an average of 5,372 House committee and subcommittee meetings; in the 1980s and 1990s the average was 4,793. In the ... 108th, the number was 2,135."

57. Numbers drawn from Ornstein, Mann, and Malbin, *Vital Statistics*. See also Mann and Ornstein, *The Broken Branch*, 18.

58. Gordon S. Wood, *Empire of Liberty: A History of the Early Republic, 1789-1815* (New York: Oxford University Press, 2009), 1272-73.

59. Steven S. Smith, "Parties and Leadership in the Senate," in Quirk and Binder, eds., *The Legislative Branch* , 274-75.

60. Andrew Seidman, "Former Members of Congress Lament Current Partisanship," McClatchy (June 16, 2010), available at link #118.

61. Makinson, *Speaking Freely*, 39-40.

62. Ibid., 6.

63. Lee Hamilton, "Will the House Come to Order?" The American Interest Online (Sept.–Oct. 2006), available at link #119.

64. To complain about distraction is not to betray doubt, as Daniel Ortiz puts it, about voters. A voter, like any employer, could well want his agent to stay focused on the job, if only to avoid the necessity of extra monitoring. See Daniel R. Ortiz, "The Democratic Paradox of Campaign Finance Reform," *Stanford Law Review* 50 (1997), arguing support for campaign finance reform is premised upon doubt about voters. The same applies to Issacharoff and Karlan's claim that a concern about "corruption" is really a concern about a "corruption of voters." For again, if the focus is on a distorted process, even if the voters could compensate for that distortion, they are rational to avoid the distraction that forces them to compensate. The fact that I double-check the cash drawer does not mean I have no good reason to avoid hiring a kleptomaniac. See Samuel Issacharoff and Pamela S. Karlan, "The Hydraulics of Campaign Finance Reform," *Texas Law Review* 77 (1998): 1723-26.

    Relatedly, Issacharoff and Karlan point to the "well-known feature of American political participation: there is a strong positive correlation between an individual's income and education level and the likelihood that she will go to the polls and cast a ballot." Ibid., 1725. In fact, the connection to policy outcomes is more complicated. As Gilens describes, though policy follows the attitudes of the elite, that is not correlated with education. Martin Gilens, *Affluence and Influence: Economic Inequality and Political Power in America* (Princeton, NJ: Princeton University Press, 2014), 94.

65. Baumgartner et al., *Lobbying and Policy Change*, 257-58.

66. This table is based, with permission, on Figure 12.1 in ibid., 258. I have re-created it using a subset of the data drawn from Table 1.4 in ibid.

67. Ibid., 258.

68. See Nicholas Stephanopoulos, "Elections and Alignment," *Columbia Law Review* 114 (2014): 283-367. Stephanopoulos extends the analysis to campaign finance in "Aligning Campaign Finance Law," working paper (October 2014), 34 (forthcoming in *Virginia Law Review* 100, 2015), available at link #120.

69. Richard L. Hall and Alan V. Deardorff, "Lobbying as Legislative Subsidy," *American Political Science Review* 100 (Feb. 2006): 69.

70. Center for Responsive Politics, *OpenSecrets.org*, Lobbying Database, available at link #121.

71. Hall and Deardorff, "Lobbying as Legislative Subsidy," 81.

72. Or as Baumgartner et al. report, almost everyone. See Laura I. Langbein, "Money and Access: Some Empirical Evidence," *Journal of Politics* 48 (1986): 1052; Kevin M. Esterling, "Buying Expertise: Campaign Contributions and Attention to Policy Analysis in Congressional Committees," *American Political Science Review* 101 (2007): 93; Clawson, Neustadtl, and Weller, *Dollars and Votes*. See also Joshua L. Kalla and David E. Broockman, "Congressional Officials Grant Access to Individuals Because They Have Contributed to Campaigns: A Randomized Field Experiment," working paper (2014), available at link #122.

73. Makinson, *Speaking Freely*, 59. See also Thompson, *Ethics in Congress*, 117.

74. Declaration of Paul Simon, *McConnell v. Fed. Election Comm'n*, No. 02-0582 (D.D.C. 2002).

75. Clawson, Neustadtl, and Weller, *Dollars and Votes*, 8.

76. Schram, *Speaking Freely*, 62.

77. Hall and Deardorff, "Lobbying as Legislative Subsidy," 80.

78. Ibid., 81.

79. Ibid.

80. Simon Johnson and James Kwak, *13 Bankers* (New York: Pantheon Books, 2010), 191–92.

81. Hall and Deardorff, "Lobbying as Legislative Subsidy," 69 (emphasis added).

82. U.S. Senate, Roll Call Vote on H.R. 6124, Food, Conservation, and Energy Act of 2008, available at link #123; U.S. House of Representatives, Office of the Clerk, Final Vote Result for Roll Call 417, available at link #124.

    A more recent example of a surprising correlation on the Right is the "Internet Freedom Act," introduced by Representative Marsha Blackburn (R-Tenn.; 2003–), H.R. 1212, 114th Cong. (2015), available at link #125. The aim of the bill was to overturn recent FCC action establishing "network neutrality." Among the thirty-one cosponsors, all but two received significant contributions from the National Cable and Telecommunications Association (NCTA). No other Republican in the House received significant contributions from NCTA, or signed on to the bill. Ben Collins, "The Campaign Cash That Can Kill the Open Internet," *Daily Beast*, Mar. 9, 2015, available at link #126.

83. Jay Cost, *A Republic No More: Big Government and the Rise of American Political Corruption* (New York: Encounter Books, Kindle Edition, 2015), 277. "Damned if the income tax isn't worse than the tariff ever was. Just like the tariff of yore, it showers its benefits upon the giant firms, which use enormous political influence to leverage the parochialism of our system to their advantage. The tariff benefited the American Sugar Refining Company and Standard Oil at everybody else's expense; the corporate income tax benefits Verizon and GE at everybody else's expense."

84. "The Cash Committee: How Wall Street Wins on the Hill," *Huffington Post*, Dec. 29, 2009, available at link #127.

85. Schram, *Speaking Freely*, 12.

86. Ibid., 48–49.
87. Ibid., 18.
88. Ibid., 93.
89. Birnbaum, *The Money Men*, 171.
90. Clawson, Neustadtl, and Weller, *Dollars and Votes*, 67.
91. Hall and Deardorff, "Lobbying as Legislative Subsidy," 79.
92. Tolchin and Tolchin, *Pinstripe Patronage*, 78. This shape-shifting is also related to an argument by Harvard professor Jane Mansbridge about why contribution studies are not likely to measure influence. As she describes, interest groups funding campaigns will fund candidates who already believe in the policies the groups favor. This produces not "quid pro quo distortion," as Mansbridge describes it, but "selection distortion," eliminating even the need for shape-shifting as the change happens as the member is selected. Jane Mansbridge, "Clarifying the Concept of Representation," unpublished manuscript, May 2011.
93. Powell, *Influence of Campaign Contributions*, Kindle Location 232.
94. General Interim Report of the House Select Committee on Lobbying Activities, H.R. Rep 3138, 81st Congress 2nd Session, 62.
95. Baumgartner et al., *Lobbying and Policy Change*, 2.
96. Interview with Larry Pressler, June 16, 2011, on file with author.
97. Powell, *The Influence of Campaign Contributions*, Kindle Location 384.
98. See generally Keith T. Poole and Howard Rosenthal, *Congress: A Political-Economic History of Roll Call Voting* (New York: Oxford University Press, 1997).
99. Larry M. Bartels, "Economic Inequality and Political Representation," working paper (2005), available at link #128.
100. Martin Gilens, "Inequality and Democratic Responsiveness," *Public Opinion Quarterly* 69 (2005): 778, 781–82. Gilens's argument has been criticized by Stuart Soroka and Christopher Wlezien; see "On the Limits to Inequality in Representation," *PS: Political Science and Politics* 41 (2008): 319–27. But as Gilens writes in response to Soroka and Wlezien, his results and Bartels's are consistent with those of a wide range of scholars, who all find "that more privileged subgroups of Americans have greater—and sometimes dramatically greater—sway over government policy." Martin Gilens, "Preference Gaps and Inequality in Representation," *PS: Political Science and Politics* 42 (2009): 335–41, 335.
101. Gilens, "Inequality and Democratic Responsiveness," 778, 788.
102. Ibid.
103. Martin Gilens and Benjamin I. Page, "Testing Theories of American Politics: Elites, Interest Groups, and Average Citizens," *Perspectives on Politics* 12 (Sept. 2014): 564, 575, available at link #129.
104. The field of this type of analysis—and it is so large now it is properly called a "field"—was born with Larry Bartels's *Unequal Democracy* (2008). That book examined the responsiveness of senators to the attitudes of low-income, middle-income, and high-income individuals. Like Gilens and Page, Bartels concluded that senators were "vastly more responsive to affluent constituents than to constituents of modest means." Larry M. Bartels, *Unequal Democracy: The Political Economy of the New Gilded Age* (Princeton, NJ: Princeton University Press, 2008), 253. Bartels's analysis was extended in the House by Christopher Ellis, Jesse H. Rhodes and Brian F. Schaffner, and Chris Tausanovitch. See Christopher

Ellis, "Representational Inequity Across Time and Space: Exploring Changes in the Political Representation of the Poor in the U.S. House," unpublished (n.d.), 9; Jesse H. Rhodes and Brian F. Schaffner, "Economic Inequality and Representation in the U.S. House: A New Approach Using Population-Level Data," working paper (Apr. 7, 2013), 29, available at link #130; Chris Tausanovitch, "Income and Representation in the United States Congress" (July 2011), 22, available at link #131, cited in Stephanopoulos, "Aligning Campaign Finance Law," 34.

105. See Ellis, "Representational Inequity," 9, finding a fivefold increase in the advantage of the affluent.

106. West, *Billionaires*, Kindle Location 126.

107. Hacker and Pierson, *Winner-Take-All Politics*, 3.

108. West, *Billionaires*, Kindle Location 113.

109. Hacker and Pierson, *Winner-Take-All Politics*, 3.

110. Ibid., 16.

111. Ibid., 24.

112. Ibid., 194.

113. Ibid., 22.

114. Ibid., 21.

115. Raghuram Rajan and Luigi Zingales, *Saving Capitalism from the Capitalists* (New York: Crown Business, 2003), 92.

116. Ibid.

117. West, *Billionaires*, Kindle Location 277.

118. Gilens, "Inequality and Democratic Responsiveness," 778, 792.

119. Joseph E. Stiglitz, "Of the 1 percent, by the 1 percent, for the 1 percent," *Vanity Fair*, May 2011, available at link #132.

120. Tyler Cowen, "The Inequality That Matters," *The American Interest* , Jan.–Feb. 2011, 4–5, available at link #133.

121. Huffington, *Third World America*, 17–18.

122. "Paywatch 2015: Executive Paywatch," *AFL-CIO*, available at link #134.

123. Barry Lynn, *Cornered: The New Monopoly Capitalism and the Economics of Destruction* (Hoboken, NJ: Wiley, 2010), 130.

124. Ibid., 130–31.

125. Hacker and Pierson, *Winner-Take-All Politics*, 151.

126. Gilens, "Inequality and Democratic Responsiveness," 778, 793–94.

127. Kaiser, *So Damn Much Money*, 355.

128. Stephanopoulos, "Aligning Campaign Finance Law," 38, citing Clyde Wilcox et al., "With Limits Raised, Who Will Give More? The Impact of BCRA on Individual Donors," in Michael J. Malbin ed., *Life After Reform: When the Bipartisan Campaign Reform Act Meets Politics* (Lanham, MD: Rowman & Littlefield, 2003), 61, carrying out survey in 2000; see Peter L. Francia, John C. Green, Paul S. Herrnson, Lynda W. Powell, and Clyde Wilcox, *The Financiers of Congressional Elections: Investors, Ideologues, and Intimates* (New York: Columbia University Press, 2003), 16, carrying out survey in 1996; Joseph Graf, Grant Reeher, Michael J. Malbin, and Costas Panagopoulos, "Small Donors and Online Giving: A Study of Donors to the 2004 Presidential Campaigns" (Washington, DC: Institute for Politics, Democracy and the Internet, George Washington University, and Campaign Finance Institute, March 2006), available at link #135, carrying out survey in 2004.

129. Stephanopoulos, "Aligning Campaign Finance Law," 36-37.
130. Benjamin I. Page, Larry M. Bartels, and Jason Seawright, "Democracy and the Policy Preferences of Wealthy Americans," *Perspectives on Politics* 11 (March 2013): 51-73.
131. Michael Barber, "Representing the Preferences of Donors, Partisans, and Voters in the U.S. Senate," unpublished working paper (Apr. 2014), 27-28, available at link #136.
132. Barber, "Representing the Preferences of Donors, Partisans, and Voters in the U.S. Senate," 22.
133. See Stephanopoulos, "Aligning Campaign Finance Law," and Stephanopoulos, "Elections and Alignment," 283-367.
134. Birnbaum, *The Money Men*, 72.
135. Ansolabehere, de Figueiredo, and Snyder, "Why Is There So Little Money in U.S. Politics?" (2003), 125-26.
136. This point is emphasized powerfully in Edward B. Foley, "Equal-Dollars-per-Voter: A Constitutional Principle of Campaign Finance," *Columbia Law Review* 94 (1994): 1204, 1226-27. "Voting is only the final stage of the electoral process. It is preceded not only by the agenda-formation stage...but also by...the "argumentative stage."...We must acknowledge that a citizen does not have equal input in the electoral process if she is denied an equal opportunity to participate in [these earlier stages]." It is also the insight that animates David Strauss's analysis. See David A. Strauss, "Corruption, Equality, and Campaign Finance Reform," *Columbia Law Review* 94 (1994): 1373. "Each dollar contribution...is a fraction of an expected vote." Strauss pushes the analogy (with all of its strengths and weaknesses) directly to the Court's redistricting cases. In my view, what's missing from this analysis is the recognition of how equality (and not just corruption) is derivative from the idea of the proper dependency within a representative democracy—upon "the People alone."
137. Gilens and Page, "Testing Theories," 575.
138. Atif Mian, Amir Sufi, and Francesco Trebbi, "The Political Economy of the US Mortgage Default Crisis," *American Economic Review* 100 (2010): 1967, 1968-70.
139. Nancy L. Rosenblum, *On the Side of the Angels* (Princeton, NJ: Princeton University Press, 2008), 251.
140. Ibid., 252.
141. Birnbaum, *The Money Men*, 70.
142. Hacker and Pierson, *Winner-Take-All Politics*, 252, quoting Naftali Bendavid, *The Thumpin': How Rahm Emanuel and the Democrats Learned to Be Ruthless and Ended the Republican Revolution* (New York: Doubleday, 2007), 156-57.
143. Ibid., 157.
144. Schram, *Speaking Freely*, 19.
145. Birnbaum, *The Money Men*, 3-4.
146. Zach Carter and Ryan Grim, "Swiped: Banks, Merchants and Why Washington Doesn't Work for You," *Huffington Post*, Apr. 28, 2011, available at link #137.
147. Ibid.
148. Baumgartner et al., *Lobbying and Policy Change*, 257, 214. Baumgartner and his colleagues craft an extensive empirical analysis of the relationship between

lobbying and policy outcomes. The short form of the conclusion is that a "direct correlation between money and outcomes...is simply not there" (214). "While no one doubts that money matters, and while there is no question that the wealthy enjoy greater access," that doesn't mean, they argue, that the wealthy "can necessarily write their ticket." But this conclusion follows because of the relationship between short-term lobbying and long-term structures. While "the wealthy" "often do not" "win in Washington," that's "not because they lack power, but because the status quo already reflects that power" (194, 20). The status quo "reflects a rough equilibrium of power...and a quite unfair equilibrium...with much greater benefits going to the privileged and wealthy than to the needy and the poor" (23). "So to see that money cannot automatically purchase shifts in the status quo does not mean that the status quo might not already reflect important biases in politics" (214).

149. Lowenstein, "On Campaign Finance Reform," 323. Addressing skepticism about the proven effects of money on results, Lowenstein writes: "The question of campaign finance is a question of conflict of interest...in the course of a relationship of trust."

150. "Public Trust in Government, 1958–2014," The Pew Research Center, Nov. 13, 2014, available at link #138.

151. Birnbaum, *The Money Men*, 10.

152. "National Election Studies: The ANES Guide to Public Opinion and Electoral Behavior," University of Michigan Center for Political Studies, available at link #139.

153. New Judicial Watch/Zogby Poll: "81.7 percent of Americans Say Political Corruption Played a 'Major Role' in Financial Crisis," *Judicial Watch*, Oct. 21, 2008, available at link #140. Gallup, "Trust in Government," available at link #141.

154. Jeanne Cummings, "SCOTUS Ruling Fuels Voters' Ire," *Politico*, Feb. 9, 2010, available at link #142. See also University of Texas, "Money and Politics Project U.S. National Survey" (2009), available at link #143, finding that 79 percent of the respondents believe that the source of a candidate's campaign contributions has a high degree of influence on how a candidate votes on legislation.

155. Huffington, *Third World America*, 129.

156. Ezra Klein, "Our Corrupt Politics: It's Not All Money," *New York Review of Books*, Mar. 22, 2012, available at link #144.

157. Rick Hasen's skepticism about the relationship between America's trust in their government and the trustworthiness of the campaign finance system is less persuasive. He points to work I cited in the first edition of this book, Nathaniel Persily and Kelli Lammie, "Perceptions of Corruption and Campaign Finance: When Public Opinion Determines Constitutional Law," *University of Pennsylvania Law Review* 153 (2004): 119, available at link #145, which found no good evidence of any correlation between campaign finance laws and public trust. But there would only be such a correlation if those laws were viewed as either effective or genuine. As the Clarus Group reports, Ron Faucheux, "U.S. Voters: Congress Is Selfish About Campaign Finance," *The Atlantic*, July 16, 2012, available at link #146, the vast majority of Americans view "campaign finance reform" as self-serving. It is no surprise that a reform viewed as untrustworthy wouldn't improve trust.

158. See Piercarlo Valdesolo, Steven Lehr, Lawrence Lessig, and Mahzarin Banaji, "Contagious Inferences in Institutional Trust," unpublished (2015). A similar result was reported by psychologists Sunita Sah, George Loewenstein, and Dayain M. Cain. In the experiments they ran, advisees were told that the person advising them had a financial conflict of interest. The consequence of the disclosure was a decrease of liking and trust. See "The Burden of Disclosure: Increased Compliance with Distrusted Advice," *Journal of Personality and Social Psychology* 104 (2013): 289–304, available at link #147.

159. Aaron Kesselheim et al., "A Randomized Study of How Physicians Interpret Research Funding Disclosures," *New England Journal of Medicine* 367 (2012): 1124, available at link #148. See also Maryam Kouchaki, Kristin Smith-Crowe, Arthur P. Brief, and Carlos Sousa, "Seeing Green: Mere Exposure to Money Triggers a Business Decision Frame and Unethical Outcomes," *Organizational Behavior and Human Decision Processes* 121 (2013): 53–61. "The mere presence of money or symbolic representation of money may have [influence on behavior and decisions]," available at link #149.

160. As Mark Warren has written, "If low trust instead indicates disaffection from the institutions that manage distrust, then the kind of distrust necessary for a democracy to work—engaged monitoring of political officials—is replaced by disengagement, undermining the transformative capacities of democratic institutions." Mark E. Warren, "Democracy and Deceit: Regulating Appearances of Corruption," *American Journal of Political Science* 50 (2006): 160, 165.

161. Birnbaum, *The Money Men*, 10.

Political scientists argue the effect could go either way. Hibbing and Theiss-Morse suggest it is the intensity of frustration that determines whether people increase participation or decrease it. Hibbing and Theiss-Morse, *Stealth Democracy*, 66. Abby Blass, Brian Roberts, and Daron Shaw suggest perceptions of corruption increase participation. "Corruption, Political Participation, and Appetite for Reform: Americans' Assessments of the Role of Money in Politics," *Election Law Journal* 11 (2012): 380, 393, available at link #150.

162. Steven J. Rosenstone and John Mark Hansen, *Mobilization, Participation, and Democracy in America* (New York: Macmillan, 1993). I am particularly grateful to Bryson Morgan for helping me frame this distinction.

163. See R. Michael Alvarez, Thad E. Hall, and Morgan Llewellyn, "On American Voter Confidence," *University of Arkansas–Little Rock Law Review* 29 (2007): 705; Robert F. Bauer, "Going Nowhere, Slowly: The Long Struggle Over Campaign Finance Reform and Some Attempts at Explanation and Alternatives," *Catholic University Law Review* 51 (2002): 741, 763. "Studies conclusively show that nonvoting does not stem from a rejection of, or hypothesized alienation from, the political process, but from a lack of interest in it." David M. Primo and Jeffrey Milyo, "Campaign Finance Laws and Political Efficacy: Evidence from the States," *Election Law Journal* 5 (2006): 1, discussing the relationship between campaign finance laws and perception of democratic rule, available at link #151. John Samples, "Three Myths About Voter Turnout in the United States," Cato Institute, Sept. 14, 2004, available at link #152. "The asserted line of causality from campaign finance to distrust of government does not exist. Given that, campaign finance cannot cause declines in voter turnout."

164. Rosenstone and Hansen, *Mobilization, Participation, and Democracy in America*, 144. This conclusion is confirmed by Kevin Chen, *Political Alienation and Voting Turnout in the United States: 1960-1988* (Lewiston, NY: Edwin Mellen Press, 1992), 214, 217.

165. Thomas E. Patterson, *The Vanishing Voter* (New York: Alfred A. Knopf, 2002), 183.

166. Golden, *Unlock Congress*, 34.

167. "Rock the Vote," *Wikipedia*, available at link #153.

168. August 2010 "Rock the Vote" survey, question 15.

169. "What Do Elected Officials Think About the Role of Money in Politics?" *Democracy Matters*, available at link #154.

170. Marc J. Hetherington, *Why Trust Matters: Declining Political Trust and the Demise of American Liberalism* (Princeton, NJ: Princeton University Press, 2005), 149.

171. Thompson, *Ethics in Congress*, 125-26.

172. Ezra Klein, "Our Corrupt Politics: It's Not All Money," *New York Review of Books*, Mar. 22, 2012, available at link #155. For a more complete response to Klein's review, see Lawrence Lessig, "Ezra's Review," LESSIG Blog V2, available at link #156. Rick Hasen makes a similar criticism in "Fixing Washington," *Harvard Law Review* 126 (2012): 550-85, available at link #157.

173. "Money and/or Polarisation," *The Economist*, Mar. 12, 2012, available at link #158.

174. Morris Fiorina, "Americans Have Not Become More Politically Polarized," *Washington Post*, June 23, 2014, available at link #159.

175. Mann and Ornstein, *Even Worse*, Kindle Location 2210.

176. Kaiser, *Act of Congress*, 105.

177. Conversation with John Sarbanes (2012).

178. Kaiser, *Act of Congress*, 232.

179. Golden, *Unlock Congress*, 176.

Chapter 9. How *So Damn Much Money* Defeats the Left

1. Speech of Barack Obama, Indianapolis, IN, Oct. 8, 2008.

2. Obama: " 'No Welfare for Wall Street': Nominee Is Inclined to Support Congress $700B Bailout Package If It Also Protects Main Street," CBS News *Face the Nation*, Sept. 28, 2008, available at link #160.

3. Speech of Barack Obama, San Diego, CA, Apr. 28, 2007.

4. Speech of Barack Obama, Washington, DC, Apr. 15, 2008.

5. Speech of Barack Obama, Columbia, SC, Jan. 26, 2008.

6. Speech of Barack Obama, Indianapolis, IN, Apr. 25, 2008.

7. Ibid.

8. Speech of Barack Obama, Philadelphia, PA, Apr. 2, 2008.

9. Ben Smith, "Hillary Defends Lobbyists, Opens Doors for Rivals," *Politico*, Aug. 4, 2007, available at link #161.

10. Speech of Barack Obama, Indianapolis, IN, Apr. 25, 2008.

11. Michael Grunwald, *The New New Deal: The Hidden Story of Change in the Obama Era* (New York: Simon & Schuster, Kindle Edition, 2013), Kindle Location 1451.

12. Crawford, *The Pressure Boys*, 7.

13. This point is related to Richard Posner's point about the willingness of monopolies to protect their monopoly. See Richard A. Posner, "The Social Costs of Monopoly and Regulation," *Journal of Political Economy* 83 (1975): 807-27.

14. Barry Lynn summarizes this concentration powerfully:

> Colgate-Palmolive and Procter & Gamble split more than 80 percent of the U.S. market for toothpaste;
>
> Almost every beer is manufactured or distributed by either Anheuser-Busch InBev or MillerCoors;
>
> Campbell's controls more than 70 percent of the shelf space devoted to canned soups;
>
> Nine of the top ten brands of bottled tap water in the United States are sold by PepsiCo (Aquafina), Coca-Cola (Dasani and Evian), or Nestlé (Poland Spring, Arrowhead, Deer Park, Ozarka, Zephyrhills, and Ice Mountain);
>
> Wal-Mart exercises a de facto complete monopoly in many smaller cities, and it sells as much as half of all the groceries in many big metropolitan markets. [It] delivers at least 30 percent and sometimes more than 50 percent of the entire U.S. consumption of products ranging from soaps and detergents to compact discs and pet food;
>
> The world's supply of iron ore is controlled by three firms (Vale, Rio Tinto, BHP Billiton);
>
> A few immense firms like Mexico's Cemex control the world's supply of cement;
>
> Whirlpool's takeover of Maytag in 2006 gave it control of 50 to 80 percent of U.S. sales of washing machines, dryers, dishwashers and a very strong position in refrigerators;
>
> Nike imports up to 86 percent of certain shoe types in the United States—for basketball, for instance—and more than half of many others;
>
> As of March 2009, Google had captured 64 percent of all online searches in the United States;
>
> TSMC and UMC have together captured 60 percent of the world's demand for semiconductor foundry service—in which a company serves as a sort of printing press for chips that are designed and sold by other firms—and have concentrated that business mainly in one industrial city in Taiwan;
>
> Corning has captured a whopping 60 percent share of the business of supplying [LCD glass].

Lynn, *Cornered*, 5-7, 258-59, n. 23.

15. The theory of regulatory capture raises questions about whether cartel-like industries will use their power to extract rents in the market or through government. And indeed, as Posner writes, the strongest examples of successful rent seeking come from relatively competitive industries. See Posner, "Theories of Economic Regulation," 335, 343-45. The success of the "deregulation" movement may have shifted the rent-seeking game toward the focus that now concerns Rajan and Zingales.

16. Rajan and Zingales, *Saving Capitalism from the Capitalists*, 296.

17. *Eastern Railroad Presidents Conference v. Noerr Motor Freight, Inc.*, 365 U.S. 127 (1961); *United Mine Workers v. Pennington*, 381 U.S. 657 (1965).

18. Obama for America, "Barack Obama and Joe Biden's Plan to Lower Health Care Costs and Ensure Affordable, Accessible Health Coverage for All" (2008), 5–6, available at link #162.

19. Remarks of President Obama, Weekly Address, July 18, 2009

20. Corporate Watch, "Pharmaceutical Industry," available at link #163.

21. Pub. L. No. 108-173, 117 Stat. 2066 (2003) (codified as 42 U.S.C.A. § 1395w-101 et seq.).

22. See 2014 Annual Report of the Boards of Trustees of the Federal Hospital Insurance and Federal Supplementary Medical Insurance Trust Funds, Centers for Medicare and Medicaid Services (2014), 109, available at link #164.

23. The Medicare Prescription Drug, Improvement, and Modernization Act of 2003 expressly prohibits the Centers for Medicare and Medicaid Services within the Department of Health and Human Services from (i) interfering with negotiations among drug manufacturers, prescription drug plans, and pharmacies, (ii) requiring prescription drug plans to use a particular formulary instituting a price structure for the reimbursement of drugs provided under Part D. Medicare Prescription Drug, Improvement, and Modernization Act of 2003, Pub. L. No. 108-173, sec. 101(a) (2), § 1395w-111, 117 Stat. 2066, 2092-99 (2003) (codified as 42 USC § 1395w-111[i] [2006]).

24. 153 Cong. Rec. S4634 (daily ed., Apr. 18, 2007), statement of Sen. Obama.

25. "[Pres.] Obama: Billy, YouTube video. Posted by "Political Realm TV" Apr. 9, 2008, available at link #165.

26. Jonathan Cohn, "How They Did It," *New Republic*, June 10, 2010, 14, 15.

27. Ibid., 14, 18.

28. Speech of Barack Obama, Indianapolis, IN, Apr. 25, 2008.

29. Speech of Barack Obama, Columbia, SC, Jan. 26, 2008.

30. Cohn, "How They Did It," 14, 21.

31. Ibid.

32. Ibid., 14, 25.

33. Speech of Barack Obama, Washington, DC, Apr. 15, 2008.

34. Ezra Klein, "Twilight of the Interest Groups," *Washington Post* (Mar. 19, 2010), available at link #166.

35. Speech of Barack Obama, San Diego, CA, Apr. 28, 2007.

36. Glenn Greenwald, "Industry Interests Are Not in Their Twilight," *Salon*, Mar. 20 2010, available at link #167.

37. Oliver Hart and Luigi Zingales, "Curbing Risk on Wall Street," *National Affairs* 3 (Spring 2010), 20–21, available at link #168.

38. Jim Puzzanghera, "Several Banks Considered Too Big to Fail Are Even Bigger," *Los Angeles Times*, Sept. 17, 2013, available at link #169.

39. Johnson and Kwak, *13 Bankers*, 180.

40. Hart and Zingales, "Curbing Risk on Wall Street," 20, 21. Elizabeth Warren, while chair of the Congressional Oversight Panel of TARP, published the Panel's December 2009 Oversight Report, titled "Taking Stock: What Has the Troubled Asset Relief Program Achieved?" In it, she credited Cato Institute Senior Fellow William Poole's estimation that the implicit federal guarantee of bank liability amounts to a $34 billion subsidy. Congressional Oversight Panel, "Taking Stock: What Has the Troubled Asset Relief Program Achieved?" 111th Cong. (Washington, DC: U.S. Government Printing Office, 2009), available at link #170.

41. "Trade Offs—National Priorities Project: Bringing the Federal Budget Home," available at link #171.

42. Hacker and Pierson, *Winner-Take-All Politics*, 1.

43. Krugman, "Zombie Financial Ideas"; Martin Wolf of the *Financial Times* has described it similarly. See Hacker and Pierson, *Winner-Take-All Politics*, 67.

44. Luigi Zingales, "A Market-Based Regulatory Policy to Avoid Financial Crisis," *Cato Journal* 30, no. 3 (Fall 2010): 535.

45. Luigi Zingales has another method not tied to controlling the size of banks. See ibid., 538-9.

46. Sebastian Mallaby has argued—powerfully, in my view—that these criticisms of Wall Street banks don't extend to hedge funds. That's not because hedge funds are populated with "saints," as Mallaby puts it, but because their "incentives and culture are ultimately less flawed than those of other financial companies." Sebastian Mallaby, *More Money Than God* (New York: Penguin Press, 2010), 375. I agree with this. The problem the past ten years has revealed is not innovation. It is innovation deployed in a context in which the risks are not borne by the gamblers. Hedge funds are not that.

47. Johnson and Kwak, *13 Bankers*, 214-15.

48. Jonathan Macey, "Reform Still Lets Banks Play Roulette," *Politico*, May 5, 2011, 2, available at link #172. See an interview with Macey in "Too Big Not to Fail," *The Economist*, Feb. 18, 2012, available at link #173.

49. Anna Kovner, James Vickery, and Lily Zhou, "Do Big Banks Have Lower Operating Costs?" *Federal Reserve Bank of New York Economic Policy Review* 20, no. 2 (Dec. 2014): 1-27, available at link #174.

50. Roger Lowenstein, *The End of Wall Street* (New York: Penguin Press, 2010), 291.

51. Tyler Cowen, "The Inequality That Matters," *The American Interest* (Jan.-Feb. 2011), 6, available at link #175.

52. Hacker and Pierson, *Winner-Take-All Politics*, 282.

53. Mallaby, *More Money Than God*, 378.

54. Kaiser, *Act of Congress*, 192.

55. James Kwak, "Cultural Capture and the Financial Crisis," in Daniel Carpenter and David Moss, eds., *Preventing Regulatory Capture: Special Interest Influence and How to Limit It* (New York: Cambridge University Press, 2013), 71-98.

56. Kaiser, *Act of Congress*, 129.

57. Ibid., 130.

58. Ibid., 338.

59. Ibid.

60. Ibid., 109.

61. Ibid., 339.

62. Maybe the best of this criticism is Anat Admati and Martin Hellwig, *The Bankers' New Clothes* (Princeton, NJ: Princeton University Press, 2013). Powerful technical (as in economic) evidence about the continued value of the implicit government guarantee comes from Bryan T. Kelly, Hanno Lustig, and Stijn Van Nieuwerburgh, "Too-Systemic-To-Fail: What Option Markets Imply About Sector-Wide Government Guarantees," NBER Working Paper No. 17149 (June 2011), available at link #176.

63. See Lisa Lerer, "Barney Frank Rips Staffer-Turned-Lobbyist," *Politico*, Apr. 10, 2010, available at link #177; Ryan Grim, "Peter Roberson, Bank Lobbyist Turned House Staffer, Is Heading Back to K Street," *Huffington Post*, May 29, 2010, available at link #178.
64. Center for Responsive Politics, *OpenSecrets.org*, "Finance, Insurance & Real Estate," last accessed July 1, 2015, available at link #179.
65. Kaiser, *Act of Congress*, 386.
66. Ibid., 370.
67. Ibid., 33.
68. Hacker and Pierson, *Winner-Take-All Politics*, 66.
69. Center for Responsive Politics, *OpenSecrets.org*, "Pro-Environment Groups Outmatched, Outspent in Battle over Climate Change Legislation," available at link #180.
70. The heart of the bill was a mandate that major sources of carbon emissions obtain a pollution permit for each ton of carbon dioxide or its equivalent that they emit. Sponsors emphasize that it required "electric utilities to meet 20 percent of their electricity demand through renewable energy sources and energy efficiency by 2020." The bill included new spending on "clean energy technologies and energy efficiency, including renewable energy ($90 billion in new subsidies by 2025), carbon capture and sequestration ($60 billion), electric and other advanced technology vehicles ($20 billion), and basic scientific research and development ($20 billion)." It also established new energy-saving standards for new buildings and appliances. "American Clean Energy and Security Act," *Wikipedia*, available at link #181.
71. James Hansen, *Storms of My Grandchildren: The Truth About the Coming Climate Catastrophe and Our Last Chance to Save Humanity* (New York: Bloomsbury USA, Kindle Edition, 2010), Kindle Location 59.
72. Center for Responsive Politics, *OpenSecrets.org*, "Lobbying Database," available at link #182.
73. Ryan Lizza, "As the World Burns: How the Senate and the White House Missed Their Best Chance to Deal with Climate Change," *The New Yorker*, Oct. 11, 2010, 12.
74. Robert Reich, "Everyday Corruption," *The American Prospect*, July/Aug. 2010, 26, available at link #183.
75. Speech of Barack Obama, Philadelphia, PA, Apr. 2, 2008.
76. Danielle Parquette, "What You Need to Know About Obamacare's Cost-Cutting Measures," *Washington Post*, Oct. 6, 2014, available at link #184. See also West, *Billionaires*, Kindle Location 2959. Obamacare "has raised income for those in the bottom fifth of the nation's income distribution."
77. Paul Krugman, "In Defense of Obama," *Rolling Stone*, Oct. 8, 2014, available at link #185; Paul Glastris, Ryan Cooper, and Siyu Hu, "Obama's Top 50 Accomplishments," *Washington Monthly*, Mar./Apr. 2012, available at link #186; Jonathon Chait, "Why History Will Be Kind to Obama," *New York Magazine*, Jan. 11, 2015, available at link #187.
78. Mann and Ornstein, *Even Worse*, 1606.

Chapter 10. How *So Damn Much Money* Defeats the Right

1. Read more at F. H. Buckley, "Republic, Regained," *American Spectator*, Feb. 2012, available at link #188.

2. This claim has been subject to some powerful econometric doubt. See Andrew Eggers and Jens Hainmueller, "Capitol Losses: The Mediocre Performance of Congressional Stock Portfolios, 2004–2008," *Journal of Politics* 75 (2013): 535–51, available at link #189.

3. Dana Milbank, "Jack Abramoff's Atonement," *Washington Post*, Feb. 6, 2012, available at link #190.

"What I did not consider then, and never considered until I was sitting in prison, was that contributions from parties with an interest in legislation are really nothing but bribes. Sure, it's legal for the most part. Sure, everyone in Washington does it. Sure, it's the way the system works. It's one of Washington's dirty little secrets but it's bribery just the same." Jack Abramoff, *Capitol Punishment*, Kindle Location 1646.

Abramoff is not the only person to refer to the system as "bribery." See, e.g., Richard A. Posner, "Business Ethics—Posner," *The Becker-Posner Blog*, Mar. 31, 2013, available at link #191 (Judge Richard Posner: "quasi-bribery"); Michael Lewis, "The Access Capitalists," *New Republic*, Oct. 18, 1993, available at link #192 (David Rubenstein: "legalized bribery"); James Allworth, "How Corruption Is Strangling U.S. Innovation," *Harvard Business Review*, Dec. 7, 2012, available at link #193 (Leon Panetta: "legalized bribery"); Ray Henry, "Jimmy Carter: Unchecked Political Contributions Are 'Legal Bribery,' " *Huffington Post*, July 17, 2013, available at link #194 (Jimmy Carter: "legal bribery"); Albert R. Hunt, "Shrinking Line Separates Campaign Donations from Bribes," *Bloomberg View*, May 25, 2014, available at link #195 (Russell Long: "hairline's difference between bribes and contributions").

4. Brugman, "Bipartisan Promise," 64.

5. John Bohlinger Jr., "More Republicans Should Support Overturning *Citizens United*," The Hill's *Congress Blog*, June 19, 2013, available at link #196.

6. "Eric Cantor," *Wikipedia*, last accessed June 14, 2015, available at link #197.

7. See, e.g., Nicholas Confessore and Megan Thee-Brenan, "Poll Shows Americans Favor an Overhaul of Campaign Financing," *New York Times*, June 2, 2015, available at link #198.

8. E-mail from Dan Weeks, Executive Director, Open Democracy, Mar. 12, 2015, reporting Bopp supporting "tax credits on small donations."

9. Loren Collins, "The Truth About Tytler," available at link #199. Something like this was certainly a concern among our Framers. John Adams, for example, feared that if democratic equality were taken too far, "debts would be abolished first; taxes laid heavy on the rich, and not at all on the others; and at last a downright equal division of everything be demanded, and voted." Hacker and Pierson, *Winner-Take-All Politics*, 77. Tocqueville, too: "The government of the democracy is the only one under which the power which votes the taxes escapes the payment of them." Alexis de Tocqueville, *Democracy in America*, ed. Francis Bowen, trans. Henry Reeve (Sever and Francis, 1835, 1863), 272.

10. U.S. Department of the Treasury, "The Debt to the Penny and Who Holds It," available at link #200.

11. U.S. Department of the Treasury, "The Debt to the Penny and Who Holds It," available at link #201 (figure obtained on Sept. 23, 2010). Brian Riedl, "New CBO Budget Baseline Shows That Soaring Spending—Not Falling Revenues—Risks

Drowning America in Debt," The Heritage Foundation, Aug. 19, 2010, available at link #202 (calculations based on Congressional Budget Office baseline calculations).

12. Hacker and Pierson, *Winner-Take-All Politics*, 78.

13. Timothy F. Geithner et al., 2009 Annual Report of the Boards of Trustees of the Federal Hospital Insurance and Federal Supplementary Medical Insurance Trust Funds, 24, available at link #203; Ed Silverman, "Will the Affordable Care Act Give Drugmakers a Boost?" *Forbes*, Dec. 26, 2013, available at link #204.

14. Cohn, "How They Did It," 14–25.

15. Peter S. Goodman, "Treasury Weighs Fixes to a Program to Fend Off Foreclosures," *New York Times*, Jan. 22, 2010, B1. The Treasury indicates it lowered the burden by $45.6 billion. "Making Home Affordable," U.S. Department of the Treasury, available at link #205.

16. Ruth Mantell, "Treasury Slapped over Shoddy Support for Homeowners," *MarketWatch*, Apr. 29, 2015, available at link #206, citing Office of the Special Inspector General for the Troubled Asset Relief Program (SIGTARP), "Quarterly Report to Congress," Apr. 29, 2015, available at link #207.

17. ProPublica, "FHA Finance Program," last accessed on June 14, 2015, available at link #208.

18. Dina ElBoghdady, "With Clock Ticking on Mortgage Relief, Homeowners Wonder What's Ahead," *Washington Post*, Mar. 10, 2014, available at link #209.

19. American Bar Association, "Lobbying Law in the Spotlight: Challenges and Proposed Improvements," Task Force on Federal Lobbying Laws Section of Administrative Law and Regulatory Practice, Jan. 3, 2011, vi, available at link #210.

20. Carter and Grim, "Swiped."

21. Scott Rasmussen, "50 percent Say 'Rigged' Election Rules Explain High Reelection Rate for Congress," Rasmussen Reports 2009, available at link #211.

22. Ibid.

23. Schram, *Speaking Freely*, 135–36.

24. Birnbaum, *The Money Men*, 66.

25. Clawson, Neustadtl, and Weller, *Dollars and Votes*, 37.

26. Ibid.

27. Robert Sitkoff, "Corporate Political Speech, Political Extortion, and the Competition for Corporate Charters," *University of Chicago Law Review* 69 (2002): 1103.

28. Birnbaum, *The Money Men*, 194.

29. Clawson, Neustadtl, and Weller, *Dollars and Votes*, 36.

30. Kaiser, *So Damn Much Money*, 315.

31. Schram, *Speaking Freely*, 134.

32. Evan Halper, "Maker of Tax Software Opposes State Filing Help," *Los Angeles Times*, available at link #212.

33. Ibid.; Liz Day, "How the Maker of TurboTax Fought Free, Simple Tax Filing" *ProPublica*, Mar. 26, 2013, available at link #213.

34. Williams and Jensen, "Tax Policy," available at link #214.

35. Brian Kelleher Richter, Krislert Samphantharak, and Jeffrey F. Timmons, "Lobbying and Taxes," *American Journal of Political Science* 53 (2009): 893, 896.

36. Ibid., 893, 906.

37. Ibid., 893, 907. And not just taxes. As they also conclude, "Firms that lobby are the primary tax beneficiaries of research and development activities" (905).
38. Ibid., 907
39. Michael J. Graetz, "Paint-by-Numbers Tax Lawmaking," *Columbia Law Review* 95 (1995): 609, 672.
40. Rebecca Kysar, "The Sun Also Rises: The Political Economy of Sunset Provisions in the Tax Code," *Georgia Law Review* 40 (2006): 335, 340.
41. Ibid., 335, 341.
42. Ibid., 335, 357-58.
43. Ibid., 335, 358.
44. Ibid., 335, 358-59
45. For related and later work, see Rebecca M. Kysar, "Lasting Legislation," *University of Pennsylvania Law Review* 159 (2011): 1007-68, available at link #215; Rebecca M. Kysar, "Reconciling Congress to Tax Reform," *Notre Dame Law Review* 88 (2013): 2121-55, available at link #216.
46. Kysar, "The Sun Also Rises," 335, 363-64.
47. Tax Byte$, "An R&D Tax Credit That Works," Institute for Policy Innovation, Jan. 20, 2011, available at link #217.
48. Mancur Olson was the father of modern public choice theory. His book *The Logic of Collective Action* (Cambridge, MA: Harvard University Press, 1965) explains most convincingly just why special interests are so powerful.
49. Kysar, "The Sun Also Rises," 335, 365.
50. John D. McKinnon, Gary Fields, and Laura Saunders, " 'Temporary' Tax Code Puts Nation in a Lasting Bind," *Wall Street Journal*, Dec. 14, 2010, available at link #218. See also Victor Fleischer, "NYU/UCLA Tax Policy Symposium Politics and Taxation: Commentary, Tax Extenders," *Tax Law Review* 67 (2014): 613.
    Professor Rob Sitkoff had described this same dynamic earlier. See Robert H. Sitkoff, "Corporate Political Speech, Political Extortion, and the Competition for Corporate Charters," *University of Chicago Law Review* 69 (2002): 1103-66.
51. Howard Gleckman, "The Perpetual, Immortal, Eternal, Never-Ending Tax Extenders," *Forbes*, May 28, 2015, available at link #219.
    See also John D. McKinnon, "Senate Votes to Extend Temporary Tax Breaks to End of 2014," *Wall Street Journal*, Dec. 16, 2014, available at link #220, describing extensions passed in 2014.
52. Clawson, Neustadtl, and Weller, *Dollars and Votes*, 76.
53. Hacker and Pierson, *Winner-Take-All Politics*, 107.
54. West, *Billionaires*, Kindle Location 2710.
55. Ibid., Kindle Location 2712.
56. Rajan and Zingales, *Saving Capitalism from the Capitalists*, 293.
57. Ibid., 276.
58. Ibid., 294.
59. Ibid., 10.
60. Adam Smith, *Wealth of Nations*, ed. Edwin Cannan, vol. 1 (Chicago: University of Chicago Press, 1976), 144, Chap. X ("Of Wages and Profit in the Different Employment of Labour and Stock"), Part II ("Inequalities Occasioned by the Policy of Europe").
61. Rajan and Zingales, 9.

62. Ibid.

63. Ibid., 13.

64. Raghuram G. Rajan, *Fault Lines: How Hidden Fractures Still Threaten the World Economy* (Princeton, NJ: Princeton University Press, 2010), 18.

65. Ronald J. Pestritto and William J. Atto, *American Progressivism: A Reader* (Lanham, MD: Lexington Books, 2008), 274.

66. James Bessen, "The Anti-Innovators," *Foreign Affairs*, Jan./Feb. 2015, available at link #221. See also James Allworth, "How Corruption Is Strangling U.S. Innovation," *Harvard Business Review*, Dec. 7, 2012, available at link #222.

67. James Bessen, *Learning by Doing: The Real Connection Between Innovation, Wages, and Wealth* (New Haven: Yale University Press, 2015).

68. Lawrence Lessig, *Free Culture: How Big Media Uses Technology and the Law to Lock Down Culture and Control Creativity* (New York: Penguin, 2004), 198-99.

69. Post, *Citizens Divided*, Kindle Locations 652-59.

70. Urofsky, *Brandeis*, 326.

71. Johnson and Kwak, *13 Bankers*, 21.

72. Pestritto and Atto, *American Progressivism*, 216.

73. Committee for Economic Development, "Investing in the People's Business: A Business Proposal for Campaign Finance Reform" (1999), 1.

74. Ibid.

75. Money in Politics Project, Committee for Economic Development, available at link #223.

76. Hart Research Associates and American Viewpoint, "American Business Leaders on Campaign Finance and Reform," Survey conducted for Committee for Economic Development (June 2013), available at link #224.

77. Schweizer, *Extortion*.

Chapter 11. How *So [Damn Little] Money* Makes Things Worse

1. Ilya Zemtsov, *The Encyclopedia of Soviet Life* (Herndon, VA: Transaction Publishers, 1991), 177.

2. Matthew Eric Glassman and Amber Hope Wilhelm, "Congressional Careers: Service Tenure and Patterns of Member Service, 1789-2015," Cong. Res. Service, Jan. 3, 2015, available at link #225.

3. James R. Ozinga, Thomas W. Casstevens, and Harold T. Casstevens II, "The Circulation of Elites: Soviet Politburo Members, 1919-1987," *Canadian Journal of Political Science* 22 (1989): 609, 614.

4. Norman Ornstein, "District of Corruption," *The New Republic*, Feb. 4, 2009, available at link #226.

5. Lisa Rein, "Federal Officials Fight Back over Criticism About Salaries," *Washington Post*, Aug. 17, 2010, available at link #227, describing debate about higher pay for federal officials.

6. Russ Choma, "One Member of Congress = 18 American Households: Lawmakers' Personal Finances Far from Average," Center for Responsive Politics, *OpenSecrets.org*, Jan. 12, 2015, available at link #228; Center for Responsive Politics, *OpenSecrets.org*, "Personal Finance Disclosure," available at link #229; Robert J.

Samuelson, "The Millionaire's Club Expands," *Washington Post*, Oct. 22, 2014, available at link #230.

7. Eric Jackson, "Evan Bayh: Hypocrisy on the Public Option," *TheStreet*, Oct. 29, 2009, available at link #231.

8. Marcia R. Jansen, "Wife's WellPoint Conflict Puts Bayh's Interests in Question," *Indianapolis Star*, May 25, 2009, A13.

9. Leadership PACS, Open Secrets.org, available at link #232.

10. Birnbaum, *The Money Men*, 233-34. This is still possible under the current ethics rules. H. Comm. on Standards of Official Conduct, 110th Cong., House Ethics Manual 47-48 (Comm. Print 2008), available at link #233.

11. "Leadership PACs: PAC Contributions to Federal Candidates," Center for Responsive Politics, Apr. 25, 2011, available at link #234.

12. Center for Responsive Politics, *OpenSecrets.org*, "Leadership PACs," available at link #235.

13. See R. Jeffrey Smith, "Money Intended to Help Candidates Often Ends Up Funding PACs Themselves," *Washington Post*, June 2, 2010, available at link #236.

14. Marcus Stern and Jennifer LaFleur, "Leadership PACs: Let the Good Times Roll," ProPublica, Sept. 26, 2009, available at link #237.

15. Prime Minister's Public Service Division, Press Release, "Modest Year-End Payments for Civil Servants," Nov. 26, 2009, available at link #238; Transparency International, "Corruption Perceptions Index 2014: Results," Dec. 2014, available at link #239; Rachel Chang, "Singapore Budget 2015: Ministerial Salaries Have Not Risen in Past Three Years," *Straits Times*, Mar. 10, 2015, available at link #240; BloombergBusiness, "SGDUSD Spot Exchange Rate," available at link #241.

16. InsideGov, Congressional Staff Directory, available at link #242; Luke Rosiak, "Congressional Staffers, Public Shortchanged by High Turnover, Low Pay," *Washington Times*, June 6, 2012, available at link #243; InsideGov, "What Is the Average Congressional Staff Salary?" Available at link #244.

17. Lynn Hume, "SEC Chair's Salary Far Below Group Execs Representing Firms, Individuals Overseen," *Bond Buyer*, Sept. 3, 2013, available at link #245.

18. Martha Neil, "Now Hiring: SEC Has Glut of Attorney Jobs, Turns to Recruiter for Help," *ABA Journal*, May 25, 2015, available at link #246.

19. Kenneth Rapoza, "How Much Do Wall Streeters Really Earn?" *Forbes*, Mar. 13, 2013, available at link #247.

20. Though the issue is not uncontested. See Eugene Kiely, "Are Federal Workers Overpaid? Both Sides in Great Pay Debate Are Misleading the Public," FactCheck .org, Dec. 1, 2010, available at link #248.

21. See generally Keith A. Bender and John S. Heywood, "Out of Balance? Comparing Public and Private Sector Compensation over 20 Years," Center for State & Local Government Excellence and National Institute on Retirement Security (2010), available at link #249.

22. Jeffrey H. Birnbaum, "The Road to Riches Is Called K Street," *Washington Post*, June 22, 2005, available at link #250; Jeanne Cummings, "The Gilded Capital: Lobbying to Riches," *Politico*, June 26, 2007, available at link #251; Arthur Delaney and Ryan Grim, "On K Street, an Ex-Senate Staffer Is Worth $740,000 a Year," *Huffington Post*, Sept. 24, 2010, available at link #252.

23. Ornstein, "District of Corruption," available at link #253.
24. See a comparable case of Joel Oswald, who works for Williams and Jensen and had twenty financial services clients as of 2010, available at link #254; Public Citizen and the Center for Responsive Politics, "Banking on Connections: Financial Services Sector Has Dispatched Nearly 1,500 'Revolving Door' Lobbyists Since 2009" (2010), available at link #255.
25. Birnbaum, *The Money Men*, 191.
26. Kaiser, *So Damn Much Money*, 343–44.
27. Eric Lichtblau, "Lobbyist Charged with Hiding Political Donations," *New York Times*, Aug. 5, 2010, A12, available at link #256; "104 Will Get You $300 Million," *New York Times*, Feb. 19, 2009, A30, available at link #257; Ryan J. Reilly and Alex Sciuto, "Despite Donations to Girl Scouts, PMA Lobbyist Gets 27 Months," *TPMMuckraker*, Jan. 7, 2011, available at link #258.
28. Judy Sarasohn, "Special Interests; Of Revolving Doors and Turntables," *Washington Post*, Feb. 17, 2000, A29; "Recording Industry Association of America," *Wikipedia*, available at link #259.
29. See, e.g., Lichtblau, "Lobbyist Charged," "104 Will Get You $300 Million."
30. Jordi Blanes i Vidal, Mirko Draca, and Christian Fons-Rosen, "Revolving Door Lobbyists," Center for Economic Performance Working Paper No. 993 (Aug. 2010).
31. Don Seymour, "House Republicans Renew Earmark Ban for 113th Congress," Speaker.gov, Nov. 16, 2012, available at link #260.
32. See Walter Pincus, "Earmarks Banned? House Members Find a New Way to Court Their Districts," *Washington Post*, June 19, 2013, available at link #261; Colby Itkowitz, "No Earmarks, but Still Plenty for Lawmakers to Take Credit For," *Washington Post In the Loop Blog*, July 22, 2014, available at link #262. CAGW claims to have identified earmarks in the federal budget, the ban notwithstanding. See Citizens Against Government Waste, "CROMNIPORK: CAGW Exposes Earmarks in CRomnibus Appropriations," Dec. 11, 2014, available at link #263.
33. Jack Abramoff, *Capitol Punishment*, Kindle Locations 2260–61.

Chapter 12. Two Conceptions of "Corruption"

1. Roberto Mangabeira Unger, *The Critical Legal Studies Movement*, 191 (Cambridge, MA: Harvard University Press, 1986).
2. Gallup, "Supreme Court," last accessed June 14, 2015, available at link #264.
3. Randal C. Archibold, "Ex-Congressman Gets 8-Year Term in Bribery Case," *New York Times*, Mar. 4, 2006, available at link #265.
4. David Stout, "Ex-Louisiana Congressman Sentenced to 13 Years," *New York Times*, Nov. 13, 2009, available at link #266.
5. *United States v. Narvaez*, 350 Fed. Appx. 355 (11th Cir. 2009), available at link #267.
6. *Buckley v. Valeo*, 424 U.S. 1, 27 (1976).
7. Professor Malcolm Salter describes and applies the idea in "Crony Capitalism, American Style: What Are We Talking About Here?" Harvard Business School Research Paper Series No. 15-025 (Oct. 22, 2014), available at link #268. See also M. Patrick Yingling, "Conventional and Unconventional Corruption," *Duquesne Law Review* 51 (2013): 263–320, available at link #269; Doron Navot, "Real Politics and the Concept of Political Corruption," (forthcoming in *Political Studies Review*), available at link #270; Renata E.B. Strause and Daniel P. Tokaji, "Between Access

and Influence: Building a Record for the Next Court," *Duke Journal of Constitutional Law and Public Policy* 9 (2014): 179-221, available at link #271.

Janine Wadel has developed a precisely analogous conception of corruption through the idea of accountability. See her fantastic book, *Unaccountable: How Elite Power Brokers Corrupt Our Finances, Freedom, and Security* (New York: Pegasus, 2014).

Unrelated to the problem of governance, Lisa Cosgrove and Robert Whitaker have applied the notion in a devastating critique of psychiatry. Robert Whitaker and Lisa Cosgrove, *Psychiatry Under the Influence: Institutional Corruption, Social Injury, and Prescriptions for Reform* (New York: Palgrave Macmillan, 2015).

For a critical review of "dependence corruption," see Richard L. Hasen, "Is 'Dependence Corruption' Distinct from a Political Equality Argument for Campaign Finance Reform? A Reply to Professor Lessig," *Election Law Journal* 12 (2013): 305-16, available at link #272; Bruce E. Cain, "Is 'Dependence Corruption' the Solution to America's Campaign Finance Problems?" *California Law Review* 102 (2014): 37-47, available at link #273.

Yasmin Dawood has powerfully located the idea in "Classifying Corruption," *Duke Journal of Constitutional Law and Public Policy* 9 (2014): 103-33, available at link #274.

Marie Newhouse develops the idea as an application of fiduciary theory in "Institutional Corruption: A Fiduciary Theory," *Cornell Journal of Law and Public Policy* 23 (2014): 553-94, available at link #275.

8. See J. Mark Ramseyer and Eric B. Rasmussen, "Skewed Incentives: Paying For Politics as a Japanese Judge," *Judicature* 83 (2000): 190.

9. James J. Sample, Charles Hall, and Linda Casey, "The New Politics of Judicial Elections," *Judicature* 94 (2010): 50, 52.

10. Alicia Bannon and Lianna Reagan, "New Politics of Judicial Elections 2011-12: 2011-2012 Supreme Court Races Spending Breakdown," Brennan Center for Justice, Oct. 23, 2012, available at link #276.

11. Justice Sandra Day O'Connor, "How to Save Our Courts," *Parade*, Feb. 24, 2008, available at link #277.

12. Ibid. (emphasis added).

13. Sample, "Justice for Sale," A24.

14. Sample, "Democracy at the Corner," 749.

15. David Pozen, James Sample, and Michael Young, "Fair Courts: Setting Recusal Standards," Brennan Center for Justice (2008), 11, available at link #278.

16. Sample, "Democracy at the Corner," 746.

17. Report of Stanford law student, spring 2009, on file with author.

18. Stephen J. Ware, "Money, Politics and Judicial Decisions: A Case Study of Arbitration Law in Alabama," *Capital University Law Review* 30 (2002): 583, 584.

19. Adam Liptak and Janet Roberts, "Campaign Cash Mirrors a High Court's Rulings," *New York Times*, Oct. 1, 2006, A1.

20. Adam Liptak, "Looking Anew at Campaign Cash and Elected Judges," *New York Times*, Jan. 29, 2008, A14, available at link #279.

21. It isn't quite accurate historically to speak of both the House and the Senate in this way, since the Senate was originally appointed by state legislatures. My analysis translates the view of the House to the norms for the now-elected Senate.

22. Sam Issacharoff advances a distinct conception of corruption that roughly parallels my sense of dependence corruption. He focuses upon the "clientelist" relation between "elected officials and those who seek to profit from relations to the state." Samuel Issacharoff, "On Political Corruption," *Harvard Law Review* 124 (2010): 121, the result of which is a "distortion of political outcomes as a result of the undue influence of wealth" (122).

23. "Public Citizen Litigation Group," *Wikipedia*, available at link #280; the case was *Virginia State Pharmacy Board v. Virginia Citizens Consumer Council*, 425 U.S. 748 (1976).

24. Post, *Citizens Divided*, Kindle Locations 1038–39.

25. Garrett Epps, *Wrong and Dangerous: Ten Right-Wing Myths About Our Constitution* (Lanham, MD: Rowman & Littlefield, 2012), 80–81.

26. *Citizens United v. Fed. Election Comm'n*, 558 U.S. 310, 345–47 (2010).

27. Deborah Hellman, "Defining Corruption and Constitutionalizing Democracy," *Michigan Law Review* 111 (2013): 1385, 1394.

28. Edwin Meese III, "The Great Debate," Speech, *The Federalist Society*, Nov. 15, 1985, available at link #281.

29. There is significant skepticism about the very idea of "originalism," and my using an originalist argument here shouldn't be confused with my believing there are not serious problems with the approach. My own work has tried to craft a version of originalism that is most responsive to the idea of interpretive fidelity. See Lawrence Lessig, "Understanding Changed Readings: Fidelity and Theory," *Stanford Law Review* 47 (1995): 395–472; Lawrence Lessig, "Translating Federalism, United States v. Lopez," *Supreme Court Review* 1995 (1995): 125–215; Lawrence Lessig, "Fidelity in Translation," *Texas Law Review* 71 (1993): 1165–68. For a powerful defense of a (small "l") liberal conception of originalism, see Jack M. Balkin, *Living Originalism* (Cambridge, MA: Belknap Press, 2011), and for an introduction to the (to many) puzzling fascination of American lawyers with originalism, see Jack M. Balkin, "Why are Americans Originalist?" in David Schiff and Richard Nobles, eds., *Law, Society and Community: Socio-Legal Essays in Honour of Roger Cotterrell* (Burlington, VT: Ashgate, 2015), 309–26, available at link #282.

30. Zephyr Teachout, *Corruption in America: From Benjamin Franklin's Snuff Box to Citizens United* (Cambridge, MA: Harvard University Press, Kindle Edition, 2014), Kindle Locations 821–22.

31. Ibid., Kindle Locations 723–24.

32. Gordon S. Wood, *The Creation of the American Republic, 1776-1787* (Chapel Hill, NC: University of North Carolina Press, Kindle Edition, 1998), 33.

33. Brugman, "Bipartisan Promise," 31.

34. J. G. A. Pocock, *Virtue, Commerce, and History: Essays on Political Thought and History, Chiefly in the Eighteenth Century* (New York: Cambridge University Press, 1985), 78.

35. The work in this section is drawn from the brief submitted as Amicus in the Supreme Court. See Brief for Lawrence Lessig as Amicus Curiae, *McCutcheon v. Fed. Election Comm'n*, 134 S. Ct. 1434 (2014), available at link #283.

36. John Joseph Wallis, "The Concept of Systematic Corruption in American History," in Edward L. Glaeser and Claudia Goldin, eds., *Corruption and Reform: Lessons from America's Economic History* (Chicago: University of Chicago Press, 2006), 23, 25.

37. *SpeechNow v. Fed. Election Comm'n*, 599 F.3d 686 (2010), available at link #284.
38. Mann and Ornstein describe a similar dynamic in *Even Worse*, Kindle Locations 1276-79. "Then there is a third element. As one Senator said to us, 'We have all had experiences like the following: A lobbyist or interest representative will be in my office. He or she will say, "You know, Americans for a Better America really, really want this amendment passed. And they have more money than God. I don't know what they will do with their money if they don't get what they want. But they are capable of spending a fortune to make anybody who disappoints them regret it." ' No money has to be spent to get the desired outcome."

   Jack Abramoff writes of self-consciously using this technique when wooing congressional staffers:

   > Once I found a congressional office that was vital to our clients...I would often become close to the chief of staff of the office. In almost every congressional office, the chief of staff is the center of power. Nothing gets done without the direct or indirect action on his or her part. After a number of meetings with them, possibly including meals or rounds of golf, I would say a few magic words: "When you are done working for the Congressman, you should come work for me at my firm...."
   >
   > With that, assuming the staffer had any interest in leaving Capitol Hill for K Street—and almost 90 percent of them do, I would own him and, consequently, that entire office. No rules had been broken, at least not yet.

   Abramoff, *Capitol Punishment*, Kindle Locations 1729-35.
39. Center for Responsive Politics, *OpenSecrets.org*, "2014 Super PACs: How Many Donors Give?" Available at link #285.
40. This pattern is consistent with findings from the Montana Supreme Court suggesting unlimited contributions reduce individual contributions. *Western Partnership Inc. v. Attorney General*, 271 P.3d 1, 11 (Mont. 2011), reversed on other grounds by *American Tradition Partnership, Inc. v. Bullock*, 132 S.Ct 2490 (2012).
41. Martin Gilens, *Affluence and Influence: Economic Inequality and Political Power in America* (Princeton, NJ: Princeton University Press, 2014), 247-48.
42. David Weigel, "In New Hampshire, Lindsey Graham Retools the Straight Talk Express," *Bloomberg*, Mar. 10, 2015, available at link #286.
43. Chris Cilliza, "Sheldon Adelson spent $93 million on the 2012 election. Here's How," *Washington Post*, Mar. 25, 2014, available at link #287; Ryan Grim, "Sheldon Adelson: Investigation into His Casinos by Justice Department Is Top Reason for Backing Romney," *Huffington Post*, Sept. 26, 2012, available at link #288.
44. None of the groups that track either donations or expenditures to either candidates or PACs track independent corporate spending. The reason according to one data maven is that it "is very rare." In 2012, *Demos* did an independent analysis of independent expenditures, aggregating categories of contributors. As Adam Lioz reported to me, they "did not find a significant enough amount of direct corporate expenditures to make it its own category in our outside spending graph." E-mail, July 1, 2015, on file with author. The minimum amount for any category in that analysis was $4.4 million.

45. Prior to 2010, the number of individuals making large (> \$1 million) expenditures in federal political campaigns was small. The Center for Responsive Politics' *OpenSecrets.org* indicates the number of individuals making large expenditures in each of these cycles between 2004 and 2014. Center for Responsive Politics, "Top Donors to Outside Spending Groups," *OpenSecrets.org*, available at link #289.

Pre-2004 data to precisely calculate the number is not available, but based on the Center for Responsive Politics' *OpenSecrets.org*'s data on total independent expenditures by individuals and entities such as PACs and 501(c)'s, we can calculate the maximum number of large contributors who could have cleared \$1 million in each of the years beginning in 1990. Center for Responsive Politics, "Total Outside Spending by Election Cycle, Excluding Party Committees," *OpenSecrets.org*, available at link #290.

The resulting data can be represented in this chart.

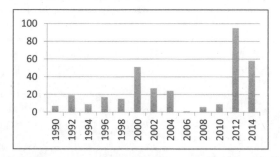

These maximums were derived from data on total independent expenditures, communication costs, and electioneering costs between 1990 and 2002.

Though these data lack the specificity of data since 2004, they nonetheless enable the calculation of the 1990–2002 maximums above with the aid of two conservative assumptions.

First, I assume individuals alone account for the entirety of each year's total independent expenditures, and other groups such as PACs and 501(c)'s account for none at all. This is plainly implausible, but it would only reduce the 1990–2002 figures above and bolster my claim that only a few rich individuals spend large.

Second, I assume that even limiting the analysis to individuals, those surpassing \$1 million account for almost all of the total expenditures. For example, *OpenSecrets.org* indicates that total independent expenditures for the 1996 cycle were \$17.9 million. To maximize the number of distinct individuals who could've spent at least \$1 million, I assumed that seventeen (the closest whole number, rounding down) individuals each spent exactly \$1 million and not a dollar more. This, too, is improbable—even if it were true that individuals account for all the spending and groups none, still it's more probable that individuals who spent at least \$1 million did not all spend exactly \$1 million. Instead, the likelier distribution, as shown in the years for which precise data are available, has a few individuals who spend more than \$1 million and many more who spend less than \$1 million.

Thus, since reality is contrary to this second assumption, too, in fact far fewer distinct individuals surpass \$1 million than the maximums estimated above.

46. Josh Duboff, "Target Issues Apology After Donation to Anti-Gay, Conservative Republican," *New York Magazine*, Aug. 5, 2010, available at link #291; CBSNEWS, "Target Spending Company Money on Candidates," July 27, 2010, available at link #292.

47. *McCutcheon v. Fed. Election Comm'n*, 134 S.Ct 1434, 1442–43 (2014).

48. *McCutcheon*, 134 S.Ct 1434, 1473–75 (2014), Breyer dissenting.

49. See Center for Responsive Politics, *OpenSecrets.org*, "Donor Demographics," available at link #293.

50. See, e.g., Richard A. Posner, *How Judges Think* (Cambridge, MA: Harvard University Press, 2008), 288, describing Justice Oliver Wendell Holmes's "puke" test.

51. *Williams-Yulee v. Florida Bar*, 135 S. Ct. 1656, 1667 (2015), available at link #294.

52. *Yulee* presents an interesting challenge to the distinction I draw between regulations of influence on the public and regulations of influence on government officials. The regulation at issue in that case was a limit on the ability of officials to solicit funds from the public. The justification for upholding that limit was the impression it would create in the public that judges were bought. But a stronger justification (from the perspective of the distinction I draw) would focus on the effect such speech might have on judges.

53. Robert G. Kaiser, *So Damn Much Money* (New York: Knopf Doubleday Publishing Group, Kindle Edition, 2009), Kindle Locations 2164–66.

54. Ibid., Kindle Location 2824.

55. Lawrence Lessig, "Democracy in Small States," *Lessig Blog V2*, May 15, 2015, available at link #295.

Part III. Unconventional Thoughts

1. Issue One, which is focused on making the funding of campaigns the first issue for every politician, has collected a list of the organizations working in the space. See Issue One, "Organizations," available at link #296.

Chapter 13. A *Proposing* Convention

1. See Matt Skurnik, "Partisan Platforms for Constitutional Amendments," Feb. 15, 2015, available at link #297 (research conducted for this book).

2. From Professor Bruce Ackerman's perspective, this claim is wrong for the most important amendments. In the three critical moments of constitutional amendment—the founding, the Civil War, and the New Deal—partisanship certainly dominated the latter two. But I've excepted the Civil War from my claim, and while I understand the sense in which the New Deal changes can be viewed as "constitutional," they are of a different (not lesser) kind from the changes reflected in the text of the document.

3. Dan Eggen, "Poll: Large Majority Opposes Supreme Court's Decision on Campaign Financing," *Washington Post*, Feb. 17, 2010, available at link #298.

4. "Article V Convention for a Balanced Budget," Mike Church, *SiriusXM Patriot*, Apr. 27, 2013, available at link #299, linking to Stalin.

5. Gordon S. Wood, *The Creation of the American Republic*, 310. See also Robert G. Natelson, "State Initiation of Constitutional Amendments: A Guide for Lawyers and Legislative Drafters," The Independence Institute, Apr. 6, 2014, 22, available at link #300. Judge Thomas E. Brennan has effectively surveyed the arguments

in *The Article V Amendatory Constitutional Convention: Keeping the Republic in the Twenty-First Century* (Lanham, MD: Lexington Books, 2014).

6. Natelson, "A Guide," 22.

7. "Provided that no Amendment which may be made prior to the Year One thousand eight hundred and eight shall in any Manner affect the first and fourth Clauses in the Ninth Section of the first Article; and that no State, without its Consent, shall be deprived of its equal Suffrage in the Senate." U.S. Const. Art V, sec. 1.

8. Natelson, "A Guide," 26. "A plenipotentiary convention is one with an unlimited mandate, or at least a mandate that is very broad. The term comes from international diplomatic practice. During the Founding Era, the in-state conventions that managed their governments in absence of the legislature enjoyed plenipotentiary authority. However, the Constitution does not authorize any plenipotentiary conventions."

9. Natelson, "A Guide," 28–29. "Unlike the Constitutional Convention, which was called by the states in their sovereign capacity, a convention for proposing amendments is called pursuant to the Constitution." Ibid., 25. "A proposing convention is charged only with proposing solutions to prescribed problems."

10. Russell L. Caplan, *Constitutional Brinksmanship: Amending the Constitution by National Convention* (New York: Oxford University Press, 1988), 27–29, quoting Max Farrand, ed., *The Records of the Federal Convention of 1787*, 4 vols. (New Haven, CT: Yale University Press, rev. ed., 1937), 1:22, 202–3, 629.

11. Ibid.

12. Wood, *The Creation of the American Republic*, 310.

13. Charles M. Roslof, "Should We Fear a 'Runaway Convention'? Lessons from State Constitutional Conventions," working paper (May 15, 2015), available at link #301.

14. Natelson, "A Guide," 27.

15. Ibid.

16. *Coleman v. Miller*, 307 U.S. 433 (1939).

17. Charles M. Roslof, "Should We Fear a 'Runaway Convention'? Lessons from State Constitutional Conventions," working paper (May 15, 2015), available at link #302.

18. This is the thrust of the truly great book by Paul J. Weber and Barbara A. Perry, *Unfounded Fears: Myths and Realities of a Constitutional Convention*, Contributions in Legal Studies, 55 (Santa Barbara, CA: Praeger, 1989). As they argue, we should approach the question of an Article V convention not as lawyers, but pragmatically. Weber and Perry's book radically changed how I thought about Article V. I am grateful for their work.

19. Akhil Amar has famously argued that, in fact, Americans could amend the Constitution outside of the Article V procedure—at least if one believes the original Constitution was properly ratified. See Akhil Reed Amar, "The Consent of the Governed: Constitutional Amendment Outside Article V," *Columbia Law Review* 94 (1994): 457, 457. "We the People of the United States have a legal right to alter our Government—to change our Constitution—via a majoritarian and populist mechanism akin to a national referendum, even though that mechanism is not explicitly specified in Article V."

20. As little as 4 percent of the population "can veto amendments if scattered throughout enough states." Peter Suber, "Population Changes and Constitutional

Amendments: Federalism Versus Democracy," *Michigan Journal of Law Reform* 20 (1987): 409, 412, available at link #303.

21. Stephen D. King, *When the Money Runs Out* (New Haven, CT: Yale University Press, Kindle Edition, 2013), Kindle Location 1347.

22. The device was developed by Stanford Professor James S. Fishkin. See, e.g., James S. Fishkin, *The Voice of the People: Public Opinion and Democracy* (New Haven, CT: Yale University Press, 1995). For a related device, see Mark E. Warren, "Two Trust-Based Uses of Minipublics in Democracy," paper prepared for the American Political Science Association Annual Meeting (Sept. 2009), available at link #304.

Deliberative polls are not necessarily inconsistent with the reform pluralism described by Cain. As he describes, properly informed, they can balance the weaknesses of direct democracy. And unlike the more difficult contexts he considers—redistricting, for example—the level of expertise necessary for the questions framed here is appropriate. See Cain, *Democracy More or Less*, 81–85.

23. Or even the capacity, at least when not properly constituted. See Cain, *Democracy More or Less*, 195–97.

Chapter 14. Referendum Politicians

1. See *Republic, Lost*, Chaps. 18, 19.

Conclusion

1. Global Strategy Group, Fund for the Republic—2013 Online Survey (Nov. 27–Dec. 12, 2013), unpublished, on file with author. The *New York Times* found 85 percent of Americans want at least a "fundamental change," with almost half calling for a "complete rebuild." Nicholas Confessore and Megan Thee-Brenan, "Poll Shows Americans Favor an Overhaul of Campaign Financing," *New York Times*, June 2, 2015, available at link #305. 84 percent think money has "too much influence." New York Times and CBS News, "A New York Times/CBS News Poll on Money and Politics," *New York Times*, June 2, 2015, 10, available at link #306. 58 percent were "pessimistic" about whether change would occur.

2. Ron Faucheux, "U.S. Voters: Congress Is Selfish About Campaign Finance," *The Atlantic*, July 16, 2012, available at link #307.

3. *Obergefell v. Hodges*, No. 14-556, slip op., 21 (June 26, 2015).

4. See e.g., Judith Bessant, *Democracy Bytes: New Media, New Politics and Generational Change* (New York: Palgrave Macmillan, 2014); Clay Shirky, *Here Comes Everybody: The Power of Organizing Without Organizations* (New York: Penguin, 2008). It was Manuel Castells's hope that this infrastructure might empower differently. Manuel Castells, *Communication Power* (Oxford, UK: Oxford University Press, 2011). We are seeing this now, if not precisely in the direction Castells (or I) would like.

For a fantastically valuable archive tracking digital activism globally, see Digital Activism Research Project, available at link #308.

5. Tom Brokaw, *The Greatest Generation* (New York: Random House, 1998).

Afterword

1. Guy-Uriel E. Charles, "Corruption Temptation," *California Law Review* 102 (2014): 25–36.

Image Credits

Figure 1: Copyright © 2015 Gallup, Inc. All rights reserved. The content is used with permission; however, Gallup retains all rights of republication.

Figure 2: Derived from Gallup data.

Figure 3: Drawn from Open Secrets.

Figures 4, 6, 15, and 16: Design by Jin Suk.

Figure 5: Copyright © 2015 *Vital Statistics on Congress* project, Brookings. All rights reserved. The content is used with permission.

Figure 7: Cunningham memo produced in prosecution.

Figures 8, 9, and 10: Derived from *Vital Statistics on Congress* project, Brookings.

Figure 11: Based on data in Frank R. Baumgartner, Jeffrey M. Berry, Marie Hojnacki, David C. Kimball, and Beth L. Leech, *Lobbying and Policy Change: Who Wins, Who Loses, And Why* (Chicago: University of Chicago Press, 2009), 258.

Figures 12, 13, and 14: Figure 1, Martin Gilens and Benjamin I. Page, "Testing Theories of American Politics: Elites, Interest Groups, and Average Citizens," *Perspectives on Politics* 12 (Sept. 2014): 564, 573.

Figure 17: Data derived from Open Secrets.

Index